SEXUAL POLITICS, SEXUAL COMMUNITIES

SEXUAL POLITICS, SEXUAL COMMUNITIES

The Making of a
Homosexual Minority
in the United States
1940–1970

JOHN D'EMILIO

The University of Chicago Press
Chicago and London

The University of Chicago Press, Chicago 60637
The University of Chicago Press, Ltd., London

Library of Congress Cataloging in Publication Data

D'Emilio, John.
  Sexual politics, sexual communities.

  Based on the author's thesis (Ph.D.)—Columbia
University, 1981.
  Bibliography: p.
  Includes index.
  1. Gay liberation movement—United States—History.
I. Title.
HQ76.8.U5D45   1983   306.7'66'0973   82-16000
ISBN 0-226-14265-5

For Estelle

Contents

Part 4. The Liberation Impulse

Acknowledgments

This book has been a long time in the making. In the course of writing it, I have incurred substantial debts to friends, teachers, and colleagues that I acknowledge more than gratefully.

I began this study as a doctoral dissertation in the history department of Columbia University, under the direction of Professor William Leuchtenburg. His formidable skill as an editor has improved the manuscript considerably. He also set consistently high standards for historical work and, without ever asking me to abandon my point of view, insisted that I use the persuasion of evidence carefully marshaled, rather than rhetoric carelessly employed, to make my argument. Estelle Freedman of Stanford University has been through more versions of the manuscript than either of us cares to remember. From the first chapter outline to the final draft, she has combined the criticism of a fine historian with the understanding of a long-time friend, to prod me along to completion. I have also benefited from readings from Kenneth Jackson, Rosalind Rosenberg, Joseph Interrante, Jim Oleson, James D'Emilio, William McLaughlin, Susan Stone Wong, Duane Tananbaum, Nancy Bernkopf Tucker, and Gary Rubin. The librarians and supporting staff at the Institute for Sex Research in Bloomington, Indiana, made a research trip there most profitable. A Kent fellowship from the Danforth Foundation, a scholarship from the Gay Academic Union of California, and financial assistance from Jim Oleson enabled me to finish the research and writing. Peter Lowy generously defrayed the cost of copying drafts, and Joe Duchac typed the final version with speed and accuracy. The members of my New York study group in the history of sexuality—Lisa Duggan, Jonathan Katz, Carole Vance, and Paula Webster—always posed incisive questions about my work and made the task of thinking and writing about sexuality an enjoyable one.

In many ways this book is also a product of the movement whose history it chronicles. I was privileged to be one of the founding members of the Gay Academic Union in New York in 1973. The men and women who sustained GAU during its first three years provided a supportive context in which it was first possible even to imagine writing about some aspect of the history of homosexuality. All of them had a part in my decision to undertake this project, but I especially want to thank Joseph Cady, Martin Duberman, and Bert Hansen. Their example convinced me that scholarship and a commitment to social change are not mutually exclusive. Activists in the homophile movement not only made the history I have written about but graciously consented to my demands on their time in the form of interviews. Several of them—Harry Hay, Chuck Rowland, James Kepner, Dorr Legg, and Frank Kameny—deserve special thanks for having saved the documents that are the raw material of this study, for inviting me into their homes to do the research, and for responding to repeated requests for another interview or letter. A number of gay publications and organizations provided me with a forum for presenting work in progress—the *Body Politic* of Toronto, *Gay Community News* of Boston, the North Shore Lesbian and Gay Alliance of Massachusetts, and the San Francisco Lesbian and Gay History Project, among others. They allowed me to test my ideas and to receive comments along the way from the community whose history I was writing.

Last but not least, there has been the help of friends. Tony Ward and David Roggensack lived with me throughout the writing of this book. They created a home environment in which concentrated work was possible and the right balance of pushing and encouragement to keep me going. Jonathan Katz and Allan Bérubé shared with me their enormous knowledge of gay history and their unswerving conviction that its study is worth pursuing. Members of the Re-Evaluation Counseling Community in New York, especially Sylvia Conant, John Bell, Dorothy Stoneman, Tom Roderick, and Elizabeth Higginbotham, were smart enough to break any writing blocks I had. Jim Oleson was there when I most needed him. My parents, Vincent and Sophie D'Emilio, always expressed confidence in my abilities and trust in my choices, and they have made a difference.

Most of all, I want to thank Estelle Freedman. As a respected colleague, a committed feminist, and my dearest friend, she shared all of the ups and downs in a way that no one else could.

Introduction

Since June 1969, when a police raid of a Greenwich Village gay bar sparked several nights of rioting by male homosexuals, gay men and women in the United States have enlisted in ever growing numbers in a movement to emancipate themselves from the laws, the public policies, and the attitudes that have consigned them to an inferior position in society. In ways pioneered by other groups that have suffered a caste-like status, homosexuals and lesbians have formed organizations, conducted educational campaigns, lobbied inside legislative halls, picketed outside them, rioted in the streets, sustained self-help efforts, and constructed alternative separatist institutions on their road to liberation. They have worked to repeal statutes that criminalize their sexual behavior and to eliminate discriminatory practices. They have labored to unravel the ideological web that supports degrading stereotypes. Like other minorities, gay women and men have struggled to discard the self-hatred they have internalized. Many of them have rejected the negative definitions that American society has affixed to their sexuality and, instead, have begun to embrace their identity with pride.

From the beginning a curious inconsistency appeared between the rhetoric of the gay liberation movement and the reality of its achievements. On the one hand, activists in the early 1970s repeatedly stressed, in their writing and their public comments, the intertwining themes of silence, invisibility, and isolation. Gay men and lesbians, the argument ran, were invisible to society and to each other, and they lived isolated from their own kind. A vast silence surrounded the topic of homosexuality, perpetuating both invisibility and isolation. On the other hand, gay liberationists exhibited a remarkable capacity to mobilize their allegedly hidden, isolated constituency, and the move-

ment grew with amazing rapidity. By the mid-1970s, homosexuals and lesbians had formed more than 1,000 organizations scattered throughout the
country. Many of these groups directed their energy outward, exerting pressure on legislatures, schools, the media, churches, and the professions. Activists proved capable of turning out tens of thousands of individuals for demonstrations, and they won impressive victories in relatively quick order. Many
lesbian and gay male organizations also looked inward, toward their constituency. Activists created newspapers, magazines, health clinics, churches,
multipurpose social centers, and specialized businesses—in short, a range of
institutions that implied the existence of a separate, cohesive gay community.

Clearly, what the movement achieved and how lesbians and gay men responded to it belied the rhetoric of isolation and invisibility. Isolated men and
women do not create, almost overnight, a mass movement premised upon a
shared group identity. In combating prejudicial attitudes and discriminatory
practices, moreover, gay liberationists encountered a quite clearly articulated
body of thought about homosexuality. And, if lesbians and homosexuals were
indeed invisible, the movement's leaders displayed an uncanny ability to find
them in large numbers.

The present study began as an effort to resolve this contradiction, specifically by searching for the roots of the gay liberation movement in the political
efforts of homosexuals and lesbians that preceded it. Militants in the early
1970s gave faint acknowledgment to the work of a previous generation, to the
men and women who composed the "homophile" movement and who staffed
organizations such as the Mattachine Society and the Daughters of Bilitis in
the 1950s and 1960s. But, almost in the same breath, modern-day liberationists glibly denied the importance of their forebears. Mattachine had a reputation as the "NAACP of our movement,"[1] a damning description during years
when groups like the Black Panther party were capturing the fancy of young
radicals. When seen from a longer historical view, however, the comparison
was intriguing since the NAACP, cautious and moderate as it may have been,
had compiled over several decades a record of achievement that helped make
possible the black civil rights movement of the 1950s and 1960s. Did the
homophile movement play a similar role for gay men and women? Did its work
perhaps prepare the ground for the victories of the 1970s?

As I researched the first phase of the gay emancipation struggle in the United
States, it became apparent that its participants, and their work, deserved more

---

1. Quoted in Merle Miller, *On Being Different* (New York, 1971), p. 38. For a similar view of
the homophile movement, see Dennis Altman, *Homosexual: Oppression and Liberation*, Discus ed.
(New York, 1971), p. 115. See Laud Humphreys, *Out of the Closets: The Sociology of Homosexual
Liberation* (Englewood Cliffs, N.J., 1972), for a more sympathetic view of the difference between
gay liberation and its homophile predecessor.

than consignment to the dustbin of history. It is true, without question, that the homophile movement had failed to attract large numbers of lesbians and homosexuals to its cause. Nor had it succeeded in substantially revising the laws and public policies that kept them in a state of second-class citizenship. But at a time when heterosexual Americans appeared virtually unanimous in their disapproval, if not condemnation, of same-sex eroticism, the first generation of gay activists did open a debate on the topic. The homophile movement targeted the same groups and institutions as would gay liberation members in the 1970s—urban police forces, the federal government, the churches, the medical profession, the press and other media—and through its persistence managed to rupture the consensus that shaped social attitudes toward homosexuality and society's treatment of gay people.

Searching for the answer to one puzzle, however, only raised another, more vexing problem. Much of what homophile activists fought against—moral condemnation by the churches and the criminal status of homosexual behavior, for instance—had existed for centuries. Why, then, did a gay emancipation movement come into existence only in the post–World War II era? And why did it not become a mass movement until the end of the 1960s? One could point to the specific proximate causes of political activism, such as the publication of the Kinsey study of male sexual behavior in 1948 and the repression of the McCarthy era or, in the case of gay liberation, to the model provided by the radical movements of black and white youth and of women in the 1960s. But these explanations still leave unresolved the question, "Why not earlier?" The United States had experienced both repression and mass militancy in earlier periods of its history. Moreover, other groups—blacks, women, workers—had a history of resistance to oppression and exploitation that stretched back for more than a century. Why had homosexuals and lesbians not taken up their own cause generations ago?

The recent historical literature on human sexuality suggested a way of approaching this problem. Motivated perhaps by the much heralded sexual revolution of the 1960s, or by the challenges to sexual ideology that the contemporary feminist and gay liberation movements have posed, historians have begun to study the erotic life of men and women as never before. Borrowing from the work of anthropologists and sociologists, some historians have discarded the view that sexuality is primarily a biological category, an innate, unchanging "drive" or "instinct" immune from the shifts that characterize other aspects of social organization. Instead, as a number of writers have argued, eroticism is also subject to the forces of culture. Human beings learn how to express themselves sexually, and the content of that learning is as varied as the societies that women and men have formed through the ages. Particular erotic practices, from heterosexual intercourse to masturbation and sodomy, have a universal existence. But how individual men and women interpret their sexual activity and desires, and the meanings that different societies affix to erotic behavior, vary enormously from one culture to another and from one historical era to the next.[2]

In studying homosexuality, some historians have begun to entertain the idea that human sexuality is a socially constructed, changing category. In recent books several writers have argued that "the homosexual" or "the lesbian"— that is, the person defined by society and by self through a primary erotic interest in the same sex—is a nineteenth-century invention.[3] Before then, in Western Europe and in the portions of North America populated by European settlers, men and women engaged in what we would describe as homosexual behavior, but neither they nor the society in which they lived defined persons as essentially different in kind from the majority because of their sexual expression. The absence of rigid categories called "homosexual" and "heterosexual" did not imply approval of same-sex eroticism. Men and women caught in such an act were severely punished, but their behavior was interpreted as a discrete transgression, a misdeed comparable to other sins and crimes such as adultery, blasphemy, and assault. By the late nineteenth century, a profound conceptual shift had occurred. Some men and women *were* homosexuals. The label applied not merely to particular sexual acts, as "sodomite" once had, but to an entire person whose nature—acts, feelings, personality traits, even body type—was sharply distinguishable from the majority of "normal" heterosexuals.

When applied to the topic of gay politics, this interpretation offers a new angle of vision that helps to illuminate both the timing and the course of the homosexual emancipation movement in the United States. The movement's history cannot be understood merely as a chronicle of how activists worked to mobilize masses of gay men and lesbians and to achieve a fixed agenda. Instead, the movement constitutes a phase, albeit a decisive one, of a much longer historical process through which a group of men and women came into existence as a self-conscious, cohesive minority. Before a movement could take shape, that process had to be far enough along so that at least some gay women and men could perceive themselves as members of an oppressed minority, sharing an identity that subjected them to systematic injustice. But before the

2. Some relevant social science studies of sexuality are found in Clellan S. Ford and Frank Beach, *Patterns of Sexual Behavior* (New York, 1951); John H. Gagnon and William Simon, *Sexual Conduct: The Social Sources of Human Sexuality* (Chicago, 1973); and Mary McIntosh, "The Homosexual Role," *Social Problems* 16 (1968): 182–92. For overviews of historical approaches to sexuality, see Robert A. Padgug, "Sexual Matters: On Conceptualizing Sexuality in History," *Radical History Review*, no. 20 (Spring/Summer 1979), pp. 3–23; and Estelle B. Freedman, "Sexuality in Nineteenth-Century America: Behavior, Ideology, and Politics," *Reviews in American History* 10 (1982).

3. See Jeffrey Weeks, *Coming Out: Homosexual Politics in Britain from the Nineteenth Century to the Present* (London, 1977); Michel Foucault, *The History of Sexuality*, vol. 1, *An Introduction*, trans. Robert Hurley (New York, 1978); Lillian Faderman, *Surpassing the Love of Men* (New York, 1981); Kenneth Plummer, ed., *The Making of the Modern Homosexual* (London, 1981); and Jonathan Katz, *Gay/Lesbian Almanac* (New York, 1982).

movement could become a significant social force, the consciousness and the conditions of daily life of large numbers of lesbians and homosexuals had to change so that they could take up the banner carried by a pioneering few. Thus activists had not only to mobilize a constituency; first they had to create one. The fact that most of them remained unaware of this task did not make it any less critical.

The study that follows, then, is more than an account of the first two decades of the gay emancipation movement and less than a history of homosexuality in American society. Although the primary focus remains the story of a movement for social change, I have attempted to situate the growth of a gay politics within the larger setting of the evolution of a gay sexual identity and an urban subculture of homosexuals and lesbians. In Part I, I present the historical background of the origins of the movement. Chapter 1 describes the transformation of homosexuality, both conceptually and in its actual expression, from a sexual act to a personal identity; and it provides an overview of the sanctions and the negative attitudes directed toward men and women who engaged in homoerotic behavior. The next two chapters detail the events, roughly from 1940 to 1960, that helped shape an urban gay subculture and the modern forms of gay oppression. Chapter 2 focuses on World War II and the boost it gave to the formation of a collective gay life, while Chapter 3 examines the intensification of antihomosexual attitudes and penalties during the McCarthy era.

Part II chronicles the first decade of the movement, when a tiny number of people struggled simply to keep gay organizations alive. In Chapter 4, I look at the founding of the Mattachine Society by a group of leftist homosexuals. Chapter 5 charts the abrupt shift in the Mattachine philosophy from an emphasis on mass militancy and homosexual difference to a stress on political gradualism and the insignificance of sexual expression. Chapter 6 describes the founding of the Daughters of Bilitis and the historical specificity of lesbian identity and life. In Chapter 7, I assess the accomplishments and limitations of the homophile movement in the latter half of the 1950s, when its leaders adopted an accommodationist approach to social change.

Part III examines the homophile movement during the 1960s, a turbulent decade in American history. As I argue in Chapter 8, the "sexual revolution" of the decade extended to homosexuality, as Supreme Court decisions removed legal barriers to the presentation of homoeroticism in print and in visual media, and a bewildering variety of images and viewpoints about homosexuality appeared. This barrage of information made it easier for people to come to a self-definition as homosexual or lesbian, strengthened the institutions of the subculture, and gave activists more opportunities for action. Chapter 9 traces the growth during the early 1960s of a militant wing of the movement in the East where, influenced by the example of the civil rights effort, gay activists adopted direct action protest techniques. Chapter 10 focuses on events in San Francisco during the decade. There an unusual set of circumstances provoked the first important stirrings of political consciousness within the subculture of gay bars, so that San Francisco's experience came to foreshadow what would happen in cities throughout America in the 1970s. Chapter 11 takes the story of the homophile movement up to the birth of gay liberation and assesses its success in ending the negative consensus about homosexuality. In Chapter 12 I describe the Stonewall riot and the emergence of gay liberation. Chapter 13 evaluates the role that the homophile movement played in fostering massive, grassroots activism among gay men and lesbians.

1   Identity, Community, and Oppression: A Sexual Minority in the Making

ONE

Homosexuality and American Society: An Overview

On a Saturday afternoon in November 1950, five men convened at the home of Harry Hay in the Silverlake district of Los Angeles. They gathered to discuss a proposal written by Hay that had as its purpose "the heroic objective of liberating one of our largest minorities from . . . social persecution."[1] All of the participants were members of the group they intended to liberate—America's homosexual minority. Out of their meeting eventually came the Mattachine Society, the organizaton whose founding heralded the beginning of the gay emancipation movement in the United States.

Embedded in Hay's proposal were certain assumptions that few contemporaries, homosexual or heterosexual, shared. Whether viewed from the vantage point of religion, law, or science, homosexuality appeared not as a mark of minority group status but as an individual problem, as evidence of moral weakness, criminality, or pathology. Nor would most Americans at that time have considered the treatment accorded homosexuals and lesbians a form of "social persecution." Instead, it seemed to constitute an appropriate response to behavior that offended common decency, violated accepted norms, and threatened the welfare of society. Rather than liberation, Americans who thought about homosexuality at all, including many gay men and women themselves, would have preferred elimination. Earlier generations would even have been puzzled by the categorization of a group of people on the basis of their erotic behavior.

Untangling the jumble of facts that make up the early history of the gay emancipation movement requires a preliminary exploration of the elements

1. See "Remarks Made by Harry Hay to First Discussion Group," November 1950, typescript, personal papers of James Kepner, Los Angeles.

that created the mid-twentieth-century construction of homosexuality. What made it possible for eroticism to become the basis for an identity that some people took on? What meanings did American society ascribe to homosexual behavior, and how did those meanings shape the experience of lesbians and homosexuals? What forces constrained them from breaking with the dominant views of their sexuality? What propelled some of them into a political movement, and why did that movement originate when it did?

I

For the North American settlers who migrated from England in the seventeenth and eighteenth centuries, the imperative to procreate dominated the social attitude toward and organization of sexuality. The production of children by each conjugal pair was as much a necessity as the planting of crops in the spring, since the cooperative labor of parents and their offspring generated the material goods that sustained life. Fertility in colonial America was extraordinarily high; the average pregnancy rate for white New England women was more than eight. "Heterosexuality" remained undefined, since it was literally the only way of life.[2]

Under such conditions, the existence of lesbians and gay men was inconceivable. Though criminal records, church sermons, and other evidence reveal homoerotic activity among the residents of the colonies, nothing indicates that men or women thought of themselves as "homosexual." Same-sex erotic behavior remained sporadic and exceptional. Even the trials of persistent offenders document daily lives that revolved around a heterosexual family role. The prevailing ideology reflected the facts of social existence. Colonists labeled what the twentieth century calls homosexual behavior a sin and a crime, an aberrant act for which the perpetrator received punishment in this world and the next. Nor did they conceive of homosexual acts as different in essence from other sexual transgressions—such as adultery, fornication, or bestiality—that occurred outside the sanctioned bonding of husband and wife.[3]

2. The literature on the colonial family and its relation to economic life is extensive. See Phillip J. Greven, *Four Generations* (Ithaca, N.Y., 1970); John Demos, *A Little Commonwealth* (New York, 1970); Lois Green Carr and Lorena S. Walsh, "The Planter's Wife: The Experience of White Women in Seventeenth-Century Maryland," *William and Mary Quarterly* 34 (1977): 542–71; Robert V. Wells, "Quaker Marriage Patterns in Colonial Perspective," *William and Mary Quarterly* 29 (1972): 415–42; Allan Kulikoff, "The Beginnings of the Afro-American Family in Maryland," in Aubrey C. Land et al., eds., *Law, Society and Politics in Maryland* (Baltimore, 1977), pp. 171–96; and Mary P. Ryan, *Womanhood in America* (New York, 1975), pp. 19–82.

3. For evidence of homosexual activity in the colonies, see Robert F. Oaks, "'Things Fearful to Name': Sodomy and Buggery in Seventeenth-Century New England," *Journal of Social History* 12 (1978): 268–81; J. R. Roberts, "The Case of Sarah Norman and Mary Hammond," *Sinister Wisdom*, no. 14 (1980), pp. 57–62; Vern L. Bullough, *Sexual Variance in Society and History* (Chicago, 1976; Phoenix Books ed., 1980), pp. 504–29; and Jonathan Katz, *Gay American History* (New York, 1976), pp. 16–24, 568–71. A second volume by Katz, *Gay/Lesbian Almanac* (New York, 1982) contains a substantial number of documents on the colonial era as well as an

During the second half of the nineteenth century, the momentous shift to industrial capitalism provided the conditions for a homosexual and lesbian identity to emerge. As a free-labor system, capitalism pulled men and women out of a household economy and into the marketplace, where they exchanged their individual labor power for wages. Throughout the nineteenth and twentieth centuries, as the socialized production of commodities spread, goods formerly made in the home could be purchased. The family, deprived of the functions that once held it together as an economic unit, became instead an affective entity that nurtured children and promoted the happiness of its members. Birth rates declined steadily, and procreation figured less prominently in sexual life. In place of the closely knit villages, the relatively small seaport towns, and the sprawling plantations of the preindustrial era, huge impersonal cities arose to attract an ever larger proportion of Americans. The interlocking processes of urbanization and industrialization created a social context in which an autonomous personal life could develop. Affection, intimate relationships, and sexuality moved increasingly into the realm of individual choice, seemingly disconnected from how one organized the production of goods necessary for survival. In this setting, men and women who felt a strong erotic attraction to their own sex could begin to fashion from their feeling a personal identity and a way of life.[4]

In America's cities from the 1870s through the 1930s, there emerged a class of people who recognized their erotic interest in members of their own sex, interpreted this interest as a significant characteristic that distinguished them from the majority, and sought others like themselves. Case histories compiled by doctors, vice commission investigations into the underworld of American cities, newspaper accounts of the scandalous and the bizarre, and, more rarely, personal correspondence and diaries testify to the wide social variety of these gay lives. The group included letter carriers and business executives, department store clerks and professors, factory operatives, civil service employees, ministers, engineers, students, cooks, domestics, hoboes, and the idle rich. Both men and women, blacks and whites, immigrants and the native born

---

interpretive essay. I am indebted to him for permitting me to see the manuscript before publication.

4. On the emergence of a gay identity in capitalist society, see Jeffrey Weeks, *Coming Out: Homosexual Politics in Britain* (London, 1977); Michel Foucault, *A History of Sexuality, vol. 1, An Introduction*, trans. Robert Hurley (New York, 1978); and Lillian Faderman, *Surpassing the Love of Men* (New York, 1981). On the development of a "personal life," see Eli Zaretsky, *Capitalism, the Family and Personal Life* (New York, 1976). On the rise of the family as an affective unit, see Paula Fass, *The Damned and the Beautiful: American Youth in the 1920s* (New York, 1977). On the spread of single-person living arrangements, see Frances E. Kobrin, "The Fall in Household Size and the Rise of the Primary Individual in the United States," *Demography* 13 (1976): 127–38. Separation of work and home is one of the central themes of nineteenth-century women's history; see Ryan, *Womanhood in America*, pp. 83-192; Nancy F. Cott, *The Bonds of Womanhood* (New Haven, Conn., 1977); and Carl Degler, *At Odds: Women and the Family in America, 1776 to the Present* (New York, 1980).

people these accounts. Some were or had been married; others were single. Many lived in relative isolation, while quite a few had formed lasting partnerships and acquired a circle of lesbian or homosexual friends. Their sexuality had propelled some toward a lifetime commitment to homoerotic relationships, whereas for others, homosexual involvements were sporadic and transitory, brief detours off a well-worn path.[5]

Gradually finding methods of meeting one another, these men and women staked out urban spaces and patronized institutions that fostered a group life. During the first two decades of the twentieth century, male homosexual transvestites and their ordinary-looking comrades made their liaisons in saloons and clubs scattered through the least respectable parts of town. In the largest cities, such places had multiplied by the 1920s to a point that permitted differentiation of clientele by social class and "type." By World War I, gay men regularly cruised certain thoroughfares and parks, from Riverside Drive in New York and Lafayette Park in Washington to the Presidio in San Francisco. Some public bathhouses and YMCAs became gathering spots for male homosexuals. In St. Louis and the nation's capital at the turn of the century, annual drag balls that brought together black gay men evinced well-developed networks among them. Lesbians and gay men formed literary societies and planned private entertainments that sustained friendships and promised dependable social interaction. Newspapers revealed the existence of working class couples, sometimes legally married, in which both members were women, with one of them passing as a man to obtain work. Occasionally a circle of such cross-dressing women would come to light. Among the faculties of women's colleges, in the settlement houses where some alumnae lived, and in the professional associations and clubs that college-educated women formed, one could find lifelong intimate relationships supported by a web of friendships with other lesbians.[6]

By 1915, one observer of male homosexual life was already referring to it as "a community distinctly organized."[7] Meeting places for public liaisons, institutions such as bars, and friendship networks dotted the urban landscape.

---

5. Unless otherwise noted, material about the lives of gay men and lesbians from 1870 to 1940 is drawn from the relevant documents in Katz, *Gay American History*.

6. For Riverside Drive, see U.S. Senate, 67th Cong., 1st Sess., Committee on Naval Affairs, *Report on Alleged Immoral Conditions and Practices at the Naval Training Station, Newport, R.I.* (Washington, 1921), p. 8; on San Francisco, see Allan Bérubé, "Lesbians and Gay Men in Early San Francisco: Notes Toward a Social History of Lesbians and Gay Men in America," typescript, in the possession of Bérubé, San Francisco, 1979; on literary societies and private social activities, see Vern Bullough and Bonnie Bullough, "Lesbianism in the 1920s and 1930s: A Newfound Study," *Signs* 2 (1977): 895–904. On college-educated women, see Judith Schwarz, "*Yellow Clover:* Katharine Lee Bates and Katharine Coman," *Frontiers: A Journal of Women Studies* 4, no. 1 (Spring 1979): 59–67; and Anna Mary Wells, *Miss Marks and Miss Woolley* (Boston, 1978).

7. Quoted in Katz, *Gay American History*, p. 52.

During the 1920s and 1930s, they acquired a measure of stability, slowly grew in number, and differentiated themselves to allow for specialization by social background and styles. Gradually a subculture of gay men and lesbians was evolving in American cities that would help to create a collective consciousness among its participants and strengthen their sense of identification with a group.

II

A society hostile to homosexual expression shaped the contours of gay identity and the gay subculture. In the Judeo-Christian tradition, homosexual behavior was excoriated as a heinous sin, the law branded it a serious crime, and the medical profession diagnosed homosexuals and lesbians as diseased. Together, they marked gay people as inferior—less moral, less respectable, and less healthy than their fellows. Exposure promised punishment and ostracism. It hovered about gay life as an ever present danger, always reminding homosexual men and women of the need for secrecy and careful management of information about their sexual preferences. Coupled with the restrictions that social custom and law placed on public discussion of homosexuality, fear of discovery kept the gay world invisible. It also erected barriers against self-awareness and made it difficult for women and men to find entry into the homosexual subculture.

Biblical condemnations of homosexual behavior suffused American culture from its origin. For seventeenth-century settlers, with only a precarious foothold on the edge of an unknown continent, the terrible destruction of Sodom and Gomorrah by an angry God evoked dread. Men who lay with men, the book of Leviticus warned, committed an "abomination; they shall surely be put to death; their blood shall be upon them." Paul considered lustful behavior between men and between women "vile passions . . . against nature." Colonial ministers railed against sodomy in their sermons. Although the world view of most twentieth-century Americans had ceased to be as biblically centered as that of their colonial predecessors, and although modern believers might be less inclined to expect ruin to pour down from heaven, religious teachings still shaped their views of sexuality and their sexual behavior to a large degree. The information Alfred Kinsey culled from 10,000 interviews convinced him that nothing in American society had "more influence upon present-day patterns of sexual behavior than the religious backgrounds of that culture. . . . Ancient religious codes are still the prime source of the attitudes, the ideas, the ideals, and the rationalizations by which most individuals pattern their sexual lives." Derrick Sherwin Bailey, a biblical scholar who undertook in the 1950s a comprehensive reevaluation of Christian theology and homosexuality, closed his book with the thirteenth century because "it does not appear that the tradition has undergone any significant alteration since that time." He found the antihomosexual interpretation of the Sodom episode "accepted without question" and at the base of "the thought and the imagination of the West in the matter of homosexual practices."[8]

The law stipulated harsh punishments for homosexual acts. Colonial legal codes, drawn either directly from the Bible or from the theologically influenced English buggery statute of 1533, prescribed death for sodomy, and in several instances courts directed the execution of men found guilty of this act. Magistrates invoked statutes prohibiting lewd behavior in order to prosecute other homosexual behavior by men and women. Although most states abolished the death penalty for sodomy in the half century after independence, all but two in 1950 still classified it as a felony. Only murder, kidnapping, and rape elicited heavier sentences. Through penal code revisions and court rulings, statutes had also become more inclusive in the course of the nineteenth and twentieth centuries. State legislatures rewrote laws and judges reinterpreted them, so that erotic activity between women and oral sex between men fell within the domain of the sodomy and "crime against nature" statutes.[9]

Although comparatively few men and virtually no women suffered the full punishment permitted under these laws, the statutes imposed the stigma of criminality upon same-sex eroticism. The severity with which legislatures and magistrates viewed homosexual behavior, moreover, buttressed the enforcement of a wide range of other penal code provisions against homosexuals and lesbians. As a gay subculture took root in twentieth-century American cities, police invoked laws against disorderly conduct, vagrancy, public lewdness, assault, and solicitation in order to haul in their victims. Gay men who made assignations in public places, lesbians and homosexuals who patronized gay bars, and occasionally even guests at gay parties in private homes risked arrest. Vice squad officers, confident that their targets did not dare to challenge their

8. Alfred Kinsey et al., *Sexual Behavior in the Human Male* (Philadelphia, 1948), pp. 465, 487; Derrick Sherwin Bailey, *Homosexuality and the Western Christian Tradition* (London, 1955), pp. viii, 27, 152. The biblical passages are Lev. 20:13 and Rom. 1:26, quoted in Bailey, p. 29. For other surveys of Christian teaching, see Michael J. Buckley, *Morality and the Homosexual: A Catholic Approach* (Westminster, Md., 1960); Robert L. Treese, "Homosexuality: A Contemporary View of the Biblical Perspective," in Sally Gearhart and William R. Johnson, eds., *Loving Women/Loving Men* (San Francisco, 1974), pp. 23–58; and John McNeill, *The Church and the Homosexual* (Kansas City, 1976). A recent book by John Boswell, *Christianity, Social Tolerance, and Homosexuality* (Chicago, 1981), argues strongly against a view of Christianity as unremittingly hostile to homosexuality, yet even Boswell is forced to admit that antihomosexual attitudes reigned supreme by the end of the Middle Ages. On colonial religious opinion, see Katz, *Gay American History*, pp. 19–20.

9. See Oaks, " 'Things Fearful to Name' "; and Roberts, "The Case of Sarah Norman and Mary Hammond"; Louis Crompton, "Homosexuals and the Death Penalty in Colonial America," *Journal of Homosexuality* 1 (1976): 277–93; Bullough, *Sexual Variance*, pp. 565–82; Morris Ploscowe, *Sex and the Law* (New York, 1951), pp. 195–213; and Karl M. Bowman and Bernice Engle, "A Psychiatric Evaluation of the Laws of Homosexuality," *Temple Law Quarterly Review* 29 (1956): 273–326. Donald Webster Cory (pseud.), *The Homosexual in America: A Subjective Approach* (New York, 1951), contains extracts from state penal codes in app. B, pp. 281–92.

authority, were free to engage in entrapment. Anxious to avoid additional notoriety, gay women and men often pleaded guilty even when the police lacked sufficient evidence to secure convictions. Court proceedings seemed designed to instill feelings of shame and obliterate self-esteem. A New York City magistrate, writing in 1951, described how the court attendant's "normally stentorian voice drops to a whisper" when reading a homosexual-related complaint, while judges commonly directed gratuitous, abusive language at defendants.[10]

Besides facing the moral condemnation of churches and the punishments imposed by law, gay men and women found themselves scrutinized by a medical profession that diagnosed homosexuality as a disease. In the 1880s and 1890s, when the scientific literature first appeared, doctors engaged in a spirited debate over whether homosexuality was a vice indulged in by weak-willed, depraved individuals, an acquired form of insanity, or a congenital defect that indicated evolutionary degeneracy. In time, advocates of the first view dropped out of the discussion, content to leave the regulation of homosexual behavior to the church and the criminal justice system. Among proponents of a medical model, a near consensus had emerged by the early twentieth century that homosexuality was hereditary in its origins.[11]

The implications drawn from the congenital framework, however, varied considerably. In Germany and Britain, for instance, a minority of doctors argued that individuals should not be punished for a biological inheritance over which they had no control, and the congenital perspective thus served as the intellectual underpinning for vigorous homosexual reform movements. In the United States, on the other hand, doctors emphasized the tainted nature of the inheritance. Homosexual impulses, the argument ran, generally remained inactive until they were inexplicably triggered in people who had been leading otherwise heterosexual lives. Its unexpected manifestation made homosexuality an especially dread disease. It provoked exaggerated descriptions of infection and danger, with some medical men even proposing and carrying out sexual surgery to prevent such defectives from passing their traits on to future

10. Ploscowe, *Sex and the Law*, p. 195; on the use of gratuitous and abusive language, see Lawrence M. Goldwyn, "Legal Ideology and the Regulation of Homosexual Behavior," Ph.D. diss., Stanford University, 1979, pp. 23–47; on law enforcement practices, see below, Chap. 3.

11. The medical model is one area that has received relatively extensive treatment in the history of homosexuality. See Vern L. Bullough, "Homosexuality and the Medical Model," *Journal of Homosexuality* 1 (1974): 99–110; Elizabeth Fee, "Science and Homosexuality," in *The Universities and the Gay Experience* (New York, 1974), pp. 35–39; Paul Robinson, *The Modernization of Sex* (New York, 1976), pp. 1–41; Weeks, *Coming Out*, pp. 23–32; Dolores Klaich, *Woman + Woman: Attitudes Toward Lesbianism* (New York, 1974), pp. 55–87; Katz, *Gay American History*, pp. 129–207; and John R. Martin, "Sexual Perversion or Vice? A Late-nineteenth-century Debate," paper delivered at the April 1980 meeting of the Organization of American Historians, San Francisco. On the development of sexuality as a field of medical science, see John S. Haller and Robin M. Haller, *The Physician and Sexuality in Victorian America* (Urbana, Ill., 1974); and Foucault, *The History of Sexuality*.

generations. Perhaps because Americans of Anglo-Saxon stock at the turn of the century feared racial "contamination" by immigrants and blacks, homosexuality stimulated worries about evolutionary degeneracy.[12]

Though a disease model exercised hegemony among doctors until the 1970s, it underwent major reformulation as Freudian psychoanalytic perspectives gained preeminence after World War I. Despite Freud's postulation of a continuum between constitutional and environmental influences on sexual development, psychoanalysis decisively shifted medical investigation of sexuality to the psyche and away from the body, where nineteenth-century science had focused its attention. Freud himself did not write extensively on homosexuality (though when he did, he tended to view it sympathetically and to refrain from categorizing it as pathological), but his theories did provide a much sharper definition of the "normal," with the libido moving in stages from polymorphous expression in infancy to genital heterosexuality in adults. Almost without exception, however, Freud's pupils and successors in psychoanalysis placed homosexuality firmly in the sphere of pathology. Adherents of libido theory argued a variety of possible causes, from unresolved Oedipal conflicts to oral fixations, that might lead to a homosexual orientation; other psychiatrists, such as Karen Horney and Harry Stack Sullivan, emphasized the importance of nonsexual needs in obstructing sexual development. Thus homosexuality might be itself the psychological malady needing treatment, or it might be the symptom of some other personality disorder. In any case, it remained a mental health problem requiring psychiatric treatment.[13]

Besides pathology, the common thread of gender differences ran through both the somatic and the psychoanalytic literature on homosexuality. Doctors of whatever theoretical persuasion pursued their study of human sexuality from the starting point of procreation. Richard von Krafft-Ebing, the most influential of the late nineteenth-century medical writers, constructed an elaborate sexual system based on the complementary nature of male and female reproductive functions. Procreative sexuality became one attribute of normal, healthy males and females who were themselves the product of a long

12. On the movements in Germany and England, see John Lauritsen and David Thorstad, *The Early Homosexual Rights Movement, 1864–1935* (New York, 1974); James D. Steakley, *The Homosexual Emancipation Movement in Germany* (New York, 1975); Weeks, *Coming Out*; and Sheila Rowbotham and Jeffrey Weeks, *Socialism and the New Life: The Personal and Sexual Politics of Edward Carpenter and Havelock Ellis* (London, 1977). On medical opinion in the United States, see Katz, *Gay/Lesbian Almanac*, which contains extensive documents and an analysis of the medical literature from 1880 to 1920. On nativist fears of "racial contamination" and "race suicide," see Linda Gordon, *Woman's Body, Woman's Right* (New York, 1976), chap. 7; and Mark Haller, *Eugenics: Hereditarian Attitudes in American Thought* (New Brunswick, N.J., 1963).

13. The psychoanalytic literature on homosexuality is vast. For a sampling, see Hendrik M. Ruitenbeek, ed., *The Problem of Homosexuality in Modern Society* (New York, 1963); and Irving Bieber et al., *Homosexuality* (New York, 1962), pp. 3–18, which provides a useful summary of competing psychoanalytic models. See Nathan G. Hale, Jr., *Freud and the Americans* (New York, 1971), for the beginnings of Freudian influence on American thought.

evolutionary process. Homosexuality, he argued, violated the "hidden laws of nature" by confusing the appropriate roles of men and women. Even such a sexual modernist as Havelock Ellis rooted his theories in the biological differentiation of the sexes. Though psychoanalysis turned away from biology, it also linked proper sexual development to notions of femininity and masculinity. As a result, homosexuality became associated with "mannishness" in women and effeminacy in men as descriptions of both physical appearance and personality. The medical profession contributed to a popular stereotype of gay men and women as generally exhibiting the characteristics of the opposite sex.[14]

The medical model played only a minor role in society's understanding of homosexuality until the 1940s. Before then, it was elaborated upon primarily in the pages of specialized journals. However, psychiatric screening of inductees ordered by the federal government during World War II catapulted the psychiatric profession into the lives of millions of Americans. Psychiatry emerged from the war with its status enhanced. Dr. William Menninger, the chief psychiatric consultant to the surgeon-general of the army, wrote afterward, "Although the shooting is over, the public interest in the profession of mental health and illness and the challenge of that interest to professional psychiatry is at an all-time high, as a result of the war."[15] Hollywood movies like *Now Voyager* and *Spellbound* introduced these doctors of the mind into the popular culture. Increasingly, Americans came to view human sexual behavior as either healthy or sick, with homosexuality falling into the latter category. Medical guides aimed at a lay audience expounded on the phenomenon of same-sex orientation and the possibilities of curing it. In the fifteen years after World War II, legislatures of more than half the states turned to psychiatrists for solutions to the problem of sex crimes, and they passed sexual psychopath laws that officially recognized homosexuality as a socially threatening disease. In the postwar era, medicine was moving toward parity with religion and law in structuring American culture's perception of homosexuality.[16]

Medical views bore a complex relation to the older perspectives of religion and law. In important ways they reinforced the cultural matrix that condemned and punished persons who engaged in homosexual activity. Whether

14. See, e.g., Richard von Krafft-Ebing, *Psychopathia Sexualis*, 12th ed., rev. and enl., trans. Frank S. Klaf (New York, 1965); Havelock Ellis, *Studies in the Psychology of Sex* (New York, 1936); and Helene Deutsch, *The Psychology of Women* (New York, 1945).

15. William C. Menninger, *Psychiatry in a Troubled World* (New York, 1948), p. vii.

16. On the impact of the war on psychiatry and its role in American society, see Menninger, *Psychiatry in a Troubled World*; and Rebecca Schwartz Greene, "The Role of the Psychiatrist in World War II," Ph.D. diss., Columbia University, 1977. On the sexual psychopath laws, see Karl M. Bowman and Bernice Engle, "Sexual Psychopath Laws," in Ralph Slovenko, ed., *Sexual Behavior and the Law* (Springfield, Ill., 1965); Edwin H. Sutherland, "The Sexual Psychopath Laws," *Journal of Criminal Law and Criminology* 40 (1950), 543–54; and Alan H. Swanson, "Sexual Psychopath Statutes: Summary and Analysis," *Journal of Criminal Law, Criminology and Police Science*, 51 (1960), 215–35.

seen as sin, crime, or sickness, homosexuality stigmatized an individual. Doctors did not ply their trade in a vacuum, moreover, and the language of the moralist permeated the scientific literature. It is difficult to imagine a physician describing pneumonia as "shocking to every sense of decency, disgusting and revolting," yet one did apply these phrases to a case of homosexuality.[17] Although the medical profession strove from the 1880s onward to wrest power over the fate of homosexuals and lesbians away from the criminal justice system, the attempt did not initially seem to benefit gay individuals. Its first results—the sexual psychopath laws of the 1940s, 1950s, and 1960s—simply added another mechanism of control that deprived some gay women and men of their freedom. A view of homosexuality as disease spelled trouble even for those who never ran afoul of the law, since some families committed their gay members to asylums. In their search for a cure, doctors experimented on their wards with procedures ranging from the relatively benign, such as psychotherapy and hypnosis, to castration, hysterectomy, lobotomy, electroshock, aversion therapy, and the administration of untested drugs. The severity of these treatments suggests a perception of homosexuality as a disease almost as threatening to society as the sin of Sodom that provoked the destruction of biblical cities. Whatever beneficent results medicine might promise, by the mid-twentieth century it had in fact branded homosexual men and women with a mark of inferiority no less corrosive of their self-respect than that of sin and criminality.[18]

Yet to a certain extent physicians also subverted the earlier approaches. Once homosexual behavior entered the realm of science, it became subject to careful investigation. No matter how solid the consensus that homosexuality was a disease, the accumulation of empirical evidence could inspire new, dissenting theories, whereas Christian teachings rested on the immutable words of the Bible. Unlike moralists and law enforcement officials, doctors had a vested interest in naming, describing, and classifying the "unmentionable vice" in all its forms. The successful treatment of disease required detailed knowledge; its prevention demanded that parents, educators, public health officials, indeed all members of society understand the causes and symptoms of the malady. In contrast to immorality and crime, illness elicited compassion, a sympathetic concern for the afflicted victim. Precautions could be taken against disease, but one did not generally blame a patient for becoming sick or interpret poor health as a result of free choice. The medical model introduced a dynamic element into discussions of same-sex eroticism that could serve the interests of reformers.

Finally, the intervention of science in the discourse on homosexuality initiated a profound reconceptualization of the phenomenon. Medical profes-

17. Quoted in Katz, *Gay American History*, p. 136.
18. For the range of treatments, see Katz, *Gay American History*, pp. 129–207; for examples of the commitment of gay men and women to asylums by their families, see the autobiographical accounts by Whitey and Rick in Nancy and Casey Adair, *Word Is Out* (New York, 1978), pp. 3–13, 29–41.

sionals were able to theorize about it because they had specific case histories to examine. Under their scrutiny, homosexuality shifted from being an aberration for which individuals were punished to a condition that inhered in a person and defined one's very nature. By transforming same-sex eroticism into a clinical entity, doctors hastened the evolution of a new form of identity that was based upon sexual expression.

In addition to the opprobrium emanating from religion, law, and medicine, American society at large revealed its disapproval of homosexual eroticism by sharply curtailing public discussion of the topic. From the Reverend Higgeson who referred in 1629 to sodomitical activity as "wickedness not to bee named" to the Illinois judge who in 1897 described the crime against nature as "not fit to be named among Christians," commentators composed their remarks according to a formula that discouraged further amplification.[19] To the general reticence of Victorian America, the purity crusades of the 1870s and later added federal, state, and municipal statutes that prohibited the importation, mailing, production, distribution, sale, and possession of obscene literature. Sex and obscenity were often seen as synonymous. Extralegal pressures supplemented the law as private citizens' groups worked in tandem with the post office and the police to enforce compliance.[20]

Although the diffusion of Freudian psychoanalysis in the 1920s helped foster a rapidly growing public discourse on sexuality that substantially replaced late nineteenth-century reserve, the decade's much heralded revolution in manners and morals was an exclusively heterosexual upheaval. Homosexuality continued to be a target of censorship forces who succeeded remarkably in holding the line against acceptance of homosexuality as an artistic theme. In the mid-1920s purity advocates in New York City managed to drive a number of plays with lesbian and gay male themes from the legitimate stage and won passage of a theatrical padlock bill outlawing the portrayal of sexual "perversion." The successful 1929 court challenge of the seizure of Radclyffe Hall's lesbian novel, *The Well of Loneliness*, was an exception that proved the rule. The National Office for Decent Literature of the Catholic Church, founded in the 1930s, placed homosexual works on its list of proscribed literature. To avoid trouble, publishers and newspaper editors engaged in a form of self-censorship that kept homosexuality virtually out of print. In 1934 the motion picture production code prohibited any depiction of homosexuality in films. Although the "conspiracy of silence" surrounding sex was losing its force, on the eve of World War II it still placed powerful inhibitions on the flow of any

19. Higgeson's remark may be found in Katz, *Gay American History*, p. 20, and those of the Illinois judge in Honselman v. People, 168 Ill. 172, 48 N.E. 304, quoted in Ploscowe, *Sex and the Law*, p. 197.

20. On the obscenity statutes, purity crusades, and early twentieth-century censorship efforts, see Robert W. Haney, *Comstockery in America* (Boston, 1960); Murray L. Schwartz, *Federal Censorship* (New York, 1961); Felice Flanery Lewis, *Literature Obscenity and Law* (Carbondale, Ill., 1976); and David Pivar, *Purity Crusade: Sexual Morality and Social Control* (Westport, Conn., 1976). See also the discussion below in Chap. 8.

information that did not conform to the most negative, condemnatory views of same-sex eroticism.[21]

III

It is much harder to reconstruct the emotions and experiences of lesbians and homosexuals who lived in the half century before the Second World War than to chart the attitudes of society and compile the catalog of penalties facing gay men and women. Prudence dictated that they remain unobtrusive and leave behind as little incriminating evidence as possible. Subcultural institutions were still rare. Much of the information that does survive comes from the outside, from prejudiced observers, and records the stories of men and women in distress. Yet fragments remain to allow one to speculate tentatively about the broad contours of a gay life in the generations before the homosexual emancipation movement.

"Coming out"—recognizing one's homosexual desires, subsequently attempting to act upon them, and acknowledging one's sexual preferences to others of the same persuasion—was a lonely, difficult, and sometimes excruciatingly painful experience. Although their sexual impulses might eventually bind gay men and women to others like themselves, initially their sexuality created a profound, even disturbing, sense of difference from family, community, and society. Lesbians and homosexuals grew up with the male/female couple as their only model of intimate erotic relationships. Unaware of sexual alternatives, they found no encouragement for same-sex eroticism. Resources even for naming their desires were meager. When information about homosexuality did surface, it rarely inspired self-esteem. Medical texts emphasizing morbidity and newspaper stories of violent crimes, infamous scandals, and social misfits offered a dismal view of the possibilities awaiting the sexually different. Often these scarce bits of negative evidence escaped the attention of gay men and women. When someone did break the silence in order to dissent publicly from prevailing views, the response of gay women and men suggests how rare such occasions were. Emma Goldman, who lectured on homosexuality during her 1915 speaking tour, commented on the numerous "men and women who used to come to see me after my lectures on homosexuality." One twenty-five-year-old woman, typical of many whom the fiery anarchist encountered, confided that "she had never met anyone . . . who suffered from a similar affliction nor had she ever read books dealing with the subject." Goldman's lecture "set her free." Few men and women who experienced homosexual desire were as lucky as those in Goldman's audience.[22]

21. On the theater controversy in New York in the 1920s, see the documents in Katz, *Gay American History*, pp. 82–91; on the specifically heterosexual character of the changes in sexual mores in the 1920s, see Fass, *The Damned and the Beautiful*; and Christina Simmons, "Purity Rejected: The New Sex Freedom of the Twenties," paper delivered at the 1976 Berkshire Women's History Conference, and "Companionate Marriage and the Lesbian Threat," *Frontiers* 4, no. 3 (Fall 1979): 54–59.
22. Quoted in Katz, *Gay American History*, p. 377.

Ironically, the medical model promoted the articulation of a gay identity and made it easier for many lesbians and homosexuals to come out. In elaborating upon their theories, doctors helped create the phenomenon that most of them wished to eliminate. They transformed an evil impulse that the morally upright strove to resist into the primary constituent of one's nature, inescapable because it permeated one's being. Thus in 1924 F. O. Matthiessen, a young Yale graduate who would one day become a well-regarded literary historian, described the impact of reading Havelock Ellis's *Sexual Inversion.* "Then for the first time it was completely brought home to me that I was what I was by *nature.* . . . How clearly I can now see every act and friendship of my boyhood interpreted from my proper sexual temperament." Thereafter, he went on, "I didn't know whether I could keep from getting morbid *without* some [sexual] expression." By the 1930s Radclyffe Hall's *The Well of Loneliness* was popularizing the medical model among its wide audience. Long after the congenital explanation had lost its credence among professionals, many gay women and men held on to it, using it to affirm and justify their sexual desires. Medical theories made homosexuality not a deed that one avoided but a condition that described who one was.[23]

Whatever the path by which gay men and women arrived at a self-definition based on their sexuality, the labeling of one's sexual desires marked but the first step in a lifelong journey of discovery that offered challenges, perils, and rewards. "We stand in the middle of an uncharted, uninhabited country," Matthiessen wrote to his lover, Russell Cheney.[24] Men and women had first of all to find their fellows. Largely invisible and still rudimentary, the gay subculture easily escaped detection. In the first decades of the twentieth century many, perhaps even most gay women and men undoubtedly spent the better part of their adulthood in relative or total isolation from their own kind. Entry into the gay world, moreover, always brought with it the possibility of exposure and trouble. The effort to conceal what one so laboriously sought to uncover often exacted a heavy emotional toll. Nor could any homosexuals or lesbians stand entirely apart from the abusive definitions that made them, as Matthiessen phrased it, "pariahs, outlaws, degenerates" in the eyes of the world."[25]

For some, the struggle to construct a viable personal life around their erotic inclinations nurtured a character sturdy enough to counter the majority viewpoint. A turn-of-the-century business executive described her attraction to women as a "divine gift of loving," while a male contemporary accepted his sexuality as "a natural, pure and sound passion . . . worthy of the reverence of all fine natures." The biographies of many college-educated women of the

23. Louis Hyde, ed., *Rat and the Devil: Journal Letters of F. O. Matthiessen and Russell Cheney* (Hamden, Conn., 1978), p. 47 (second emphasis added). For an example of disastrous consequences of the medical model's influence on individual consciousness, see Katz, *Gay American History,* pp. 258–79.

24. Hyde, *Rat and the Devil,* p. 71.

25. Ibid., p. 29.

early twentieth century reveal the empowering effect of lifelong intimate relationships that encompassed both a female lover and a support network of lesbian couples. Other men and women collapsed under the weight of social opprobrium, engaging in violent antisocial behavior, falling into insanity, or delivering themselves into the hands of doctors in the hope of a cure. In trying to maneuver the narrow space between extreme self-hate and external troubles, the majority probably managed to escape the latter, but at the price of internalizing a negative view of their sexual identity.[26]

For some, particularly gay men and women in the largest cities, the 1920s and 1930s brought a modest easing of their difficulties. There was more open discussion of sexuality in sophisticated circles; and in cities such as New York, Chicago, and San Francisco, a small but stable group life was forming. Neither of these developments ameliorated society's hostility to homosexuality, but at least the chances of sharing one's predicament were increasing. Although participation in an urban gay subculture remained exceptional in the period between the two world wars, it suggested the shape of things to come.

On the eve of World War II, contradictory forces structured the phenomenon of same-sex eroticism in America. On the one hand, cumulative historical processes—the spread of capitalist economic relations, industrialism and the socialization of production, and urban growth—were shaping a social context in which homosexual desire might congeal into a personal identity. As men and women who were inclined toward their own sex took on a self-definition as homosexual or lesbian, they searched for others like themselves and gradually created a group life. On the other hand, a pervasive hostility, expressed through religion, law, and science, kept homosexuality submerged and constrained gay people from openly acknowledging their presence in society. Restrictions on public discussion of homosexual eroticism inhibited coming out, making it difficult not only to formulate a self-definition as gay but also, more importantly, to locate the inchoate subculture of lesbians and homosexuals. For men and women who surmounted these hurdles and managed to stumble upon collective manifestations of gay life, the prevailing ideology imposed a burden of self-hate and encouraged them to interpret their sexuality in individualistic terms as an aberration, a flaw, or a personal failing. Few would have predicted the launching at mid-century of a gay emancipation movement.

26. The quotation is from Katz, *Gay American History*, pp. 374–76. On college-educated women, see Schwarz, "Yellow Clover"; Nan Bauer Maglin, "Vida to Florence: 'Comrade and Companion,' " *Frontiers* 4, no. 3 (Fall 1979): 13–20; and Faderman, *Surpassing the Love of Men*.

TWO

Forging a Group Identity: World War II and the Emergence of an Urban Gay Subculture

The mobilization of American society for victory during World War II seriously upset patterns of daily life. Following in the wake of a depression that saw both marriage and birth rates drop precipitously, the war further disrupted family stability and social relations between the sexes. It uprooted tens of millions of American men and women, many of them young, and deposited them in a variety of nonfamilial, often sex-segregated environments. Men left home as conscripts or volunteers to spend years in the armed forces, while millions of women entered the paid labor force for the first time. The relocation of civilians of both sexes to the burgeoning centers of defense industry typically involved a shift from rural and small-town residences to impersonal metropolitan areas. Young adults who in peacetime might have moved directly from their parents' home into one with their spouse experienced instead years of living away from kin and away from settings where easygoing intimacy with the opposite sex led to permanent ties. Families endured prolonged separations, divorce and desertion occurred more frequently, and the trend toward greater sexual permissiveness accelerated.[1]

1. On domestic society during the war years, see Richard Polenberg, *War and Society* (Philadelphia, 1972); Francis Merrill, *Social Problems on the Home Front* (New York, 1948); Henry Shryock and Hope Eldridge, "Internal Migration in War and Peace," *American Sociological Review* 12 (1947): 27–39; Ruth Milkman, "Women's Work and the Economic Crisis: Some Lessons from the Great Depression," in Nancy F. Cott and Elizabeth H. Pleck, eds., *A Heritage of Her Own* (New York, 1979); William H. Chafe, *The American Woman* (New York, 1972), chaps. 6–8; Geoffrey Perrett, *Days of Sadness, Years of Triumph* (New York, 1973); Roy Hoopes, *Americans Remember the Home Front* (New York, 1977); and Richard R. Lingeman, *Don't You Know There's a War On?* (New York, 1970).

In releasing large numbers of Americans from their homes and neighbor-hoods, World War II created a substantially new "erotic situation" conducive both to the articulation of a homosexual identity and to the more rapid evolution of a gay subculture. For some gay men and women, the war years simply strengthened a way of living they had previously chosen. People who had already come to a self-definition as homosexual or lesbian found greater opportunities during the war to meet others like themselves. At the same time, those who experienced strong same-sex attraction but felt inhibited from acting upon it suddenly possessed relatively more freedom to enter into homosexual relationships. The unusual conditions of a mobilized society allowed homosexual desire to be expressed more easily in action. For many gay Americans, World War II created something of a nationwide coming out experience.[2]

I

Men and women felt the impact of the war in different ways. For men, the demands of the armed forces shaped their experiences. The Selective Training and Service Act of 1940 led to the immediate registration of more than 16,400,000 males between the ages of twenty-one and thirty-five. As teenagers came of age and the limits were extended to include both older and younger men, others came into contact with the military apparatus. At their peak strength the services held more than 12 million men. Although the military cast a wide net in order to meet its manpower needs, it preferred men who were young, single or with few dependents: a population group likely to include a disproportionate number of gay men.

The intrusion of the military into the lives of American men brought with it questions concerning homosexuality. From the beginning of the war, psychiatrists examined potential inductees to weed out the unfit. Since a history of homosexual behavior or even tendencies toward it constituted grounds for exclusion, medical personnel interrogated recruits about their sexual inclinations. In an era when silence most typically characterized socie-ty's approach to same-sex eroticism, the military medical examination was a significant exception. For gay and nongay men alike, it represented the first and perhaps the only time that they faced such inquiries in a public setting.[3]

Although intended in part to keep homosexuals out of the armed forces, psychiatric screening proved relatively ineffective in doing so. Given the patriotic fervor that the war elicited and the stigma attached to a rejection for neuropsychiatric reasons, few gay men willingly declared themselves in order to avoid service. Moreover, the medical questioning averaged only a few

---

2. The description of wartime and military life as a new "erotic situation" comes from Colin J. Williams and Martin S. Weinberg, *Homosexuals and the Military* (New York, 1971), p. 57.

3. For a thorough analysis of psychiatric screening, see Rebecca Schwartz Greene, "The Role of the Psychiatrist in World War II," Ph.D. diss., Columbia University, 1977.

minutes in duration and depended upon the most superficial signs of homosexuality. As their means of identification, doctors often relied on body type or recruits' recognition of homosexual slang. In general, only the most effeminate, those with arrest records, or those especially worried about the strain of living in an all-male environment with stringent sanctions against homosexual behavior found themselves rejected because of their sexuality. In evaluating the success of the screening process, Doctor William Menninger concluded that, "for every homosexual who was referred or came to the Medical Department, there were five or ten who never were detected." Other authorities estimated that the proportion who served without discovery was much higher.[4]

Even for those gay men who slipped by the psychiatrists, the experience brought their sexuality into bold relief. Anticipation of the examination bred anxious introspection, and afterward the screening remained a vivid memory. Troubled by his sexual inclinations, Merle Miller had made strenuous efforts at concealment, including participation in attacks upon "queers" in his campus newspaper, *The Daily Iowan*, to divert suspicions. The induction procedure worried him. "I was afraid I would never get into the army," he recalled, "but after the psychiatrist tapped me on the knee with a little hammer and asked how I felt about girls, before I really had a chance to answer, he said 'Next' and I was being sworn in." The brief encounter stayed with him, however, and Miller spent his four years in service carefully masking his identity. For homosexual soldiers, induction into the military forced a sudden confrontation with their sexuality that highlighted the stigma attached to it and kept it a matter of special concern.[5]

The sex-segregated nature of the armed forces raised homosexuality closer to the surface for all military personnel. Soldiers indulged in buffoonery, aping in exaggerated form the social stereotype of the homosexual, as a means of releasing the sexual tensions of life in the barracks. Such behavior was so common that a towel company used the image of a GI mincing with a towel draped around his waist to advertise its product. Army canteens witnessed men dancing with one another, an activity that in peacetime subjected homosexuals to arrest. Crowded into port cities, men on leave or those waiting to be shipped overseas shared beds in YMCAs and slept in each other's arms in parks or in the aisles of movie theaters that stayed open to house them. Living

4. William C. Menninger, *Psychiatry in a Troubled World* (New York, 1948), p. 227. On homosexuality, the military, and psychiatric screening, see Menninger, pp. 221–31; Lewis J. Loesser, "The Sexual Psychopath in the Military Service: A Study of 270 Cases," *American Journal of Psychiatry* 102 (July 1945): 92–101; *Newsweek*, June 9, 1947, p. 54; L. B. Hohman and B. Schaffner, "The Sex Lives of Unmarried Men," *American Journal of Sociology* 52 (1947): 501–7; and Williams and Weinberg, *Homosexuals and the Military*, pp. 26–27. For a higher estimate, see Alfred Kinsey et al., *Sexual Behavior in the Human Male* (Philadelphia, 1948), pp. 621–22.

5. Merle Miller, *On Being Different* (New York, 1971), pp. 19–20. For a contemporary account of the screening procedure, see Donald Vining, *A Gay Diary, 1933–1946* (New York, 1979), pp. 224, 227.

in close quarters, not knowing whether they would make it through the war, and depending on one another for survival, men of whatever sexual persuasion formed intense emotional attachments. In this setting, gay men could find one another without attracting undue attention and perhaps even encounter sympathy and acceptance by their heterosexual fellows. Bob Ruffing, a chief petty officer in the navy, recalled the ease with which he met other homosexuals:

> When I first got into the navy—in the recreation hall, for instance— there'd be eye contact, and pretty soon you'd get to know one or two people and kept branching out. All of a sudden you had a vast network of friends, usually through this eye contact thing, some through outright cruising. *They could get away with it in that atmosphere.* [Emphasis supplied.]

At a basic training camp in the Midwest, several young homosexual soldiers in their teens and early twenties quickly formed a tight circle of friendship that solidified their emerging gay identities and sustained them through the stress of the ensuing years. Though the military officially maintained an anti-homosexual stance, wartime conditions nonetheless offered a protective covering that facilitated interaction among gay men.[6]

The diary of Donald Vining reveals how the war years affected male homosexual life. Born in 1917, the precocious Vining accepted his homosexuality early in his adolescence, yet when the war started he had had few homosexual experiences and had made only one gay friend. A pacifist by inclination, after much soul-searching he finally chose to admit his homosexuality to his draft board, since his mother needed his earnings, and they could not afford the cost of his placement in a camp for conscientious objectors. Early in the war, Vining hinted at its sexual significance. "The war is a tragedy to my mind and soul," he confided to his diary, "but to my physical being, it's a memorable experience. I can understand how Walt Whitman felt when nursing during the Civil War."[7] Moving from his small-town residence in New Jersey to New York City, he found employment at Sloane House, a YMCA on 34th Street, and worked as a volunteer in the Stage Door Canteen. Diary entries record erotic encounters in New York and for a time in Los Angeles.

6. Irving L. Janis, "Psychodynamic Aspects of Adjustment to Army Life," *Psychiatry* 8 (May 1945): p. 170; Vining, *A Gay Diary*, p. 312; Alan Stephenson, "The Homosexual: Another Untold Story, an Oral History of Bob Ruffing," typescript, in the possession of Allan Bérubé, San Francisco, 1980; "World War II Letters," correspondence of gay soldiers, in the possession of Allan Bérubé, San Francisco; Allan Bérubé, "Marching to a Different Drummer: Coming out During World War II," paper presented at the December 1981 annual meeting of the American Historical Association, Los Angeles. The towel ads may be found in the *Saturday Evening Post*, December 20, 1943, inside front cover; and *Life*, January 3, 1944, p. 1, and June 26, 1944, p. 1. I am indebted to Allen Bérubé for calling my attention to them, as well as for letting me read the World War II letters.

7. Vining, *A Gay Diary*, p. 220.

Vining had affairs with soldiers, sailors, and marines as well as with civilians. Many of them took place at Sloane House, where 60 percent of the residents were military personnel on leave; but he also met men at the canteen, in movie theaters on 42d Street, in Pershing Square in Los Angeles and Central Park in New York, on the street, and in gay bars filled with men in uniform. Many of his partners were self-acknowledged homosexuals, who told Vining stories about their gay friends and lovers in service; others, usually heterosexually inclined, willingly shared Vining's bed for a night of physical intimacy. The war years drastically altered the shape of his life. By 1945 he had an active sex life, several gay friends, and knowledge of homosexual meeting places and of a spectrum of gay lives; and he was embarking on a relationship that would become permanent. His diary suggests that countless other gay men underwent equally significant transformations.

Although fewer than 150,000 women served in the armed forces during World War II, the military played an especially prominent role in fostering a lesbian identity and creating friendship networks among gay women. *The Well of Loneliness*, already a classic among many self-acknowledged lesbians, created an almost magical aura around military life through its description of the experience of Stephen Gordon, the book's heroine, in the women's ambulance corps in World War I. In an era that frequently associated homosexuality with the reversal of gender roles, the Women's Army Corps became the almost quintessential lesbian institution. As its official historian ruefully admitted, the WACS labored under a "public impression that a women's corps was the ideal breeding ground" for lesbianism. Ironically, military policy contributed to a situation that it took pains to deny. Recruitment centered on a population group statistically likely to include a disproportionate number of lesbians and women whose sexuality was most malleable: in mid-1943, 70 percent of the women in the WACS were single; 83 percent were childless; 40 percent were under twenty-five years of age, and 67 percent were under thirty. Anxious to counter its reputation of moral laxity, the military sought to avoid unwanted pregnancies by keeping its female personnel segregated, often having women-only nights at canteens or providing separate space for women to socialize. A training manual for officers praised the desire for intense "comradeship" in service as "one of the finest relationships" possible for women. But with emotional attachment serving as a powerful stimulus to female eroticism, such bonding might lead toward unintended results. Taken together, popular stereotypes, army policy, and the special conditions of military life may have kept women of confirmed heterosexual persuasion away from enlistment, while drawing in an unusually large proportion of lesbians.[8]

8. Mattie E. Treadwell, *The Women's Army Corps* (Washington, D.C., 1954), pp. 625–26, 767, 777–78; War Department, *Sex Hygiene Course: Officers and Officer Candidates, Women's Army Auxiliary Corps*, Pamphlet no. 35-1 (Washington, D.C., 1943), p. 3; Vining, *A Gay Diary*, pp. 329, 353; and Bérubé, "Marching to a Different Drummer." I am indebted to Bérubé for calling my attention to the sex hygiene pamphlet.

Pat Bond's experience illustrates the configuration of forces that drew lesbians to the military. Raised in Davenport, Iowa, she became aware of "gay feelings" while in high school. She "practiced" necking with a girl friend, developed a crush on her French teacher, and then suffered through an unrequited love for a somewhat older woman who soon married. Having read *The Well of Loneliness*, and weighed down by what she called "the certain knowledge that most gay women have: that you are forever alone," Bond decided to "escape into the Women's Army Corps." She received a taste of what was in store for her at the Blackhawk Hotel, where the recruiting sergeant reminded her of all her "old gym teachers in drag. Stockings, little earrings, her hair slicked back and very daintily done so you couldn't tell she was a dyke, but *I* knew!" Many of the women whom she saw there were extremely "masculine" in appearance and dress. The army psychiatrists asked recruits whether they had ever been in love with a woman, but denial brought the questioning to an end. It did not take Bond long to find other gay women. During her tour in the Pacific, most of her friends and associates, including several officers, were lesbians. From the "certain knowledge" that her homosexuality doomed her to isolation, Bond had moved in short order to participation in a community of gay women.[9]

The war also created pressures that temporarily suspended the normally harsh military attitude toward female homosexuals. Officers in the WACS received careful instructions not to engage in "witchhunting or speculating," to ignore "hearsay," and to approach the problem with an "attitude of fairness and tolerance." A training manual eschewed menacing stereotypes and minimized the differences between heterosexuals and lesbians. "They are exactly as you and I, except that they participate in sexual gratification with members of their own sex." When incontrovertible evidence of homosexual activity did surface, officers were advised to counsel rather than punish, and only those "not amenable to successful guidance" were to receive discharges. Sometimes officers ignored even these directives. Rita Laporte joined the WACS in 1943. Previously she had viewed her sexual desires as "criminal," but she reevaluated them in the service when she fell in love with another woman and her passion was reciprocated. After her lover's transfer to a distant base and her own failure to obtain an assignment in the same location, Laporte tried to secure a discharge by confessing her homosexuality to her commanding officer. The tactic failed. "We argued. I pleaded. But it was useless," she recalled. An acknowledged lesbian, she remained in the service for the duration of the war. The army needed women in its ranks. It could not afford either the loss of personnel or the scandal that would result from stringent enforcement of its own regulations. For a time, many women in the military enjoyed a

9. See the interview with Pat Bond in Nancy and Casey Adair, *Word Is Out* (New York, 1978), pp. 55–65.

measure of safety that permitted their sexuality to survive relatively unharassed.[10]

The military provoked dramatic, intense changes in the sexual lives of many of its female recruits, but the economy's production requirements affected far more women. The female paid labor force rose by more than 6 million during the war years. For the first time, white married women and mothers of young children left their homes in large numbers to take remunerative employment. Two million women filled jobs, normally available only to men, in war-related heavy industries; they crowded the expanded payrolls of factories, offices, and retailers that traditionally employed females. Women made up the bulk of the civilians who migrated during the war. They moved to distant cities, away from the watchful eyes of male kin, lived in makeshift residences that accommodated the influx of laborers, worked night shifts, and in general engaged in a range of activities that marked their independence and signaled their departure from the normative female role.[11]

Focusing attention on the large-scale entry of white married women into the work force and on Rosie the Riveter, who labored alongside men in typically male endeavors, has obscured the significance of the home front experience for women of lesbian inclination. With millions of males in the armed forces and with many more women earning wages, a female world beyond the confines of household and family spread enormously during the war years. Some women assembled aircraft and built ships, but the numbers employed in traditionally female work places, in clerical jobs and consumer industries, showed a greater absolute increase. Women who relocated to answer the call of an impersonal labor market often found residence in boarding-houses, trailer parks, and apartment complexes filled with other women. The dearth of young men that conscription imposed necessarily encouraged many women to structure their social lives around their female companions. This shift toward sex segregation may or may not have affected the erotic focus of women with a long history of heterosexuality. But, by expanding the social space in which women predominated, the war opened possibilities for lesbians to meet at the same time that it protected all-female environments from the taint of deviance.[12]

One woman who benefited from the temporary changes induced by the war was "Lisa Ben." Growing up on a ranch in northern California during the 1920s and 1930s, she lived in relative isolation, with the nearest neighbor a quarter mile away. In high school she developed a "mad crush" on a girl friend

10. War Department, *Sex Hygiene Course*, pp. 24–28; Rita Laporte, "Living Propaganda," *Ladder*, June 1965, pp. 21–22; and Bérubé, "Marching to a Different Drummer."

11. See Milkman, "Women's Work and the Economic Crisis"; Chafe, *The American Woman*, chaps. 6–8; Shryock and Eldridge, "Internal Migration"; and Roy Hoopes, *Americans Remember the Home Front*, pp. 239–79.

12. On the expansion of female sex-segregated occupations, see Milkman, "Women's Work and the Economic Crisis."

but was "too naive" at the time to appreciate its implications for her sexuality. The war gave her new opportunities for social activities. "I used to hitchhike to San Francisco to see a movie," she recalled. "Nobody thought of hitchhiking in the terms they do today. There were no men around then, it was wartime, and so I'd wait till a carload of women came by and I'd extend my thumb." Episodes like these made her desirous of more freedom from parental control. During the last year of the war, Lisa Ben moved to Los Angeles, found work as a secretary, and lived in a rooming house populated by women. There she made her first acquaintance with lesbians. She and her neighbors, she reminisced,

> were all sunbathing on the garage roof, and they got to talking . . . and I thought, "Gee, I wonder if these are some of the girls that I would very dearly love to meet"—because by that time I realized . . . exactly what I want. . . . I started talking and finally they asked me, "Do you like boys, or do you go out strictly with girls?" and I said, "If I had my rathers I'd go out strictly with girls." . . . It was like a Victorian melodrama!

Her new friends took her to a women's softball game and soon brought her to lesbian bars in Los Angeles—The If Club, The Flamingo, and another on Pico Boulevard. That, she said, "was when I met *lots* of girls."[13]

These new opportunities coexisted with old forms of trouble. In the course of the war, Donald Vining was arrested twice and spent four nights in jail, though he was guilty of nothing but sitting on a park bench. "It was obvious that [the police] just had to make a few arrests to look busy," he protested in his diary. "It was a travesty of justice and the workings of the police department." Active cruising carried other risks. One sexual partner ("trade," as Vining described the man) robbed him, while on another occasion he narrowly avoided serious injury when someone tried to assault him after engaging in sex with him. Pat Bond too experienced good and bad. Stationed in Japan among the occupying forces in the months after the war, she found herself swept up in a massive purge of lesbians. Bond used the escape hatch of a marriage of "convenience" to a homosexual to obtain a speedy separation from the service, but scores of women whom she knew fell victim to the witchhunt. Throughout the war and its aftermath, gays continued to face the laws, attitudes, and dangers that ordinarily plagued their existence.[14]

Heterosexuality, moreover, continued as the predominant form of sexual expression. For every GI away from home who experienced a same-sex erotic relationship, many more turned to women, whether prostitutes or women whom they met during leaves at home and abroad. Pinups of Hollywood stars

13. Leland Moss, "An Interview with Lisa Ben," *Gaysweek*, January 23, 1978, pp. 14–16; and Lisa Ben (pseud.), interview with the author, January 9, 1977, Los Angeles.

14. Vining, *A Gay Diary*, pp. 284–87, 324–25, 336–38, 347–48; and Nancy and Casey Adair, *Word Is Out*, pp. 60–61.

like Betty Grable, Lana Turner, and Rita Hayworth provided the material for a rich heterosexual fantasy life. Correspondence kept alive ties with fiancées and wives. Many women also remained faithful to husbands and sweethearts, while some took advantage of their independence and mobility to initiate new intimate relationships with men. Others no doubt simply refrained from erotic activity. Though the war disrupted old sexual ways, the change cannot primarily be defined as a shift from heterosexuality to homosexuality.

Yet, despite both the persistence of antihomosexual oppression and the continuing dominance of male/female sexuality, the social conditions of wartime profoundly affected same-sex eroticism. The war temporarily weakened the patterns of daily life that channeled men and women toward heterosexuality and inhibited homosexual expression. Some Americans could react to the new situations in which they found themselves by embarking upon gay relationships. For men and women conscious of a strong attraction to their own sex but constrained by their milieu from acting upon it, the war years eased the coming out process and facilitated entry into the gay world. Finally, the war allowed men and women who already identified themselves as homosexuals or lesbians to strengthen their ties to a gay life.

II

The return of peace could neither undo nor immediately halt these changes. Vining, for instance, remained in New York, and Lisa Ben in Los Angeles. Excited by "how open" gay life was in San Francisco when he passed through during the war, Bob Ruffing settled there after his discharge from the navy. Rather than return to Iowa, Pat Bond also sank roots in San Francisco, along with many of the other women ejected from the WACS. During the day she worked in a factory alongside other lesbians and at night participated in the subculture of lesbian bars. Vining's lover-to-be, a man in his mid-thirties, abandoned his sexually ascetic prewar existence. On joining the service, he left the small Maine community where his Yankee ancestors had resided for generations. After demobilization, he moved to New York. Three years away from home and savings from his military pay gave him the freedom to embark upon a new life, and he plunged eagerly into the gay social activities that the city offered. Many other homosexuals and lesbians who had savored the pleasures of self-discovery and companionship during the war also found ways in peacetime to maintain their ties with their own kind. In particular, they swelled the gay population of port cities or centers of war industry, such as Los Angeles, New York, and the San Francisco Bay area, to which the war years had exposed them.[15]

The transformations induced by the war added up to more than the sum of the individual lives involved. Homosexuals and lesbians in association with

15. Vining, *A Gay Diary*, and *A Gay Diary, Volume Two: 1946–1954* (New York, 1980); author's interview with Lisa Ben; Alan Stephenson, "The Homosexual: Another Untold Story"; and Nancy and Casey Adair, *Word Is Out*, pp. 61–63.

one another created institutions that bolstered their identity. During the 1940s exclusively gay bars appeared for the first time in cities as diverse as San Jose, Denver, and Kansas City. In Cleveland the number of gay bars increased to four by the end of the decade. Even the relatively small industrial city of Worcester, Massachusetts, had its own homosexual bar. In New York City several honorably discharged gay men formed the Veterans Benevolent Association in 1945. Functioning as a social club for gay ex-servicemen, it held dances and parties that sometimes attracted 400 to 500 homosexuals. A different kind of social organization was formed in Los Angeles in the late 1940s. There the Knights of the Clock offered a safe environment for interracially involved homosexuals and their families to meet, enjoy themselves, and discuss mutual problems. Also in Los Angeles, Lisa Ben commenced publication during 1947 of *Vice Versa*, a magazine for lesbians. She published nine issues before the burden of the one-woman operation became too heavy to carry.[16]

The postwar decade also witnessed a minor efflorescence of literature with gay themes. Claire Morgan's *The Price of Salt* (1951) and Jo Sinclair's *The Wasteland* (1946) presented strong lesbian characters who accepted their attachments to women. Some gay male works, such as Charles Jackson's *The Fall of Valor* (1946) and John Horne Burns's short story "Momma" (1947), were grounded in the social conditions of wartime. Though admittedly much of the writing exhibited the mores of contemporary society, portraying sexually different characters pursued by tragedy and unhappiness, it still held up a mirror that reflected a gay image to its readers. The friendship networks, the bars, the social clubs, and the literature of the postwar decade sustained the sense of belonging to a group at the same time that, for those who were just coming out, they enhanced the chances of stumbling upon collective expressions of gay life.[17]

Of all the changes set in motion by the war, the spread of the gay bar contained the greatest potential for reshaping the consciousness of homosexuals and lesbians. Alone among the expressions of gay life, the bar fostered an identity that was both public and collective. Among lesbians, a primary relationship with a lover, a circle of friends, or social activities held in the home may have offered emotional sustenance, but they also structured a view of

16. On the spread of gay bars, see Gene Tod, "Gay Scene in Kansas City," *Phoenix* (newsletter of the Phoenix Society), August 1966, pp. 5–6; and John Kelsey, "The Cleveland Bar Scene in the Forties," and Jim Jackman, "Missing the Ports O Call," both in Karla Jay and Allen Young, eds., *Lavender Culture* (New York, 1978), pp. 146–54. On the Veterans Benevolent Association, see Jonathan Katz, *Gay American History* (New York, 1976), p. 635; and Edward Sagarin, "Structure and Ideology in an Association of Deviants," Ph.D. diss., New York University, 1966, pp. 64–67. On the Knights of the Clock, see Marvin Cutler, ed., *Homosexuals Today* (Los Angeles, 1956), pp. 93–94; See also author's interview with Lisa Ben. Copies of *Vice Versa* may be found in the National Gay Archives in Los Angeles and in the Lesbian Herstory Archives, New York City.

17. On lesbian and gay male literature, see Jeannette Foster, *Sex Variant Women in Literature*, 2d ed. (Baltimore, 1975), pp. 324–41; and Roger Austen, *Playing the Game: The Homosexual Novel in America* (Indianapolis, 1977), pp. 93–142.

one's sexuality as an exclusively private matter. On the other hand, cruising by gay men, though occurring in public spaces, held the risk of chance encounters with nongay acquaintances. Consequently, participants had to remain always on guard, ready to mask their purposes and abandon at once their quest for an erotic liaison. But the bars offered an all-gay environment where patrons dropped the pretension of heterosexuality, socializing with friends as well as searching for a sexual partner. When trouble struck, as it often did in the form of a police raid, the crowd suffered as a group, enduring the penalties together. The bars were seedbeds for a collective consciousness that might one day flower politically.[18]

One important indication that changes had occurred in gay life during the 1940s was the publication of *The Homosexual in America*, by Donald Webster Cory. The pseudonymous Cory composed his subjective account from the perspective of twenty-five years of experience as a homosexual. He described the hostility gay men encountered, the persecution and discrimination they faced, the variety of homosexual lifestyles, and the institutions of the gay subculture. Above all, however, Cory intended his book as a polemic, an argument designed to win acceptance for a new view of the homosexual. "We who are homosexual," he asserted,

> are a minority, not only numerically, but also as a result of a caste-like status in society. . . . Our minority status is similar, in a variety of respects, to that of national, religious and other ethnic groups: in the denial of civil liberties; in the legal, extra-legal and quasi-legal discrimination; in the assignment of an inferior social position; in the exclusion from the mainstream of life and culture.[19]

The appearance of Cory's book not only provided gay men and women with a tool for reinterpreting their lives; it also implied that the conditions of life had changed sufficiently so that the book's message might find a receptive audience.

III

With the lives of many homosexual men and women already in flux, the publication of the Kinsey reports on male and female sexual behavior, in 1948 and 1953, offered scientific evidence conducive to a reevaluation of conventional moral attitudes. Conceived and written by a scientist whose high professional reputation rested on a meticulous study of the gall wasp, the two books permanently altered the nature of public discussion of sexuality as well as

18. For a discussion of the contrast between the gay bar and other aspects of gay life, see Donald Webster Cory (pseud.), *The Homosexual in America* (New York, 1951), pp. 120–21. For other analyses of bars, see Nancy Achilles, "The Homosexual Bar," M.A. thesis, University of Chicago, 1964; and Evelyn Hooker, "Male Homosexuals and Their 'Worlds,'" in Judd Marmor, ed., *Sexual Inversion* (New York, 1965), pp. 83–107. See also below, chaps. 3, 6, and 10.

19. Cory, *The Homosexual in America*, pp. 3, 13–14.

society's perception of its own behavior. Nothing like them had ever appeared before. Using the technique of face-to-face interviews, Alfred Kinsey and a small, carefully trained staff collected the erotic histories of more than 10,000 white American men and women. Scientists detailed for America, in charts, graphs and tables, the frequency and variety of its sexual experiences—inside and outside of marriage; alone and with others; in youth and old age; with the same sex, the opposite sex, and animals. Kinsey treated his sensitive subject in the matter-of-fact manner more typical of the bug collector than of the writer on sex. Although his data challenged many dearly held, almost sacred beliefs about American manhood and womanhood, the stance of dispassionate scientific objectivity that Kinsey adopted allowed him to assert that his book offered value-free facts devoid of moral content.[20]

No other books on sex in the twentieth century had received as wide a circulation as the Kinsey reports. After commissioning a market analysis of the book's potential audience, the publisher ordered a first run of 5,000 copies of *Sexual Behavior in the Human Male*. But the huge demand for the 804-page tome brought the number of copies in print to 185,000 within two weeks of its official publication date of January 3, 1948. Both volumes spent several months high on the *New York Times* bestseller list, and each sold almost a quarter of a million copies. The male study stimulated more than 200 major symposia among professionals in 1948 and 1949, while more than fifty other books capitalized on the notoriety of the Kinsey reports. The Indiana zoologist appeared on the cover of *Time*, newspapers made headlines out of critiques of his work, and a Hollywood producer tried to secure movie rights to the scientific treatises. "Kinsey" became a household word, almost synonymous with sex itself and symbolic of what seemed to be a relentless push toward the liberation of human sexuality from the constraining morality of a Victorian past.[21]

For those who explored behind the headlines, the picture Kinsey provided of the sexuality of ordinary white Americans must have been startling. Among men he found that masturbation was a nearly universal practice, that virtually all had established a regular sexual outlet by the age of fifteen, that half of the

20. See Kinsey et al., *Sexual Behavior in the Human Male* (hereafter referred to as *SBHM*); and *Sexual Behavior in the Human Female* (Philadelphia, 1953) (hereafter referred to as *SBHF*). On Kinsey and the studies, see the memoir by one of his staff members, Wardell Pomeroy, *Dr. Kinsey and the Institute for Sex Research* (New York, 1972); the in-house biography by Cornelia V. Christenson, *Kinsey: A Biography* (Bloomington, Ind., 1971); Paul Robinson, *The Modernization of Sex* (New York, 1976), pp. 42–119; and Regina Markell Morantz, "The Scientist as Sex Crusader: Alfred C. Kinsey and American Culture," *American Quarterly* 29 (1977): 563–89.

21. Pomeroy, *Dr. Kinsey*, esp. pp. 265, 280–82, 301–4, 338–43; and Christenson, *Kinsey*, esp. pp. 141–42, 153–54. Kinsey appeared on the cover of *Time* on August 24, 1953. Among other books published about the Kinsey reports, see Donald Porter Geddes and Enid Curie, *About the Kinsey Report* (New York, 1948); Albert Deutsch, ed., *Sex Habits of American Men* (New York, 1948); Jerome Himeloch and Sylvia Fava, eds., *Sexual Behavior in American Society* (New York, 1955); and Seward Hitner, *Sex Ethics and the Kinsey Reports* (New York, 1953).

husbands in the survey engaged in extramarital intercourse, and that 95 percent of white American males had violated the law in some way at least once along the way to an orgasm. After studying the sexual experiences of women, Kinsey concluded that, contrary to prevailing belief, females were no slower in responding to physical stimuli than males. Ineffective techniques of male partners, rather than innate female biological characteristics, accounted for the differences between the responses of men and women. He labeled the vaginal orgasm, identified by psychoanalysts as the mark of female sexual maturity, a "biologic impossibility"; minimized the significance of the penis in women's sexual arousal; and asserted that male and female orgasms were essentially similar physiological phenomena. Kinsey reported that 90 percent of American white women had engaged in premarital petting, half had had premarital intercourse, and 25 percent of American wives had had extramarital sexual relations. Moreover, the study identified a trend toward greater incidence of each of these activities among younger women. Kinsey presented all of his findings in dry, unsensational prose, without a trace of moral disapproval for the sexually active, regardless of their source of sexual outlet.[22]

Of all Kinsey's statistics, none challenged conventional wisdom as much as his data on homosexuality. He uncovered an incidence of homosexual behavior that dwarfed all previous estimates of its prevalence. Among males he found that 50 percent admitted erotic responses to their own sex, 37 percent had had at least one postadolescent homosexual experience leading to orgasm, 4 percent were exclusively homosexual throughout adulthood, and, in one out of eight cases, same-sex eroticism predominated for at least a three-year period. For women the proportions, though lower, still revealed extensive lesbian activity. Twenty-eight percent responded erotically to their own sex, and 13 percent had experienced orgasm with another woman, while the percentage of women either exclusively or primarily homosexual in orientation was between one-third and one-half of the corresponding male figures. The data disputed the common assumption that all adults were permanently and exclusively either homosexual or heterosexual and revealed instead a fluidity that belied medical theories about fixed orientations. To highlight these variations, Kinsey constructed a seven-point rating scale, ranging from exclusive heterosexuality at one end to exclusive homosexual behavior at the other.[23]

Kinsey's findings on homosexuality departed so drastically from traditional notions that he felt compelled to comment on them. In his male study Kinsey acknowledged that he and his colleagues "were totally unprepared" for such high incidence data and "were repeatedly assailed with doubts" about their validity. Checking and cross-checking their tabulations only widened the distance separating their results from the estimations of others. "Whether the histories were taken in one large city or another," Kinsey wrote,

22. Kinsey, *SBHM*, pp. 301, 392, 499, 585; and *SBHF*, pp. 164, 233, 286, 416, 468, 584.
23. For the findings on homosexual behavior, see Kinsey, *SBHM*, pp. 610–66; and *SBHF*, pp. 446–501.

whether they were taken in large cities, in small towns, or in rural areas, whether they came from one college or from another, a church school or a state university or some private institution, whether they came from one part of the country or from another, the incidence data on the homosexual have been more or less the same. . . . Persons with homosexual histories are to be found in every age group, in every social level, in every conceivable occupation, in cities and on farms, and in the most remote areas of the country.[24]

The evidence from personal interviewing forced a repudiation of physical stereotyping, while the information volunteered by many male respondents with homosexual histories indicated that a dearth of information about where to make contacts severely limited their sexual activity. The prevalence of homosexual behavior "in spite of the severity of the penalties that our Anglo-American culture has placed upon it through the centuries" led Kinsey to suggest that "such activity would appear in the histories of a much larger portion of the population if there were no social restraints." Dismissing views of homosexual behavior as abnormal, unnatural, or neurotic, he concluded that it represented instead an "inherent physiologic capacity."[25]

Not surprisingly, Kinsey came under heavy fire from many quarters. Some critics disputed the adequacy of his sample or expressed doubts about the reliability of his statistical method. Others, like the literary scholar and humanist Lionel Trilling, dissented in a reasoned way from what appeared to be a two-dimensional approach that reduced human sexuality to an "outlet," something one could comprehend through numbers alone. But much of the reaction took the form of moral outrage. Harold Dodds, president of Princeton University, likened the male report to "the work of small boys writing dirty words on fences"; the head of Union Theological Seminary in New York, Henry Van Dusen, viewed Kinsey's statistics as evidence of a "degradation in American morality approximating the worst decadence of the Roman era." Both volumes aroused indignation, but the female study unleashed the most intense emotional outbursts. Louis Heller, a New York congressman, charged Kinsey with "hurling the insult of the century against our mothers, wives, daughters and sisters" and, though he had not read the book, urged the postmaster general to ban it from the mails. Kinsey stood accused of aiding world communism, and in 1954 a congressional committee singled out the reports as examples of scientific research that produced "extremely grave" social effects.[26]

24. Kinsey, *SBHM*, pp. 625, 627.

25. Ibid., pp. 637, 632, 659–60; and *SBHF*, p. 447.

26. See Lionel Trilling, *The Liberal Imagination* (New York, 1950); Harold Dodd, quoted in Pomeroy, *Dr. Kinsey*, p. 287; and Henry P. Van Dusen, "The Moratorium on Moral Revulsion," *Christianity and Crisis*, June 21, 1948, p. 81. Heller and the House Committee are quoted in Christenson, *Kinsey*, pp. 161, 165.

No amount of vilification, however, could erase the impact of Kinsey's work on postwar American culture. He had mapped the unsurveyed sexual landscape of the nation. Kinsey provided the most complete, detailed picture of white American sexuality yet recorded. By revealing the wide divergence between ideals and actual behavior, he informed ordinary men and women that their private "transgressions" marked them as neither deviant nor exceptional. In this respect, Kinsey implicitly encouraged a revision of existing norms to correspond to common practice. Opinion polls indicated that his research met with approval from the vast majority of Americans who believed that sexual behavior was a fit subject for scientific investigation. Newspapers discovered that articles about sex did not provoke an outraged response from the majority of their readers. Ironically, the barrage of criticism as much as the reports themselves hastened the demise of Victorian taboos that still limited public discourse about the erotic life of men and women. The outpouring of words about the reports legitimated sexuality as a topic of discussion in the popular, mass-circulation press.[27]

Kinsey's studies had contradictory effects upon attitudes toward homosexuals and lesbians. Kinsey himself used his statistics to suggest that such a common sexual activity ought not be punished. Resting on the misinformed view that homosexual behavior was confined to a small number of individuals, society's treatment of homosexuals, he argued, was socially destructive. As with the rest of his findings, his data on homosexuality seeped into popular consciousness. At the time, however, the information served not to ameliorate hostility toward gay men and women, but to magnify suddenly the proportions of the danger they allegedly posed. Yet in the long run the information provided by Kinsey would become an important element in the rationale for law reform.[28]

Among homosexuals and lesbians themselves, Kinsey had a more clearly beneficial impact. Scientific evidence appeared to confirm what many gay people in the 1940s were experiencing—the sense of belonging to a group. Moreover, by revealing that millions of Americans exhibited a strong erotic interest in their own sex, the reports implicitly encouraged those still struggling in isolation against their sexual preference to accept their homosexual inclinations and search for sexual comrades. In effect, Kinsey's work gave an added push at a crucial time to the emergence of an urban gay subculture. Kinsey also provided ideological ammunition that lesbians and homosexuals might use once they began to fight for equality.

27. See Donald B. Hileman, "The Kinsey Report: A Study of Press Responsibility," *Journalism Quarterly* 30 (1953): 434–35; Paul D. Brinkman, "Dr. Alfred Kinsey and the Press," Ph.D. diss., Indiana University, 1971; and Pomeroy, *Dr. Kinsey*, pp. 340–43.

28. Kinsey, *SBHM*, pp. 663–66.

IV

The disruptive social conditions induced by World War II did not last long after demobilization. In the succeeding decade, personal life returned to time-honored patterns. After fifteen years of depression and war, many Americans wanted little more than to construct a tranquil family environment. Especially among the young, traditional sex roles were reasserted. GIs shed their khakis and became breadwinners as they took back the jobs that women had filled during the national emergency. Millions of men and women married. The birth rate, having declined for more than a century, shot upward as the war came to a close. Generous educational benefits and home-buying arrangements gave millions of veterans the wherewithal to marry and support a family at a younger age than usual. A barrage of propaganda from business and government informed women that, with the war ending, they must relinquish their places in the work force to make room for returning soldiers. Opinion surveys indicated that most women in heavy industry wanted to keep their jobs, yet employers routinely dismissed them in the months after VE Day. In the media, pictures of sparkling, well-equipped kitchens occupied by young mothers with babies in their arms replaced images of women in hard hats surrounded by heavy machinery. Popular psychology books and women's magazines equated femininity with marriage and motherhood. In the baby boom years of the late 1940s and 1950s, the man or woman choosing to pursue same-sex intimacy was more than ever going against the grain. The reaffirmation of normative gender roles and stable heterosexual relationships made those who lived outside them appear more clearly deviant.

Still, one can scarcely overestimate the significance of the 1940s in restructuring the social expression of same-sex eroticism. The war years allowed the almost imperceptible changes of several generations, during which a gay male and lesbian identity had slowly emerged, to coalesce into a qualitatively different form. A sexual and emotional life that gay men and women previously experienced mainly in individual terms suddenly became, for the war generation, a widely shared collective phenomenon.

World War II promoted this transformation not so much by permanently encouraging more homosexual behavior, a proposition that in any case would be impossible to prove, but by shifting its location and changing its context. As the Kinsey studies demonstrated, same-sex eroticism could be an exclusive lifetime commitment, the preferred form of sexuality for a few years, an occasional activity over decades, or a rare event. Because the war removed large numbers of men and women from familial—and familiar—environments, it freed homosexual eroticism from some of the structural restraints that made it appear marginal and isolated. Many of the nongay men with whom Donald Vining enjoyed physical intimacy during the war resumed a heterosexual existence in peacetime, but the occurrence of what for them was an unusual homosexual encounter intensified for men like Vining the sense of being gay. Millions of heterosexual women returned to a domestic environment after demobilization, but their temporary presence in the public sphere made it safer for women like Lisa Ben to be in the company of lesbians.

Demobilization did not turn back the clock. For many homosexual men and women their wartime experiences became the foundation upon which they built a postwar life. Individual decisions not to return home, to settle in large cities where anonymity permitted gay socializing more easily, and to maintain the friendships of the war years helped forge a group existence. During the 1940s an urban gay subculture took shape.

THREE

The Bonds of Oppression: Gay Life in the 1950s

The emergence of an urban gay subculture carried with it the potential for disaster. The shifts that occurred in gay life during the 1940s were not paralleled by a growing social tolerance of homosexuality. The matrix of religious beliefs, laws, medical theories, and popular attitudes that devalued and punished lesbians and homosexuals remained intact. Although greater ease of association improved the quality of existence for many gay men and women, it also made them more vulnerable. Should society find a reason to persecute its homosexual members actively, the changing structure of gay life guaranteed that it would locate them.

The Cold War and its attendant domestic anticommunism provided the setting in which a sustained attack upon homosexuals and lesbians took place. In the eyes of political leaders of both parties, Soviet Communism in the postwar years replaced German Nazism as an immediate and major threat to the country's safety. Having just defeated the Axis powers, Americans were asked to muster their resources against another enemy. Moreover, Communist successes in Europe and Asia bred fears of internal subversion by a fifth column that was sapping the nation's vitality. Democrats and Republicans, liberals and conservatives alike sought ways to expose the disloyal and to bolster the country's security. In 1947 President Truman established a loyalty program for federal employees, and the Justice Department issued a list of allegedly subversive organizations. The House Un-American Activities Committee conducted highly publicized hearings in their search for traitors. The conviction of Alger Hiss for perjury about his alleged role in passing government documents to the Russians confirmed for many the belief that Washington was riddled with spies. Many states established special committees to investigate the loyalty of their employees. Several unions purged suspected communists from positions of authority, while the national Congress of Industrial Organizations expelled entire unions and some statewide affiliates because of suspected communist leadership. As the anticommunist wave in American politics rose, it carried homosexuals with it. Gay men and women became the targets of a verbal assault that quickly escalated into policy and practice.[1]

I

A chance revelation by a State Department official during congressional hearings on the loyalty of government employees led to the entanglement of homosexuality in the politics of domestic anticommunism. Facing sharp interrogation by members of the Senate Appropriations Committee, Under Secretary John Peurifoy testified on February 28, 1950, that most of ninety-one employees dismissed for moral turpitude were homosexuals. Republicans were making the national security issue the centerpiece of their strategy to discredit the Truman administration, and, eager to exploit any weak spot, they pounced upon Peurifoy's remarks.[2]

In the succeeding months, the danger posed by "sexual perverts" became a staple of partisan rhetoric. Senator Joseph McCarthy, just embarking upon his career as an anticommunist crusader, charged that an unnamed person in the State Department had forced the reinstatement of a homosexual despite the threat to the nation's safety. Styles Bridges, a conservative senator from New Hampshire, assailed the laxity of the executive branch in ferreting out spies and homosexuals. After the head of the District of Columbia vice squad told a Senate committee that thousands of "sexual deviates" worked for the government, the Republican floor leader, Kenneth Wherry, demanded a full-scale Senate inquiry. In May Governor Thomas Dewey of New York, who had been the party's presidential candidate in 1948, accused the administration of tolerating the employment of sex offenders. Seven thousand Republican party workers received a newsletter from their national chairman, Guy Gabrielson, alerting them to the new "homosexual angle" in Washington. "Sexual perverts . . . have infiltrated our Government in recent years," he warned, and they were "perhaps as dangerous as the actual Communists." Gabrielson implied that party loyalists had a special responsibility to arouse the country's ire over

1. The literature on anticommunism in American politics during the postwar era is extensive. See, e.g., David Caute, *The Great Fear: The Anti-Communist Purge Under Truman and Eisenhower* (New York, 1978); Victor Navasky, *Naming Names* (New York, 1980); Robert Griffith and Athan Theoharis, *The Specter* (New York, 1974); Norman Markowitz, *The Rise and Fall of the People's Century* (New York, 1973); Richard M. Freeland, *The Truman Doctrine and the Origins of McCarthyism* (New York, 1972); Alan Harper, *The Politics of Loyalty: The White House and the Communist Issue, 1946–1952* (Westport, Conn., 1969); Robert Griffith, *The Politics of Fear* (Lexington, Ky., 1970); and Athan Theoharis, *Seeds of Repression: Harry S. Truman and the Origins of McCarthyism* (Chicago, 1971).

2. *New York Times*, March 1, 1950, p. 1.

the issue, since "decency" constrained the media from "adequately presenting the facts" to the American people. Finally, in June 1950 the full Senate bowed to mounting pressure and authorized an investigation into the alleged employment of homosexuals "and other moral perverts" in government.[3]

The unprecedented inquiry cast a revealing light on the complex of attitudes about homosexuality that often remained hidden because of the constraints on public discussion. In its report published in December, the committee took for granted that the employment of homosexuals was undesirable. The criminality of homosexual acts and the religious consensus that such behavior was grossly immoral dictated the committee's view of homosexual men and women as "outcasts" thoroughly unsuitable for government service. Testimony by doctors that homosexuals and lesbians needed medical care did not lead the senators to suggest that treatment ought to replace punishment. Instead, the claims that homosexuality was inherently pathological bolstered the committee's belief that the "sexual pervert" should be denied federal employment. To support its own assumptions, the committee even marshalled evidence intended to challenge the negative evaluation of homosexuality. Thus the senators culled information from the Kinsey study of the American male—that homosexual behavior was widespread, that homosexuals came from all walks of life, and that they did not conform in appearance or mannerism to the popular stereotype—in order to argue that the problem was far more extensive and difficult to attack than they had previously thought.[4]

In drawing its grim picture of the menace of homosexual employment in government, the Senate report developed two overlapping lines of reasoning to justify their exclusion from government service. The first concerned the "character" of the homosexual. "Those who engage in overt acts of perversion lack the emotional stability of normal persons," the report asserted. "Indulgence in acts of sex perversion weakens the moral fiber of the individual." The presence of homosexuals was debilitating and threatening to everyone around them. Even one "sex pervert in a Government agency," the committee warned,

tends to have a corrosive influence upon his fellow employees. These perverts will frequently attempt to entice normal individuals to engage in perverted practices. This is particularly true in the case of young and impressionable people who might come under the influence of a pervert. . . . One homosexual can pollute a Government office.

The government would be assuming a grave burden if it allowed such morally contaminated persons to remain in its service.[5]

3. *New York Times*, March 9, 1950, p. 1; March 15, 1950, p. 1; April 19, 1950, p. 25; April 25, 1950, p. 5; April 26, 1950, p. 3; May 5, 1950, p. 15; May 20, 1950, p. 8; and June 15, 1950, p. 6.
4. U.S. Senate, 81st Cong., 2d sess., Committee on Expenditures in Executive Departments, *Employment of Homosexuals and Other Sex Perverts in Government* (Washington, D.C., 1950).
5. Ibid., pp. 3–5.

The committee also argued that "sexual perverts" imperiled national security. "The social stigma attached to sex perversion" was so great that detection could ruin an individual for life. "Gangs of blackmailers," the report continued, took advantage of this vulnerability by making "a regular practice of preying upon the homosexual." Espionage agents "can use the same type of pressure to extort confidential information." Immature, unstable, and morally enfeebled by the gratification of their perverted desires, homosexuals lacked the character to resist the blandishments of the spy. They would betray their country, the committee asserted, rather than live with the consequences of exposure. As evidence for their contention about blackmail, the Senators relied on the case of an Austrian intelligence officer whose homosexuality made him a tool of the Russians in the years before World War I. Besides, the committee concluded, homosexuals "seldom refuse to talk about themselves," and foreign agents willing to embark upon clandestine liaisons could easily extract sensitive information while preserving blackmail as a last resort.[6]

The committee's evaluation of the government's response to the situation offered scant comfort to the security conscious. The report charged federal agencies with adopting a "head-in-the-sand" attitude. Personnel officers acted in "outright disregard of existing rules and they handled the problem in accordance with their individual feelings or personal judgments." Some actually "condoned" the continued employment of homosexuals, while others allowed them to resign without public exposure. The committee uncovered numerous instances of known homosexuals who were able to move from one government department to another because their supervisors had refrained from including information about sexuality in their personnel records. Strict enforcement of regulations could prevent future delinquencies, and careful investigation by the FBI might keep most homosexual men and women off the federal payroll; but detection was not an easy task, the committee reluctantly admitted, because too many of them lacked the "outward characteristics or physical traits that are positive as identifying marks of sex perversion." The report concluded, "Even the most elaborate and costly system of investigating applicants for Government positions will not prevent some sex perverts from finding their way into Government service."[7]

The homosexual menace continued as a theme of American political culture throughout the McCarthy era. Legislators questioned federal officials closely in committee hearings about the enforcement of security measures, while agency heads, anxious to avoid charges of negligence, publicized cases to demonstrate their watchfulness. Right-wing organizations combined their attacks on communists with calls for the ejection of homosexuals from government. A series of *Confidential* books by Lee Mortimer, a columnist for the Hearst-owned New York *Daily Mirror*, combined the conclusions of the Senate committee with the statistics in the Kinsey report and embellished

6. Ibid.
7. Ibid., pp. 8–10.

them considerably. Homosexuality became an epidemic infecting the nation, actively spread by communists to sap the strength of the next generation. Lesbians were organizing cells in high schools and colleges to prey upon the young; they infiltrated the WACS and the WAVES, where they seduced the pliant and "raped" the unwilling. Mortimer announced that "10,000 faggots" had escaped detection by the FBI. The government remained "honeycombed in high places with people you wouldn't let in your garbage-wagons."[8]

Stricter enforcement of sanctions accompanied the attacks in print. From 1947 through April 1, 1950, when the sexual pervert issue arose, dismissals of homosexuals from civilian posts in the executive branch had averaged five per month. Over the next half year, the figure increased to more than sixty. In April 1953, soon after Eisenhower's inauguration, the new president issued Executive Order 10450, which revised the Truman administration's loyalty-security program. One section explicitly listed "sexual perversion" as sufficient and necessary grounds for disbarment from federal jobs, thus narrowing the wide discretionary authority over firing that personnel officers had previously enjoyed. In its first sixteen months of operation, the Eisenhower program removed homosexuals from government at a rate of forty per month. By all accounts, however, these figures understate the number of gay men and women penalized for their sexuality. At the very least, they exclude employees still allowed to resign quietly through the compassion of a friendly supervisor. Many more individuals never made it on to the federal payroll, since all applicants for government employment faced security investigations. From 1947 through mid-1950, 1,700 job seekers were denied employment because of homosexuality. After that period, the government expanded its screening procedures.[9]

The military too intensified its search for homosexuals and lesbians in its ranks. In contrast to its rebuke of civilian agencies, the 1950 Senate investigation lavished praise on the armed forces for their stringent approach to the problem. During the late 1940s discharges for homosexuality had averaged slightly more than 1,000 per year. But in the atmosphere of heightened concern about national security, the military also worked overtime to purge homosexuals. Separations averaged 2,000 per year in the early 1950s and rose

8. *New York Times*, March 28, 1951, p. 1; October 5, 1951, p. 2; June 26, 1952, p. 4; and April 13, 1953, p. 20; *Senator McCarthy's Methods*, pamphlet published by the Constitutional Educational League Committee FOR McCarthyism (New York City, 1954), copy in Herbert Lehman papers, Columbia University (I am indebted to Duane Tananbaum for calling my attention to this pamphlet); Lee Mortimer, *Washington Confidential Today* (New York, 1952; Paperback Library ed., 1962), pp. 110–19; and Jack Lait and Lee Mortimer, *U.S.A. Confidential* (New York, 1952), pp. 43–45.

9. *Employment of Homosexuals*, pp. 7–9, 12–13; Executive Order 10450, reprinted in the *Bulletin of the Atomic Scientists*, April 1955, pp. 156–58; *New York Times*, January 4, 1955, p. 14; Eleanor Bontecou, *The Federal Loyalty-Security Program* (Ithaca, N.Y., 1953), pp. 272–99, 323–35; Ralph S. Brown, Jr., *Loyalty and Security: Employment Tests in the United States* (New Haven, Conn., 1958), pp. 256–60; and Karl M. Bowman and Bernice Engle, "A Psychiatric Evaluation of the Laws of Homosexuality," *Temple Law Quarterly Review* 29 (1956): 299–300.

by another 50 percent by the beginning of the 1960s. Moreover, the armed services employed methods for dealing with gay men and women that seriously circumscribed the rights of its personnel. The military generally bypassed the court martial proceedings required for a dishonorable discharge and instead used administrative mechanisms that terminated members as "undesirable." This route eliminated the need to substantiate charges with hard facts. Defendants lacked the right to question or even to meet their accusers, and they had no access to the sources used against them. Sometimes individuals who had won an acquittal by a court martial on the grounds of insufficient proof found themselves discharged as undesirable on the same inadequate evidence. Though technically less serious than a bad conduct separation, the undesirable label carried similar punitive effects after discharge. Homosexuals and lesbians who left the military under these conditions carried a burden that one study called "a life stigma."[10]

The cost in human suffering hidden behind the numbers of discharged women and men was great. The indignities of interrogation, the sense of helplessness before military authorities, the mounting terror as a witchhunt spread, the assault on one's self-esteem, and the expectation of permanent stigmatization tested even the sturdiest. Late in 1950 the military began a "housecleaning" of lesbians at Keesler Air Force base in Biloxi, Mississippi. "Eleven girls were called in," one corporal under investigation reported,

and questioned as to their alleged homosexuality. . . . The girls being sick of the worry and strain of being under suspicion and being promised by a very likable chap Capt. Dickey of the OSI (Office of Special Investigation) that they would receive General Discharges if they confessed, all proceeded to do so and after confessing were informed that it wasn't enough to incriminate only themselves—they must write down also someone else with whom they had homosexual relations—this done they waited and at the end of January they were all out with Undesirables.

Named in a confession, the corporal soon faced grilling by an officer, who, she said, "tells you that you don't have to say anything but does it in such a way that you are sure if you don't the consequences will be little short of fatal." Nonetheless, she requested the opportunity to prove her innocence at a court martial; but the Air Force denied her request and discharged her administratively. A commander who advised her squadron of its rights under military law was relieved of her post.

In addition to the eleven women at Keesler, the military separated at least twenty others at Lackland Air Force base and several more at Wright-

10. *Employment of Homosexuals*, p. 8; Williams and Weinberg, *Homosexuals and the Military* (New York, 1971), pp. 31–36, 45–47, 53; Clifford A. Dougherty and Norman B. Lynch, "The Administrative Discharge: Military Justice?" *George Washington Law Review* 33 (1964): 498–528; and Jerome A. Susskind, "Military Administrative Discharge Boards: The Right to Confrontation and Cross-Examination," *Michigan State Bar Journal* 46 (1965): 25–32. The phrase "life stigma" comes from Williams and Weinberg, p. 36.

Patterson on the basis of confessions it extracted. One of the women discharged at Wright-Patterson assessed the results. "I am refused forever the
right to wear the uniform of my country. . . . I may never hold a position of
trust in this country because I am a 'bad security risk.' Anytime I want to apply
for a civil service job, it will be right there. . . . To Washington, I [am] a
nonentity with a homosexual contact." Still, she counted herself "one of the
luckier ones, with an understanding family." In contrast, she reported, "two
of the girls discharged for homosexuality have committed suicide and one
other has disappeared completely."[11]

The hunt for homosexuals and lesbians extended far beyond a search for
those in the military and the federal bureaucracy. The obsessive concern with
national security spurred the growth of an immense system of tests and
standards to determine the suitability of employees. More than 12,600,000
workers, or slightly more than 20 percent of the labor force, faced loyalty-
security investigations. States and municipalities followed the lead of the
federal government in demanding from their personnel not only loyalty but
traditional moral probity as well. The states also used rigorous standards in
licensing a number of occupations. Private industries under government
contract applied to their workers the security provisions of the Eisenhower
administration. The coast guard enforced a similar system of regulations for
merchant sailors, longshore workers, and other maritime laborers. One study
predicted that the use of security measures would "probably expand and
intensify." With the role of the federal government in American life growing
rapidly during the Cold War era, the exclusion of gay women and men from its
service seriously limited their economic choices.[12]

Once the government assumed the position that homosexuals and lesbians
threatened the welfare of the country, it had to devise methods to cope with the
problem that gay people could conceal their identity. Since hidden homosexuals allegedly posed the most serious danger, national security seemed to
depend on the ability to break their cover. In 1950 the FBI, charged with the
responsibility of supplying the Civil Service Commission with background
information on employees and applicants, took the initiative of establishing
liaison with police departments throughout the country. Not content with
acting only on requests to screen particular individuals, it adopted a preventive
strategy that justified widespread surveillance. The FBI sought out friendly
vice squad officers who supplied arrest records on morals charges, regardless
of whether convictions had ensued. Regional FBI offices gathered data on gay
bars, compiled lists of other places frequented by homosexuals, and clipped

11. Barbara J. Scammell to ACLU, February 15, 1951: and June Fusca to ACLU, March 16,
1951 and April 23, 1951; all in General Correspondence, vol. 16, 1951, ACLU papers, Princeton
University.
12. See Ralph S. Brown, Jr., "Loyalty-Security Measures and Employment Opportunities,"
Bulletin of the Atomic Scientists, April 1955, pp. 113–17, and *Loyalty and Security*; Bontecou, *The
Federal Loyalty-Security Program*; and Walter Gellhorn, ed., *The States and Subversion* (Ithaca,
N.Y., 1952).

press articles that provided information about the gay world. Friendship with a known homosexual or lesbian subjected anyone to investigation. The Post Office, exploiting its authority to prevent the dissemination of obscene material through the mails, joined the antihomosexual campaign. The department established a watch on the recipients of physique magazines and other forms of gay male erotica. Postal inspectors subscribed to pen pal clubs, initiated correspondence with men whom they believed might be homosexual, and, if their suspicions were confirmed, placed tracers on victims' mail in order to locate other homosexuals.[13]

Federal investigators engaged in more than fact finding; they also exhibited considerable zeal in using the information they collected. A professor in Maryland and an employee of the Pennsylvania department of highways, for example, lost their jobs after the Post Office revealed to their employers that the men received mail implicating them in homosexual activity. Neither of the victims ever met his accusers. In a statement submitted to the American Civil Liberties Union in 1964, B. D. H. described how the FBI had hounded him for more than a decade. Expelled from the University of Illinois in 1942 after a security guard apprehended him for making a "pass" at another student, the young man went to Washington, where he worked in a federal agency for several years as a clerk-typist. His troubles began after he left his government job to return to the Midwest. An FBI agent visited the University of Illinois and obtained the records of the former student. Subsequently, a friend who worked for the State Department was charged with sexual perversion on the basis of the two men's association. B. D. H., meanwhile, experienced FBI harassment while working in office jobs at the International Shoe Company and Mound City Business College in St. Louis and the Hilton Hotel in Chicago. Fellow employees and supervisors, apprised of his homosexuality, ridiculed him mercilessly. In 1960, after an arm injury left him unable to type, he applied for retraining with the Illinois Division of Vocational Rehabilitation, but he was refused aid because of his sexual orientation. As late as the early 1960s, FBI agents visited B. D. H. at his home in an attempt to extract the names of homosexual acquaintances.[14]

The consensus on homosexuality supplied a lethal weapon for unscrupulous individuals to wield with impunity. Charges of sexual perversion, like the accusation of communism, could be employed as a tactic to discredit one's

13. See J. Edgar Hoover, "Role of the FBI in the Federal Employee Security Program," *Northwestern University Law Review* 49 (1954): 333–47. The information on the FBI surveillance program comes from several hundred pages of documents obtained from the FBI under the Freedom of Information Act, File Classification nos. 94-843, 94-1001, 94-283, 100-37394, and 100-45888. I am indebted to Bill Hartmann of San Francisco for sharing these documents with me. The postal surveillance came to light in the mid-1960s. See memo of Alan Reitman to Affiliates, September 1, 1965; Ernest Mazey to Reitman, September 10, 1965; and Spencer Coxe to Reitman, August 5, 1965; all in General Correspondence, vol. 1, 1965, ACLU papers.

14. *New Republic*, August 21, 1965, pp. 6–7; *Newsweek*, June 13, 1966, p. 24; and B. D. H., "Personal and Confidential History," in General Correspondence, vol. 43, 1964, ACLU papers.

political adversaries or a cause that one opposed. In 1958, for example, a legislative committee headed by Charley Johns, a conservative state senator from northern Florida, appropriated police functions and spearheaded a sensationalistic investigation of homosexual activity at the state university in Gainesville. The committee collected several thousand pages of testimony, grilled hundreds of witnesses, and exhibited little compunction about releasing information based on hearsay and unsubstantiated accusations. Called in by some of the victims, the Florida Civil Liberties Union surmised that motives other than a concern for sexual morality were at work. Civil rights forces were beginning to resume the offensive in the South. The first black student had recently enrolled in the university's law school, and the FCLU recognized that the Johns committee's "intimidation of the faculty and student body would serve as a deterrent against racial integration on the campus or [the establishment of] a university chapter of the FCLU." The American Civil Liberties Union was on record supporting the constitutionality of sanctions against homosexuality because, it argued, the government had the right to regulate behavior. As a result, the strongest objection its Florida affiliate could muster against Johns was concern over the "tremendous and permanent damage your inquest will bring to the reputation of professors and students who are *innocent* of any participation in homosexual activity" (emphasis supplied). Liberal newspapers in the state also editorialized against the investigation's excesses, but to no avail. Their scruples lacked persuasive power when juxtaposed with the alleged corruption of Florida's youth, and Charley Johns proceeded unhindered. Sixteen staff and faculty members eventually lost their positions on charges of homosexuality; all had been active in the civil rights movement.[15]

Although the meagerness of evidence to sustain the charge that homosexuals and lesbians threatened national security makes the preoccupation with sexual "perversion" appear in retrospect bizarre and irrational, the incorporation of gay women and men into the demonology of the McCarthy era required little effort. According to extreme anticommunist ideologues, left-wing teachers poisoned the minds of their students; lesbians and homosexuals corrupted their bodies. Communists bore no identifying physical characteristics. Able to disguise their true selves, they infiltrated the government where, as the Hiss and Rosenberg cases seemed to demonstrate, they committed treason against their country. They exhibited loyalty only to a political ideology and a foreign

15. Weekly Bulletin no. 2015, October 26, 1959; Stuart Simon to Charlie Johns, February 5, 1959; and other material on the Johns Committee, all in General Correspondence, vol. 55, 1959, ACLU papers. For press coverage, see *Miami News*, February 10 and 16, 1959; and March 3, 1959, p. 5; *Daytona Beach News*, February 19, 1959; *New York Herald Tribune*, April 4, 1959 (clippings in General Correspondence, vol. 55, 1959, ACLU papers). For the final report of the investigation, which continued for several years, see *Homosexuality and Citizenship in Florida: A Report of the Florida Legislative Investigating Committee* (Tallahassee, Fla., 1964). For the ACLU's 1957 position on homosexuality, see "Homosexuality and Civil Liberties," *Civil Liberties*, March 1957, n.p. For additional discussion of the ACLU, see below, chaps. 7, 9, and 11.

power that inspired fanatical, unreasoning passion. Homosexuals too could escape detection. Coming from all walks of life, they insinuated themselves everywhere in society, including the highest reaches of government. Allegedly slaves to their perverted desires, they stopped at nothing to gratify their sexual impulses. The satisfaction of animal needs dominated their lives until it atrophied all moral sense. Communists taught children to betray their parents; mannish women mocked the ideals of marriage and motherhood. Lacking toughness, the effete, overly educated male representatives of the Eastern establishment had lost China and Eastern Europe to the enemy. Weak-willed, pleasure-seeking homosexuals—"half-men"—feminized everything they touched and sapped the masculine vigor that had tamed a continent. The congruence of the stereotypical communist and homosexual made scapegoating gay men and women a simple matter.

II

The widespread labeling of lesbians and homosexuals as moral perverts and national security risks gave local police forces across the country a free rein in harassment. Throughout the 1950s gays suffered from unpredictable, brutal crackdowns. Men faced arrest primarily in bars and cruising areas such as parks, public restrooms, beaches, and transportation depots, while women generally encountered the police in and around lesbian bars. But even the homes of gay men and women lacked immunity from vice squads bent on increasing their arrest records. The utmost caution did not guarantee protection from the hand of the law. Many of those lucky enough to escape arrest had friends or acquaintances captured in a raid. Newspaper headlines announced that the police were combing the cities for nests of deviates. Editors often printed the names, addresses, and place of employment of men and women arrested in bar raids. Police parked their squad cars in front of homosexual taverns to intimidate patrons. Every evening spent in a gay setting, every contact with another homosexual or lesbian, every sexual intimacy carried a reminder of the criminal penalties that could be exacted at any moment. The only safety lay in forswearing all contact with other gay women and men, yet even the final resort of utter isolation could not quiet internalized fears. A gnawing insecurity pervaded the lives of gay men and women.[16]

Arrests were substantial in many cities. In the District of Columbia they exceeded 1,000 per year during the early 1950s. Washington police frequently

16. With the exception of the Boise scandal, local police activities against gay men and women did not receive coverage beyond the pages of local papers. It is accordingly a laborious process to uncover incidents of harassment. The most accessible sources are the publications of gay organizations that, beginning in the mid-1950s, covered police practices extensively. *ONE* magazine is by far the best source, with news items from around the country, but the *Ladder* and the *Mattachine Review*, as well as newsletters from local chapters of the Mattachine Society and the Daughters of Bilitis, also gave space to police practices. James Kepner, who wrote the articles on police practices for *ONE*, has saved the clippings from local newspapers that readers of *ONE* sent to him. These may be found in the National Gay Archives, Los Angeles (hereafter referred to as NGA).

resorted to entrapment by plainclothesmen in Lafayette Park and downtown movie houses to arrest male homosexuals. In Philadelphia during the 1950s, misdemeanor charges against gay men and women averaged 100 per month. Arrests could fluctuate enormously in response to shifting police priorities. Salt Lake City officers took no actions against male homosexuals in May 1957, but they apprehended twenty-five gay men during the first four months of 1958 and twenty-three in the next four weeks. Bar raids suddenly swelled the totals of arrests and spread panic throughout the gay populaton of a city. Thirty-six women went to jail on a single night in September 1956, when police descended on the Alamo Club, a lesbian bar in San Francisco. One resident reported "a paralyzing fear," with lesbians "seeking cover once again." In New Orleans in 1953 vice officers packed Doris Lunden and sixty-three other women into vans after clearing them from a lesbian club in the French Quarter. The next day, Lunden found the court overflowing with men and women brought in from other bars in the city. A raid by the Baltimore police in October 1955 netted 162 gay men. Wichita, Dallas, Memphis, Seattle, and Ann Arbor were among the cities in the 1950s that witnessed sudden upsurges in police action against gays. A survey of male homosexuals conducted by the Institute for Sex Research revealed how far police action extended into the gay world: 20 percent of the respondents had encountered trouble with law enforcement officers.[17]

Any one of a variety of circumstances could provoke a sudden intensification of police harassment. During the New York City mayoral campaign of 1953, a gay man reported that "the situation here . . . is getting worse, instead of better, with the elections coming along: raids on gay bars, arrests on the beaches this summer, and cops chasing [homosexuals] out of Sutton Place where they cruise in the evenings on the river's edge." Six years later, when Lee Mortimer castigated the police in the *Daily Mirror* for laxity about gay bars, another round of citywide raids ensued. Baltimore police closed bars and broke up parties in private homes to deflect attention from a grand jury investigation into police corruption. After the kidnap and murder of a young boy, the county attorney in Sioux City ordered the detention of known local homosexuals. Invoking the provisions of Iowa's sexual psychopath law, which

17. On the District of Columbia see *Employment of Homosexuals*, pp. 15–19; Kelly v. U.S., 194 F .2d 150 (D.C. Circuit, 1952); 90 A .2d 233 (D.C.Munic. Ct. App., 1952); and McDermott v. U.S., 98 A .2d 287 (D.C. Munic, Ct. App., 1953). On Philadelphia see *The Challenge and Progress of Homosexual Law Reform* (San Francisco, 1968), p. 18. On Salt Lake City see *Salt Lake Tribune*, May 29, 1958. On San Francisco see *Ladder*, November 1956, p. 5. On New Orleans see Elly Bulkin, "An Old Dyke's Tale: An Interview with Doris Lunden," *Conditions: Six* (1980), p. 28. On Baltimore see *ONE*, December 1955, p. 10; and *Baltimore Evening Sun*, October 3 and 5, 1955 (clippings in NGA). On Wichita see *Wichita Eagle*, November 16, 1954 (clippings in NGA). On Ann Arbor see *Ann Arbor News*, December 22, 1959, p. 17; and *Chicago Daily Tribune*, December 23, 1959, pt. 2, p. 9. On the other cities see *ONE*, November 1955, p. 8; November 1958, p. 17; December 1958, p. 15; and June 1959, p. 13. For the ISR survey see John H. Gagnon and William Simon, *Sexual Conduct* (Chicago, 1973), pp. 138–39.

permitted interment without trial or conviction, he had twenty-nine men committed to asylums. "At least word is out that they're not welcome in Sioux City any more," the prosecutor commented. In Boise, the arrest of three men in November 1955 on charges of sexual activity with teenagers precipitated a fifteen-month-long investigation into the city's male homosexual subculture. Gay men fled Boise by the score as the police called in 1,400 residents for questioning and pressured homosexuals into naming gay friends. In 1954 the murder of two homosexuals in Miami by "queerbashers" who had picked up their victims in a gay bar led the mayor to reverse a longstanding policy of closing his eyes to the existence of the establishments. Police made sweeps of the bars and beefed up their patrols of Bay Front Park and other meeting places. Like prostitutes, who also violated conventional sexual morality, gay men were subjected to VD inspections and verbal abuse by the police. In a strange twist, the individuals most in need of protection had become the targets of the police.[18]

The stigma attached to homosexuality also made gay men and women the easy prey of petty criminals. Seedy characters haunted male homosexual cruising areas in order to beat and rob their victims. "Pickups" suddenly metamorphosed into thieves, seizing the valuables in one's home, secure in the knowledge that the incident would not be reported. Gangs of men stalked lesbian bars to attack women who rebuffed their sexual overtures. The police, if they intervened, were more likely to arrest the women than their male assailants. In many cities organized crime invested in gay bars. Vice squad officers received from the owners lucrative payoffs that came out of the pockets of customers who paid excessive prices for watered drinks. Extortionists posed as plainclothes detectives to obtain quick cash from defenseless homosexuals. Blackmail became a profitable racket, sometimes engaged in by nationwide rings, often with the cooperation of the police. Money, not classified secrets, was the object.[19]

Although the treatment accorded gay men and lesbians in the 1950s grew out of a cultural tradition clearly hostile to homoerotic activities, nonetheless it

18. On New York see *ONE*, November 1953, p. 19; and Lee Mortimer's columns in the *Daily Mirror*, August 12, 1959; November 3, 1959; and January 26, 1960. On Baltimore see *ONE*, April 1955, p. 14; and December 1955, p. 10. On Sioux City see *ONE*, November 1955, p. 9; and February 1956, p. 11; and the *Des Moines Register*, November 25, 1955. On Boise see *Time*, December 12, 1955, p. 12; John Gerassi, *The Boys of Boise* (New York, 1966); Jonathan Katz, *Gay American History* (New York, 1976), pp. 109–19; and Washington Mattachine *Newsletter*, January 1957, pp. 1–3. On Miami see "Miami Junks the Constitution," *ONE*, January 1954, pp. 16–21; "Miami Hurricane," *ONE*, November 1954, pp. 4–8; and John Orr to Herbert Levy, September 13, 1954, in General Correspondence, vol. 19, 1954, ACLU papers. See also the extensive NGA collection of clippings from the *Miami Herald* and the *Miami Daily News*, August and September 1954.

19. For examples, see Donald Vining, *A Gay Diary, Volume 2, 1946–1954*; the interview with Pat Bond in Nancy and Casey Adair, *Word Is Out* (New York, 1978), pp. 61–62; Buffalo Lesbian

marked a significant departure from the past. During the 1950s antihomosexual forces took an aggressive stance. For the first time, the phenomenon rose to the surface of American life, to become a subject of serious concern.

The targeting of gay men and women in the 1950s testified to the depth of the changes that had occurred in the previous decade, for without them it is difficult to imagine the homosexual issue carrying much weight. In 1920, for instance, the Senate investigated "immoral conditions" of a homosexual nature at the naval training station in Newport, Rhode Island.[20] The political context resembled that of the McCarthy era—a world war had recently ended, a major communist revolution had taken place, and the nation was in the midst of a red scare. Yet, although the report expressed intense loathing for sexual "perverts," it reserved its severest condemnation for the corrupt methods used to detect them and made no effort to arouse an antihomosexual campaign. During the 1940s, however, homosexuality assumed significantly greater visibility. Armed forces medical personnel questioned all recruits about their sexual inclinations. The shift toward sex segregation affected far larger numbers of Americans than it had in World War I, and the mobilization effort lasted longer. Homosexuality became less of an abstraction for the many individuals who encountered gay men and women for the first time. As homosexuals and lesbians constructed an urban subculture, the phenomenon of same-sex eroticism appeared to take on larger proportions. Finally, the Kinsey reports, especially the study of the male, informed Americans that homosexual behavior was far more common than conventional wisdom believed. Although a centuries-long cultural antagonism toward homoeroticism underlay the oppression of gay men and women, recent changes in the structure of homosexual life and a growing awareness of its presence in society propelled the antigay campaigns of the 1950s.

Systematized oppression during the 1950s exerted contradictory influences on gays. In repeatedly condemning the phenomenon, antigay polemicists broke the silence that surrounded the topic of homosexuality. Thus the resources available to lesbians and homosexuals for attaching a meaning to otherwise dimly understood feelings expanded noticeably. The attacks on gay men and women hastened the articulation of a homosexual identity and spread the knowledge that they existed in large numbers. Ironically, the effort to root out the homosexuals in American society made it easier for them to find one another.

Oral History Project, "Lesbian Bars in Buffalo, 1930–1960," paper presented at the June 1981 Berkshire Women's History Conference Vassar College, Poughkeepsie, N.Y.; and Wardell Pomeroy, *Dr. Kinsey and the Institute for Sex Research* (New York, 1972), pp. 347–48. For information on a blackmail ring that operated from the early 1950s through the mid-1960s, see *New York Times*, February 18, 1966, p. 19; and March 3, 1966, p. 1.

20. See U.S. Senate, 67th Cong., 1st sess., Committee on Naval Affairs, *Alleged Immoral Conditions at Newport (R.I.) Naval Training Station* (Washington, D.C., 1921).

At the same time, the harsh reality of oppression shaped the contours of gay identity and the gay world. The condemnations that did occur burdened homosexuals and lesbians with a corrosive self-image. The dominant view of them—as perverts, psychopaths, deviates, and the like—seeped into their consciousness. Shunted to the margins of American society, harassed because of their sexuality, many gay men and women internalized the negative descriptions and came to embody the stereotypes. Moreover, even as some of them participated in an urban subculture that sustained the sense of belonging to a group, they confronted an ideology that viewed their situation as an individual problem. Whether seen from the vantage point of religion, medicine, or the law, the homosexual or lesbian was a flawed individual, not a victim of injustice. For many, the gay world was reduced to a setting where they shared an affliction.

2   The 1950s:
Radical Visions and
Conformist Pressures

FOUR

Radical Beginnings of the Mattachine Society

Formidable obstacles stood in the way of launching a homosexual emancipation movement. Although the growth of an urban subculture was bringing gay men and lesbians into a community bound by shared experience, the phenomenon was still too recent in origin and too small in scope to counteract the centrifugal forces in their lives. The dominant view of homoeroticism as sin, sickness, or crime accustomed homosexual men and women to seeing their situation as a personal problem, not a cause for political action. The overwhelming majority of them, moreover, had the option of "passing," of keeping their sexual identity a closely guarded secret. As Donald Webster Cory phrased it in *The Homosexual in America*, the ability to wear the mask of heterosexuality trapped gays "in a particularly vicious circle." The punishment that came with acknowledging one's homosexuality openly was

> so great that pretense is almost universal; on the other hand, only a leadership that would acknowledge [it] would be able to break down the barriers. . . . Until the world is able to accept us on an equal basis as human beings entitled to the full rights of life, we are unlikely to have any great numbers willing to become martyrs. . . . But until we are willing to speak out openly and frankly in defense of our activities, and to identify ourselves with the millions pursuing these activities, we are unlikely to find the attitudes of the world undergoing any significant change.[1]

As the antihomosexual impulse in American society gathered strength during the 1950s, pressure to remain invisible and isolated became even more acute,

1. Donald Webster Cory (pseud.), *The Homosexual in America* (New York, 1951), p. 14.

while the McCarthy era fostered a political climate generally inhospitable to movements for social change.

However, despite the odds against it, a homosexual emancipation movement did take root in the mid-twentieth century. The founding of the Mattachine Society in Los Angeles in 1951 marked the beginning of what would grow into a nationwide effort.[2] The society's leadership came from several male homosexuals who were either members of the Communist party or traveled in left-wing circles. Standing outside the political mainstream, they also broke with accepted notions of homoerotic behavior and pioneered in conceiving homosexuals as an oppressed minority. Mattachine struggled to find ways to develop in its members a strong group consciousness free of the negative attitudes that gay men and women typically internalized. The founders argued that homosexuals were indeed different from the heterosexual majority. But they affirmed the uniqueness of gay identity, projected a vision of a homosexual culture with its own positive values, and attempted to transform the shame of being gay into a pride in belonging to a minority with its own contribution to the human community. Above all, the Communist party experience of some of the founders gave them organizational skills especially relevant to the situation of homosexuals and lesbians. The Mattachine Society adopted a secret, cell-like structure that, by protecting members from exposure, allowed them to participate with relative safety in a gay organization.

I

Henry Hay was the man most responsible for the founding of the Mattachine Society. Born of American parents in England in 1912, he spent most of his childhood and adolescence in southern California. After graduating from high school in 1929, he worked for a year in a law office in Los Angeles. During that time Hay, who had felt a strong sexual desire for males before puberty, had his first homosexual experiences with men whom he met on the street in downtown Los Angeles. In the fall of 1930 he enrolled in Stanford University, where he developed an interest in drama. Professional and personal concerns soon became intertwined, as he discovered gay male friendship circles in San Francisco among the city's actors, musicians, artists, and writers. When Hay returned to Los Angeles, friends from San Francisco provided introductions that gave him entree to homosexual networks in southern California.[3]

2. The decision to begin the history of the movement with the founding of the Mattachine Society is not meant to imply that it was the first homosexual emancipation group in the United States. There may have been several other earlier groups, and the existence of at least one—in Chicago in the 1920s—has been documented. But the founding of the Mattachine Society does mark the start of an *unbroken* history of homosexual and lesbian organizing that continues until this day. For information on the Chicago group, see Jonathan Katz, *Gay American History* (New York, 1976), pp. 385–93.

3. The biographical information about Hay contained in this and the following paragraphs comes from my interviews with him during October 16–19, 1976, in San Juan Pueblo, N.M. Unless otherwise specified, quotations are from those interviews. For another interview with Hay, see Jonathan Katz, *Gay American History* (New York, 1976), pp. 406–20.

In 1933 Hay took a step that greatly changed the course of his life. In the depression-ridden years of the early 1930s, he found it difficult to secure steady work as an actor, and so he accepted the invitation of a friend to join a group that performed agitational, propagandistic theater at the sites of strikes and other demonstrations. The experience awakened in him a political consciousness, and when he discovered that many of his associates were Communist party members, Hay joined too. Sent by the party to San Francisco in May 1934, he participated in the July general strike called by labor leaders. The strike, he reminisced,

> was just something tremendous! And I was committed from then on, man. That was it! That did it! The commitment was not an intellectual one to start with. It was pure emotional, a gut thing. You couldn't have been a part of that and not have your life completely changed.[4]

For the next fifteen years, the Communist party absorbed Hay's energy. Initially assigned to the artists and writers branch of the party, Hay was a union organizer for a time during World War II, but after 1945 he returned to cultural work. Active in the Los Angeles chapter of People's Songs, a leftist organization of songwriters and musicians, Hay represented the group at the People's Educational Center, a workers' education project whose directors ranged from AFL representatives to Communist party members. Early in 1948 he began teaching a class there on the history of popular music.[5]

Hay's allegiance to the party also profoundly affected his personal life. By the 1930s Stalin had reversed the policy of tolerance toward homosexuality that had characterized Soviet Communism during its early years in power, and he was persecuting homosexuals with a vengeance.[6] Unable to reconcile his sexual and political identities, Hay revealed his homosexuality to party superiors, who counseled him to repress it. He accepted their advice and in 1938 married another party member, Anita, with whom he had worked closely for a long time. As he described it years later in a letter, "I determined that I would simply close a book and never look back. For fourteen years I lived . . . in an exile world." But Hay failed to make as complete a break with his homosexual

4. Hay's description of the birth of a strong commitment to the party bears a remarkable similarity to those provided by other party members. For the testimony of others who joined the Communist party in the 1930s and 1940s, see Vivian Gornick, *The Romance of American Communism* (New York, 1978), esp. pp. 28–106.

5. For an outline of Hay's music course, see his "Tentative Outline to 'Music—Barometer of the Class Struggle,'" January 2, 1948, mimeo, personal papers of James Kepner, Los Angeles. On People's Songs, Inc., see R. Serge Denisoff, *Great Day Coming: Folk Music and the American Left* (Urbana, Ill., 1971), pp. 107–18; on the People's Educational Center, see Edward L. Barrett, Jr., *The Tenney Committee* (Ithaca, N.Y., 1951), pp. 105–21.

6. As with most of American society, the attitude of the Communist party toward homosexuality was reflected mostly by its silence. Standard histories of the party in the 1930s and 1940s give it no mention at all. But the position of the Soviet Union, from which the American party generally took its lead, is known. On Soviet policy under Stalin, see John Lauritsen and David Thorstad, *The Early Homosexual Rights Movement, 1864–1935* (New York, 1974), pp. 62–70.

inclinations as he pretended; occasionally he had sexual encounters with men. However, he did deliberately isolate himself from gay social circles and ostensibly conformed to the party's—and society's—sexual mores.[7]

An unexpected occurrence during the summer of 1948 upset this precarious equilibrium. The Communist party was concentrating much of its effort that summer on the Henry Wallace presidential bid, and Hay was working on the campaign while continuing to do research for his history of music class at the People's Educational Center. Early in August, he attended a social gathering where he was expecting to meet another musicologist. When he arrived, he found that all of the guests were gay. Hay began talking about the Wallace campaign, and before long he and several others were jokingly spinning out the design of an organization to mobilize gay men behind the Progressive party. Calling it "Bachelors for Wallace," they imagined the group gathering support among male homosexuals in return for a sexual privacy plank in the Wallace platform. Although Bachelors for Wallace never moved beyond the stage of idle talk, Hay took the notion of a political organization of homosexuals seriously. In the months that followed, he mulled over the idea of a gay organization. As he thought about it, Hay found himself moving toward a change in his life as extreme as the one that took place when he joined the Communist party. He began to realize that "somehow or another, my [life] as a heterosexual, a pseudo-heterosexual, was coming to an end." The time had come when "suddenly I was forced to admit that the relentless difference between me and the world of my choice had grown imperceptibly into an unscalable barrier." Having once abandoned gay life for the Communist party, Hay would soon use the organizing skills he had acquired in the party to launch a homosexual emancipation movement.[8]

Almost two years elapsed before Hay elicited any glimmers of enthusiasm about his idea for a homosexual organization. First he approached his professional heterosexual acquaintances—doctors, lawyers, ministers, educators— in various progressive organizations and sounded out their opinions on the "plight" of homosexuals; but their tepid response convinced him that a campaign on behalf of homosexuals would have to be initiated by the oppressed themselves. Finally, in the spring of 1950, he spoke to Bob Hull and Chuck Rowland about his idea. Hull was a student in Hay's music class; Rowland was Hull's roommate and closest friend. The three men met one evening at a concert; and Hay, who suspected that the pair might be gay, decided to broach the subject of a homosexual rights organization. As it turned out, they had

7. Hay to Donald Webster Cory, Kepner papers. Hay's letter to Cory is undated, but in it he answers questions posed by Cory in a letter to him dated May 1, 1952, also in Kepner papers.

8. Ibid. Hay's observation about the value of his party experience for other activities is echoed in Gornick, *The Romance of American Communism*, p. 31. For a more detailed account of one person's experience with a similar theme, see Jessica Mitford's memoir, *A Fine Old Conflict* (New York, 1977).

more in common than their homosexuality, since Rowland and Hull had also been Communist party members.[9]

Born in 1917, Rowland was raised in a small town in South Dakota. He grew up feeling confused and isolated by homosexual urges that he could discuss with no one. Going away to college at the University of Minnesota provided the opportunity for him to come out, to meet other men like himself and begin the process of self-acceptance. But Minneapolis in the 1930s also provided fertile soil for the growth of political activism, and Rowland found himself participating in campus demonstrations in support of the Loyalists in the Spanish Civil War and against compulsory military training for students.

Hull attended the university in the same years as Rowland, although the two men did not know each other as students. Hull had a graduate degree in chemistry but had rejected a career in science to pursue his interest in music. When he met Rowland in 1940, he was just beginning to break into Twin Cities music circles as a pianist. The two men became lovers and, when that relationship ended, moved easily into a close friendship that would last for twenty years.

Rowland served in the army during World War II and toward the end of the war became a charter member of the American Veterans Committee. The AVC tended to attract New Deal liberals and progressives who were determined, as Rowland described it, "to build a world in our own, idealistic image." After his discharge, he worked as a field representative for the AVC in the Midwest and traveled throughout the region. However, he did not remain with the American Veterans Committee for long.[10] Throughout 1946 national officers in New York charged that Communists had infiltrated the organization. Rowland's own inquiries established that Communists were prominent among AVC organizers, but in his opinion they invariably turned out to be "the most dedicated workers and soundest strategists." He decided to join the party (recruiting his friend Hull in the process) and, when finally forced out of the veterans' group because of his politics, returned to Minneapolis to work for American Youth for Democracy, a Communist-dominated organization. During 1948 he took part in Henry Wallace's presidential campaign. Discouraged by its disastrous outcome and worried about mounting anticommunism, he left the party and migrated to Los Angeles at the end of the year.[11]

---

9. Rowland gave an account of the initial meeting in his keynote speech at the Mattachine Society's convention in Los Angeles, April 11, 1953 (copy in personal papers of Don Lucas, San Francisco). The information about Rowland and Hull in the following paragraphs comes from a series of letters from Rowland to the author: December 5 and 11, 1976; January 4 and 17, 1977; May 19, 1977; July 9, 1977; and December 1, 1977.

10. Rowland to author, January 17, 1977. For information on the founding of the American Veterans Committee and its goals, see *New York Times*, April 15, 1945, p. 7; and *New Republic*, November 27, 1944, p. 695.

.11. Rowland to author, January 17, 1977; and July 9, 1977. On anticommunism in the AVC, see *New York Times*, May 11, 1946, p. 7; November 11, 1946, p. 22; January 15, 1947, p. 6;

Hull followed Rowland to Los Angeles, but he maintained his party affiliation. He joined one of its cultural units in southern California and participated in the activities of the People's Educational Center, enrolling in Hay's music class. Hull and Rowland were both excited by what Hay suggested on the evening of the 1950 concert, and a few more conversations ensued. However, their informal discussions ended when the men temporarily lost contact with one another after the conclusion of Hay's music class.

Early in July 1950, Hay met R. at a rehearsal of the Lester Horton Dance Theatre. A Jewish costume designer and dancer with Horton's company, R. had fled Austria in 1938 with his mother to escape Nazi persecution and settled in Los Angeles. He found the company an intensely political milieu; Horton's work frequently had a theme of social injustice, and troupe members who did not share such concerns quickly left. Hay spoke to R. about a political organization to defend the rights of homosexuals. R. expressed interest and, upon reading Hay's prospectus, committed himself to the venture. After almost two years of cautious effort, Hay had found his first recruit at last.[12]

Not quite sure how to begin to develop their organization, Hay and R. decided to try to find homosexuals who shared their political sympathies. In an attempt to locate other leftists, they obtained copies of a Communist party petition against the Korean war and took them to the gay male beaches in Los Angeles. During the next two months, the two men collected the signatures of several hundred homosexuals opposed to the war. But when they used the opportunity also to talk about current government investigations of homosexuals in federal employment and to suggest that something ought to be done, Hay and R. encountered a terrified silence. No one was willing to risk exposure of his sexual identity by joining a homosexual rights organization.[13]

Hull, meanwhile, had enrolled in another of Hay's music classes, and Hay decided to show him the prospectus. Hull and Rowland passed it on to another gay friend, Dale Jennings, a writer active in campaigns to defend the civil liberties of Japanese-Americans. Hull arranged a meeting with Hay, and on a Saturday afternoon in November 1950 the five men—Hay, R., Hull, Rowland, and Jennings—gathered at Hay's home to discuss the formation of a homosexual rights organization. Frequent meetings over the next several months led to the formation of the Mattachine Society.

January 16, 1947, p. 27; and January 17, 1947, p. 11. See also *Newsweek*, June 24, 1946, p. 27; and *Nation*, June 14, 1947, pp. 706–8.

12. On the Lester Horton Dance Theatre, see *Dance Perspectives*, vol. 31 (Autumn 1967). For Hay's prospectus, see Eann MacDonald, "Preliminary Concepts," July 7, 1950, Kepner papers. "Eann MacDonald" was the pseudonym initially used by Hay in some of his Mattachine activities.

13. "America's Peace Poll," flyer issued by the Los Angeles Committee, American Peace Crusade; and Harry Hay, undated note to James Kepner describing the petition activity at the gay beaches, Kepner papers.

II

Several features of the early Mattachine Society reflected the leftist orientation of its founders and distinguished it from most of its successor organizations. Its secret, cell-like, hierarchical structure was inspired by the experience of Hay, Rowland, and Hull in the Communist party. The society exhibited a concern for understanding the cause of gay oppression and developed an analysis of homosexuals as an oppressed cultural minority. As believers in a theory of social change that stressed action by masses of people on their own behalf, the founders kept the society focused on mobilizing a large gay constituency and welding it into a cohesive force capable of militancy.

The founders' perception of the need for secrecy grew out of the political climate of the times. By 1950 American Communists and their sympathizers were an embattled, increasingly isolated political minority, subject to repression. The popular front of the 1930s, in which Communists, New Deal liberals, and other radicals frequently worked together, had fragmented. In 1949 the government indicted Communist party leaders under the Smith Act, and in September 1950 Congress passed a tough new Internal Security Act, requiring party members and front organizations to register with the Justice Department and providing for the internment of Communists in case of national emergency. Many states also enacted laws aimed at suppressing the party. American Communists, meanwhile, believed that America was moving rapidly toward fascism.[14] Although this conclusion proved fanciful, the first-hand experience of the Mattachine founders made the assertion appear plausible. Rowland had lost his position with the American Veterans Committee because of anticommunism; Jennings's involvement with Japanese-Americans in California made him appreciate the threat of internment; and R. had fled his native country to escape a fascist regime bent on exterminating Jews, leftists, and homosexuals. Hay above all was fearful of repression. With much of his party work centered on cultural activities, he was acutely aware of the targeting of leftists in Hollywood by the House Un-American Activities Committee. Moreover, California had its own anticommunist investigating committee, and the two organizations in which Hay was most active had already come under its scrutiny. Finally, the homosexual issue had just recently surfaced in Washington, and as they debated the structure of the organization, the Senate released its report on "sexual perverts."[15]

---

14. On anticommunist measures and the isolation of the Communist party in the postwar period, see David Caute, *The Great Fear: The Anti-Communist Purge Under Truman and Eisenhower* (New York, 1978); Robert Griffith and Athan Theoharis, eds., *The Specter: Original Essays on the Cold War and the Origins of McCarthyism* (New York, 1974); and Joseph Starobin, *American Communism in Crisis, 1943–1957* (Berkeley, 1972). On state legislation aimed at Communists, see Walter Gelhorn, ed., *The States and Subversion* (Ithaca, N.Y., 1952).

15. On the investigation of People's Songs, Inc., see Denisoff, *Great Day Coming*, pp. 123–24.

The structure that Hay and the others finally devised for the Mattachine Society was modeled on the Communist party, in which secrecy, hierarchical structures, and centralized leadership predominated. The founders created a pyramid of five "orders" of membership, with increasing levels of responsibility as one ascended the structure and with each order having one or two representatives from a higher order of the organization. As the membership of the Mattachine Society grew, the orders were expected to subdivide into separate cells so that each layer of the pyramid could expand horizontally. As the number of cells increased, members of the same order but in different cells would be largely unknown to one another. A single fifth order consisting of the founders would provide the Mattachine Society with a centralized leadership whose policies flowed downward through the lower orders.[16]

Hay and his partners also brought to their discussions an interest in uncovering a systemic analysis for social problems. As Marxists they believed that injustice and oppression came not from simple prejudice or misinformation but from relationships deeply embedded in the structure of society. This led them to reject a narrowly pragmatic approach to the situation of the homosexual, focusing only on a set of reform goals, and pushed them instead to seek a theoretical understanding of the homosexual's inferior status. Although the motivation for this exploration came from their party background, the failure of Communist ideology in the mid-twentieth century to address questions about human sexuality freed Hay and the others from the dogmatism that often characterized American Communist thought.

The lack of an already developed analysis of the oppression of homosexuals forced the founders to generate one by scrutinizing their own lives. Throughout the winter of 1951 the five men met frequently to share their histories, focusing especially on their gay experiences. They exchanged stories of coming out, of discovering cruising places and bars, of the years of loneliness. Trying

---

On the People's Educational Center, see Barrett, *The Tenney Committee*, pp. 105–21. The Tenney Committee also focused attention on campaigns to defend the civil liberties of Japanese-Americans; see Barrett, pp. 81–88. On HUAC's investigations into Communist influence in Hollywood, see Victor Navasky, *Naming Names* (New York, 1980); Robert K. Carr, *The House Committee on Un-American Activities, 1945–1950* (Ithaca, N. Y., 1952), esp. pp. 55–78; and Walter Goodman, *The Committee* (New York, 1968), esp. pp. 298–309. See also Mitford, *A Fine Old Conflict*, for an account of day-to-day harassment of Communists in California; as well as Gornick, *The Romance of American Communism*, and Lillian Hellman, *Scoundrel Time* (Boston, 1976). Federal legislation aimed at the Communist party became a major issue as early as 1948, and its prime sponsor, Richard Nixon, was a U.S. Representative from southern California. In 1951, moreover, several leaders of the party in California were indicted under the Smith Act. Taken together, these incidents help explain the Mattachine founders' intense preoccupation with repression.

16. I was unable to uncover any written documents describing the structure of the early Mattachine Society. But the accuracy of my description is supported by the consistency with which the structure was outlined by all of the participants whom I contacted: Hay, Gruber, Stevens, Jackson, Legg, Brissette, Kepner, and Rowland.

to find patterns in their individual experiences, they posed questions: How did one become a homosexual? Was homosexuality an adopted trait, or was it innate? Were homosexuals sick? Did the five exhibit the psychopathology that supposedly characterized the homosexual personality? If not, why were some homosexuals so disturbed? Were there special cultural traits that developed in a gay life? Were homosexuals merely a conglomeration of individuals sharing only a sexual orientation, or did they perhaps have in common something more that made it feasible for them to work together?[17]

Out of their discussions an analysis gradually emerged of homosexuals as an oppressed cultural minority. Individuals, they argued, drew their identity from their participation in heterosexual nuclear families where they learned a "socially predetermined pattern" for human relationships. Raised in families as virtually all Americans were, men and women unquestioningly accepted as "natural" a system of social roles "which equates male, masculine, man ONLY with husband and Father . . . and which equates female, feminine, woman ONLY with wife and Mother." Rigid though these definitions of gender were, they did nonetheless generate what the founders called "an adequate sense of value," appropriate to guide the lives of heterosexuals. Homosexuals, however, "did not fit the patterns of heterosexual love, marriage, children, etc., upon which the dominant culture rests." But with no socially approved models for their life-style, homosexuals "mechanically superimposed the heterosexual ethic" on their own situation "in empty imitation of dominant patterns." The result was a daily existence predicated upon "self-deceit, hypocrisy, and charlatanism" and a "sense of value . . . disturbed, inadequate, and undesirable." Victimized by a "language and culture that does not admit the existence of the Homosexual Minority," homosexuals remained "largely unaware" that they in fact constituted "a social minority imprisoned within a dominant culture."[18]

Their definition of homosexuals as a minority "unaware" of its existence put the founders on more familiar ground and suggested to them an initial course of action. Their formulation resembled the Marxist distinction between a class "in itself" and a class "for itself." The difference between these two was one of consciousness. In the former case, workers constituted an objective social category; in the latter, they recognized their common interests. According to Marxist theory, the transformation from one to the other made the working

---

17. The content of these meetings, and especially the questions that the participants raised, was discussed by Rowland in a letter to the author, January 17, 1977.

18. See "Sense of Value," September 6, 1951; "Sense of Value (II)," September 20, 1951; and "Social Directions of the Homosexual," October 4, 1951; all in Kepner papers. See also Eann MacDonald, "A Speculation on the Dialectics of Homosexual Social Directions," September 18, 1951, in Mattachine Society—Los Angeles file, Institute for Sex Research, Bloomington, Ind. (hereafter referred to as ISR); Harry Hay, "Preface to the Communication of Homosexual Values," December 1952, Kepner papers; and Charles Rowland, "Opening Speech," April 11, 1953, Lucas papers.

class a cohesive force able to fight on its own behalf. Homosexuals, too, were trapped by false consciousness, by a hegemonic ideology that labeled their eroticism an individual aberration. The first task of a homosexual emancipation movement, then, was to challenge the internalization of this view by homosexuals and to develop among the gay population an awareness of its status as an oppressed minority. Out of that awareness homosexuals could then evolve a "highly ethical homosexual culture" and "lead well-adjusted, wholesome, and socially productive lives." The result would be a "new pride—a pride in belonging, a pride in participating in the cultural growth and social achievements of . . . the homosexual minority." And from the cohesiveness that such a self-image would create, in time the founders expected to forge a unified movement of homosexuals ready to fight against their oppression.[19]

In order to initiate this process and recruit gays into the Mattachine Society, the founders decided to sponsor semipublic discussion groups. Early on, they had recognized the value of their private meetings as a means of cementing relations among themselves and discarding many conventional attitudes about homosexuality. Consequently, even before they had formalized their structure or their goals, they began inviting selected gay friends and acquaintances to a biweekly discussion group on homosexuality. But the discussions never seemed to take off, and few people returned more than once.[20]

The open meetings did lead, however, to the addition of a pair of lovers to the original group of five. James Gruber was an ex-serviceman studying at Occidental College; Konrad Stevens was a photographer. When they appeared at one gathering during the winter of 1951, they exhibited an enthusiasm absent among the other guests. Rowland approached them after the gathering, told them about the effort to form a homosexual rights organization, and invited them to the next closed meeting. Gruber and Stevens accepted. Although they had never before taken part in political causes and recalled feelings of "terror" aroused by the "communist jargon" of the founders, the two men were attracted by the concern for justice behind the rhetoric. By the end of the evening, they were firmly committed to the as yet undeveloped organization.[21]

With the involvement of Gruber and Stevens, the Mattachine Society finally

---

19. Mattachine Society, "Missions and Purposes," April 1951, Mattachine Society—Los Angeles file, ISR; and Rowland, "Opening Speech," April 11, 1953, Lucas papers. Marx made the distinction between a class in itself and for itself in *The Poverty of Philosophy*; see Robert C. Tucker, ed., *The Marx-Engels Reader*, 2d ed. (New York, 1976), p. 218.

20. The information in this paragraph is drawn from my interview with Hay, October 16, 1976.

21. Interview with Konrad Stevens, Los Angeles, January 5, 1977; and interview with James Gruber, Mountain View, Calif., December 28, 1976. Years later, in recalling the impact of Gruber's and Stevens's appearance and subsequent involvement, Rowland said, "That was the night the Mattachine was born" (Rowland to author, December 5, 1976). Hay too emphasized their importance in my interviews with him.

took shape. The name itself was suggested by Gruber after Hay had talked about "mattachines," mysterious mediaeval figures in masks whom Hay speculated might have been homosexuals. The presence of Gruber and Stevens also forced the others to frame their ideas in language accessible to non-Marxists. In April 1951 they wrote a succinct, one-page document setting out their goals and some of their thinking about homosexuals as a minority. The purpose of the society, it read, was to unify isolated homosexuals, educate homosexuals to see themselves as an oppressed minority, and lead them in a struggle for their own emancipation. During the spring the seven members of the "fifth order" agreed on the structure of the organization and tried to revive the almost lifeless discussions that they were still holding. After the disappointing attempts of the winter and spring, the semipublic meetings suddenly caught on and the number of groups proliferated as summer approached.[22]

A questionnaire compiled by the fifth-order members facilitated discussion. The lengthy document covered a range of subjects, including experiences of discrimination or trouble with the law, frequency of sexual encounters and visits to bars, and knowledge of an individual's sexual identity by family and co-workers. Few participants had ever before been asked such questions systematically, and the questionnaire fueled extended discussions. Group members speculated on causes of homosexuality, reasons for social hostility to it, and whether sexual "deviants" could lead well-adjusted lives. They described the pain of discovering their sexual identities and the surrounding tragedies, as well as the strengths that survival in a hostile society had produced. Together they imagined how life might be different, how a gay subculture might emerge to provide emotional sustenance, and how homosexuals and lesbians might act to change social attitudes.[23]

The discussion groups provoked startling changes in the individuals who attended. Konrad Stevens remembered that initially fear of exposure dominated the meetings. Participants were "petrified that the government might get a list" of their names and fully expected that "the cops would come barging in and arrest everybody." Many of them even used pseudonyms at first. But as time passed and no raids materialized, men and women dropped their defenses, friendships formed, and the meetings took on the character of intimate gatherings. Geraldine Jackson, who became active in the society, recalled how "people were able to bloom and be themselves. . . . [It] was something we didn't know before." At last, she said, there was the opportunity to "say what you wanted to say and feel accepted." James Gruber also attributed the success of the groups to the atmosphere of acceptance. "All of us," he reminisced,

---

22. "Missions and Purposes," April 1951, Mattachine Society—Los Angeles file, ISR.

23. A copy of the questionnaire can be found in the Kepner papers. At the time, Hay wrote that the questionnaires "stirred up tremendous interest" and were used as "points of departure" in the groups (Hay to Kepner, n.d., Kepner papers).

had known a whole lifetime of not talking, of repression. Just the freedom to open up . . . really, that's what it was all about. We had found a sense of belonging, of camaraderie, of openness in an atmosphere of tension and distrust. . . . Such a great deal of it was a social climate. A family feeling came out of it, a nonsexual emphasis. . . . It was a brand new idea.

Men whose gay relationships remained mostly confined to a series of sexual encounters and women who led relatively isolated existences, with barely a scattering of lesbian acquaintances, found themselves meeting with dozens of other gay men and women and frankly affirming their homosexuality. For the first time, many members felt a sense of self-worth. By offering them a positive alternative to the traditional patterns of gay life, the Mattachine discussions succeeded in drawing frightened men and women into an organizational network.[24]

The discussion groups also exerted a profound influence on how the participants viewed themselves in relation to society. For instance, in trying to understand the "emotional stress and mental confusion" that so many gays experienced, one group rejected theories interpreting homosexuality as a pathological condition. Members argued that the psychological state of the gay individual was "socially conditioned," a product of the externally imposed pressure to hide for self-protection. To remove this pressure, the group concluded, homosexuals had to band together, since "it is doubtful that individuals, working as such, can affect any noticeable change." As the founders of the Mattachine Society had intended, the discussions were transforming the consciousness of participants, who began to see themselves as members of a minority group with a need to act collectively.[25]

By the early autumn of 1951, the seven fifth-order members, no longer able to handle the dozen or so discussion groups then in existence, began to establish first-order units which they also called "guilds." They selected articulate individuals who had the ability to lead groups skillfully and invited them to become guild members. To imbue them with a sense of special purpose, the fifth order devised what one described as "almost a religious ceremony" to initiate guild members. Standing in a circle and holding hands in a candlelit room, new and old members pledged themselves to the work ahead:

Our interlocking, sustaining and protecting hands guarantee a reborn social force of immense and simple purpose. We are resolved that our people shall find equality of security and production in tomorrow's world. We are sworn that no boy or girl, approaching the maelstrom of deviation,

24. Interview with Stevens; interview with Geraldine Jackson (pseud.), Los Angeles, October 13, 1976; interview with Gruber. For another emotional description of the impact of the discussion groups, see the undated three-page typescript of one anonymous participant's reactions in the Lucas papers.

25. "Discussion Group: Chairman—Steve," September 6, 1951, Kepner papers.

need make that crossing alone, afraid and in the dark ever again. In these moments we dedicate ourselves once again to each other in the immense significance of such allegiance, with dignity and respect, proud and free.

For women and men who remembered well the loneliness and fear of their own coming out, the power of these sentiments inspired an intense loyalty. "You felt like you had a mission in the world," Geraldine Jackson reminisced. "You felt that you were doing something terribly worthwhile for our people."[26]

First-order members did more than simply facilitate the discussion groups. At the meetings of their own guilds and later, in interguild conferences arranged by the fifth order, they debated at length the concept of gays as a minority, the notion of a "homosexual culture," and the forms that political action should take. First-order members brought their perspectives to the discussion groups that they were running and encouraged participants to see their situation as a product of social forces larger than the individual and her or his family configuration. They put forward concepts of minority group culture and oppression, urged participants to develop the cohesion and loyalty to one another that other minorities exhibited, and stressed the importance of formulating collective approaches to improve their lot. Guild members played a critical role in creating among the discussion groups a common point of view that would serve as a foundation for unified action.[27]

As the Mattachine Society became more of a commitment for its founders, Hull and Hay, who still had Communist ties, severed their connection with the party. Hull, whose participation had been of short duration and relatively marginal, simply stopped attending party meetings. But for Hay the involvement had extended for most of his adulthood, encompassing both work and personal relationships and inspiring strong passions. He reported to his party superiors that he was now leading an organization of homosexuals and, in view of the current homosexual scapegoating by the anticommunist right wing, recommended that he be released from membership in order not to place further onus on the party in southern California. Since the Communist party had little sympathy for homosexuality, there was probably never any doubt that they would do so. The revelation also provoked the breakup of Hay's marriage of thirteen years. Deprived suddenly of the attachments that had

26. "Induction Ceremony," Lucas Papers; interview with Jackson. About the induction ceremony, Rowland later wrote, "No one felt that our rituals were empty, frivolous or lugubrious, and I think the reason is that they were *not* any of those things. Rather, they solemnized a dedication, a devotion, and a promise. A ceremony marked a person as Chosen, elevated" (Rowland to author, December 11, 1976).

27. Gruber especially remarked upon this last aspect of the relationship between the discussion groups and the higher orders. He emphasized that much of the thinking of the members of the first-order guilds and the fifth order came from taking stray comments or insights expressed by individuals at the discussion groups, exploring them further, and elaborating on them in the closed meetings of the various orders (interview with Gruber).

sustained him since the 1930s, Hay focused all of his energy on the Mattachine Society.[28]

III

With the discussion groups and guilds functioning smoothly, the fifth order turned its attention to the large, uncharted area of political action. Eager as they were to move beyond the stage of talking, Hay and the others had no clear idea of where to begin. But in February 1952, the issue of police harassment struck home and precipitated a plunge into public action. One of Mattachine's original members, Dale Jennings, became a victim of police entrapment. Arrested by a plainclothes officer who, Jennings claimed, accosted him in a Los Angeles park, he was held for several hours in the local police station and charged with lewd and dissolute behavior. After he was released on bail, he called his Mattachine associates, who hastily scheduled an emergency meeting of the fifth order. After much debate they agreed to fight the charges, using Jennings's arrest to expose police entrapment practices against homosexuals and to mobilize the discussion groups around the issue. Throughout the spring the upcoming trial became the prime topic of discussion among group participants.[29]

Hesitant about revealing the existence of Mattachine to outsiders, the fifth order created an ad hoc Citizens Committee to Outlaw Entrapment in order to publicize the case. When press releases and letters to broadcast media and newspapers failed to secure any response, the Citizens Committee decided to use the informal communications network of the gay male subculture to make the upcoming trial known. The leadership wrote several flyers about the case and circulated them throughout Los Angeles. Mattachine's membership distributed the leaflets, probably the first in America to raise the homosexual issue, in areas frequented by homosexuals—at gay beaches in Santa Monica and bars in Los Angeles, in restrooms known to be cruised by gay men, and at park benches and bus stops in homosexual areas of the city. Fifth-order members met with gay male shop owners in West Hollywood and elicited their cooperation in informing homosexual patrons about the case. Hay humorously recalled that Mattachine even had a couple of supermarket clerks in the Hollywood area who surreptitiously dropped flyers into the packages of their gay customers. The literature struck a responsive chord among many of its homosexual readers, and the Citizens Committee was soon receiving a good

28. The information about Hull leaving the party comes from my correspondence with Rowland. The information about Hay comes from my interviews with him; an interview with Dorothy Healey, who was head of the party in Southern California at the time (Los Angeles, June 3, 1977); and a May 1979 interview with a party member who was a close friend of Anita Hay and wishes to remain anonymous.

29. On the circumstances surrounding the arrest, see Dale Jennings, "To Be Accused, Is to Be Guilty," ONE, January 1953, pp. 10–13.

deal of mail containing financial contributions to defray legal fees and offers to become involved in the committee's work.[30]

When the trial began on June 23, 1952, Jennings admitted that he was a homosexual but denied that he was guilty of the charges against him. It was a courageous—and dangerous—stand to take. After thirty-six hours of deliberation, the jury reported that it was deadlocked, with one member holding fast to a verdict of guilty. The district attorney's office decided to drop the charges. Given the prevalent attitudes toward "sexual deviance," the Citizens Committee was justified in calling the outcome "a GREAT VICTORY for the homosexual minority."[31]

A year of rapid growth followed the Jennings trial. The circulation of Citizens Committee flyers and the open defense of the right to be homosexual sparked considerable interest in the Mattachine Society. Chuck Rowland recalled that after the Jennings victory, "Mattachine really took off. . . . We moved into a broad sunlit upland filled with whole legions of eager gays. Mattachine was suddenly IN! No combination of people in our limited leadership could handle them."[32] Doubling their size from one meeting to the next, discussion groups subdivided, to repeat the process a few weeks later as the number of participants continued to multiply. The network of groups soon stretched throughout southern California. By the beginning of 1953, it extended along the coast from San Diego to the beach communities north of Santa Monica and inland to San Bernardino. New guilds were formed to handle the proliferating discussion groups, and the structure of Mattachine expanded to include second-order units. In May 1953, the fifth order estimated total participation in the society at more than 2,000, with the number of discussion groups approaching a hundred.[33]

The Mattachine Society also grew beyond its southern California place of origin. In February 1953 a young man named Gerry Brissette, who worked as a lab technician at the University of California at Berkeley, wrote a letter of inquiry to the society. Describing himself as a pacifist who was active in the Fellowship of Reconciliation, he spoke of his dissatisfaction with the gay subculture, his "dream of freedom" for homosexuals, and his recognition of "*my* responsibility to work for the kind of world I believe in, to help create in the hearts of people like me a belief in themselves, a dignity, and a capacity for

30. See "An Anonymous Call to Arms," "NOW Is The Time to Fight," "An Open Letter," and "VICTORY!" all flyers in the Kepner papers.

31. On the trial and its outcome, see Hay to Jay Clark, October 6, 1952, Kepner papers; and "VICTORY!"

32. Rowland to author, January 17, 1977.

33. On the geographical spread of the discussion groups, see Romayne Cox to Donald Webster Cory, January 28, 1953; the creation of the second-order units had occurred by early autumn—see "Second Order Minutes," September 12, 1952, and October 3, 1952; the estimate of more than 2,000 participants comes from a Mattachine Foundation circular of May 24, 1953; all in Kepner papers.

loving." He concluded, "If Mattachine means this, then I am with you all the way." At the invitation of Rowland, Brissette came to Los Angeles to meet with the fifth-order members. He returned to Berkeley eager to start the Mattachine Society there. Before long he had set up groups in Berkeley, Oakland, and San Francisco, with sixty or more persons coming to meetings. As Brissette wrote to Rowland, gay men and women continued to "flock to us in hordes, hungry, anxious, eager to DO something, SAY something, get started."[34]

As the Mattachine Society grew, its membership became more diverse. In southern California it was overwhelmingly male, with only a few groups containing more than token lesbian representation. In the north, however, Brissette had several lesbian friends whom he quickly invited into leadership roles, and women consequently composed a substantial proportion of the Bay area branch of the society. The Laguna group drew in what Rowland described as "Junior Chamber of Commerce" types; a Long Beach unit was composed mostly of "swishy" homosexuals; another attracted a contingent of factory workers; and, near UCLA, a group took shape from the ranks of the school's faculty.[35]

With the growth in membership came an expansion of activities, as well-established discussion groups began assuming new functions. The group composed mostly of UCLA faculty members embarked upon studying the literature of the natural and social sciences in an attempt to make sense of current theories about homosexuality. Another group surveyed creative literature with homosexual and lesbian themes. Others compiled clipping files on vice squad actions and morals arrests, and most of them gathered affidavits from participants who had suffered from abusive police behavior.[36]

The most significant development, however, was the decision by a few members of a discussion group to launch a homosexual magazine. The publication of the first issue of *ONE* in January 1953 represented a major step forward for the young movement. As the Jennings case seemed to demonstrate vividly, homosexuals could not depend on the press or other media to publicize

34. Gerard Brissette to Mattachine Foundation, February 15, 1953; Brissette to David Freeman, March 1, 1953; Brissette to Rowland, May 6, 1953; all in Kepner papers. See also the letters of Brissette to Rowland of March 29 and April 19, 1953, for detailed descriptions of the rapid spread of the discussion groups in the San Francisco Bay area (Kepner papers). "David Freeman" was the pseudonym used by Rowland in correspondence to persons as yet unknown to him.

35. The contrast between southern California, where men predominated, and northern California, where lesbian involvement was substantial, was confirmed by all of the participants in the early Mattachine Society whom I interviewed. On the diverse membership of the various discussion groups, see Rowland to Hay, March 11, 1953, Kepner papers.

36. On the activities of the discussion groups, see Romayne Cox to Donald Webster Cory, September 17, 1952; "A Quick Guide to Conducting Discussion Groups;" and "Dear Friend," form letter from Romayne Cox to Mattachine Foundation mailing list; all in Kepner papers. See also "Bases of Mammalian Sexual Feeling," typescript presented for discussion, Lucas papers; and interview with James Kepner, September 27–30, 1976, Los Angeles.

their grievances. The men and women who established *ONE* intended it as a forum where the gay minority could present its views to the public and to other homosexuals and lesbians. Although *ONE* was formally independent of the Mattachine Society, most of the editorial board were guild members, and Dale Jennings served as the magazine's first editor. Early issues featured articles about the Mattachine Society, and the discussion groups provided the editors with a large pool of potential subscribers. Within a few months, *ONE's* sales passed 2,000 copies per month, with a readership substantially larger than that. Since, as letters to the editor revealed, the magazine was circulating throughout the country, it also helped spread word that a homosexual emancipation organization had formed.[37]

Emboldened by the positive response that the Citizens Committee generated, the fifth order resolved late in the summer of 1952 to take a further step into the open. Hay and his associates decided to incorporate in California as a not-for-profit educational organization. They saw the Mattachine Foundation, as they called it, as a means of advancing their work in several ways. It would offer an acceptable front for reaching out to society, especially to professionals and public officials. The foundation might eventually succeed in winning heterosexual allies. It could also become the vehicle for conducting research into homosexuality and for using the results of this research as part of an educational campaign for the rights of homosexuals. Finally, the existence of the foundation offered a simple answer to the many anxious newcomers about whether participation in a homosexual organization was illegal.[38]

The fifth order had modest success in obtaining professional backing for the foundation. Through Gruber and Stevens, it arranged a meeting with novelist and screenwriter Christopher Isherwood and with a research psychologist from UCLA, Dr. Evelyn Hooker. Both professed support for what the Mattachine leaders were attempting, although they declined to join the board of directors. According to Stevens, Isherwood bowed out on the grounds that he was not a "joiner," but he did contribute money to the foundation and informed others of its existence. Hooker, who was just beginning to study male homosexuality, felt that membership would compromise her research in the eyes of her colleagues. She did keep in close touch with her Mattachine friends, however, and in 1953 Mattachine provided Hooker with a large pool of gay

---

37. Minutes of the fall 1952 meetings that led to the publication of *ONE* may be found in *ONE Confidential*, Fall 1958, pp. 2–7. Participants included fifth-order members Jennings and Rowland, first-order members Dorr Legg and Geraldine Jackson, and a few individuals who were not involved in Mattachine activities. See also William Lambert, "How ONE Began," *ONE*, February 1955, pp. 8–15. Paid circulation figures come from the July 1953 issue of *ONE*, inside front cover.

38. See "By-Laws of the Mattachine Foundation, Inc.," July 29, 1952; and Romayne Cox to Donald Webster Cory, September 17, 1952, Kepner papers. Both Hay, in my interviews with him, and Rowland, in his letter of December 11, 1976, elaborated on the rationale for the foundation.

men for her study of the male homosexual personality. Other efforts secured the involvement of a clergyman, Wallace de Ortega Maxey, pastor of the First Universalist Church in Los Angeles, which supported a variety of political causes; and a physician from San Bernardino, Richard Gwartney.[39]

By the winter of 1953 the tiny group of leftist homosexuals who had founded the Mattachine Society could assess their work with satisfaction. Since the days two years earlier when they were a few men meeting secretly and puzzling over what to do, they had created an apparently thriving organization that was growing rapidly. Konrad Stevens recalled that, in the months after the Jennings trial, "we were meeting very often. We just lived Mattachine. We didn't do anything else. We never went anywhere just for pleasure. When we went, it was organizing." Scores of discussion groups, membership that included first- and second-order units, a monthly magazine, and the Mattachine Foundation not only kept the founders busy but encouraged their conviction that the future was bright. From being "pioneers in a hostile society," as Rowland wrote to Hay, the leadership could claim that they had "set a movement in motion."[40]

39. Isherwood and Hooker were both friends of Gruber and Stevens. Isherwood was approached by the Mattachine leaders as soon as the idea of a foundation was first discussed in the spring of 1952. Isherwood and Hooker were formally invited to join the board of directors in the same spring (Hay to Cory, undated but probably written ca. May 2, 1952, and "Second Order Minutes," October 3, 1952, Kepner papers; interviews with Gruber and Stevens). In an interview with the author in Santa Monica on November 4, 1976, Hooker said that her gay friends, all of whom were living proof of the inadequacy of the medical literature on homosexuality, provided the motivation for her subsequent research on the topic. On Gwartney, see R. H. Gwartney, "The Mattachine Foundation, Inc.: Reorganization Study," Kepner papers. On Maxey's church, see Barrett, *The Tenney Committee*, p. 52.

40. Interview with Stevens; Rowland to Hay, March 11, 1953, Kepner papers.

FIVE

Retreat to Respectability

The organizational growth and steps toward visibility that inspired Rowland's optimistic assessment also presented the Mattachine founders with serious problems. Hay and the others expected the society to draw its strength from unity around the propositions that homosexuals were an oppressed minority and that only militant, collective action on their own behalf could win equality. Both ideas required a leap in consciousness, and the fifth order relied on the discussion groups to convince participants to make the leap. Rapid expansion made it difficult, however, to achieve this goal. The continuing influx of new members subverted the effort to build a consensus, while the pressing need for group leaders forced the Mattachine Society to induct into the guilds men and women who did not necessarily share the perspective of the founders. In their attempt to construct a gay organization as single-minded in outlook as the Communist party, Hay and his fellows failed to appreciate a fundamental difference between the two. Where the party won recruits who agreed with its political philosophy, Mattachine attracted its constituency on the basis of a common sexual identity. Since gay men and women reflected the diversity of the American population, the bond of sexuality could easily lose its strength in the face of other differences.

As the Mattachine Society slowly moved into the open, the former Communist affiliation of some of its founders became a serious liability. The political background that gave Hay and the others the skill to build a secret organization and allowed them to break with comparative ease from mainstream views of homosexuality also made Mattachine doubly vulnerable to attack. Not only was the society trying to mobilize social outcasts, but it apparently placed its trust in a leadership that stood beyond the boundaries of political legitimacy. Furthermore, many of the new participants had not met the members of the fifth order. Should the past history of the founders become known, the complex secret structure would only heighten suspicions.[1]

I

The tensions posed by visibility and growth suddenly exploded in March 1953, when Paul Coates, a Los Angeles newspaper writer, made Mattachine the subject of his column. The Mattachine Foundation had mailed to candidates for the Los Angeles city council and school board letters inquiring about their views on police harassment of homosexuals and sex education in the public schools. Coates received a copy of the letters and, sensing a good story, searched for more information about the foundation. He reported in his column that the Mattachine legal adviser, Fred Snider, had been an "unfriendly witness" before the House Un-American Activities Committee; that is, he had taken the Fifth Amendment and refused to answer its questions. Coates reminded his readers that homosexuals had been "found to be bad security risks in our State Department," and he painted a threatening picture of "sexual deviates" banding together to "swing tremendous political power." With an alleged 200,000 homosexuals in the Los Angeles area alone, he asserted, "a well-trained subversive could move in and forge that power into a dangerous political weapon." He concluded, "If I belonged to that club, I'd worry."[2]

The Coates column hit the Mattachine Society where it was most vulnerable, and the charges provoked a swift reaction throughout the organization. One Los Angeles discussion group appealed to the foundation's directors to "make themselves known" and bring an end to "subterfuge." The Laguna group called for "a loyalty oath as a condition of membership" in Mattachine. Marilyn Rieger, a guild member from Los Angeles, reported that "many members of the meetings . . . feel that Mr. Coates asked legitimate questions . . . and that explanations are definitely in order." To continue working for a cause, Rieger said, she needed "complete faith in the people . . . who set forth policies, principles, aims and purposes."[3]

1. The description in these two paragraphs of the problems faced by the Mattachine Society is drawn from the following sources: Rowland to Hay, March 11, 1953, and Brissette to Rowland, April 29 and 26, 1953, personal papers of James Kepner, Los Angeles; author's interview with Harry Hay, October 16, 1976, in San Juan Pueblo, New Mexico; and author's interviews with James Kepner, September 27–30, 1976, in Los Angeles.

2. Paul Coates, "Well, Medium and Rare," Los Angeles *Mirror*, March 12, 1953, clipping in National Gay Archives, Los Angeles. For Snider's appearance before HUAC, see U.S. Congress, House, Committee on Un-American Activities, *Communist Activities Among Professional Groups in the Los Angeles Area—Part III, Hearings*, 82d Cong., 2d sess., October 1, 1952, pp. 4001–4. Copies of the questionnaire and letter to candidates may be found in the Mattachine—Los Angeles file, Institute for Sex Research, Bloomington, Ind. (hereafter cited as ISR).

3. "Notes of Discussion Group Meeting," March 20, 1953, personal papers of Don Lucas, San Francisco; Rowland to Brissette, March 29, 1953, Kepner papers; Rieger to Mattachine Foundation, March 23, 1953, Lucas papers.

To understand the intensity of the reaction within the Mattachine Society, one must remember the context in which the Coates column appeared. Senator McCarthy, who had become chairman of the Government Operations Committee and its permanent subcommittee on investigations in January 1953, was at the height of his influence. In February he began his widely publicized investigation into alleged Communist influence in the State Department, its overseas information program, and the Voice of America. Moreover, the House Un-American Activities Committee, which had conducted numerous inquiries into Communist influence in Hollywood over the preceding six years, was in Los Angeles in March and April 1953, holding public hearings on the operations of the Communist party in Los Angeles. The timing of the Coates article could not have been less auspicious for the Mattachine leadership.[4]

With the pressures upon them increasing rapidly, the fifth order sought to quiet the furor by calling a "democratic convention" to restructure the Mattachine Society as an aboveground organization. The fifth order invited the hundred or so first- and second-order members to a two-day conference in April at the Reverend Maxey's Universalist Church in order to draw up a constitution, adopt by-laws, and elect officers for an open membership organization. Still, the founders came to the convention expecting to do battle over the Communist issue. "Come hell or high water," Rowland wrote to one member, "we will oppose all idea of a non-Communist statement by any group using the name Mattachine . . . [and] will have nothing to do with any group which has a loyalty oath as a condition of membership."[5]

Rowland and Hay staked out the fifth order's positions at the opening session of the convention. In a keynote speech Rowland argued for recognition of homosexuals as members of a minority with a culture of its own. "We must disenthrall ourselves of the idea," he said, "that we differ only in our sexual directions and that all we want or need in life is to be free to seek the expression of our sexual desires." The heterosexual mores of the dominant culture had excluded them, he continued, and "as a result of this exclusion [we] have developed differently than have other cultural groups." Rowland urged Mattachine members to affirm with him a pride in their distinctive identity and to embrace the task of consciously creating "an ethical homosexual culture." Hay followed with a spirited defense of the Mattachine lawyer's refusal to testify before HUAC. He reminded his listeners that, with the federal government removing homosexuals and lesbians from its payroll, each of them had something to hide from investigators. Hay urged Mattachine members to see that it was in their interest to defend the Fifth Amendment rights of everyone,

4. See Robert Griffith, *The Politics of Fear: Joseph R. McCarthy and the Senate* (Lexington, Ky., 1970), pp. 188–220; and U.S. Congress, House, Committee on Un-American Activities, *Investigation of Communist Activities in the Los Angeles Area, Hearings*, 83d Cong., 1st sess., March 23–April 8, 1953.

5. "A Call to All Members of the Mattachine Society"; Rowland to Hay, March 11, 1953; and Rowland to Brissette, March 29, 1953; all in Kepner papers.

regardless of political belief, since some day they might be the target of Congressional questioners.[6]

Kenneth Burns, a Los Angeles guild member, emerged during the convention as the de facto leader of those at odds with the founders. Burns presided over a guild whose members, one of them recalled, had been as upset by the questionnaire to local candidates as they had been by the innuendos of Communist subversion. They felt that any open intervention in politics was "likely to destroy the organization." Nor did they look with favor on Rowland's and Hay's opening speeches, which they considered rabble-rousing and radical. Burns, who was a safety engineer for the Carnation Company, dressed the part of a Brooks Brothers executive. He was also young and sexually attractive, with a soft-spoken manner that commanded attention. Burns had an ability, one participant reminisced, "to get people to quiet down and let their emotions cool." His adeptness with the labyrinthine rules of parliamentary procedure quickly distinguished him from the mass of delegates, who selected him to chair the committee charged with drafting a constitution.[7]

Burns was joined on the committee by Marilyn Rieger. Unlike Burns, whose guild was virtually unanimous in its opposition to the fifth order's control, Rieger found herself isolated. Although she had mobilized her own Los Angeles discussion group to challenge the Mattachine leadership, her guild remained loyal to the society's founders and the views they espoused. However, Rieger and Burns quickly made contact at the convention and together canvassed other delegates to determine their views.[8]

They found a receptive listener in Hal Call, a San Francisco delegate. Call had a degree in journalism from the University of Missouri and had worked for a number of Midwestern newspapers. Arrested in Chicago in 1952 on a homosexual morals charge, he had lost his job and migrated to San Francisco, which he had first visited during World War II. There he joined the first Mattachine discussion group in the city. Gruff and aggressive in manner, the outspoken Call came to the convention already suspicious of the fifth order. The keynote speeches did nothing to allay his fears. Rumors that Rowland was a Communist youth organizer aroused Call's ire, and he resolved to remove any radical elements from Mattachine.[9]

6. Charles Rowland, "Opening Speech," April 11, 1953, Lucas papers. Hay's speech was reprinted in *ONE*, April 1953, pp. 5–13. Rowland's speech is an extraordinary document, expressing sentiments that did not receive wide currency until the gay liberation movement of the 1970s. For a further elaboration of the idea of a distinct homosexual culture, see Rowland's article, written under the pseudonym of David Freeman, in *ONE*, May 1953, pp. 8–11.

7. Interview with Kepner; interview with Gerard Brissette, November 17, 1976, in El Cerrito, Calif., and interview with Hal Call, November 16, 1976, in San Francisco. See "Minutes of California State Constitutional Convention of the Mattachine Society," April 11–12, 1953, Lucas papers.

8. See the Interim Constitutional Committee "Convention Call," Kepner papers; Marilyn Rieger, "Notes of Discussion Group Meeting," March 20, 1953, Lucas papers; and interview with Kepner.

9. Interview with Call; for a biographical sketch of Call, see *Mattachine Review*, June 1958, pp. 28–29.

Although criticism of the founders remained relatively muted at the April convention, the opposition was vocal and better organized at a second session held in May to complete work on the constitution. Rieger delivered an extended critique of the minority group concept. "We know we are the same," she began, "no different than anyone else. Our only difference is an unimportant one to the heterosexual society, *unless we make it important.*" Rieger argued that the emphasis on a homosexual culture separate and distinct from the dominant heterosexual one would only accentuate the hostility of society, and she pleaded with the delegates to reject it. Equality for gay men and women would come, she said, "by declaring ourselves, by integrating . . . not as homosexuals, but as people, as men and women whose homosexuality is irrelevant to our ideals, our principles, our hopes and aspirations." Only then, she concluded, will we "rid the world of its misconcepts of homosexuality and homosexuals."[10]

Rieger's argument had both flaws and strengths. On the one hand, to claim that homosexuality was an unimportant difference—in the face of laws, government policy, religious belief, medical opinion, and popular prejudice to the contrary—clearly missed the mark. On the other hand, her position carried enormous emotional appeal. Gay men and women in mid-twentieth-century America lived with an ever present awareness of their difference, of being set apart from society. When Rieger said to the audience that "we are first and foremost people," she touched a deeply felt need on the part of many delegates to have their humanity affirmed. The emphasis that proponents of the gay minority thesis placed on being different aroused the antagonism of individuals who yearned above all for simple acceptance of who they were. It mattered little that advocates of a minority group analysis saw their position as strategic, as a means for homosexuals and lesbians eventually to win acceptance by society and achieve equality. At present it raised for some the specter of a more pronounced separation from an already hostile culture.[11]

Charges of Communist subversion also surfaced at the May convention. In particular, the San Francisco delegation, led by Hal Call and David Finn, a newly recruited friend of his, attacked the fifth order for their political affiliations. Call introduced a motion, approved by the membership of the San Francisco discussion groups, that "a very strong statement concerning our stand on subversive elements" be inserted into the new constitution. "We are already being attacked as Communistic," he reminded his audience, and the proposed resolution "guarantees us that we will not be infiltrated by Communists." Should anyone make such charges again, he argued "we can insist that

10. Marilyn Rieger, "Delegates of the Convention," May 23, 1953, Kepner papers.

11. Ibid. In supporting Rieger's position, one delegate said, "Never in our existence as individuals or as a group should we admit to being a minority. For to admit being a minority we request of other human beings that we so desire to be persecuted" (unsigned speech at the convention, May 1953, Lucas papers).

[the resolution] be printed and our stand would then be clear." Finn joined the
fray with accusations of Communist infiltration and manipulation.[12]

The convention produced paradoxical results. The delegates rejected the
views of the opposition, and the founders emerged victorious on every vote.
The convention defeated Call's motion for an anticommunist declaration, and
it approved a preamble to the organization's constitution affirming the need for
a homosexual minority to develop "a highly ethical homosexual culture."
However, the concern of some delegates about Communist subversion troubled the founders, who had every reason to believe that such a fear would
continue to haunt the Mattachine Society. "We were aware," Gruber recalled,
"that Communism had become such a burning issue. We all felt, especially
Harry, that the organization and its growth was more important than any of the
founding fathers. . . . We had to turn it over to other people." Self-interest was
at stake, too. The anticommunism of the McCarthy era was reaching its peak
in 1953, and Hay, Rowland, and Hull did not relish being officers of an
organization whose members might focus attention on their politics. The
fifth-order members therefore agreed among themselves not to seek office in
the newly structured Mattachine and announced their decision at the final
session.[13]

The rest was anticlimactic. The convention approved a simple membership
organization headed by an elected Coordinating Council with the authority to
establish working committees. Regional branches of the Mattachine Society,
called "area councils," would elect their own officers and be represented on the
main council. The unit for membership participation became the task-
oriented chapter. Perhaps because time was short, or perhaps because the
opposition had taken such a visible role in the proceedings, the delegates chose
Burns head of the Coordinating Council and Rieger, Call, and Finn to other
positions of leadership, even though the delegates had earlier rejected the
dissenters' stands on key philosophical issues.[14]

For the members of the fifth order, their decision to relinquish leadership
had the impact of a "personal calamity," according to Gruber's recollection.
Hull, Gruber, and R. dropped their Mattachine involvement altogether. For a
time, Jennings shifted his energy to *ONE* magazine, which he edited and
which stayed independent of Mattachine. Stevens and Rowland maintained
their membership in the society until the end of the year, when the former quit
in frustration and the latter joined the staff of *ONE*. The outcome proved most
difficult for Hay to handle. For twenty years his life had revolved around

12. "Minutes of General Convention of the Mattachine Society," May 23–24, 1953, Lucas
papers; interviews with Hay, Kepner, Call, and Brissette. For other accounts of the convention,
see *ONE*, January 1954, pp. 4–8; and March 1954, pp. 16–18.

13. "Minutes," May 23–24, 1953; and "Constitution of the Mattachine Society," adopted
May 24, 1953 (both in Lucas papers); and interview with James Gruber, December 28, 1976, in
Mountain View, Calif.

14. "Minutes," May 23–24, 1953; and "Constitution," May 24, 1953.

radical politics. Having ended both his Communist party ties and his marriage in order to return to gay life as an organizer, he found himself hamstrung by his political past. With his emotional props gone, Hay sank into a paralyzing depression and came close to committing suicide. Though he returned years later to the gay movement, he never again occupied a central role.[15]

II

The May convention initiated changes in the Mattachine Society reaching far beyond the transfer of leadership from one group to another and the shift from secrecy to open membership. Over the next several months, the new officers firmly imprinted their mark upon the organization. They erased every trace of the founders' influence upon the Mattachine Society and charted a direction distinctively their own.

Burns, Rieger, Call, and others of the new leadership proceeded from a set of interlocking, mutually reinforcing assumptions that formed as definite a world view as that held by Hay and the other leftist founders. Decisively rejecting the notion of a homosexual minority, they took the contrary view that "the sex variant is no different from anyone else except in the object of his sexual expression." They also evinced hostility to the corollary idea of a homosexual culture and to the effort to fashion a special ethic for gay life. Rather, the new leadership urged homosexuals to adjust to a "pattern of behavior that is acceptable to society in general and compatible with [the] recognized institutions . . . of home, church, and state." Believing that the pervasive sanctions against homosexuality resulted from "false ideas about the variant," Burns and the others concluded that Mattachine's "greatest and most meaningful contribution . . . will consist of aiding established and recognized scientists, clinics, research organizations and institutions . . . studying sex variation problems." Their reliance on professionals as the agents of social change pushed them to abandon collective, militant action by the Mattachine Society. In sum, accommodation to social norms replaced the affirmation of a distinctive gay identity, collective effort gave way to individual action, and confidence in the ability of gay men and lesbians to interpret their own experience yielded to the wisdom of experts. Under its new officers, the Mattachine Society shifted its focus from mobilizing a gay constituency to assisting the work of professionals.[16]

15. The information in this paragraph is drawn from my interviews with Hay, Gruber, Stevens, Legg, and Kepner, and from my correspondence with Rowland. On Jennings, see also "Minutes," Mattachine Convention for the Adoption of By-Laws, November 14–15, 1953, Los Angeles, Lucas papers; on Rowland, see Church of One Brotherhood file, Homosexual Information Center, Los Angeles. Confirmation of Hay's account came from an interview in Los Angeles on June 3, 1977, with Dorothy Healey, who had been head of the party in Los Angeles at the time; and from a May 1979 interview with a close friend (also a party member) of Anita Hay who wishes to remain anonymous.

16. Ken Burns to Dale Jennings, March 1, 1954, Kepner papers; *The Mattachine Society Today* (Los Angeles, 1954), p. 1 (copy in Mattachine—Los Angeles file, ISR); Ken Burns, "Opening

The impact of the new leadership's perspectives hit the discussion groups first. Initially conceived by Hay as places to forge homosexuals and lesbians into a cohesive, self-respecting, and self-conscious minority, they became under Burns individualistic in tone, a "means of therapy" for distraught homosexuals. Without the sense of almost missionary zeal attached to their deliberations, by and large the discussion groups withered and died. The San Diego group, for example, collapsed within weeks after the May convention. The East Bay Mattachine, which in May 1953 had three thriving groups that attracted as many as sixty participants each, shrank into two tiny chapters with a total of eight members by the autumn. In the Los Angeles area, the far-flung network of discussion groups shriveled to a mere five by the autumn.[17]

A few of the discussion groups with some of the early Mattachine Society's most committed members reconstituted themselves as task-oriented chapters. Rowland and Stevens, for instance, remained active in a Los Angeles chapter that voted to take on entrapment cases. Under their leadership, the group agreed to search out cases "of significance to the whole minority" and "to fight the charges aggressively."[18] But Burns and the Coordinating Council vetoed the chapter's decision. The Mattachine Society's new attorney advised Burns that

> the very existence of a Legal Chapter, if publicized to society at large, would intimidate and anger heterosexual society. . . . It would be detrimental to the [Mattachine] Society to let the public know of the existence and activities of the Legal Chapter; and it would probably bring more pressures on the Society if the heterosexual felt that the homosexual, whom he hates, was trying to change the laws to suit himself.[19]

Burns accepted this estimation and argued that the Mattachine Society had to "consider what the outside society feels toward us at this time." The Coordinating Council cautioned the membership to be "realistic" and to recognize that the organization was "not yet strong enough" to embark upon an "aggressive program." Instead, it offered to refer entrapment victims to sympathetic and reputable lawyers.[20]

Similar reasoning also inhibited the society from seeking penal code reform. Despite the fact that the Mattachine convention had authorized the creation of

Speech," Proceedings of the First Annual Convention of the Mattachine Society, May 15–16, 1954, San Francisco, Kepner papers; and The Mattachine Society Today, pp. 2, 10, 7.

17. Ken Burns, "Opening Speech," May 15–16, 1954, Kepner papers; "Minutes of Meeting of Mattachine Society Coordinating Council" (hereafter referred to as CC Minutes), August 21, 1953, Lucas papers; and "Minutes of East Bay Area Meeting," October 20, 1953, and "Call to Convention," November 14–15, 1953 (both in Kepner papers). The "Call" listed only five surviving chapters in Los Angeles.

18. Southern Area Council Newsletter, November 2, 1953; and CC Minutes, October 23, 1953, Kepner papers.

19. CC Minutes, August 28, 1953, Lucas papers.

20. CC Minutes, October 23, 1953, Kepner papers.

a legislative committee to pursue sodomy law repeal, the leadership sidestepped the issue. Dave Finn, the chairman of the Committee, and Call, a committee member, effectively forestalled action. In August 1953 they published a pamphlet that declared,

> Any organized pressure on lawmakers by members of the Mattachine Society as a group would only serve to prejudice the position of the Society. . . . It would provide an abundant source of hysterical propaganda with which to foment an ignorant, fear-inspired anti-homosexual campaign.

Rather, they proposed for Mattachine a policy of "merely acquainting itself" with legislation and informed members that the "burden of activity must rest upon the individual."[21]

The retreat from collective action stemmed in part from the leadership's acceptance of society's evaluation of gays. "We didn't have much confidence at that time," Burns later acknowledged. "We felt we had to work through people . . . who could better present what [homosexuality] was all about—better than ourselves. . . . [We made] a definite decision that by working through research projects and people in education and religion that we would get acceptance." And, as Call conceded, they felt the need to work through professionals "to give ourselves credibility. To be just an organization of upstart gays, we would have been shattered and ridiculed and put down."[22]

Such attitudes explain the strategy that the leadership did pursue—to rely, as Call said, on people "in places of influence." The Mattachine Society offered its services to researchers in the hope that they would eventually "give the public information that was valid" and "dispel fiction with fact."[23] In June 1953, the Research Committee arranged a meeting with several professors at UCLA to discuss ways the society could aid them in their research. In northern California the organization contacted Dr. Karl Bowman, head of the Langley-Porter clinic at Berkeley, who had just completed studies on sex deviation for the California state legislature. Bowman expressed interest in obtaining cases of "normal" homosexuals for further research, and the Mattachine Society agreed to cooperate.[24] Anxious, as Call put it, "to ride on the shirttails" of professionals, the leadership sought out state public health officials and law enforcement personnel, attorneys, sociologists, clerics, and mental health workers in an effort to enlist the support of those who they believed would effect social change.[25]

The contact with professionals tended to reinforce the leadership's caution. Alfred Kinsey, for instance, advised Mattachine officers to avoid "special pleas

21. San Francisco Area Council, "Mattachine: What's It All About?" August, 1953, Kepner papers.

22. Interview with Kenneth Burns, January 10, 1977, in Los Angeles; interview with Call.

23. Interview with Call; Ken Burns, "Opening Speech," May 15–16, 1954, Kepner papers.

24. CC Minutes, June 26, 1953, and July 10, 1953, Lucas papers.

25. Interview with Call.

for a minority group" and to restrict themselves to aiding "qualified research experts." Evelyn Hooker too considered reference to homosexuals as a minority "a misnomer" and dismissed the question of gay identity and consciousness, since "only the mode of sexual behavior would differentiate and distinguish a homosexual." Burns used such counsel to underline the judiciousness of his leadership. "Responsible persons in public life tell us," he wrote, that if the Mattachine Society did not "grow up with good manners" and an "attitude of responsibility," then "we can only expect to fail."[26]

As the new leadership imprinted its views on the Mattachine Society during the summer and fall of 1953, the Communist issue remained alive. Just two weeks after the May 1953 convention, Finn wrote to Burns that the FBI had contacted him in San Francisco. Finn reportedly gave the government investigators copies of the Mattachine constitution and detailed his own efforts and those of others to eliminate any Communist influence from the society. Though Burns later announced that the organization had "expressed itself satisfactorily to the FBI," the matter did not come to rest. Much of the Coordinating Council's attention continued to revolve around the Communist question.[27] Both the Los Angeles and San Francisco Area Councils released pamphlets under the society's name announcing that Mattachine was "unalterably opposed to Communists and Communist activity." In expressing such sentiments, the pamphlets made further statements that suggested a connection between the leadership's anticommunism and its other perspectives. "Homosexuals," the Los Angeles group wrote, "are not seeking to overthrow or destroy any of society's existing institutions, laws or mores, but to be assimilated as constructive, valuable, and responsible citizens." With homosexual behavior a violation of both law and social mores, the position left the Mattachine Society with little room in which to act.[28]

III

The conflict between the remnants of the old Mattachine and the emerging direction of the new leadership peaked in November 1953, at an organization-wide convention held in Los Angeles. Burns and several other officers came prepared to complete the transition begun in the spring. Though the issues were the same as before—the definition of homosexuals as a minority and its corollary of a homosexual culture, militant and aggressive political action, and

26. San Francisco Area Council *Newsletter*, no. 25 (June 1955) and no. 28 (September 1955), National Sex Forum, San Francisco; Ken Burns, "The Mattachine on Cooperation," *ONE*, March 1954, p. 14.

27. CC Minutes, June 5, 1953, Lucas papers; Burns to Jennings, March 1, 1954, Kepner papers. For other discussions of the Communist "threat," see CC Minutes, July 4, August 7, and November 6, 1953, Lucas papers; "Northern California Area Council Meeting Minutes," July 23, 1953, Lucas papers; "Southern California Area Council Meeting , Minutes," August 31, 1953; and "East Bay Area Meeting, Minutes," October 20, 1953 (all in Kepner papers).

28. Southern California Area Council, "Aims and Principles"; and San Francisco Area Council, "Mattachine: What's It All About?" August 1953 (both in Kepner papers).

Communism—the balance of power in the organization had shifted. When Burns spoke now, he did so as head of the Mattachine Society.

The leadership successfully disposed of what was left of the founders' perspective. Still chafing over the preamble adopted in May, which committed the society to developing "a highly ethical homosexual culture," Burns urged the convention to eliminate the "very peculiar language" that "the influence of the old leadership at the last convention forced . . . upon us." In its place he offered, and the membership accepted, a statement that not only dropped the reference to a homosexual culture but also avoided any mention of homosexuals.[29] Burns also proposed, again successfully, a resolution disavowing "any direct, aggressive action" by the society. Instead, the organization voted to "limit its activities to . . . working with and through . . . persons, institutions, and organizations which command the highest possible public respect."[30]

Though the changes proposed by Burns were accepted, the debate surrounding them provoked an uproar. When Rowland attempted to speak against revising the preamble, Dave Finn, who was parliamentarian and whose anticommunism bordered on the vituperative, ruled him out of order. Finn then announced angrily that he would turn over to the FBI the names of everyone in attendance if the convention failed to reject the "communistic" principles imposed by the old leadership. His announcement created havoc. Many delegates were outraged that anyone would dare violate the almost sacred guarantee of anonymity.[31]

Finn's behavior ruined the scenario planned by Burns and some of the other officers. They had prepared a number of resolutions to deal with the question of "subversive" elements within the Mattachine Society. One simply declared that "this Society unconditionally subscribes to the American creed." Another, a loyalty oath, required each member to sign a statement that included the following: "I believe it is my duty to my country to love it; to support its constitution; to obey its laws; to respect its flag; and to defend it against all enemies." A third resolution mandated the creation of a "Committee for Investigating Communist Infiltration," with the power to summon any member before it and to suspend anyone who failed to answer "satisfactorily" questions concerning Communist party membership. Whether the majority of the delegates opposed the resolutions out of considered conviction or out of anger over the attempt at intimidation remains unclear. But they did defeat all of the resolutions aimed at extirpating "subversive" influences.[32]

29. Mattachine Society Convention for the Adoption of By-Laws, "Minutes," November 14–15, 1953, Los Angeles, Lucas papers.

30. Ibid.

31. Ibid.; Jeff Winters, "Can Homosexuals Organize?" ONE, January, 1954, pp. 4–8; David L. Freeman, "Who Is This Man?" ONE, March 1954, pp. 16–18; interview with Kepner; and interview with Dorr Legg, October 6, 1976, in Los Angeles.

32. "Call to Convention," November 14–15, 1953, Kepner papers; and Mattachine Society Convention, "Minutes," November 14–15, 1953, Lucas papers.

The convention, however, closed a chapter in the history of the Mattachine Society. Despite the rejection of loyalty oaths and other paraphernalia of the McCarthy era, the membership had decisively abandoned the radical, militant impulse that had characterized the first three years of the organization. The cost of the new direction was high. Since the early summer, the organization's work had been "immeasurably hampered," as Burns admitted, by a series of resignations coming from officers and members who shared the vision of the founders. "Too many committees," one officer reported in July 1953, are "at present trying to function with a minimum of personnel." In September, Brissette and almost all of the East Bay membership in northern California quit.[33]

The November convention accelerated the decline. Konrad Stevens, who finally left the organization after the convention, described his reasons:

> It was dull and wasting time. The fighting, the beginnings, the revolution, was over. I felt we were dragging our feet. Everything was so watered down that nothing courageous would ever be done. They wanted to do nice things to make society accept them.[34]

Others agreed. Ben Tabor, an officer in southern California, submitted his resignation to Burns shortly after the convention. There were "two premises," he wrote, "which comprise the essence of our organization. . . . We are predominantly an organization of homosexuals [and] we are interested primarily in demanding our civil rights. But from where I sit, it looks like the Coordinating Council is devoting all its energy to denying both of these premises."[35]

Over the next year and a half, the Mattachine Society continued to decline in size. At its first annual convention in May 1954, only forty-two members were in attendance. Burns attempted to give an optimistic appearance to the situation by telling his audience that "what the Society requires as members is quality—not quantity," but it was hard to ignore the change from the convention a year earlier, when the organization had been expanding rapidly and the hundred delegates represented a much larger constituency in the discussion groups. The turnout for the annual meeting the following year was even

33. Ken Burns, "Opening Speech," Proceedings of the First Annual Convention of the Mattachine Society, Kepner papers; CC Minutes, July 10, 1953, Lucas papers; and interview with Brissette. The resignation of officers and active members is mentioned in CC Minutes, June 26, July 10, July 31, August 7, and October 16, 1953; and in the reports of the chairmen of the Northern and Southern Area Councils, Mattachine Society Convention Minutes, November 14–15, 1953, Lucas Papers.

34. Interview with Kepner; interview with Konrad Stevens, January 5, 1977, in Los Angeles.

35. Tabor to Burns, November 30, 1953, Lucas papers. After resigning from the Mattachine Society, Tabor began working with *ONE*. Others, such as Kepner and Rowland, also chose that option rather than remain with the Mattachine Society.

smaller, reflecting a further drop in membership. The presence of women in the society, formerly a minority, fell to token representation.[36]

Along with the decrease in numbers went a program that was at once cause and effect of the decline. Relying on the good offices of individuals in the fields of medicine, law, religion, and mental health, the Mattachine Society had opted for a relatively passive, long-term strategy of education undertaken by others. The society urged homosexuals to adjust to the mores of the community, yet homosexuality remained outside the boundaries of acceptable behavior. Rather than undertake consciousness raising, challenges to police practices, political action, and efforts to achieve penal code reform, the organization sponsored activities—blood drives; the collection of clothes, books, and magazines for hospitals; and the like—to demonstrate that homosexuals were solid citizens. It even began to deny that the Mattachine Society was an organization of homosexuals. The new Mattachine offered too little to persuade gay men and women to take the risk of joining a homosexual group. And, as membership figures fell, the society had too little strength to do anything but depend on sympathetic professionals.[37]

IV

While Mattachine took a more cautious, conservative direction, *ONE* strove to keep alive the militant spirit of the society's early years. The group of men and women who ran it kept the magazine independent of Mattachine. With Jennings as editor and Rowland as one of its main writers, *ONE* published articles harshly critical of Mattachine's new policies and perspectives. After Jennings and Rowland left the magazine at the end of 1954 and 1955, respectively, *ONE*'s attacks upon the society stopped, but its outlook remained different from Mattachine's.

Much of *ONE*'s character came from Dorr Legg, the magazine's business manager. Legg, who was raised in the academic milieu of Ann Arbor's university community, traced his family roots back to Michigan's pioneer days and before that to seventeenth-century New England. Acceptance of his homosexuality came easily to him, he claimed, since his intellectual precocity and a Yankee confidence in his own superior breeding allowed him to dismiss the theorizing of the medical profession and what he considered the "ravings of organized religion." With advanced degrees in urban planning and in music, Legg settled in New York in the 1930s, later taught at a state university in Oregon, and then, during the war, moved to Detroit to be near his ailing

36. "Proceedings of the First Annual Convention of the Mattachine Society," Kepner papers. Thirty-one were in attendance at the 1955 convention. See San Francisco Area Council *Newsletter* no. 23, June 1955, National Sex Forum, San Francisco.

37. "Report of Southern Area Council to General Convention," May 15–16, 1954, San Francisco, Kepner papers. At one meeting Mattachine officers debated whether the organization should "broaden into heterosexual problems or the problem of the human being, not just the sex variant"; see "Minutes, Board of Directors Meeting," September 13, 1954, Lucas papers.

parents. His lover at the time was black, and though the two men met with acceptance in Detroit's black community, elsewhere they suffered "terrible traumas of prejudice and hatred." An interracial pair of men, Legg recalled, "would be stopped on the streets. . . . The police simply assumed criminal purposes." After the war they migrated to Los Angeles, hoping that the fluid society of southern California might offer them freedom from harassment. In the early 1950s they participated in the Knights of the Clock, a private interracial social club for gay couples in Los Angeles.[38]

Legg joined the Mattachine Society in 1952, shortly after the Jennings trial. Quickly invited into guild membership, he was a participant in the discussion group that decided to publish a magazine and was thus involved with *ONE* from its inception. Legg energetically hawked the slim monthly at Mattachine discussion groups, searched out newsstand and bookstore outlets in other cities, and aggressively pushed the magazine in correspondence with readers. Soon after *ONE* began publishing, Legg abandoned his career as an urban planner. Living on savings and a small private income, he became the movement's first fulltime worker. With an unalloyed confidence in his own intelligence, Legg played a key role in giving *ONE* its assertive, brash, and often irreverent tone.[39]

During the 1950s at least, *ONE* managed to remain a mixed group, including both men and women. Its iconoclastic outlook bred a tolerance for wide, even incompatible differences in viewpoint and experience, since no one exhibited a desire to impose his or her own views upon others. Moreover, the number of persons involved was small, and the sense of being pioneers in a gay publishing venture, coupled with the vast amount of work required of everyone, encouraged mutual respect. Besides Legg, those who kept *ONE* going were Eve Ellorree, Jim Kepner, Ann Carll Reid, Sten Russell, and Don Slater.[40]

ONE adopted a stance of combative pride in being gay. It always held firmly to the position that homosexuals and lesbians were the only real authorities on gay life. The magazine regularly attacked the proponents of the medical model. Police practices also came under heavy criticism. Kepner especially sought to arouse readers' indignation at the treatment accorded gay men, through a monthly column that exposed blatant examples of police harassment. *ONE* encouraged the self-examination and criticism that had charac-

38. Interview with Legg, October 6, 1976. On the Knights of the Clock, see Marvin Cutler, ed., *Homosexuals Today: A Handbook of Organizations and Publications* (Los Angeles, 1956), pp. 93–94.

39. Interview with Legg; interview with Kepner. For examples of Legg's writing, see the following articles published by him under pseudonyms: "The Case of the Well-Meaning Lyncher," *ONE*, November 1953, pp. 10–11; and "I Am Glad I Am Homosexual," *ONE*, August 1958, p. 6.

40. Interviews with Legg; with Kepner; and with Sten Russell, October 24, 1976, in Costa Mesa, Calif.

terized the early Mattachine discussion groups. Its editors relished controversy and published provocative articles intended to spark debate. Writers
argued back and forth about whether homosexuals were superior to heterosexuals or merely different from them, whether gays formed a cultural minority,
whether the gay subculture strengthened its members or reinforced shame
about being gay, and whether homosexuals and lesbians would ever rise up in
large numbers to challenge prejudice and discrimination. Throughout the
1950s the magazine remained an open forum in which homosexual men and
women freely expressed their opinions about gay life and gay identity. Although *ONE* eschewed the task of organizing gays into what it called the
"homophile movement," it played a role in reshaping the consciousness of
some of them.[41]

V

By the end of 1955, Mattachine's decline in membership had ended, and the
organization was slowly expanding again. Small chapters existed in New York
and Chicago, and the society had promising contacts with gay men in a number
of other cities. In January 1955 the organization began publishing its own
magazine, the *Mattachine Review*, and the San Francisco chapter, headed by
Hal Call, assumed primary responsibility for publishing it, a task that helped
spur the chapter's growth. The southern California group, in contrast, never
regained its original dynamism; and at the end of 1956 San Francisco became
the headquarters for the society's national office. Side by side with Call worked
Don Lucas, a bespectacled, balding accountant. The two presented a sharp
contrast in personality: Call was raucous, aggressive, authoritarian in manner,
and given to off-color language; Lucas was reserved, timid, sober in his habits,
and absorbed in the minutiae of running an organization. Yet they managed to
work quite well together. In 1954, with the *Mattachine Review* about to
commence publication, the two men formed Pan-Graphic Press, a small
business that printed the *Review* and other work as well. The press allowed
Call and Lucas to combine movement work with earning a living, and Mattachine remained their primary commitment until well into the 1960s.[42]

The New York Mattachine Society owed its existence to the initiative of
Tony Segura and Sam Morford. Born in Cuba, Segura received his training as
a research chemist in the United States. During a business trip to Cleveland in
1954, he came across a copy of *The Homosexual in America*. "Everything in
Cory's book excited me," he remembered. "It gave me a strong sense of the
existence of homosexuals as a [minority] group which I had never thought
about before." Segura wrote to the publisher and eventually made contact with
a discussion group composed mostly of gay men in the professions. Calling

41. The conclusions in this paragraph are drawn from my reading of *ONE*, for the period
1953–1961. For a discussion of specific articles and topics, see below, Chap. 7.
42. Interview with Call; interview with Don Lucas in San Francisco, November 23, 1976.

itself The League, the group was an outgrowth of the now defunct Veterans Benevolent Association. "The heavens opened wide for me," Segura recalled, and he attended the meetings faithfully. The comings and goings at night in the warehouse district of the lower east side, however, aroused the suspicions of a neighboring business tenant, who alerted the police. When a note arrived from the local precinct, "people became terrified. Someone called me at home in great agitation. The thought was to disband immediately." Members began to fade away, and the incident convinced Segura of the need for an open organization that would be less susceptible to crises.[43]

Segura's desire for an aboveground organization had the support of Sam Morford, another member of The League. A clinical psychologist in his late forties, he had come out in New York in the 1920s. The intervening decades brought changes that impelled Morford toward political action. "It was much harder to find gay life then," he recalled. "But once you did you were relatively safe, since no one knew anything about it. . . . In the fifties the police harassed us constantly. That's why we formed Mattachine." At a convention of psychologists, he encountered Evelyn Hooker, who reported on her research among male homosexuals and told Morford about the Mattachine Society. After a trip to San Francisco over the Labor Day weekend in 1955, Morford obtained the approval of Call and Lucas to start a Mattachine branch in New York. He and Segura, along with a few friends from the moribund League, commenced meeting in December.[44]

Those who became affiliated with Mattachine after 1954 learned nothing about its political origins. Although officers acknowledged the society's beginnings as a secret organization, they withheld information about the left-wing background of the founders, their analysis of homosexuals as an oppressed minority, and their goal of building a militant mass movement. Newcomers were joining an organization whose purpose was primarily "education"—education of the homosexual about responsible citizenship and education of society, through professionals, about the homosexuals in its midst.

In its first few years, the Mattachine Society had confronted issues that would surface again and again as areas of heated debate in the gay movement—whether homosexuality was an unimportant characteristic or an aspect of a person's life so significant that it bound gay men and women together as a minority group; whether homosexuals and lesbians should accommodate themselves to the mores of society or assert their difference; whether they were victims of prejudiced opinion or of a system of oppression inherent in the structure of American society; whether patient educational work or militant

43. Interview with Tony Segura in New York City, May 24, 1977, conducted by Jonathan Katz. I am indebted to Katz for letting me use his interview material. On The League, see Edward Sagarin, "Structure and Ideology in an Association of Deviants," Ph.D. diss., New York University, 1966, pp. 73–75.

44. Interview with Sam Morford in San Francisco, December 18, 1976; and interview with Segura.

political action was the key to social change; and finally whether, in their quest for equality, gay people should rely on the leadership of professionals or their own independent efforts. The first round of conflict pitted "radicals" against "conservatives," with the two camps standing on opposite sides of each question. But in later years the set of issues would prove capable of a variety of alignments.

The outcome of the early Mattachine's internal struggles cannot be understood in isolation from the larger currents in postwar American society. The intensity of anticommunism in the early 1950s made it highly unlikely that a group of men who had ties or sympathies with the Communist party would successfully retain leadership of a constituency that was not in itself a leftist one. The harsh reality of Stalinist rule in the Soviet Union, combined with the strength of McCarthyism in the United States, tended to discredit any political perspectives associated with Communists. Thus it is not surprising that the changes in the Mattachine leadership went hand in hand with a rejection of the founders' outlook. Hay and his fellows espoused militant action during a conservative era and an analysis of the homosexual's situation that emphasized the shortcomings of American society, and this rendered it easier to discard their views. Accommodation and consensus best characterized political life during the 1950s. The founders of the Mattachine Society had advocated neither of the two.

The conditions of gay life in the postwar era also played a part in the demise of Mattachine's early radicalism and the decline in the number of its participants. Before they can win acceptance and motivate people to act upon them, new ideas need to explain convincingly the actual experience of men and women. Although a gay subculture was taking form in the 1940s and early 1950s, it remained relatively rudimentary and undeveloped, especially when compared with the group life of other minorities such as Jews and blacks. The claim that homosexuals were a minority with a distinctive culture was still too much at odds with the situation of gay men and women. The dominant view of homosexuality, with its emphasis on the individual nature of the phenomenon, more accurately described gay existence. Moreover, by 1953 the right-wing attacks upon "sexual perverts" had gathered full force, and police harassment was on the rise. Both of these seemed to magnify the risks of joining a gay organization and discouraged individuals from espousing anything that smacked of radicalism. For a gay emancipation movement to grow and become strong, the conditions of gay life and the political climate in America would have to change.

SIX

Dual Identity and Lesbian Autonomy: The Beginning of Separate Organizing among Women

Although the early Mattachine Society portrayed itself as representing *the* homosexual minority, in fact it primarily attracted men. Throughout its brief history, the fifth order remained an exclusively male preserve. Women like Geraldine Jackson and Marilyn Rieger did achieve guild membership, but there were only a few other lesbians in leadership positions. Except for those headed by women, the discussion groups also drew an overwhelmingly male membership. With knowledge of the Mattachine Society spreading by word of mouth, the initial preponderance of men tended to become self-perpetuating. After Mattachine's change of course, even the small number of women who had been loyal to the society left.[1]

Male solipsism contributed enormously to this state of affairs. The defense of Dale Jennings, trumpeted by the society as a victory for the homosexual cause, carried little immediate relevance for lesbians, who seldom engaged in the public cruising that subjected gay men to police harassment. Many of the topics that preoccupied the discussion groups failed to strike at the heart of lesbian existence. The problem of promiscuity, so central to men struggling over the question of an ethical homosexual culture, was of less concern to women who had far fewer sexual partners. Gay men in the Mattachine debated earnestly whether it was even possible for homosexuals to build an exclusive couple relationship, while among lesbians paired intimacies of long duration were not uncommon. In numerous, often unconscious ways, male homosex-

---

1. All of my interviews with participants in the early Mattachine Society confirmed the preponderance of men. For the exception—discussion groups headed by women—see Marilyn Rieger, "Notes of Discussion Group Meeting," March 20, 1953, personal papers of Don Lucas, San Francisco.

uals defined gayness in terms that negated the experience of lesbians and conspired to keep them out of the Mattachine Society.[2]

Success in mobilizing lesbians for their own emancipation depended upon recognition of their dual identity—as homosexuals and as women. Like gay men, lesbians suffered from religious condemnation, the stigma of criminality, and the morbidification of their eroticism by the medical profession; but they encountered antihomosexual opprobrium from the vantage point of their gender. The same forces that allowed a gay identity to coalesce from the late nineteenth century onward—the shift to wage labor, the growth of industrialism and urbanization, the removal of production from the home, and the restructuring of the family—affected both men and women, but in decidedly different ways. Lesbian life took on forms that, although resembling those of gay men in some respects, constituted a unique social experience. Cultural definitions of female sexuality, prescriptions about women's proper place in society, and limits upon their opportunities to earn a livelihood profoundly affected the evolution of a lesbian identity and molded the contours of the subculture in which some lesbians moved.

I

A commitment to lesbianism—to an existence characterized by a primary sexual and emotional attachment to women—demanded a much sharper break from traditional expectations of "proper" womanhood than did the corresponding choice for men. At a minimum, it required the ability to earn a living and to survive without the economic resources that a husband provided. However, far fewer women than men possessed the wherewithal to live beyond the boundaries of the nuclear family. In 1910, only 25 percent of all American adult females worked outside the home, a figure that remained almost unchanged for the next thirty years. Black and white women of the working class were more likely to engage in paid labor, but low-paying jobs made their survival dependent upon attachment to networks of kin. Since the socially prescribed role of motherhood, at least until the 1940s, virtually ended a woman's participation in the labor force, the vast majority of women in the generations before World War II had little chance to shift course and come out later in life. Gayness also implied an affirmation of female eroticism divorced from procreative potential, initiated and consummated without male participation. During much of the nineteenth century, however, Victorian sexual ideology had defined women as "passionless"; and although twentieth-century writers from Havelock Ellis to Sigmund Freud affirmed female eroticism, they defined it in ways that tied a woman's sexual desires inevitably to the activating presence of a man. Taken together, these factors inhibited the articulation of a lesbian identity and the evolution of an urban lesbian subculture. As Kinsey's

---

2. On the contrast between male and female patterns, see Alfred Kinsey et al., *Sexual Behavior in the Human Female* (Philadelphia, 1953), pp. 456–58.

studies of male and female sexual behavior revealed, women were much less likely than men to have a history of homoerotic expression.[3]

When a lesbian identity did finally emerge, it came from two distinct sources, one middle class and the other working class, reflecting the disparity in women's existence in the nineteenth century. One style of lesbian life had its roots in what has been called "the female world of love and ritual," the normative role of proper Victorian women. The other evolved out of the "deviant" experience of some working-class women who "passed" as men in the public sphere while constructing a private life with a female-centered erotic and emotional focus.[4]

White middle-class women in Victorian America inhabited a private sphere of domesticity. Although the doctrine of separate male and female spheres helped to rationalize the confinement of women to the role of wife and mother, it also affirmed women's moral superiority and implicitly endorsed close relationships between them. Middle-class Victorian women often turned to one another for intimacy and understanding. Intense attachments that began in adolescence continued after marriage, and women expressed their affection for one another in the passionate phrases generally associated with romantic love. These bonds of womanhood extended beyond paired friendships. Women constructed a "homosocial" world that not only encompassed the home but included as well far-flung networks of female kin, religious benevolence groups, and reform societies.[5]

Toward the end of the nineteenth century, the expansion of both higher education and occupational opportunities made it possible for some middle-class women to structure a female-oriented life, inclusive of eroticism, outside the limits that marriage had imposed on previous generations. Female college graduates pioneered in a variety of professional roles. Their ability to pursue a career gave them the choice of whether to marry, and in fact a disproportionate

3. On women's labor force participation, see Lois Banner, *Women in Modern America* (New York, 1974); William H. Chafe, *The American Woman* (New York, 1972); and Elizabeth H. Pleck, "A Mother's Wages: Income Earning Among Italian and Black Women, 1896–1911," in Michael Gordon, ed., *The American Family in Social-Historical Perspective* (New York, 1978), pp. 490–510. On sexual ideology, see Nancy F. Cott, "Passionlessness: An Interpretation of Victorian Sexual Ideology, 1790–1850," *Signs* 4 (1978): 219–236; Havelock Ellis, *Studies in the Psychology of Sex*, 2 vols. (New York, 1936); Sigmund Freud, *New Introductory Lectures on Psychoanalysis*, trans. J. Rivière (New York, 1935); and Helene Deutsch, *The Psychology of Women*, 2 vols. (New York, 1945). On the differences in male and female incidence rates of homosexual expression, see Kinsey et al., *Sexual Behavior in the Human Male* (Philadelphia, 1948), pp. 610–66, and *Sexual Behavior in the Human Female* (hereafter referred to as *SBHF*), pp. 446–501.

4. See Carroll Smith-Rosenberg, "The Female World of Love and Ritual: Relations Between Women in Nineteenth-Century America," *Signs* 1 (1975): 1–29. The term "passing" was coined by Jonathan Katz in *Gay American History* (New York, 1976).

5. On nineteenth-century middle-class white women, see Smith-Rosenberg, "The Female World of Love and Ritual"; Nancy F. Cott, *The Bonds of Womanhood* (New Haven, Conn., 1977); Mary P. Ryan, *Womanhood in America* (New York, 1975); and Barbara Welter, "The Cult of True Womanhood, 1820–1860," *American Quarterly* 18 (1966): 151–74.

number of college-educated women embraced paid work rather than domesticity. During the Progressive Era, significantly lower birth rates among the white middle class and the noticeable reluctance of college women to marry stimulated nativist fears of "race suicide." On the eve of World War I, roughly half of the alumnae of women's colleges were unattached to men through matrimony; in 1940 30 percent of all white, native-born, college-educated women between the ages of forty and forty-five had never married. When Katharine B. Davis investigated the sex lives of women in the late 1920s, she found a surprisingly extensive incidence of homosexual expression among female college graduates. Kinsey's statistics on female homosexual behavior demonstrated a positive correlation with education: the more years in school, the greater the likelihood that a woman would have same-sex relations. Higher education—and the better occupational choices that it offered—apparently enhanced the possibility of a woman-centered erotic life.[6]

The biographies of notable women from the 1890s through the 1920s offer clues about the nature of lesbian experience within the professional class. Paired relationships of long duration were not uncommon among administrators and faculty members of women's colleges, among those who worked in other female institutions and professions, and among women who entered the predominantly male realm of business and politics. Lesbian couples like Katharine Lee Bates and Katharine Coman or Mary Woolley and Jeannette Marks moved within female networks that gave them emotional strength to pursue their public activities and nurtured intimacy between themselves. They received approval and validation from each other. Having broken decisively with the normative female role by embarking upon a career, these women maintained a discreet private life. To the world around them, they were beyond reproach, euphemistically described as close friends and devoted companions. The female separatism that they inherited from Victorian society and that a vigorous feminist movement affirmed safeguarded their relationships from the taint of deviance.[7]

The decline of the feminist movement and the diffusion of Freudian psychoanalytic perspectives in the years after 1920 transformed society's evaluation of these female attachments. After suffrage, "new women" opted

6. On marriage and birth rates and the race suicide controversy, see Linda Gordon, *Woman's Body, Woman's Right* (New York, 1976), pp. 136–58, esp. p. 139; and Daniel Scott Smith, "Family Limitation, Sexual Control, and Domestic Feminism in Victorian America," in Mary Hartman and Lois W. Banner, eds., *Clio's Consciousness Raised* (New York, 1974), p. 120. See also *SBHF*, pp. 459–60; and Katharine B. Davis, *Factors in the Sex Life of Twenty-two Hundred Women* (New York, 1929), p. 259.

7. See Blanche Wiesen Cook, *Women and Support Networks* (New York, 1979); Judith Schwarz, " 'Yellow Clover': Katharine Lee Bates and Katharine Coman," *Frontiers* 4, no. 1 (Spring 1979): 59–67; Anna Mary Wells, *Miss Marks and Miss Woolley* (Boston, 1978); Lillian Faderman, *Surpassing the Love of Men* (New York, 1981), esp. pp. 157–230; and Nan Bauer Maglin, "Vida to Florence: 'Comrade and Companion,' "*Frontiers* 4, no. 3 (Fall 1979): 13–20. On female separatism, see Estelle Freedman, "Separatism as Strategy: Female Institution Building and American Feminism, 1870–1930," *Feminist Studies* 5 (1979): 512–29.

for assimilation into the male world of work and politics and rejected the separatist strategy of female institution building that had earlier helped sustain lesbian relationships among middle-class women. The writings of sexual modernists shifted the definition of woman's nature from the passionlessness of the Victorian era to one that emphasized an eroticism pervading the lives of human beings of both sexes from infancy. Many younger women in the decades after suffrage adopted the values of those sexual theorists who stressed the importance of erotic companionship between men and women as a requisite of personal fulfillment. Middle-class women reaching maturity after 1920 were far more likely to engage in coitus before marriage than previous generations. The new affirmation of eroticism in male/female relationships implicitly devalued all-female networks. Lesbians lost the protection that came from a distinct culture of women and a Victorian sexual ideology that placed constraints upon heterosexual expression. Moreover, the attention that Freudian theory focused upon sexual motivation in human relationships cast suspicion upon female couples. Paired intimacies between women became morbidified, a sign of sexual pathology. Thus, in the years between the two world wars, a lesbian identity that had emerged ironically out of the normative roles of middle-class Victorian women was reinterpreted as deviant.[8]

II

The conditions of life among working-class women encouraged the evolution of a significantly different pattern of lesbianism. Victorian notions of separate spheres for men and women and of female passionlessness exerted less influence upon their consciousness. Working-class women more frequently engaged in paid labor—in factories, sweatshops, or domestic employment when single, in the home after marriage. The cramped quarters in which they dwelled offered little chance to pursue a cult of domesticity or to create an all-female world, while the lack of privacy that the urban poor experienced made sexual activity among adults more visible to the young. Moreover, the presence of prostitutes in their neighborhoods served as evidence of female eroticism. Although the poorly paying jobs available to women imposed obvious constraints upon their autonomy, and the sexual values of the working class did not endorse female pairings, working-class women did not face the same cultural inhibitions on erotic expression that affected middle-class women. On the other hand, neither did they enjoy the support that the bonds of womanhood provided to the middle class.[9]

8. See Freedman, "Separatism as Strategy"; Faderman, *Surpassing the Love of Men*, pp. 231–331; Christina Simmons, "Purity Rejected: The New Sex Freedom of the Twenties," paper delivered at the 1976 Berkshire Women's History Conference, and "Companionate Marriage and the Lesbian Threat," *Frontiers* 4, no. 3 (Fall 1979): 54–59; and Paula Fass, *The Damned and the Beautiful: American Youth in the 1920s* (New York, 1977), esp. 53–118 and pp. 260–90.

9. On working-class women, see Thomas Dublin, *Women at Work: The Transformation of Work and Community in Lowell, Massachusetts, 1826–1869* (New York, 1979); Susan J. Kleinberg,

In the nineteenth and early twentieth centuries, the phenomenon of passing offered working women both an immediate, substantial improvement in their economic status and a protective covering for a lesbian relationship. Some women dressed as men, adopted male mannerisms, and entered the public male sphere. Lucy Ann Lobdell, a woman who passed for almost thirty years, explained the pecuniary motives behind her decision to begin cross-dressing in the 1850s.

As hard times were crowding upon us, I made up my mind to dress in men's attire to seek labor, as I was used to men's work. And as I might work harder at house-work, and get only a dollar a week, and [as] I was capable of doing men's work, and getting men's wages, I resolved to try.

Lobdell's masquerade gave her the freedom to leave her family and construct a personal life of her own choosing. Eventually she met a woman who lived as her spouse for over a decade. In the early twentieth century, Cora Anderson donned male attire to obtain work. Upon her exposure in Milwaukee in 1914, she too cited economic motives for passing. "Is it any wonder that I determined to become a member of this privileged sex, if possible?" she asked. "The woman who must work is a slave. . . . With the present wage conditions there are thousands of young women who are living in a state of semi-starvation." Like Lobdell, Anderson had spent several years married to a woman. Occasionally groups of passing women worked together and socialized in male preserves such as the saloon. In the process, they helped to create a public, albeit hidden, lesbian identity. Not all passing women were lesbians, and the masquerade always carried the risk of discovery; but for at least some women of the working class cross-dressing promised economic independence as well as allowing lesbian couples to live together under the guise of husband and wife.[10]

After the 1920s, working-class lesbian life assumed a more public, undisguised expression that included as its central feature bars for gay women. As a subcultural institution, bars for lesbians appeared later than bars for male homosexuals. Throughout the nineteenth century the tavern had been a domain of men; prostitutes were the main exceptions to male exclusivity.

"Technology and Women's Work: The Lives of Working Class Women in Pittsburgh, 1870–1900," *Labor History* 17 (1976): 58–72; and David M. Katzman, *Seven Days a Week: Women and Domestic Service in Industrializing America* (New York, 1978). On the contrast between working-class and middle-class women's lives, see Estelle B. Freedman and Erna Olafson Hellerstein, "The Adult Woman: Personal Life–an Introduction," in Hellerstein et al., *Victorian Women* (Stanford, 1981), pp. 118–33.

10. Quoted in Katz, *Gay American History*, p. 219, pp. 256–57; see also the entire section in Katz, "Passing Women," pp. 209–79, for other cases; and the San Francisco Lesbian History Project, "Lesbian Masquerade: Some Women Who Passed as Men in Early San Francisco," slide lecture presented at the June 1981 Berkshire Women's History Conference, Vassar College, Poughkeepsie, N.Y.

Women played a conspicuous part in the temperance movement, and organizations like the Woman's Christian Temperance Union attracted millions of members and conducted major campaigns against saloons. Ironically, the Prohibition era witnessed a relaxation of the cultural sanctions against women's consumption of alcohol, while the flapper simultaneously provided a visible image of a woman who enjoyed her nights about town. The end of Prohibition in 1933 set the stage for the spread of bars patronized exclusively by gay women. In the nation's largest cities, a bar subculture took root from the 1930s onward.[11]

The world of lesbian bars never assumed the proportions of its male equivalent. In medium-sized cities and towns, where the lesbian population was too small to support its own taverns, gay women and men mingled in mixed establishments. But even in the biggest metropolitan areas, the number of lesbian bars remained small. In Boston, for instance, about two dozen male homosexual taverns appeared in the course of the 1950s, but throughout the decade one bar served an all-female clientele. In 1963 Donald Webster Cory estimated that only thirty exclusively lesbian bars were operating in America, while San Francisco alone had almost that many establishments for gay men.[12]

The disparity in numbers had several sources. Given the constraints upon female autonomy, the pool of women from whom patrons might be drawn was undoubtedly smaller; there were simply fewer lesbians than gay men to fill the bars. Whereas married men could engage in casual sexual encounters with relative ease and thus form a large periphery around a central core of male homosexuals, marriage virtually excluded women from lesbian life. Like all businesses, the tavern depended on customers with money to spend; women of the working class had extremely limited resources. Although bar attendance in the mid-twentieth century no longer defined a woman as beyond the pale, it still bore connotations of disreputable behavior. The questionable legality of establishments that catered to "sexual perverts" encouraged underworld investment, a management that contributed to a seedy atmosphere, and the opening of lesbian bars in run-down parts of town. Women had to be willing to travel in unsafe areas of the city at night without a male escort, risking harassment and assault. Going to bars also implied a comparatively open acknowledgment of one's sexual identity. Although gay men could reach that point in stages by participating in street cruising and other forms of public

11. See Mary Jane Lupton, "Ladies' Entrance: Women and Bars," *Feminist Studies* 4 (1979): 571–588; Jon M. Kingsdale, "The 'Poor Man's Club': Social Functions of the Urban Working-Class Saloon," in Elizabeth H. Pleck and Joseph H. Pleck, eds., *The American Man* (Englewood Cliffs, N.J., 1980), pp. 255–83; and Fass, *The Damned and the Beautiful*, pp. 310–24. For evidence of lesbian bars before World War II, see Caroline Ware, *Greenwich Village* (New York, 1935; Harper paperback ed., 1965), p. 96; Vern Bullough and Bonnie Bullough, "Lesbianism in the 1920s and 1930s: A Newfound Study," *Signs* 2 (1977): 902; and J. R. Roberts, "Lesbian Hoboes," *Dyke: A Quarterly*, no. 5 (Fall 1977), pp. 36–50.

12. Boston Area Lesbian and Gay History Project, "Our Boston Heritage," slide lecture presented in New York City, March 1, 1981; and Donald Webster Cory (pseud.), *The Lesbian in America* (New York, 1964), p. 153.

liaisons, the structure of the lesbian subculture lacked these transitional opportunities. In an era when exposure of an individual as a homosexual promised harsh penalties, involvement in the world of gay bars marked a critical dividing line that many lesbians hesitated to cross.[13]

All these reasons, however, ultimately accented the importance of the bars. As the only clearly identifiable collective manifestation of lesbian existence, the bars filled a unique role in the evolution of a group consciousness among gay women. They alone brought lesbianism into the public sphere. The entire setting emphasized a lesbian's difference from heterosexual women at the same time that it bound her to her gay sisters. No matter how closeted a woman might be in other areas of her life, in the bars she took a step out and affirmed her erotic preferences.

One particular feature of lesbian bar culture deserves special comment, since virtually all firsthand accounts call attention to it: the butch-femme dichotomy. Many gay women took on polarized roles, perhaps originating in the earlier phenomenon of passing, that encompassed dress, appearance, and mannerisms and sometimes extended into their home life and intimate relationships. Newcomers to the bars faced questions about which role they took; old-timers expected them to make a choice. Women responded to the demands of their peers in different ways. Shirley Willer, a registered nurse who came out in Chicago during the 1940s, recalled that she "frequently encountered suspicion among lesbians" during her early forays into the bars because she did not take a clearly defined role. "I never desired or approved of [role playing]," she said, "but we had to live with it." By her own testimony, she became more and more butch to achieve acceptance. In New Orleans in the early 1950s, Doris Lunden found much the same thing. "If you didn't pick a role—butch or femme—and stick with that, people thought you were mixed up and you didn't know who you were and you were laughed at and called 'ki-ki'—a sort of queer of the gay world." The butch "seemed to fit with my notion of having boys' feelings," she said, and Lunden moved easily into a part that she took quite seriously. In contrast, Barbara Gittings felt alienated from the New York bar scene of the mid-1950s and, rather than choose a role, she simply stopped going to the bars. For many other women, however, the butch role in particular served as a visible mark of their identity, a way of saying to society that they were indeed sexually different. The desire for acceptance in the one social institution available to lesbians perpetuated the system of roles, while the ostracism that resulted from their failure to conform kept away the recalcitrant.[14]

13. On the impact of marriage on homosexual behavior among women see *SBHF*, p. 454. On the contrast between methods of meeting one another among male homosexuals and lesbians, compare Donald Webster Cory, *The Homosexual in America* (New York, 1951) and *The Lesbian in America*.

14. Interview with Shirley Willer, conducted by Toby Marotta, 1975; Elly Bulkin, "An Old Dyke's Tale: An Interview with Doris Lunden," *Conditions: Six* (1980), pp. 26–27; and "Barbara Gittings," in Kay Tobin and Randy Wicker, *The Gay Crusaders* (New York, 1972), pp. 209–10.

The social changes induced by World War II and the reaction in the postwar decade affected lesbians in a particularly direct way. The large-scale entry of women into the work force, the geographic mobility that many of them experienced, the removal of millions of young men from the home front, and the concentration for the first time of substantial numbers of women in the armed forces created a qualitatively new and unique situation in which women might come out and lesbians might meet one another. For the working-class butch, the temporary changes in styles of feminine attire and the presence of more women in male occupations made her appear less unusual and ameliorated the hostility she would otherwise encounter on the streets. After the war, just as suddenly, social patterns reverted to heterosexuality, but in an exaggerated fashion. The average age at marriage lowered, the birth rate jumped sharply, and the rate of marriage reached a peak unsurpassed in the nation's history. Among women born between 1921 and 1930, a greater percentage married than any previous female cohort. Although women's participation in the paid labor force never declined to its prewar level, for the most part women lost the high-paying industrial jobs that had temporarily enhanced their prospects of financial security. The resurgence of prescriptive literature on women's proper place intensified the psychological pressures that lesbians confronted. By the early 1950s, American society had assumed a posture that accentuated the deviance of women who pursued a female-centered life.[15]

In 1955, when a few gay women in San Francisco commenced autonomous organizing for their own emancipation, their efforts reflected the particularities of lesbian experience. The extreme isolation and invisibility of gay women projected concerns about social life to the forefront of their goals. A smaller subculture made recruitment more difficult, while the precarious economic circumstances of women and their limited options heightened the risks of participating in a movement. The conservative tenor of American society during the 1950s posed special problems for lesbian organizations, since many

---

My own interviews with Del Martin, Phyllis Lyon, Sten Russell, and Helen Sanders confirmed this picture. For other descriptions of lesbian bar life, see the interview with Pat Bond in Nancy and Casey Adair, *Word Is Out* (San Francisco, 1978), pp. 61–64; Sidney Abbott and Barbara Love, *Sappho Was a Right-on Woman* (New York, 1972), pp. 69–82; and Buffalo Lesbian Oral History Project, "Lesbian Bars in Buffalo, 1930–1960," paper presented at the 1981 Berkshire Women's History Conference. A recent, positive evaluation of the bar scene and roles is given by Joan Nestle, "Butch-Fem: Sexual Courage in the 1950s," paper presented at the June 1981 Berkshire Women's History Conference, Vassar College, Poughkeepsie, N.Y. A shorter version of Nestle's paper can be found in *Heresies*, no. 12 (1981), pp. 21–24.

15. For the proportion of women born between 1921 and 1930 who married, see Gordon, *Woman's Body, Woman's Right*, p. 49. On the status of women in the postwar decade, see Betty Friedan, *The Feminine Mystique* (New York, 1963); Banner, *Women in Modern America*, pp. 211–27; Chafe, *The American Woman*, pp. 199–225; and Ryan, *Womanhood in America*, pp. 282–87, 301–3, 318–20, 335–61. For an example of postwar prescriptive literature, see Ferdinand Lundberg and Marynia F. Farnham, *Modern Woman: The Lost Sex* (New York, 1947). For the impact of World War II on working-class lesbian life, see Buffalo Project, "Lesbian Bars."

women with a strong sense of their lesbian identity, the butch patrons of gay bars, embodied the least acceptable image of womanhood.

III

Del Martin and Phyllis Lyon deserve most of the credit for launching the Daughters of Bilitis (DOB) and keeping the first lesbian political organization afloat during its early years. At one time or another the couple held every office in DOB. They edited its monthly publication, the *Ladder*, provided much of the copy for the magazine, and answered faithfully the many letters that arrived from lesbians around the country. Martin and Lyon kept DOB solvent with contributions from their own pockets; opened their home for countless meetings; and played mother, confidante, nurse, and counselor for women who came to the Daughters for help. For the two lovers, DOB became a full-time occupation that consumed far more hours than either of them spent earning a living.[16]

Born in San Francisco in 1921, Del Martin entered her adolescence aware of a strong attraction to girls, but she had no words to describe her desires and knew better than to confide in anyone about them. At nineteen she married a college classmate and dropped out of school shortly afterward, when she became pregnant. The family moved to a suburb of San Francisco, and her husband, Jack, commuted to the city, where he worked long hours during the war as a civilian employee of the army. When Martin fell in love with a woman neighbor, she knew that the time had come to get a divorce. Her husband, who had found some "mushy notes" that she had written to her friend, threatened to contest the divorce, but the proceedings went smoothly, and Martin won custody of her young daughter, Janey.[17]

The next few years were difficult ones, in which Martin had to juggle working, raising her child, and coming to terms with her nascent identity as a lesbian. She read *The Well of Loneliness*, and "for the first time she was able to put a name to what she had been feeling . . . and experienced a release she had never known before. . . . She was a homosexual—a Lesbian." Her elation did not last long. As she searched for more information, Martin encountered ugly stereotypes and derogatory evaluations. "I'd go to the library," she recalled, "and look up whatever was there and it was horrifying to read the stuff they were saying. How could you identify with that? How could you call yourself [a lesbian] when it was so awful? It was a real struggle." She finally confided in two female friends at work, who went with her to the lesbian bars in the North Beach section of San Francisco. These places at least offered the assurance that other women shared her preference, but the bars were not to her liking.

16. The best sources of information about Martin and Lyon are their partly autobiographical book, *Lesbian/Woman* (San Francisco, 1972; Bantam ed.), and the interview with them in Tobin and Wicker, *The Gay Crusaders*, pp. 47–64.

17. Tobin and Wicker, *The Gay Crusaders*, pp. 47–50; Martin and Lyon, *Lesbian/Woman*, pp. 24–25, 151.

Meanwhile, Martin had relinquished custody of her daughter to her ex-husband, who had remarried, and in 1949, after one lesbian affair, she took a job in Seattle for a firm that published trade journals.[18]

Phyllis Lyon was one of her co-workers in Seattle. Three years younger than Martin, she had been born in Tulsa. Her family migrated to the San Francisco area, and Lyon enrolled in the University of California at Berkeley. In college, though she shied away from serious involvements with men, she did date and have heterosexual relationships, with lesbianism never entering her consciousness. "It never occurred to me there was any option," she recalled. "If you were a woman, you had to have a man! There was no other way." Lyon studied journalism at Berkeley, and, with the ranks of male students depleted because of the war, she was able to circumvent the barriers women usually faced and became an editor of the *Daily Californian*. After graduating, she worked for a time as a crime reporter for a paper in Chico before moving to Seattle.[19]

By this time Martin was exhibiting somewhat more openness about her sexuality, and she told several of her fellow female employees, including Lyon, that she was a lesbian. This information provoked many conversations. Martin assumed that Lyon was heterosexual. Over the succeeding three years, the two women became close friends and, finally, lovers. In 1953 they returned to San Francisco and set up house together. For a short while they adopted the butch-femme roles that were "the only models we knew. . . . We played the roles in public, and then we went home and fought about them." They also made a few unsuccessful forays into the bar subculture, in their search for gay female friends, but found them composed of "mostly in-groups, where everybody knew each other, and they seemed to be wary of strangers." After two years in San Francisco, Martin and Lyon had only a few superficial acquaintances among lesbians, and these had come through the good services of a gay male couple in their neighborhood.[20]

The desire to socialize with gay women propelled the Daughters of Bilitis into existence. When one of their lesbian acquaintances invited them to a meeting to discuss starting a social club, Martin and Lyon accepted with enthusiasm. "What we were looking for was a *safe* place, where we could meet other women and dance, . . . an alternative to the gay bar scene," Lyon reminisced. On September 21, 1955, eight women—four couples—gathered and within a few weeks had formed DOB. "Songs of Bilitis," an erotic poem by Pierre Louys, inspired the name. It would carry special meaning for lesbians but also "would sound like any other women's lodge" and thus mask the identity of the group's members.[21]

18. Tobin and Wicker, pp. 47–50; Martin and Lyon, pp. 25–26, 51, 140; author's interview with Del Martin in San Francisco, November 19, 1976.

19. Tobin and Wicker, pp. 47–50; Martin and Lyon, pp. 5, 56, 97.

20. Martin and Lyon, pp. 6, 91–94, 108, 140.

21. Tobin and Wicker, pp. 50–51; Martin and Lyon, pp. 238–40; Phyllis Lyon, remarks at "Gay History Night," a panel discussion sponsored by the Harvey Milk Democratic Club, San

Disagreements soon emerged over what direction the fledgling club should take. The group's evenings together often turned into discussions about the problems faced by lesbians, and before long Martin and Lyon were arguing that DOB should broaden its goals to include the educational work of changing the public's attitude toward lesbianism. By this time the two women had discovered the Mattachine Society in San Francisco, which became a model for their proposal to expand the purposes of DOB. The group split in half over the suggestion, with the blue-collar workers leaving to form another social club.[22]

The six women who remained in DOB joined forces with the Mattachine Society and with ONE, Inc., in what the other two organizations were by then calling the "homophile" movement. In January 1956 several DOB women traveled to Los Angeles to attend ONE's midwinter institute of educational seminars. In April the group participated in its first public event, when it co-sponsored a forum with Mattachine on the different problems faced by gay women and gay men. Shortly thereafter, with membership hovering around a dozen, DOB decided to commence its own "public discussions" to attract new women. As Martin explained it, "we thought it would cut down the fear. Lesbians could go there and pretend to be the 'public.' " In October DOB published the first issue of the *Ladder* and sent the run of 200 copies to every lesbian whom any of its members knew and to lawyers, psychologists, and other professionals culled from the pages of the San Francisco telephone directory.[23]

For the most part, the Daughters of Bilitis, the Mattachine Society, and ONE worked closely and cooperatively throughout the 1950s. "We had to stand shoulder to shoulder," Dorr Legg explained, "because the movement was so small, and we knew we had to protect each other." Mattachine's inability to attract women made it welcome the appearance of the Daughters, which acknowledged that its "growing pains would have been a great deal more excruciating had it not been for the full cooperation and support of the Mattachine Society." On their side, the founders of DOB expressed the wish that "our venture will encourage the women to take an ever-increasing part in the . . . fight for understanding of the homophile minority." Moreover, a basic similarity in outlook bound the organizations together. Each saw education— the dispelling of myths, misinformation, and prejudice—as the primary means of improving the status of lesbians and homosexuals. The phrasing of DOB's statement of purposes, with its call for education of the public, the adjustment of the "variant" to society, participation in research projects by professionals, and the modification of the penal code, bore an extremely close resemblance to

Francisco, March 25, 1980; and Del Martin, "Daughters of Bilitis," typescript, 1956, DOB file, Homosexual Information Center, Los Angeles.

22. Martin and Lyon, pp. 240–42, 248–49; *Mattachine Review*, August 1956, pp. 14, 39; and *Ladder*, October 1956, pp. 2–3.

23. Interview with Martin; Martin and Lyon, pp. 241–42; *Mattachine Review*, August 1956, p. 14; and San Francisco Mattachine *Newsletter*, December 1957, p. 4.

Mattachine's language and suggests the influence of the Society on DOB in its formative stages.[24]

However, close association with the Mattachine Society and ONE did not prevent DOB from retaining distinctive qualities traceable to the particular situation of lesbians. The greater isolation and invisibility of gay women had pushed Martin and Lyon into the endeavor in the first place, and these factors continued to exert an influence on DOB's activities. Though the women's group exhibited a concern with law reform and with changing attitudes toward homosexuality, it also preserved a commitment to the personal needs of lesbians. DOB existed as a self-help effort for women, a haven where they could experience a sense of belonging, put their lives in order, and then, strengthened and regenerated, venture forth into society. It was, as a circular for new members explained, "a home for the Lesbian. She can come here to find help, friendship, acceptance and support. She can help others understand themselves, and can go out into the world to help the public understand her better."[25]

The contents of the *Ladder* evidenced the priority DOB attached to the individual lesbian. The editors consciously aimed the magazine at "the lonely isolated lesbians away from the big cities." Although the *Ladder* reported political news, Helen Sanders, an editor of the magazine and an officer of DOB, insisted that it was "never meant to be a political journal. Politics was for the active members of the organization," and the women who published the magazine carefully refrained from advocacy and editorializing. Instead, the monthly devoted much of its space to poetry, fiction, history, and biography. It also allowed lesbians to give voice to an experience that society suppressed and distorted.[26]

As women, DOB members also had a set of concerns different from those of their male counterparts in the movement. Many lesbians in the organization were mothers, still shouldering the responsibility of child rearing, and how best to raise youngsters in a lesbian household surfaced frequently as a topic for discussion. Quite a few subscribers to the *Ladder* remained locked in heterosexual marriages, and the magazine gave attention to the special problems of married lesbians. The low salaries and restricted job opportunities that most women faced throughout their adult years kept alive anxieties about money that led DOB to provide advice about employment and such matters as insurance and taxes.[27]

24. Interview with Legg; and *Ladder*, October 1957, p. 6, and October 1956, p. 3. For DOB's statement of purpose, see *Ladder*, October 1956, p. 4. For Mattachine's goals, see "The Mattachine Society Today," typescript, 1954, Mattachine Society–Los Angeles file, Institute for Sex Research, Bloomington, Indiana.

25. "What Is DOB?" DOB file, Lesbian Herstory Archives, New York. The primacy of DOB's commitment to the individual lesbian and the sense of DOB as a self-help organization was expressed strongly and consistently by Martin, Lyon, Sanders, and Russell in interviews.

26. Interview with Helen Sanders in Costa Mesa, Calif., October 24, 1976.

27. See, e.g., *Ladder*, October 1956, p. 9; January 1957, p. 4; March 1957, pp. 5–6; April 1957, pp. 8–11; June 1957, pp. 6–7; May 1958, p. 10; and June 1958, pp. 12–13.

Differences in the experiences and concerns of gay women and men, the prior presence of men in the movement, and male attitudes of superiority created tensions between male and female homophile groups. DOB found gay male promiscuity and the police harassment that accompanied it an encumbrance that seemed to make lesbians guilty by association in the eyes of society. They resented the time taken in mixed gatherings on problems that had little to do with the lives of women. DOB also had to guard its autonomy against male encroachment. Mattachine's leaders often exhibited a condescending, patronizing attitude toward the lesbian organization. As Helen Sanders recalled, "they immediately saw us as their ladies' auxiliary. We said 'Up yours!' and wrote into our constitution that the Daughters could not join or affiliate with any other organization." At jointly sponsored events, the issue of a separate women's group arose with regularity, as new male recruits to the movement questioned the need for it. Sometimes DOB panelists responded in a conciliatory manner, but occasionally the unwillingness of gay men to accept women's autonomy provoked angry retorts. At a Mattachine convention in 1959, for instance, Del Martin exploded.

> At every one of these conventions I attend, year after year, I find I must defend the Daughters of Bilitis as a separate and distinct women's organization. . . . What do you men know about Lesbians? In all of your programs and your "Review" you speak of the male homosexual and follow this with—oh, yes, and incidentally, there are some female homosexuals too and because they are homosexuals all this should apply to them as well. ONE has done little better. . . . Neither organization has recognized the fact that Lesbians are *women* and that this 20th century is the era of emancipation of woman. Lesbians are not satisfied to be auxiliary members or second-class homosexuals.[28]

Mutual dependence and similarity of purpose kept these strains below the breaking point throughout the 1950s; but later, as the movement grew stronger, the possibility of a rupture would increase. The commitment of the Daughters of Bilitis to preserving women's autonomy within the movement and to defining a distinctly lesbian perspective guaranteed that male-centered views of homosexuality would not go unchallenged.

IV

DOB attracted significantly fewer members than gay male organizations throughout the 1950s and 1960s. In part this stemmed from a smaller number of potential constituents and in part from the more precarious position of women in the work force. The Daughters, Martin and Lyon reflected, never succeeded in attracting lesbians in the professions, who felt they had every-

---

28. Interview with Sanders; Del Martin in *Ladder*, October 1959, p. 19. For other instances of DOB members defending an autonomous women's organization, see *Ladder*, June 1957, p. 8; December 1957, p. 19; and October 1958, p. 5.

thing to lose from identification with a gay group. "Women who have attained some measure of professional status," they commented,

> zealously guard . . . their reputations. . . . Some root for us from the sidelines and make infrequent donations of time or money. Others damn us for bringing Lesbianism into the open, fearing that as the public becomes more aware people might take a second look at them. And, unfortunately, there are many whose attitude is "I've got it made. What can DOB offer me?"

DOB's chosen focus on self-help also contributed to the paucity of members in the professions. Lesbians who had achieved occupational security were unlikely to seek its services. Sten Russell was active in both ONE and DOB; as she explained it, the Daughters functioned as "a revolving door" for women in need. They joined the group, put their lives in order, acquired pride and self-respect, and then "graduated." The turnover not only kept DOB small; it also deprived the organization of women with leadership ability since, as Russell remarked, "the non-leaders stayed."[29]

Class prejudices also compromised DOB's ability to attract larger numbers of lesbians. The founders and leaders of DOB were for the most part white-collar semiprofessionals disenchanted with a bar subculture, whose population included many women who labored in factories and appeared butch in dress and behavior. The Daughters looked askance at both bar life and the butch lesbian. To Russell the bars were "just slightly removed from Hell. I would like to see a better meeting place for those who wish more from life than a nightmare of whiskey and sex, brutality and vanity, self-pity and despair," she wrote. DOB tried to wean patrons away from the bars. After a police raid in San Francisco that resulted in the arrest of three dozen women, the *Ladder* announced in an editorial that DOB offered a safer, more reputable outlet for meeting others. It counseled members that "their attire should be that which society will accept." Barbara Gittings, who joined DOB in 1958, recalled an incident in which

> a woman who had been living pretty much as a transvestite most of her life was persuaded, for the purpose of attending [a DOB convention], to don female garb, to deck herself out in as "feminine" a manner as she could, given that female clothes were totally alien to her. Everybody rejoiced over this as though some great victory had been accomplished—the "feminizing" of this woman.

Russell justified this approach on pragmatic grounds. "If you weren't willing to dress up at that time you couldn't get a decent job." Many of these women

---

29. Martin and Lyon, *Lesbian/Woman*, pp. 210–11; interview with Sten Russell in Costa Mesa, Calif., October 24, 1976.

worked in factories, however, and it is doubtful whether employment as an office worker or sales clerk would have represented an improvement in their circumstances sufficient to outweigh the estrangement from the one group in which they found acceptance. Involvement in the bar subculture may have restricted the options of its participants, but it also sustained among patrons a strong sense of their identity as lesbians. Women who went to the bars belonged to a group that was larger, more stable, and more familiar than what DOB offered them. For lesbian organizations to swell their ranks, either they would have to effect a rapprochement with the world of the bars or the conditions of women would have to change in ways that expanded the number who were able to claim a lesbian identity.[30]

30. *ONE*, February 1954, pp. 18–19; *Ladder*, November 1956, pp. 9, 4; interview with Barbara Gittings in Katz, *Gay American History*, p. 429; interview with Russell. On the working-class nature of lesbian bar life, see Buffalo Project, "Lesbian Bars"; and Nancy and Casey Adair, *Word Is Out*, pp. 61–64.

SEVEN

The Quest
for Legitimacy

By 1956 the homophile movement had taken the organizational shape it would retain for the rest of the decade. ONE, Inc., the Mattachine Society, and the Daughters of Bilitis were the movement's standard bearers. ONE kept as its primary task the publishing of a monthly magazine, but it added a scholarly journal and sponsored classes in "homophile studies."[1] Although DOB and Mattachine also published magazines, as membership organizations they aspired to create a nationwide structure of chapters whose coordinated efforts would gradually produce significant change in the social status of gay men and women.

The three organizations agreed that education was their overriding, immediate goal, but they were divided over the question of who needed instruction and what the content of that education should be. ONE, which cared only to reach a gay constituency, deliberately sought to provoke its audience. It placed itself in opposition to the culturally dominant view of same-sex eroticism and rejected the notion that anyone other than gay men and women possessed the authority to make judgments about homosexuality. Writers in *ONE* magazine projected an image of defiant pride in their identity; they intentionally tried to shake their readers out of a resigned acceptance of the status quo.

In contrast, DOB and Mattachine took a far more moderate position. Convinced that they needed to accommodate themselves to a society that

---

1. The first issue of *Homophile Studies* appeared in the spring of 1958. For information on ONE's classes, see Robert Gregory, "ONE Institute of Homophile Studies, 1955–1960: A Report," *Homophile Studies* 3 (1960): 214–20.

excoriated homosexual behavior, the two organizations spoke in neutral tones rather than assuming the stance of impassioned partisans. Unlike ONE, they tried to sway two audiences simultaneously. With professionals, whom they considered the makers of public opinion, Mattachine and DOB strove to initiate a dialogue. By opening their meetings and journals to "experts" who espoused a range of attitudes toward homosexuality, they attempted to demonstrate their own reasonableness and thereby to encourage heterosexual authorities to reassess their own assumptions. At the same time, the leaders of the two groups repeatedly impressed upon their gay constituency the need to adjust to normative standards of proper behavior. By persuading gay men and women of the importance of conformity and by minimizing the differences between homosexuality and heterosexuality, the two organizations expected to diffuse social hostility as a prelude to changes in law and public policy.

I

The homophile movement placed publishing at the center of its activities, and its willingness to commit scarce resources of money and labor testified eloquently to the importance the movement attached to the printed word. From their own experiences of coming out, activists knew how little written material on homosexuality appeared outside the pages of specialized journals. When articles did find their way into the press or periodicals, they tended to focus on scandal, tragedy, or stereotypical images of homosexual and lesbian life. Gay women and men rarely enjoyed the opportunity to express in print their own views about their lives. Movement leaders intended their magazines to remedy that deficiency.

Homophile organizations published under enormous constraints. Each was quite small when it decided to issue its own magazine. DOB had a membership of about fifteen when the *Ladder* first appeared; Mattachine was still declining in size when it initiated the *Mattachine Review*; and ONE, Inc., was a tiny collective of at most a dozen men and women. Deprived of access to any significant advertising revenue, DOB and Mattachine allocated membership dues to support their periodicals, but even that did not suffice. All three monthlies depended on substantial out-of-pocket contributions from those working on the magazines to stay solvent, and only volunteer labor made even this effort possible. Gay groups also published under the shadow of the censor. Although court decisions in the decade after World War II had restricted somewhat the application of federal and state obscenity statutes, the United States still operated under laws enacted during the Victorian era. In the late 1940s and early 1950s, moreover, censorship forces took the offensive. Groups like the Catholic-sponsored National Organization for Decent Literature campaigned against the display and sale of sexually oriented reading matter. Cut off from the usual channels of distribution, gay organizations had to be satisfied with sales from subscriptions and through the few bookstores and newsstands that specialized in pornography. Finally, fear of having their sexual identity discovered kept most homosexuals and lesbians from receiving in the mail or even buying gay-related material, and this further inhibited the movement's publishing ventures.[2]

As a result, circulation of the magazines remained quite small. *ONE* reported over 5,000 per month, the *Mattachine Review* 2,200, and the *Ladder* only 500. Admittedly the readership was larger than these numbers suggest, since subscribers passed copies from friend to friend. Letters to the editor also revealed that the audience was spread across the country. Yet one cannot escape the fact that, despite their best efforts, homophile publications did not succeed in attracting many readers.[3]

The magazines served a variety of purposes. They attempted to expose and document the injustices suffered by gay men and women. Through bibliographies, book reviews, and essays on history and literature, the publications filled an informational void and became valuable tools for self-education. They also had a more directly propagandizing goal, as the editors focused attention on whatever favorable developments occurred during the 1950s. Finally, the periodicals enabled gay men and lesbians to engage in dialogue among themselves. Through the pages of the gay press, subscribers articulated definitions of their experience, struggled toward new perceptions about their lives, and created an incipient sense of community.

ONE led the way in the exposure of police harassment of male homosexuals. With indignation and moral righteousness, it attacked the "flagrant infringement of civil rights" by "corrupt politicians and opportunistic demagogues" who posed as defenders of public morals.[4] Assisted by readers from around the country who sent clippings about police activities, James Kepner wrote detailed reports on the latest "witch hunts." Sweeps of public beaches in Miami, entrapment at burlesque theaters in Dallas, the closing of gay bars and house-to-house searches in Baltimore, citywide roundups of male homosexuals in Sioux City and Boise, and stories from countless other cities in every part of the United States regularly filled the pages of *ONE*.[5]

2. For the problems of publishing, see *ONE*, August 1955, p. 17; *Mattachine Review*, May 1956, pp. 23–26; and *Ladder*, October 1959, pp. 21–22, and November 1959, p. 19. On censorship in the postwar era, see Felice Flanery Lewis, *Literature, Obscenity and Law* (Carbondale, Ill., 1976); and William B. Lockhart and Robert C. McClure, "Literature, the Law of Obscenity, and the Constitution," *Minnesota Law Review* 38 (1954):295–395, and "Censorship of Obscenity: The Developing Constitutional Standards," *Minnesota Law Review* 45 (1960): 5–121. See also the discussion in Gay Talese, *Thy Neighbor's Wife* (New York, 1980), esp. chaps. 3–7.

3. Circulation figures for the entire period have proved difficult to come by. The figure for *ONE* is from the May 1954 issue, p. 2; the number for *Mattachine Review* (hereafter referred to as *MR*) is taken from "Minutes of Meeting of Daily Committee of Board of Directors," October 13, 1960, New York Mattachine Society Archives (hereafter NYMS); for the *Ladder* I have based my estimate on the fact that 500 questionnaires for their lesbian survey were sent to subscribers in June 1958 (see *Ladder*, September 1959, p. 4).

4. *ONE*, November 1954, p. 8.

5. On Miami, see "Miami Junks the Constitution," *ONE*, January 1954, pp. 16–21, and "Miami Hurricane," November 1954, pp. 4–8; on Dallas, November 1955, p. 8; on Baltimore,

Both the *Mattachine Review* and the *Ladder* approached the problem of police harassment with more restraint. In the case of the *Ladder*, lack of concern with entrapment and arrests in public places stemmed in part from the fact that lesbians rarely found themselves in such predicaments. But the caution with which both organizations tackled the area of law enforcement also reflected their conviction that they had to accommodate as much as possible to the status quo. Since laws in every state prohibited homosexual behavior, DOB and Mattachine avoided anything that smacked of advocating illegal activity.[6] Instead, their publications targeted the constraints placed on the right of homosexuals and lesbians to associate, especially police raiding of gay bars and the revocation of their liquor licenses. DOB's president, Del Martin, called the closing of gay taverns an unconstitutional infringement on the right of assembly and defended "the civil right of the homosexual to socialize." The *Mattachine Review*, emphasizing expediency rather than justice, argued that the shutdown of bars would only "increase the policing problem in the parks, on the streets, and in the public toilets" and suggested that it was preferable to keep patrons segregated in bars where they would offend "the least number of heterosexuals."[7]

The belief that ignorance and misinformation sustained a negative self-image among gay men and women impelled the editors of homophile publications to make their magazines unique educational resources. The *Ladder* featured a regular "Lesbiana" column—an annotated list of new and old books, fiction and nonfiction, with lesbian themes. Barbara Grier, a Kansas City resident who wrote under the pseudonym of Gene Damon, compiled a yearly survey of lesbian literature that summarized the contents of hardcover and paperback novels, evaluated changes in the portrayal of lesbians, and assessed trends in the publishing industry. With Marion Zimmer Bradley, a science fiction writer, she put together a bibliography of more than 500 titles that the *Ladder* made available to its readers. The *Mattachine Review* also produced a major bibliography with more than 1,000 entries. Eager to legitimate homosexuality as a significant and pervasive component of human experience, the magazines printed articles ranging from biographical portraits of literary figures such as Radclyffe Hall and Walt Whitman to explorations of homosexuality in European history and in non-Western cultures.[8]

April 1955, p. 15; on Sioux City, November 1955, p. 9; on Boise, January 1956, pp. 12–14. Kepner's articles often appeared under the pseudonyms of Lyn Pedersen or Dal McIntire. In Kepner's case the use of pseudonyms was not motivated by fear of exposure, since his name appeared in print frequently. The purpose, as he explained in an interview, was to conceal how few staff writers *ONE* had (interview with Kepner in Los Angeles, September 27, 1976).

6. See, e.g., "What Does Mattachine Do?" *MR*, April 1957, p. 22; and "What About the DOB?" *Ladder*, November 1959, p. 18.

7. Del Martin, "Editorial—the Gay Bar: Whose Problem Is It?" *Ladder*, December 1959, pp. 4–13; and Hal Call, "Why Perpetuate This Barbarism?" *MR*, June 1960, pp. 11–19.

8. For Damon's lesbian literature surveys, see *Ladder*, March 1958, p. 18; February 1960, pp. 14–15; and April 1961, pp. 12–13. For the lesbian bibliography, see *Ladder*, April 1960, p. 16. The first installment of the Mattachine bibliography appeared in *MR*, August 1957, pp. 24–29. See also

Movement leaders also used their publications in a directly propagandizing way by giving special prominence to the few positive developments occurring in the 1950s. When in 1955 the American Law Institute, a prestigious organization of jurists and attorneys, released a draft of a new model penal code that eliminated the sodomy statutes, the *Mattachine Review* praised its liberality. The *Ladder* congratulated the American Civil Liberties Union for the stand it took in 1957 against the denial of due process to homosexuals, even though the same policy statement upheld the constitutionality of statutes criminalizing homosexual behavior.[9] The magazines focused a great deal of attention on developments in England, where a series of homosexual scandals led to the formation in 1954 of a government committee to investigate the effect of the laws against homosexuality. The 1957 Wolfenden report recommendation to eliminate criminal penalties for private consensual acts between adults obtained scant coverage in the American press, but gay periodicals heralded it as a harbinger of a more humane future and a model for American legislators.[10] Lower court rulings in the United States upholding the right of bars to serve homosexuals and lesbians and overturning convictions in entrapment cases also received notice.[11] The editors discussed in detail the findings of research psychologist Evelyn Hooker, who produced during the 1950s a series of papers disputing the sickness theory of homosexuality.[12] Taken together,

---

Gene Damon, "Radclyffe Hall," *Ladder*, December 1959, pp. 8–9; David Russell and Dalvan McIntire [James Kepner], "In Paths Untrodden: A Study of Walt Whitman," *ONE*, July 1954, pp. 4–16; Philip Jason, "Homosexuals in a Related Culture: A Brief Investigation," *MR*, July 1958, pp. 8–10, and August 1958, pp. 9–11; and Lyn Pedersen [James Kepner], "England and the Vice of Sodom," *ONE*, May 1954, pp. 4–17. *MR* published three issues devoted solely to international events and literature: October 1956, October 1957, and November 1958.

9. On the American Law Institute's penal code, see *MR*, July–August 1955, p. 4, and November–December 1955, p. 2; and *ONE*, July 1955, p. 4. For the ALI's proposed revisions in the penal code, see American Law Institute, *Model Penal Code, Tentative Draft No. 4* (Philadelphia, 1955). On the ACLU, see *Ladder*, March 1957, pp. 8–9. For the text of the statement "Homosexuality and Civil Liberties," adopted by the ACLU board of directors on January 7, 1957, see *Civil Liberties*, March 1957, n.p.

10. Discussions of the Wolfenden report may be found in the *Ladder*, August 1957, p. 16; September 1957, pp. 16–17, November 1957, p. 21; and August 1958, p. 11. See also *MR*, November 1957, pp. 12–18; December 1957, pp. 19–31; January 1958, pp. 12–15; July 1958, pp. 5–7; and January 1959, pp. 4–12. The *Ladder* and *MR* contained more articles on the subject than are indexed in the *Readers's Guide to Periodical Literature*. For the full text of the recommendations, see *The Wolfenden Report: Report of the Committee on Homosexual Offenses and Prostitution*, authorized American ed. (New York, 1963), pp. 187–89. For an account of the English situation, see Jeffrey Weeks, *Coming Out: Homosexual Politics in Britain* (London, 1977), chaps. 14 and 15.

11. Martin, "The 'Gay' Bar: Whose Problem Is It?" and "Sequel to 'Gay' Bar Problem," *Ladder*, February 1960, pp. 5–9; and Mack Fingal, "Police May Not Incite to Crime," *MR*, December 1956, pp. 10–11. The court cases referred to are the following: on bars, Stoumen v. Reilly 234 P. 2d 969; Kershaw v. Department of Alcoholic Beverage Control 318 P. 2d 294; Nickola v. Munro 328 P. 2d 271; and Vallerga v. Department of Alcoholic Beverage Control 347 P. 2d 909, on entrapment, Guarro v. U.S. 116 A. 2d 408.

12. See Evelyn Hooker, "Adjustment of the Male Overt Homosexual," *MR*, December 1957, pp. 32–39, and January 1958, pp. 4–11; and "Value-Conflict and Value-Congruence of a

these made hardly a dent in the structure of oppression, but activists exploited them as much as possible with an eye toward impressing professionals who received the magazines and instilling hope among gay readers.

Above all, homophile publications allowed lesbians and homosexuals to find their own voices. In letters and articles contributors touched upon every aspect of their lives and expressed every imaginable point of view. They told stories about coming out and discussed relationships with lovers, friends, family members, and co-workers. As in the early Mattachine discussion groups, men and women speculated on the origins of their sexual proclivities, the causes of social hostility, and prospects for the future. Writers also tackled what they saw as the most controversial features of the gay world—male and female transvestism, stereotypical behavior, role-playing in relationships, marriages of convenience, and bar life. Each virulent attack on gay mores provoked someone to rise to the defense.

Interestingly, the debates that occurred in the *Ladder* and the *Mattachine Review* revealed a gulf separating the leaders of DOB and Mattachine from much of their potential membership. The officers of the two organizations used the journals to publicize their perspective. Again and again, they minimized the differences between heterosexuals and homosexuals, attempted to isolate the "deviant" members of the gay community from its "respectable" middle-class elements, stressed the responsibility of lesbians and gay men for their second-class status, and urged self-reformation. Del Martin, for instance, stated about the lesbian that "her only difference lies in her choice of a love partner"; Bob Bishop, who headed the Long Beach, California, chapter of Mattachine, asserted that gay men were basically indistinguishable from heterosexuals, "average people in all other respects outside of our private sexual inclinations." Mattachine president Ken Burns informed readers of the *Review* that "we must blame ourselves for much of our plight. When will the homosexual ever realize," he asked, "that social reform, to be effective, must be preceded by personal reform?" In a similar vein, editorials in the *Ladder* castigated lesbians who wore pants and kept their hair short, suggesting that they begin to do "a little 'policing' on their own." DOB took special pains to dissociate most lesbians from patrons of the bars. Gay women "aren't bar-hoppers," one officer declared, "but people with steady jobs, most of them good positions."[13]

Homosexual Group in a Heterosexual Society," *Ladder*, February 1960, p. 10. Hooker wrote prolifically, and her work was widely reprinted. See, e.g., "The Adjustment of the Male Overt Homosexual," *Journal of Projective Techniques* 21 (1957): 18–31, reprinted in Hendrik M. Ruitenbeek, ed., *The Problem of Homosexuality in Modern Society* (New York, 1963); "Male Homosexuality in the Rorschach," *Journal of Projective Techniques* 22 (1958): 33–54, reprinted in Murray H. Sherman, ed., *A Rorschach Reader* (New York, 1960); "A Preliminary Analysis of Group Behavior of Homosexuals," *Journal of Psychology* 42 (1956): 217–25; and "Homosexuality—Summary of Studies," in Evelyn M. and Sylvanus M. Duvall, eds., *Sex Ways in Fact and Faith: Basis for Christian Family Policy* (New York, 1961).

13. Bob Bishop, "Discard the Mask," *MR*, April 1958, p. 15; D. M., "The Positive Approach—Editorial," *Ladder*, November 1956, p. 9; Ken Burns, "The Homosexual Faces a

Many readers dissented from the views expressed by organizational leaders. Women objected strongly to the advice that they conform to conventional standards of female apparel. A lesbian couple from New York City who described themselves as "mild transvestites"—they wore pants in nonworking hours—called dresses, high heels, and stocking holders "uncomfortable contraptions men have invented to restrict the movements of women." One writer suggested that DOB would do better to campaign for equality of the sexes, so that women could wear whatever they wished. Others disagreed with the assertion that lesbians were to blame for the persecution they suffered. The black writer Lorraine Hansberry urged an end to the "lecturing . . . about how to appear acceptable to the dominant social group. . . . One is oppressed or discriminated against," she argued, "because one is different, not 'wrong' or 'bad.' "[14] Opinions contrary to those of the Mattachine leadership tended to get aired in *ONE* rather than in the *Review*. "The so-called 'gay life' is not for me to reform and I hesitate to define the 'very worst elements,' " a man from Nevada wrote. "If we must have a crusade it must be for civil rights and equality. . . . Getting all homosexuals to act like bourgeois gentlemen is not going to get those rights for me." Many others took issue with the criticism of stereotypical gay men. "When we are led by our life-long fear of being considered a sissy into contempt for effeminate homosexuals, we cease being able to respect ourselves," one man declared. Another deplored the tendency to "excommunicate any homosexual who belies the . . . thesis that we aren't different."[15]

Although the debates in homophile periodicals were superficially similar to debates between writers and subscribers in any magazine, in one crucial way they were different. The gay press of the 1950s was inventing a form of public discourse. As the only place where homosexuals and lesbians could express in print their attitudes about their sexuality, the magazines became a laboratory for experimenting with a novel kind of dialogue. The awkward phrasing that characterized much of what was published derived in part from the inability of contributors to draw upon a written tradition. In this respect it resembled the medical literature of the late nineteenth century, when doctors too were groping toward new ways of describing homosexuality. Despite the limited circulation of the magazines, they played a part in creating a common vocabulary. In evolving a shared language to articulate their experiences, gay men and women came a step closer to emerging as a self-conscious minority.

Challenge," *MR*, August 1956, p. 27; *Ladder*, November 1956, p. 4; June 1959, p. 25; and January 1957, p. 9.

14. See A. C., New York, letter, *Ladder*, July 1957, pp. 27–28; Barbara Stephens, "Transvestism—a Cross-Cultural Survey," *Ladder*, June 1957, p. 13; and L. H. N., New York City, letter, *Ladder*, May 1957, p. 27.

15. "Response to R. L. M., Reno, Nevada," *ONE*, September 1953, p. 12; "Response to R. L. M.," *ONE*, September 1953, p. 13; and Lyn Pedersen [James Kepner], "The Importance of Being Different," *ONE*, March 1954, pp. 4–6.

The pioneering effort to publish magazines about homosexuality brought the gay movement its only significant victory during the 1950s. In October 1954 the Los Angeles postmaster seized copies of *ONE* and refused to mail the magazine, on the grounds that it was "obscene, lewd, lascivious and filthy." The editors decided to contest the government's view. In 1956 a federal district judge sustained the postmaster's action, and the following year, an appeals court dealt *ONE* another blow when it characterized the magazine as "cheap pornography." But in January 1958 the United States Supreme Court unanimously reversed the findings of the lower courts. Although the justices did not issue a written opinion, *ONE* could reasonably claim that their action represented a "legal and publishing landmark." Activists inferred that the ruling sanctioned the discussion of homosexuality, and in fact homophile publications escaped any further legal action by postal authorities or local law enforcement agencies.[16]

II

The Mattachine Society and the Daughters of Bilitis made only minimal progress in their effort to establish chapters across the country. During the 1950s DOB added branches in New York, Los Angeles, Chicago, and, briefly, Rhode Island. Mattachine did somewhat better. Besides San Francisco and Los Angeles/Long Beach, groups formed in New York, Boston, Denver, Philadelphia, and for a time Detroit, Chicago, and Washington, D.C. Most chapters remained distressingly small in size and, except for California and New York, never exceeded a score of active participants. By 1960 membership in the Mattachine Society stood at a mere 230; in DOB, at only 110.[17]

The fear of exposure that kept homosexuals and lesbians from subscribing to homophile publications loomed even larger as an obstacle to joining either Mattachine or DOB. Reluctance to reveal one's sexual identity asserted itself at every stage of a chapter's life, inhibiting growth and activity. It took months for some groups even to obtain a mailing address, since, as a Chicago Mattachine member reported, "such a simple matter as the procuring of a post-office box under the name of the Society seems to us to threaten possible grave consequences." The Boston chapter of the society stumbled in contacting professionals because of the fear of unwittingly approaching a hostile individual. Members finally decided to post flyers outside psychology department offices at local universities and wait for someone to get in touch with them. The Mattachine group in Detroit never obtained public facilities for its meetings, even though one member was active in a congregation of the liberal Unitarian

16. For the offending contents, see *ONE*, October 1954, pp. 12, 18. For the full text of the Appeals Court decision, see *ONE*, March 1957, pp. 5–20. The Appeals Court decision may be found at 241 F. 2d 772. For the Supreme Court decision, see 355 U.S. 371. *ONE*'s brief before the Supreme Court may be found in *Homophile Studies* 1 (1958): 60–64.

17. "Minutes of Meeting of Daily Committee of Board of Directors," October 13, 1960, NYMS; and Jaye Bell (DOB president), "An Official Statement," *ONE*, April 1961, p. 10.

Church. He was unwilling to test the consequences of exposing his sexual preference by asking for the use of church space. Many members of chapters used aliases rather than have their own names on an organization's roster.[18]

Most DOB and Mattachine chapters remained inward looking and rarely moved beyond mutual support and self-education. Meetings usually consisted of a discussion, so that members might articulate in a safe environment their thoughts and feelings about their sexual identity. Sensitive to the difficulty of finding books in libraries and stores and to the qualms that often kept gays from requesting homosexual-related material, chapters assembled their own libraries. Sometimes members read and studied together. Every branch of DOB and Mattachine also published a newsletter. The size and quality varied considerably, from the two-page mimeos of the Chicago Mattachine and the Los Angeles DOB to the more elaborate, highly literate newsletter of the Denver Mattachine. The newsletter gave a sense of accomplishment to chapters that were often at a loss about what to do. A newsletter also offered the easiest way to let other gay men and lesbians know about the movement as well as to reach out to professionals.[19]

For those chapters with the courage and numbers to venture into the world, the national leadership of DOB and Mattachine in San Francisco offered clear guidelines for action. Homosexuals and lesbians, they reasoned, lacked the credibility and the strength to campaign for equality on their own behalf; gays needed to find allies who would speak for them and serve as a buffer between a hostile society and the gay minority in its midst. Given its conviction that the professional community held the key to social change, the movement searched for sympathetic doctors, lawyers, ministers, social workers, and public health officials.

The belief that the support of experts was necessary to legitimate the movement's aims often led homophile groups into encounters with individuals who harbored some of society's most negative attitudes toward homosexuality. A minister who addressed the Chicago Mattachine in 1955, for instance, told his audience that "homosexuality is not part of God's plan for man" and that "no homosexual who persists in following his desires can achieve ultimate peace." In San Francisco, DOB members listened as a local therapist, Basil Vaerlen, informed them that "the true biological function of the female is to have children." By denying herself this role, he said, "the Lesbian is unfulfilled and is hampering her health and happiness." Mattachine officers in New

18. On Chicago, see Robert Kirk, "Report of Chicago Area Council to Mattachine Convention," May 1954, personal papers of James Kepner, Los Angeles. See also Curtis Dewees to Ralph Gillies, January 14, 1958; and Hal Lawson to Dewees, October 27, 1958, both in NYMS.

19. For examples of discussion topics and chapter libraries, see Chicago Mattachine *Newsletter*, July 20, 1954, pp. 2–3, and May 31, 1955, p. 4. See also *Ladder*, October 1956, p. 9; April 1957, p. 9; and November 1957, pp. 4–7; *MR*, May 1956, p. 10; Denver Mattachine *Newsletter*, June 1959, p. 1; and October 1958, p. 5; Boston Mattachine *Newsletter*, June 1958, n.p., and May 1959, n.p.; and Lawson to Dewees, October 27, 1958, NYMS.

York, awed by the stature of psychoanalyst Richard Robertiello, were delighted to have him address one of their monthly meetings, despite his well-known advocacy of the sickness theory of homosexuality. And in fact he lectured that homosexuality was "an emotional disturbance, . . . a character defense," in which the patient often did not recognize that he was sick.[20]

However, local chapters did eventually uncover professionals who became allies of the movement. Evelyn Hooker spoke before DOB and Mattachine chapters when her work required her to travel. At professional conventions she informed colleagues of the existence of homophile organizations and put chapters in touch with sympathetic psychologists. Wardell Pomeroy, a New York–based sex therapist who had worked on the ground-breaking Kinsey studies, also supported the movement's educational efforts. In San Francisco Blanche Baker, a local psychiatrist, addressed the groups frequently and put forward a strong, unambiguous message: "Stop despising yourselves, stop being ashamed," she said. "Learn to take out your resentments on those responsible for them. Otherwise you will eventually take them out on yourself." Baker aided the San Francisco groups by arranging a meeting for them with some thirty of her professional acquaintances.[21]

There were others, too: in San Francisco, Ernest Besig and Albert Bendich of the Northern California Civil Liberties Union and John O'Connell and Phillip Burton of the California state assembly; in Chicago, attorney Pearl Hart, who composed for the Mattachine chapter a brochure on the legal rights of homosexuals in case of arrest; in Denver, William Reynard, a board member of the Colorado ACLU, and Robert Allen, majority leader of the Colorado house of representatives; in New York, George Rundquist of the New York Civil Liberties Union and Donal Macnamara, dean of the New York Institute of Criminology. Although the number of such professionals remained small during the 1950s, local chapters were slowly accumulating allies who later, when the movement grew stronger, would contribute to the emancipation struggle of gay men and women.[22]

20. Chicago Mattachine *Newsletter*, April 1955, n.p.; *Ladder*, January 1957, p. 5; *MR*, June 1960, pp. 4–6. In announcing Robertiello as an upcoming speaker, the New York Mattachine billed the event as "a sign, we feel, of the progress we have made and the professional recognition we are receiving. . . . We know you will find him to be an extremely sympathetic and perceptive man, who makes a serious attempt to understand and aid the homosexual" (NYMS *Newsletter*, December 1959, p. 3). Robertiello was the author of *Voyage from Lesbos: The Psychoanalysis of a Female Homosexual* (New York, 1959). The book was a detailed examination of the psychoanalysis of a lesbian who, as the title suggests, was "cured."

21. See Chicago Mattachine *Newsletter*, August 24, 1954, p. 1; San Francisco Mattachine *Newsletter*, August 1955, n.p.; NYMS *Newsletter*, October 1958, p. 5. The quote from Baker is in the *Ladder*, May 1957, pp. 6–7.

22. See San Francisco Mattachine *Newsletter*, July 1956, n.p.; *Ladder*, July 1960, pp. 12–14, and October 1960, p. 16; *MR*, May–June 1955, pp. 36–37, and May 1956, pp. 7–8; Chicago Mattachine *Newsletter*, March 26, 1960, n.p.; Denver Mattachine *Newsletter*, October 1959, pp. 8–9; and "New York Mattachine Lectures, 1957–1959," Mattachine New York file, Institute for Sex Research, Bloomington, Ind.

One invaluable service that even a few professionals could perform was to accept referrals from homophile organizations. Many men and women urgently required ministers who would provide them solace and guidance and mental health workers who were more interested in their clients' self-acceptance than in promoting "cures." Lesbian mothers wanted advice on child rearing, and gay men often needed doctors to treat cases of venereal disease in confidence, as well as lawyers who would not charge exorbitant fees in cases of entrapment. Mattachine and DOB sought out such individuals and referred men and women to them in times of crisis.[23]

Beyond these ameliorative social service efforts, homophile groups eagerly promoted themselves as material for research. Having accepted the authority of scientists to make pronouncements about homosexuality, they encouraged medical and social scientists to use their membership to study "sexual deviance." Except for Evelyn Hooker, however, no one of stature accepted their offer. Frustrated by the lack of response, DOB decided to undertake its own study—not because it felt qualified to do research but because it believed that even an amateurish effort would reveal the rich possibilities that its membership offered to professionals. Florence Conrad prepared an extensive questionnaire that was sent to *Ladder* subscribers and Mattachine members. But the survey data failed to elicit any interest from professionals.[24]

In other minor ways, homophile chapters during the 1950s made some small advances in their quest for legitimacy. In Boston, New York, and San Francisco, meetings were held in public rented facilities rather than members' homes. ONE, Inc., in Los Angeles, DOB in San Francisco, and Mattachine in San Francisco and New York maintained offices and telephones. The frequent requests for information, assistance, and a friendly ear and a bit of consolation seemed to prove the value of even the most limited visibility. Similarly, the few radio spots secured by the New York and San Francisco Mattachine chapters led to phone calls, letters, and visits to their offices in the days following each broadcast. But visibility came too infrequently to achieve significant effects, and what it did accomplish had more to do with social welfare work than with political reform.[25]

23. On referrals, see Denver Mattachine *Newsletter*, November 1959, p. 12; *Ladder*, March 1959, p. 5; and *MR*, February 1959, pp. 27–28.

24. On contacts with professionals interested in research, see *MR*, January–February 1955, p. 16; and Denver Mattachine *Newsletter*, July 1959, p. 6. One article that was published in part because of the assistance rendered by Mattachine is Brenda A. Dickey, "Attitudes Toward Sex Roles and Feelings of Adequacy in Homosexual Males," *Journal of Consulting Psychology* 25 (1961): 116–22. The results of the lesbian survey were published as a special issue of the *Ladder*, September 1959; the male homosexual survey may be found in the *Ladder*, September 1960.

25. *ONE*, November 1953, p. 23; *MR*, May 1956, p. 8; August 1957, p. 14; April 1958, pp. 24–25; and December 1958, p. 27; Boston Mattachine *Newsletter*, May 1958, n.p.; *Ladder*, February 1957, p. 1; and January 1959, pp. 7–14; Denver Mattachine *Newsletter*, April 1959, n.p., Detroit Mattachine *Newsletter*, October 1959, n.p.

III

The small size and minimal accomplishments of local chapters gave special importance to the annual gatherings of gay activists. ONE held a midwinter institute each January, the Mattachine Society a yearly convention, and DOB a biennial general assembly initiated in 1960. Members of all the organizations attended each other's events. Movement participants judged that the benefits of the gatherings justified the traveling expenses. Tiny chapters with only a few members gained confidence from contact with the rest of the organization. In mimicking the rituals of mainstream voluntary associations, those in attendance gave themselves comforting proof of their own legitimacy. Respectably dressed in their best attire, delegates sat through keynote speeches, award banquets for distinguished service, elections of new officers, and debates over constitutional revisions. The organizations rented hotel space, placed ads in local newspapers, listed the events with convention bureaus, catered meals, and printed programs available to onlookers—assertions of the right to associate in public which the movement perceived as setting precedents.[26]

The Mattachine Society's 1959 convention illustrates the value of these gatherings as well as the dangers posed by even limited visibility. Held in Denver over the Labor Day weekend, it marked the only time that a convention took place outside of California or New York. The movement made breakthroughs in both publicity and the stature of the speakers, but it also experienced its most serious external attack.

"Carl Harding" was the moving spirit behind the Denver chapter. Born and raised in a small Wyoming town, the red-haired, slightly built, thirty-three-year-old Harding was working for a welfare agency in Denver in 1953 when he came across a copy of *ONE* magazine. An article about the Mattachine Society impelled him to relocate in the San Francisco area, where he landed a job as a social worker in Oakland. Fired a few months later when his superiors discovered his homosexuality, Harding remained in San Francisco to work with the Mattachine Society, and he wrote frequently for the *Review*. In the summer of 1956 he returned to Denver, began teaching in one of its suburban public schools, and with the help of two long-time friends, "Rolland Howard" and "Harley Beckman," founded a chapter of the society.[27]

During the summer of 1958 Harding suggested that Mattachine hold its next convention in Denver, and at the September gathering in New York the membership eagerly approved the request. The Denver chapter quickly began

26. For accounts of the annual gatherings, see *Ladder*, September 1957, pp. 3–14; October 1958, pp. 6–10; March 1959, pp. 4–20; October 1959, pp. 5–20; March 1960, pp. 5–9; and July 1960, pp. 6–20. See also *MR*, May 1956 issue; September 1957, pp. 5–14; and September 1960, pp. 10–14.

27. Biographical information on Harding comes from the Denver *Post*, February 17, 1965, p. 50; and Elver Barker to author, January 9, 1977. "Harding" was the pseudonym used by Barker in his Mattachine activities.

its preparations, taking advantage of the convention as an excuse to contact professionals. Letters went out to 112 potential speakers in the Denver area, and the chapter eventually secured commitments from Robert Allen, majority leader in the Colorado state assembly, and William Reynard, a member of the board of directors of the Colorado ACLU.[28]

With Allen and Reynard as drawing cards, Harding proposed a "radical" approach to publicity for the convention. Calling previous efforts "a farce," he challenged Mattachine officers to approve "certain steps some members have feared to take in the past." Harding suggested holding a public press conference during the convention, in which officers would be photographed and interviewed under their own names. "When are we going to stop fearing our own fears?" he asked. "Granted there is an element of risk involved . . . but if we really believe in our cause, then shouldn't we be willing to take that risk? . . . Denver is a modern, progressive city," he concluded, "and can take it!"[29]

Harding's proposals won approbation, and his assertiveness paid off. The convention received excellent coverage in the Denver *Post*, with three articles that quoted from participants at length and treated the homophile movement fairly and seriously. The publicity brought many new faces to the convention and a jump in membership in the following days. Activists recognized the significance of the achievement. "Mattachine Breaks Through the Conspiracy of Silence," a *Ladder* article headlined, and the New York Mattachine newsletter glowingly reported that the "Sixth Annual Convention Makes Mattachine History."[30]

A few weeks later, however, a somber mood took hold as the movement had its worst fears confirmed. The Denver newsletter had humorously reported the presence of "two burly gentlemen" at the convention's opening session who "proved to be just what they looked like—morals officers." The police listened quietly as majority leader Robert Allen described the vice squad as "all too often the most ignorant" in matters of sexual behavior. On October 9 the police struck back and raided the homes of Harding, Bill Matson, the librarian for the Denver chapter, and another member. In Matson's case they found photos of male nudes and promptly arrested him for violating a local antipornography statute. The following day the *Post* carried a story that prominently mentioned Matson's Mattachine connection, the confiscation of mailing lists found in his apartment, and his place of employment. Matson lost his job at a local hospital, served sixty days in jail, and eventually had to leave

28. Harding to Joe McCarthy, July 30, 1958, NYMS; Denver Mattachine *Newsletter*, August 1959, p. 2.

29. Harding to members of the board of directors of the Mattachine Society, June 11, 1959, NYMS; the responses to Harding's letters may be found in the Denver *Newsletter*, August 1959, pp. 6–8.

30. Denver *Post*, September 4, 1959, p. 32; September 5, p. 3; September 6, p. 8; Denver Mattachine *Newsletter*, September 1959, p. 7; *Ladder*, October 1959, p. 5; and NYMS *Newsletter*, October 1959, p. 4.

Denver in order to find new work. Another Mattachine member employed at the same hospital quietly resigned on the advice of his supervisor rather than be fired and have his sexual orientation exposed. Harding tried to reassure members, but the police seizure of names and addresses from Matson's residence sent many men scurrying for cover. Harding acknowledged that "a wave of fear" swept over the membership and that several individuals had "broken contact with the organization." On the verge of expansion after the success of the convention, the Denver chapter instead stagnated and never regained its momentum.[31]

While the Denver chapter coped with its crisis, events in San Francisco were taking a rather bizarre twist. On October 7, 1959, the San Francisco *Progress*, a weekly neighborhood newspaper, carried a front-page banner headline warning that "Sex Deviates Make San Francisco Headquarters." The story featured accusations by Russell Wolden, who was challenging Mayor George Christopher in the upcoming election. According to Wolden, under Christopher the Mattachine Society had made San Francisco "the national headquarters of the organized homosexuals in the United States." It is "a sordid tale," the paper reported. "Homosexualism has been allowed to flourish to a shocking extent, and under shocking circumstances." The story described luridly how "the number of sex deviates in this city has soared by the thousands . . . while other communities in this area have virtually eliminated them." Gay bars had proliferated to the point where "no neighborhood is immune." Under the Christopher administration, Wolden charged, "this unsavory wicked situation is allowed to fester and spread like a cancerous growth on the body of San Francisco."[32]

Although Wolden expected to inject momentum into his own campaign and to discredit his opponent with the charges, he soon came to regret the whole affair. Over the next week, San Francisco's three dailies covered the story in detail and roundly condemned Wolden for stooping to such tactics. In dramatic front page editorials, the *Chronicle* and the *News-Call-Bulletin* both called on Wolden to withdraw from the race, the former declaring that Wolden had put himself "beyond the pale of decent politics." As it turned out, Christopher trounced Wolden in the November election.[33]

As one of the few instances during the 1950s when homosexuality became a major local political issue, the whole affair offers revealing insights into attitudes toward "sexual deviates." The San Francisco press criticized Wolden not because he had attacked a persecuted minority but because, as the *Exam-*

31. The quotes are from the Denver Mattachine *Newsletter*, October 1959, p. 3, and November 1959, p. 12. Accounts of the arrest and its aftermath may be found in the Denver *Post*, October 10, 1959, p. 3, and October 13, p. 37; in the Denver Mattachine *Newsletter*, October 1959, p. 2, and November 1959, p. 6; and in Barker to author, January 9, 1977.

32. San Francisco *Progress*, October 7, 1959.

33. For coverage by San Francisco dailies, see *News-Call-Bulletin*, the *Examiner*, and the *Chronicle*, for October 9, 1959, and the days that followed.

iner put it, he had "stigmatized the city" by suggesting that it tolerated such life-styles. When Wolden repeated the charges on the radio, the *News-Call-Bulletin* labeled the speech "the most distasteful pottage of slime, innuendo, and falsehood ever cooked up and piped into San Francisco homes." In an editorial the paper declared, "His wild charge that a moral offender finds easy tolerance in San Francisco is a resort to the extremes of irresponsible demagoguery and an affront to the truth. . . . He has insulted San Francisco." The *Chronicle*, too, called the charge "preposterous" and said that the candidate had "degraded the good name of San Francisco."[34]

For the Mattachine Society and the Daughters of Bilitis in San Francisco, the unexpected controversy had positive results. The Christopher administration did not want to give credence to the charges of a homosexual menace, so it left the organizations alone and made no attempt at the time to round up homosexuals in a cleanup campaign. On the other hand, the affair generated more publicity for the movement than it had received in all its previous years. With such a barrage of headlines and editorials, it is doubtful that many gay men and women in San Francisco remained ignorant of the movement's existence. As in other cases, visibility led to a rash of phone calls and letters requesting information.

However, if the particular circumstances of the affair allowed the San Francisco chapters, unlike the Denver Mattachine, to escape harmful repercussions from the publicity, the same could not be said elsewhere. The sudden visibility provoked panic among Detroit Mattachine members. Hal Lawson, who chaired the local chapter, wrote New York member Curtis Dewees that he was resigning from the organization "because things are too hot right now, and I value my new job." Lawson had also been intending to reactivate the moribund Chicago chapter, but of those plans he now said, "You can count me out." In January 1960 the Detroit group suspended operations and never became reactivated. Visibility, though a basic movement objective, was obviously a two-edged sword.[35]

IV

Almost a decade after the founding of the Mattachine Society, gay activists still had few achievements to encourage them. True, the movement had survived its birth pangs, and the organizational impulse had spread beyond its place of origin in southern California. Three monthly magazines and several newsletters gave expression to the movement's views, while the Supreme Court had sustained the right to publish material about homosexuality. The movement had also established contact with some liberal professionals. But the paucity of membership in DOB and Mattachine mocked their claim that they spoke for

34. *Examiner*, October 10, 1959; *Chronicle*, October 10, 1959; *News-Call-Bulletin*, October 9, 1959.

35. Lawson to Dewees, November 5, 1959, NYMS; and Detroit Mattachine *Newsletter*, January 1960, pp. 2–4.

America's second largest minority. By 1960, the homophile movement remained at best marginal to the lives of homosexuals and lesbians. It had failed to mobilize a constituency and had made virtually no progress toward its minimal goal of opening a dialogue about social attitudes and public policy toward gay men and women.

Failure among the tiny band of activists engendered internecine warfare that further weakened the already fragile condition of the movement. ONE, Inc., and DOB traded insults over the topic of ONE's January 1961 midwinter institute, "A Homosexual Bill of Rights." Del Martin attacked it as implying "a demanding attitude toward society" and accused ONE of exploiting "the subject of injustice to and prejudice against the homosexual *ad infinitum* and *ad nauseam.*" Dorr Legg, editor of *ONE* magazine, responded by calling lesbians "brainwashed" and DOB "so narrowly focused an in-group" that its members lacked understanding of "the brutal realities" of police harassment and job bias that male homosexuals faced. By the time the dust settled, the women who had made *ONE* a co-sexual magazine had departed, and DOB and ONE, Inc., preserved only the most minimal contact.[36]

Meanwhile, factionalism within the Mattachine Society provoked the dissolution of the organization's national structure, as a simmering rivalry between the New York and San Francisco chapters finally boiled over. By 1960 the New York group had surpassed San Francisco as the largest of the society's chapters. The New Yorkers resented the fact that their membership dues disappeared into the national office, and frustration led them to accuse organization officers Hal Call and Don Lucas of fiscal irregularities. At the September 1960 Mattachine convention in San Francisco, charges flew back and forth. Finally, in March 1961 an exasperated Call persuaded a majority of the national board to dissolve the organization, leaving each chapter to fend for itself, with the San Francisco group in charge of the *Review*. However, local branches had drawn strength from their connection to a larger organization. With that taken away, the Boston and Denver groups collapsed, the Chicago chapter limped along, and the Philadelphia group reorganized itself as the Janus Society. The New York Mattachine, ignoring demands from San Francisco that it change its name, went its own way as an independent organization.[37]

Why, after several years of hard, persistent work, did the homophile movement remain so weak that it indulged in self-defeating conflict? Above

36. Del Martin, "Editorial—How Far Out Can We Go?" *Ladder*, January 1961, pp. 4–5; W. Dorr Legg, "ONE Midwinter Institute: A Report," *ONE*, April 1961, p. 7; interview with Sten Russell, October 24, 1976, in Costa Mesa, Calif. See also "Homosexual Bill of Rights Sizzles and Fizzles," *Ladder*, March 1961, pp. 8–26.

37. See *MR*, August 1961, pp. 26–27, for a description of the board's action and its rationale. On the conflict at the 1960 convention, see Dewees to Lawson, May 12, 1960, NYMS; "Minutes of Meeting of Mattachine Board of Directors," September 5, 1960, NYMS; *Interim*, October 25, 1960, p. 8; and Ralph Trask, "Factionalism Is Not the Answer," Boston Mattachine *Newsletter*, February 1961, n.p.

all, the explanation must be sought in external constraints, in the social conditions in which homosexuals and lesbians lived and the movement operated. From local police harassment to job discrimination, gay men and women faced severe penalties if their sexual identities became known. Anxieties about discovery inhibited them from joining gay organizations. Membership in a homophile group increased the chance of exposure while offering seemingly little in the way of compensation. The best efforts of a few courageous activists could not overcome this terror.

The fear that kept homosexuals and lesbians out of the movement was not unwarranted. During the 1950s the FBI engaged in widespread surveillance of the gay world. Not only did it collect from local vice squads the names of men arrested on homosexual morals charges; it also placed a watch on gay bars and infiltrated the Mattachine Society and the Daughters of Bilitis. Informants provided the FBI with organizational documents, transmitted the names of members, and reported on meetings and other activities. The post office, too, engaged in covert activities against gay men. Whether the FBI harassed members of the homophile movement remains unknown, but it did use the information it amassed to keep homosexuals and lesbians out of federal jobs, while postal officials revealed to some employers the homosexual identity of workers.[38]

A decision to participate in the movement also implied that individuals had rejected, at least in part, the society's dominant attitude toward same-sex eroticism. But antihomosexualism pervaded American culture, and it infected the consciousness of gay men and women no less than heterosexuals. Homosexuals and lesbians absorbed views of themselves as immoral, depraved, and pathological individuals; many accepted harassment and punishment as well deserved. Such a self-image would hardly propel men and women into a cause that required group solidarity and the affirmation of their sexuality, nor would it encourage them to entertain the idea that their efforts might create a brighter future.

However, part of the responsibility for the movement's ineffectiveness must rest with the leaders of the Mattachine Society and the Daughters of Bilitis. Although in one way they had scorned their own fears by taking part in the movement, they still harbored anxieties and had internalized a belief in their own inferiority. As Del Martin and Phyllis Lyon recalled in an interview,

> It wasn't until [much later] that we realized we knew a whole lot more about homosexuality than Joe Psychiatrist and Joe Lawyer. Back then we didn't know. We needed support. We needed support from the establish-

---

38. On FBI and post office surveillance of gays and their meeting places, see above, chap. 3. Information on FBI surveillance of the homophile movement may be found in FBI file nos. 94–834, 94–283, 94–1001, 100–37394, and 100–45888, obtained under the Freedom of Information Act. I am indebted to Bill Hartmann of San Francisco for supplying me with copies of these documents.

ment, from heterosexuals. We were at a point where [we asked] how *we* could be the ones to deal with the public. If you could only understand the fear! You just can't begin to realize the fear that was involved and how scared we were. And we [the leadership] were just as scared as everybody else.[39]

Fear, along with the lack of confidence in their own ability to speak with authority about homosexuality, created a crippling dependency. In their search for allies and their quest for legitimacy in the eyes of the establishment, movement leaders often bowed to an apparently superior professional wisdom that was part of the problem they needed to confront. It led them to open their publications to articles classing homosexuals with rapists, child molesters, and exhibitionists as sexual psychopaths, articles arguing that homosexuals were "almost invariably neurotic or psychotic" and advising gays at least to "*try* to get cured."[40]

Fear also blocked the movement from taking action. Thus, when a Boston Mattachine member, Prescott Townsend, suggested that his chapter might work for the repeal of Massachusetts's sodomy statute, Don Lucas vetoed the proposal because of the alleged danger involved. During the summer of 1958 Randy Wicker, a white student active in the civil rights movement in the South, came to New York and attended Mattachine meetings. Wicker printed posters announcing a Mattachine lecture and distributed them to shops in Greenwich Village and on Manhattan's West Side. The publicity attracted an audience of 300 to the lecture, triple the usual number. But when Wicker returned to school in the fall, no one else would risk making the rounds of neighborhood stores.[41]

Finally, the movement took upon itself an impossible burden—appearing respectable to a society that defined homosexuality as beyond respectability. In trying to accommodate social mores, DOB and Mattachine often reflected back to their potential constituency some of society's most condemnatory attitudes. Their criticisms of the bars and the gay subculture undoubtedly alienated many of the men and women with the strongest commitment to gay life. If fear kept most homosexuals and lesbians away from the movement, contempt for its seeming acceptance of a negative view of the gay world may well have turned off the rest.

39. Interview with Del Martin and Phyllis Lyon in San Francisco, November 19, 1976.

40. James Phelan, "Sex Variants Find Their Own Answers," *MR*, September–October 1955, pp. 15–17; *Ladder*, February 1959, p. 8; and Kenneth Fink, "The Psychodynamics of the Homosexual," *MR*, July 1960, p. 11. For other examples, see *Ladder*, November 1956, p. 4, and October 1958, p. 15; and *MR*, November–December 1955, p. 7, and February 1956, p. 15.

41. Lucas to Townsend, December 15, 1959, NYMS. Dewees expressed an essentially similar position in a letter to Townsend on December 7, 1959, NYMS. On Wicker's publicity effort, see NYMS *Newsletter*, September 1958, p. 4.

3

The 1960s:
Civil Rights and the
Pursuit of Equality

EIGHT

Gay Life in
the Public Eye

As long as the ideological configuration of sin, sickness, and crime retained its dominance, homophile activists fought a losing battle. Any claims that gay men and women formed an unjustly persecuted minority lacked the persuasive power to mobilize a constituency or to alter the conditions of gay life. On one side, the prevailing view of homosexuals and lesbians as essentially flawed individuals, responsible for their predicament, inhibited the development of a group consciousness. On the other, it justified the penalties attached to homosexual behavior and reinforced the tendency to keep any discussion of it within narrow parameters. Without a mass movement, the prospects of a significant improvement in the status of gay men and women appeared dim, and yet without a change in the social perception and understanding of same-gender sexuality, a mass movement had little chance of developing.

During the 1960s a noticeable shift took place in both the sheer quantity of discourse about homosexuality and lesbianism and the social interpretation of the phenomenon. The reticence that activists of the 1950s characterized as a conspiracy of silence yielded to a fascination with this exotic, unexplored realm of American society. In pornography, literature, and the mass media, portrayals of gay life multiplied. And with the growing volume of material came new angles of vision. A significant minority of opinion began to view lesbians and homosexuals not as isolated, aberrant individuals but as members of a group.

I

Until the 1950s, a Victorian heritage of law and social custom largely governed the sexual content of the literature available to Americans. Prodded by

Anthony Comstock, a lobbyist for the YMCA, in 1873 Congress prohibited the importation and mailing of lewd, lascivious, or obscene materials. Over the next half century, many municipalities and all but one state adopted laws restricting the production, distribution, and sale of obscene literature. In their rulings on obscenity, the courts adopted the standard enunciated in *Queen v. Hicklin*, an 1868 English case: "The test of obscenity is this, whether the tendency of the matter . . . is to deprave and corrupt those whose minds are open to such immoral influences." As late as the 1930s, most American judges based their decisions on whether isolated passages of a book might adversely affect groups in the population, such as the young, who were considered most receptive to pernicious influences.[1]

The efforts of citizens' groups supplemented the work of local police and the federal government in enforcing the obscenity statutes. In the same year that Congress adopted Comstock's proposal, the moral crusader founded the New York Society for the Suppression of Vice, and the state legislature endowed the organization with the power to inspect bookstores and make arrests. Boston had its Watch and Ward Society, while Chicago citizens formed the Law and Order League to guard against allegedly obscene material. Censorship forces in the late nineteenth and early twentieth centuries targeted not only contemporary pornography but also Greek, Roman, and Renaissance classics; marriage manuals; pamphlets about birth control; and other forms of sex education literature. Since New York and Boston were the centers of the publishing trade, anti-obscenity groups in those cities wielded an influence out of proportion to their size.[2]

The vigor with which obscenity laws were enforced encouraged self-censorship. Although some book dealers and publishers challenged their convictions under the statutes, most preferred to avoid trouble. For book dealers, the cost of an appeal could easily mean bankruptcy. Wisdom dictated that they quietly pay their fines and exercise discretion in the future. Publishers commonly rejected sexually suggestive manuscripts or insisted that authors tidy up their texts to avoid the censor's wrath. With the rise of film and photography in the twentieth century, such informal self-regulating procedures spread. Hollywood responded to external pressure by setting up its own production code in the 1930s, while corporations such as Eastman Kodak exhibited caution in accepting film for processing.[3]

1. Hicklin quoted in Robert W. Haney, *Comstockery in America: Patterns of Censorship and Control* (Boston, 1960), p. 16; see also James C. N. Paul and Murray L. Schwartz, *Federal Censorship: Obscenity in the Mail* (New York, 1961), pp. 18–24; Charles Rembar, *The End of Obscenity: The Trials of "Lady Chatterley," "Tropic of Cancer" and "Fanny Hill"* (New York, 1968), pp. 17–22; and Felice Flanery Lewis, *Literature, Obscenity and Law* (Carbondale, Ill., 1976), pp.7–12.

2. Haney, *Comstockery in America*, pp. 22–23; Rembar, *The End of Obscenity*, pp. 21–22; and Gay Talese, *Thy Neighbor's Wife* (New York, 1980; Bantam ed.), pp. 71–81.

3. Lewis, *Literature, Obscenity and Law*, pp. 68, 102, 136; Paul and Schwartz, *Federal Censorship*, p. 108; and Haney, *Comstockery in America*, pp. 111–16.

However, beginning in the 1930s, judicial opinions slowly narrowed the operation of obscenity laws. In 1934 a federal appellate court for the first time explicitly rejected the *Hicklin* rationale. In a case involving James Joyce's *Ulysses*, Judge Augustus Hand ruled that the dominant theme of the work as a whole, not particular passages, should determine the obscenity of a book. Twelve years later, the Supreme Court invalidated the action of the postmaster general who had revoked second-class mailing privileges for *Esquire*, a slick men's magazine considered salacious by many at the time. Other appellate decisions of the 1940s and early 1950s reversed convictions on obscenity charges. The Bureau of Customs, more than the post office, responded by pursuing a less restrictive enforcement policy. Though customs officials still seized some contemporary works, they generally avoided the confiscation of classics.[4]

Despite these changes, support for censorship remained strong, as a new set of organizations replaced the moribund ones of the Victorian era. During the 1930s the Catholic church established the Legion of Decency to evaluate movies and the National Office for Decent Literature to pass judgment on books, magazines, and comics. Both groups amassed considerable power and welded successful alliances with Protestant and secular proponents of censorship. One critic described the result as "a system of interlocking directorates" in the anti-obscenity field. NODL's list of proscribed literature in the 1950s included *Ten North Frederick*, *The Blackboard Jungle*, *Catcher in the Rye*, *From Here to Eternity*, *Tobacco Road*, and *The Naked and the Dead*. Investigations of the pornography industry by the House and Senate in the mid-1950s added grist to the book banners' mill. Local censorship groups in the postwar era picketed newsstands and bookstores, while many urban vice squads exhibited considerable zeal in their enforcement of municipal statutes. Moreover, court decisions revealed a lack of consensus on the definition of obscenity, and many judges continued to apply the standards of an earlier era. As a result, a haphazard pattern of enforcement developed, perpetuating confusion among publishers and book dealers.[5]

Homosexuality was a special target of censorship forces. Surfacing prominently as a theme in literature in the years after World War I, it almost invariably provoked legal action. In the 1920s plays dealing with lesbianism, such as *The Captive* and *The God of Vengeance*, were driven from the New York stage despite their condemnatory point of view. Book dealers suffered reprisals for selling such material. "The most casual reference" to same-gender love, one study concluded, "could trigger an extreme reaction." The favorable

4. United States v. One Book Entitled Ulysses, 5 F. Suppl. 182 (S.D. N.Y. 1933), affirmed 72 F. 2d 705 (2d Circ. 1934); Hannegan v. Esquire, 327 U.S. 146 (1946); Paul and Schwartz, *Federal Censorship*, pp. 69–84; and Lewis, *Literature, Obscenity and Law*, p. 44.

5. Haney, *Comstockery in America*, pp. 87–91, 116–21; Paul and Schwartz, *Federal Censorship*, pp. 85–104; Lewis, *Literature, Obscenity and Law*, pp. 135–36, 158–61; and Talese, *Thy Neighbor's Wife*, pp. 62, 86–88, 148.

court decision in the *Well of Loneliness* trial in 1929 was exceptional. As late as 1954 a Louisiana appeals court upheld a ban on Mark Tryon's novel, *Sweeter than Life*, because it graphically described lesbian eroticism, while NODL's list of obscene literature included *The Well of Loneliness* and *Tea and Sympathy*. In 1934 the motion picture production code prohibited any depiction of homosexuality in films. When its administrators finally revised the code in 1956, the new version still specified that "sex perversion or any inference of it is forbidden."[6]

In June 1957 the Supreme Court confronted the obscenity issue squarely for the first time. In the case of Sam Roth, a dealer in erotica who had suffered imprisonment in the 1930s for selling novels like *Ulysses* and *Lady Chatterley's Lover*, the court tackled the constitutional question of whether the First Amendment shielded obscene literature from censorship. Sustaining Roth's conviction, Justice William Brennan unequivocally stated the majority opinion: "We hold that obscenity is not within the area of constitutionally protected speech or press." The court attempted, too, to give some semblance of clarity to a definition of obscenity. "Sex and obscenity are not synonymous," Brennan wrote. "Obscene material is material which deals with sex in a manner appealing to prurient interest." The court substituted a standard different from *Hicklin*: "whether to the average person, applying contemporary standards, the dominant theme of the material taken as a whole appeals to prurient interest."[7]

Although the *Roth* decision appeared to support the forces favoring censorship, it proved in retrospect to be a pyrrhic victory. Over the next ten years an array of cases involving pornographic classics, erotic films, contemporary fiction, pulp novels and nude photo magazines reached the Supreme Court. The obscenity issue split the Warren Court to a greater extent than any other problem in constitutional law. The justices rarely reached unanimity, and many cases produced several conflicting opinions among the court. But in passing judgment the Supreme Court effected a revolution in the sexual content of material available to the average American even while denying obscenity the protection of the First Amendment.

The high court's decisions progressively contracted the scope of the obscenity statutes until it appeared that nothing warranted the label. In 1959 the court overturned the conviction of a Los Angeles book dealer on the grounds that the police must prove that he had knowledge of the contents of the book. That same year the justices reversed the decision of the New York State Board of Regents denying its seal of approval to a film that depicted adultery in a

6. Lewis, *Literature, Obscenity and Law*, p. 94; the film code is quoted in Haney, *Comstockery in America*, p. 128; information on the works cited in this paragraph may be found in Lewis, pp. 79–81, 94, 103–4, 108–9, 179–83; on *The Captive* and *The Well of Loneliness*, see the documents in Jonathan Katz, *Gay American History* (New York, 1976), pp. 82–91, 397–405; on Hollywood, see Vito Russo, *The Celluloid Closet* (New York, 1981).

7. Roth v. United States, 354 U.S. 476 (1957). Biographical information on Roth may be found in Talese, *Thy Neighbor's Wife*, pp. 111–28.

favorable light. In the case of *Manual Enterprises v. Day*, involving photo magazines of male nudes, the court ruled that, even though the material clearly appealed to the prurient tastes of male homosexuals and was "dismally unpleasant, uncouth, and tawdry," it lacked "patent offensiveness" and therefore could not be considered obscene. A 1964 decision voiding the conviction of an Ohio theater manager for showing a French film with an explicit love scene argued that a work must be "utterly without redeeming social importance" in order to be censored. The Supreme Court also cleared the Grove Press edition of Henry Miller's *Tropic of Cancer*, a novel with a long history of entanglement with the censors. In 1966, Justice Brennan pulled together the different strands of the court's decisions in a ruling on the pornographic classic, *Fanny Hill*:

> A book cannot be proscribed unless it is found to be *utterly* without redeeming social value. This is so even though the book is found to possess the requisite prurient appeal and to be patently offensive. Each of the three federal constitutional criteria is to be applied independently; the social value of the book can neither be weighed against nor canceled by its prurient appeal or patent offensiveness.[8]

The opinion in *Redrup v. New York*, decided in May 1967, hinted that almost anything could claim some redeeming value. Confronted with several cheap hard-core pulp paperbacks, the justices ruled that they were not obscene. In the next eight months the court reversed without opinion eleven lower court convictions in pulp cases. For the next six years, it cleared every book that came before the bench.[9]

The Warren Court neither caused the explosive spread of sexually explicit material nor created the demand for it. Rather, the proliferation of challenges to the obscenity statutes suggests that the books, magazines, and films were already being produced and finding an audience. "Girlie" magazines such as *Playboy* were rolling off presses before *Roth*, while the scandal magazine *Confidential*, which titillated readers with intimate details of the lives of the famous, had a circulation of over 4 million in 1955. When Congress investigated the pornography industry in the mid-1950s, it uncovered the existence of 225 producers of mail order pictures, with annual receipts estimated at $100 million by the post office. Moreover, the sexual content of literature, at least since the early twentieth century, had been steadily albeit slowly increasing.[10]

---

8. A Book Named "John Cleland's Memoirs of a Woman of Pleasure" v. Massachusetts, 383 U.S. 413 (1966). For the other cases, see Smith v. California, 361 U.S. 147 (1959); Kingsley International Pictures Corp. v. Regents, 360 U.S. 684 (1959); Manual Enterprises v. Day, 370 U.S. 478 (1962); Jacobellis v. Ohio, 378 U.S. 184 (1964); and Grove Press, Inc. v. Gerstein, 378 U.S. 577 (1964).

9. Redrup v. New York, 388 U.S. 767 (1967); and Lewis, *Literature, Obscenity and Law*, pp. 191–97.

10. Paul and Schwartz, *Federal Censorship*, pp. 109–15.

The Supreme Court rulings, however, did sweep away legal barriers to the production and consumption of such materials. The boundaries of discussion and presentation of human sexual behavior spread far in the direction of explicitness. At one extreme, as the President's Commission on Obscenity and Pornography noted in 1970, the sex content of pulp novels and pictorial magazines had grown "progressively stronger" during the 1960s, largely, it claimed, as a result of the court's stand. At the other end, sex of a less lurid, less exploitive variety became a staple of items intended for a wide audience—movies, popular novels, mass circulation magazines, even the daily metropolitan press. Though the Warren Court was responding to already existing social pressures, its decisions did effect, as one authority concluded, "a sudden revolution" in what the average American could read.[11]

The Supreme Court decisions on obscenity did not occur in isolation from other shifts in both behavior and attitudes. The findings of the Kinsey studies made it apparent that many Americans engaged in erotic activity for reasons other than reproduction and that increasingly larger numbers of women were having sex outside of marriage. Mental health professionals from psychoanalysts to social workers argued for the importance of sexual expression in promoting the well-being of men and women. The work of birth control advocates was making contraception socially acceptable. In 1960, the Food and Drug Administration gave its approval to the marketing of oral contraceptives, and within a few years several million women were using the pill. Five years later, in the *Griswold* decision, the Supreme Court overturned Connecticut's anticontraception law, thus eliminating restrictions dating from the nineteenth century on the sale and distribution of contraceptive devices. By sanctioning sexual explicitness in books, magazines, and films, the Warren Court in effect brought cultural products in the public sphere into conformity with private sexual behavior. In doing so, it may also have helped to hasten attitudinal changes that affirmed a nonprocreative eroticism among heterosexual men and women.[12]

II

Nowhere, perhaps, were changes more evident than in the proliferation of material about male and female homosexuality. Across the spectrum, from pornography to the mass media, a bewildering variety of descriptions and images appeared in the 1960s that exposed the life-style and sexuality of gay women and men. Much of it was exploitive and derogatory; some was sympathetic; occasionally one could even find celebrations of homosexual life. But

11. Commission on Obscenity and Pornography, *Report* (New York, 1970), pp. 112, 115; Charles Rembar, introduction to Leon Friedman, ed., *Obscenity: The Complete Oral Arguments Before the Supreme Court in the Major Obscenity Cases* (New York, 1970), pp. ix–xxii.

12. See the discussion of Kinsey above, Chapter 2; Linda Gordon, *Woman's Body, Woman's Right* (New York, 1976), pp. 359–90; James C. Mohr, *Abortion in America* (New York, 1978), pp. 250–51; and Griswold v. Connecticut, 381 U.S. 479 (1965).

the significance of the content paled in comparison with the importance of the sheer quantity of material that portrayed, dissected, and argued about the gay experience in America.

The evolution of the lesbian pulp novel—books originally published in cheap paperback editions—offers one startling measure of change during the decade. Barbara Grier, a librarian from Kansas City who began collecting lesbian literature at the age of sixteen, meticulously examined in the *Ladder* each year's outpouring of fiction. For 1957, the first year of Grier's survey and, coincidentally, the year of the *Roth* decision, she found four paperback originals whose plots revolved around lesbianism. Two years later the figure jumped to thirty-four. By 1964–1965, the total skyrocketed to 348, a larger number of works than Jeannette Foster had uncovered in her study of 2,500 years of Western literature, *Sex Variant Women in Literature*.[13]

Although the leap in numbers in itself is staggering, the meaning of the lesbian pulp phenomenon requires closer analysis. The quality ranged, according to Grier, "from nearly pornographic tripe to lyric and beautiful writing. . . . The poorest are so poor they are indescribable, yet even the cheapest paperback publishers are issuing some quite well written, fairly realistic and highly sympathetic novels."[14] Lurid covers with sensationalistic copy encased stories that were written most often by men to excite a male heterosexual audience. The plots frequently reflected stereotypical views of lesbianism, with characters plagued by self-hate and submerged in lives of alcoholism, violence, and despair. But others were written by lesbians, and though editors might tack on unhappy endings, the final versions still retained strong, brazen, rebellious women who embraced a lesbian identity. Novels by Valerie Taylor, Ann Bannon, Paula Christian, and Dallas Mayo became underground classics, treasured by their lesbian owners. They provided characters that allowed readers to identify with other gay women and offered as well descriptions of bars, cities, and resorts where lesbians gathered.[15]

Yet probably few women read these paperbacks without twinges of fear and guilt. Lesbian consumers of pulp fiction had little chance to discriminate in their selections. How was one to know that inside the covers of *Guerrilla Girls*, *The Savage Salomé*, and *The Twisted Ones* could be found, according to Grier, "interesting, sympathetic studies" of lesbian characters? Sally Gearhart, a lesbian activist of the 1970s, recalled driving down Highway 59 in Texas with a hundred of her lesbian novels. Fearful of exposure, embarrassed to possess them, she "tore them into shreds and threw them out the window." Another

13. Grier's surveys of lesbian literature appeared in the *Ladder* under the pseudonym of Gene Damon. See *Ladder*, March 1958, p. 18; February 1960, pp. 14–15; April 1961, pp. 12–13; February 1962, pp. 6–11; January 1963, pp. 6–13; February 1964, pp. 12–19; February–March 1965, pp. 19–23; and March 1966, pp. 22–26.

14. "Lesbian Literature in 1959," *Ladder*, February 1960, pp. 14–15.

15. For an evaluation of lesbian pulp novels, see Fran Koski and Maida Tilchen, "Some Pulp Sappho," in Karla Jay and Allen Young, eds., *Lavender Culture* (New York, 1978), pp. 262–74.

avid reader of the genre, Kate Millett, hoarded her "library of cheap paper-back lesbian affairs full of sentiment . . . because they were the only books where one woman kissed another." But, Millett recalled, at the same time she recognized them as "books about grotesques." She kept them "hidden in a drawer so visitors would never spy me out" and eventually burned them rather than risk having the novels, and her identity, discovered by others. Thus pulp novels may have given sustenance to lesbian readers, but they also stimulated contradictory emotions. Their mere possession reminded their owners of the lesbian's outcast status.[16]

The collapse of legal barriers against sexually explicit magazines and books also affected the output of gay male pornography. The 1950s, wrote one student of gay male literature, had seen "a rash of pulps that were more homophobic than homosexual . . . edited and packaged to induce the straight reader to take a disdainful peek at those naughty, neurotic homosexuals." By the mid-1960s, however, fly-by-night firms were directing their wares to a male homosexual audience. A pulp novel such as Richard Amory's *Song of the Loon*, perhaps the most popular of the genre, not only contained graphic descriptions of sexual activity but placed them in an idyllic wilderness setting populated by gay fur trappers and Indian braves.[17] The gay characters were presented as pure and noble, choosing to remain beyond the edges of a corrupt civilization that condemned and punished their love. The Supreme Court decision in the *Manual Enterprises* case, by clearing male physique magazines of obscenity charges, opened the way to the genre's unrestricted production. Herman Womack, founder and owner of Manual Enterprises and the largest producer of such material, was selling 40,000 copies of his magazines per month when the post office seized them in 1960. The reversal of his conviction eliminated prohibitions against the publication and distribution of pictorials, and by 1965 total monthly sales of physique magazines topped 750,000.[18] Quasi-pornographic novels with some claim to literary merit also owed a debt to the Supreme Court. Within a year after the court ruled favorably on the Grove Press edition of the heterosexually oriented *Tropic of Cancer*, the avant-garde publishing house released several books with gay male themes, including Jean Genet's *Our Lady of the Flowers*, Hubert Selby's *Last Exit to Brooklyn*, William Burroughs's *Naked Lunch*, and John Rechy's *City of Night*. Unlike the pulps, all of these commanded the attention of critics.

Same-sex love also weaved its way into the popular literature of the 1960s. Grier's survey of contemporary novels from the late 1950s uncovered the

16. Gene Damon, "Lesbian Literature—1961," *Ladder*, February 1962, p. 7; "Interview with Sally Gearhart," *Gay Community News*, December 15, 1979, p. 8; and Kate Millett, *Flying* (New York, 1974), p. 202.

17. Roger Austen, *Playing the Game: The Homosexual Novel in America* (New York, 1977), p. 192; and Richard Amory, *Song of the Loon* (San Diego, 1966).

18. Friedman, *Obscenity: The Complete Oral Arguments*, p. 131; Clark Polak, "The Story Behind Physique Photography," *Drum*, October 1965, pp. 8–15.

beginnings of a slow but steady increase in the number of books with lesbian-ism as a major theme. By 1966 the situation had so changed that Grier announced the demise of lesbian fiction per se. "There is no such thing as a separate Lesbian literature," she wrote. Gay women, she claimed, so popu-lated the pages of contemporary fiction, their existence so "taken-for-granted" as an aspect of social life, that a "complete integration" of lesbianism into the mainstream had been achieved. Bestsellers of the decade—Allen Drury's *Advise and Consent*, James Baldwin's *Another Country*, and Mary McCarthy's *The Group*—highlighted the trend toward inclusion of gay characters and subplots in stories that were not homosexual "problem" novels.[19]

Change also beat a path to Hollywood. Buffeted by competition from television and from foreign films whose frankness appealed to an adult audi-ence, American movie makers successfully pressed for a revision of the indus-try's production guidelines. The new 1956 code, however, failed to modify the ban on "sex perversion." Only later, after a number of major producers like Otto Preminger and William Wyler had launched projects with gay themes, did the Production Code Administration ease its stand. In October 1961 it ruled that homosexuality might be portrayed on the screen "provided any references are treated with care, discretion and restraint."[20]

The first test of the new code soon clarified the meaning of discretion and restraint. In November 1961 the PCA denied its seal of approval to a British import, *Victim*, a dramatized version of the Wolfenden report that received praise from critics in Europe. The film sympathetically depicted male homosexuals as victims of outmoded laws that subjected them to blackmail by unsavory characters. The hero of the movie, a married homosexual who risks his career and family ties to bring the extortionists to justice, stood out as a man of integrity, courage, and compassion. In withholding its endorsement, the film regulators rebuked *Victim* for its "candid and clinical discussion of homosexuality" and its "overtly-expressed plea for social acceptance of the homosexual."[21]

Hollywood producers avoided such reproaches. Several films dealing with homosexuality reached American movie houses in 1962 and 1963—*The Chil-dren's Hour, Advise and Consent, Walk on the Wild Side*, and *The Best Man*—and each one had received the PCA's seal. The suicide of a tortured lesbian school teacher redeemed *The Children's Hour*, while Barbara Stanwyck's sinis-ter characterization of a lesbian madam in *Walk on the Wild Side* exhibited the

19. Gene Damon (pseud.), "Lesbian Literature, 1966," *Ladder*, April 1967, pp. 8–13; "Les-bian Literature in 1964," *Ladder*, March 1966, pp. 22–26; "Lesbian Literature in 1963," *Ladder*, February 1964, p. 12. On the fate of the gay male novel in the 1960s, see Austen, *Playing the Game*, pp. 199–225.

20. *New York Times*, October 4, 1961, p. 41; October 23, 1961; and October 29, 1961, Section II, p. 7. See also Russo, *The Celluloid Closet*, pp. 118–22.

21. *New York Times*, November 16, 1961, p. 45; December 12, 1961, p. 54; February 6, 1962, p. 27; and February 11, 1962, Section II, p. 1. See also Russo, *The Celluloid Closet*, pp. 128–31.

moral stance required for approval. Similarly, by portraying the gay bar as a demonic netherworld filled with leering, half-crazed men, *Advise and Consent* escaped censure. Unlike *Victim*, moreover, the American films assiduously avoided the use of words like "homosexual" or any of its colloquial variations. Although a few other European imports, such as John Schlesinger's *Darling*, treated homosexuality in a noncondemnatory way, the growing number of Hollywood movies in the 1960s that touched upon the subject continued to present it in a harsh light. No longer invisible, homosexuality nonetheless remained for Hollywood a perversion.[22]

Along with fictional presentations of lesbianism and homosexuality came the journalistic discovery of the gay world. For the first time, the metropolitan press and the mass circulation weeklies made forays into the gay subculture. In December 1963, when the *New York Times* offered readers a front page feature on the city's "most sensitive open secret," a flourishing male homosexual underground of bars and cruising areas, the story itself became a news item, with *Newsweek* running an article on it.[23] Other urban papers printed series that explored gay life, summarized medical and legal opinions, and gave space to the views of homophile leaders. *Life* and *Look* presented extensive photo reviews, *Time* offered an essay on the topic, and monthlies such as *Harper's* let their readers steal a glimpse inside the gay male bar.[24]

This first wave of newspaper and magazine coverage varied considerably in content and viewpoint. Some, like the Washington *Post* and *Life*, acknowledged a range of opinions, including those of homophile leaders and mental health professionals who took issue with the sickness theory. Others, such as the *Times*, emphasized the stance of vice squad officers and the segment of the medical profession that categorized homosexuals as "crippled psychically." Some were quite antagonistic toward homosexuality. As a *Time* magazine essay concluded,

it is a pathetic little second-rate substitute for reality, a pitiable flight from life. As such it deserves fairness, compassion, understanding and, when possible, treatment. But it deserves no encouragement, no glamorization, no rationalization, no fake status as minority martyrdom, no sophistry about simple differences in taste—and, above all, no pretense that it is anything but a pernicious sickness.[25]

22. *Life*, February 23, 1962, pp. 88–102.

23. Robert Doty, "Growth of Overt Homosexuality in City Provokes Wide Concern," *New York Times*, December 17, 1963, p. 1; and *Newsweek*, December 30, 1963, p. 42.

24. *Washington Post*, January 31–February 3, 1965; *Atlanta Journal and Constitution*, January 3–8, 1966; *Denver Post*, February 14–19, 1965; "Homosexuality in America," *Life*, June 26, 1964, pp. 66–74; "The Sad 'Gay' Life," *Look*, January 10, 1967, pp. 30–33; "The Homosexual in America," *Time*, January 21, 1966, pp. 40–41; and "New York's 'Middle-Class' Homosexuals," *Harper's*, March 1963, pp. 85–92.

25. *Time*, January 21, 1966, p. 41.

Even the most vituperative articles, however, served as resources for homosexuals and lesbians in search of a subculture. They frequently pinpointed the location of bars, cruising areas, and residential concentrations of gays, as well as evaluations of which cities offered the most hospitable environment for homosexual men and women.

The early 1960s also witnessed the appearance of a new genre in nonfiction book publishing, an inside view of the gay world intended for a lay audience. Like the articles in the press, these exposés ranged widely in tone and attitude. At one extreme, Jess Stearn penned an account of gay male life, *The Sixth Man*, that dripped with venom and contempt.[26] The book, which spent three months on the *New York Times* bestseller list, blamed homosexuals for social maladies ranging from the rising divorce rate to juvenile crime and the defeminization of women. Its catalog of industries infested with gay men was so lengthy that a reader could only wonder whether Stearn's estimate of every sixth man was not grossly conservative. At the other end, Donald Webster Cory wrote a sympathetic account of lesbian life.[27] Though Cory remained wedded to a view of homosexuality as psychopathology, his book contained three-dimensional character sketches, took for granted that gay women were victims of unjust discrimination and deserved full civil rights, and had fine words of praise for the Daughters of Bilitis. In between, one could find a host of hastily composed accounts in which consistency, logic, or evidence played second fiddle to sensationalism.[28]

A common thread ran through much of the literature on homosexuality and lesbianism. From lesbian pulp novels set in a metropolitan milieu of bars and private parties to a photo essay in *Life* that depicted male homosexual meeting places came the implicit recognition that gay men and women existed in groups with a network of institutions and resources to sustain their social identity. The shift suggests an alteration not merely in attitudes—a willingness to acknowledge the presence of a gay subculture in American cities—but also a change in social reality, the rapid maturation in postwar America of a stable gay world that could no longer escape detection.[29]

26. Jess Stearn, *The Sixth Man* (Garden City, N.Y., 1961).

27. Donald Webster Cory [pseud.], *The Lesbian in America* (New York, 1964); Cory also co-authored a book on male homosexuality during the 1960s: see Cory and John P. LeRoy, *The Homosexual and His Society: A View from Within* (New York, 1963).

28. See, e.g., R. E. L. Masters, *The Homosexual Revolution* (New York, 1962); Roger Blake, *The Homosexual Explosion* (North Hollywood, Calif., 1966); Eric Karlson, *The Homosexual Uprising*, 2 vols. (San Diego, 1967); Benjamin Morse, *The Homosexual* (Derby, Conn., 1961); and Ken Worthy, *The Homosexual Generation* (New York, 1965) and *The New Homosexual Revolution* (New York, 1965). Jess Stearn also wrote a book about lesbians; see *The Grapevine* (Garden City, N.Y., 1964).

29. A. M. Rosenthal, the metropolitan editor of the *New York Times* who was responsible for the paper's front-page article on homosexuality, remarked that he decided to run such a feature after stumbling upon a gay male cruising area on the East Side of Manhattan and realizing that "never before had [I] seen so much unexotic open homosexuality" (quoted in *Newsweek*, December 30, 1963).

III

The relatively sudden emergence of gay life into public view brought with it opportunities for a redefinition of homosexuality. Embedded in the ideological configuration of sin, sickness, and crime was the assumption that the homosexual man or woman lived in isolation, as a maladjusted pathological personality, occasionally coupling with a partner in sin or crime. Such a perspective assimilated information about lesbians and homosexuals in association with one another simply by multiplying the cast of characters, by crowding the stage with actors playing out their individual dramas. However, as evidence accumulated that gay subcultures were thriving in the urban environments of the United States, the possibility grew of conceptualizing homosexuality from the vantage point of social science.

Ironically, the first significant moves toward interpreting homosexuality from a social rather than an individual perspective came from the psychoanalytic profession. Perplexed by the apparent increase in male homosexuality in the 1940s and thereafter, and the new ease with which their patients could find other homosexuals after World War II, some analysts turned away from Freudian explanations for the genesis of sexual "inversion." Discarding libido theory, with its emphasis on the individual's sex drive and family relationships, they sought, as Lionel Ovesey phrased it, to "recast the psychodynamics of homosexuality within an adaptational context in order to demonstrate the crucial role of societal forces."[30] As often as not, a male homosexual orientation, according to several psychoanalysts, emanated from the disorders of the mid-twentieth century—depression and war, the generalized anxiety of the nuclear age, intense competitive demands placed on males, pressure to conform, the rapid pace of technological change, shifting roles and increased expectations of American women.[31] Under such conditions, male homosexuality became not a defensive response against immature infantile desires or unresolved Oedipal conflicts but, in Abram Kardiner's words, a large-scale "flight from masculinity" induced by external stresses.[32]

The shift in focus had important implications. Although the psychoanalytic community by and large persisted in its categorization of homosexuality as pathological, adaptational theory removed the spotlight from the individual. "Cure" remained the goal, but a society that produced homosexuals faster than professionals could treat them became the patient. Solutions could no longer be found on the analyst's couch. In turning their attention toward society, moreover, adaptational analysts easily slipped into advocating reform. Individuals whose sexual orientation stemmed from an inability to cope with

30. Lionel Ovesey, "The Homosexual Conflict: An Adaptational Analysis," *Psychiatry* 17 (1954): 243–50.
31. See the essays by Abram Kardiner, Robert Lindner, Hendrik Ruitenbeek, and Lionel Ovesey in Hendrik M. Ruitenbeek, ed., *The Problem of Homosexuality in Modern Society* (New York, 1963).
32. Abram Kardiner, *Sex and Morality* (Indianapolis, 1954).

modern life, the argument ran, should not face censure, arrest, and discrimination, since punishment would only exacerbate their problems.

A lack of theoretical unity within the psychoanalytic community gave added weight to the work of Evelyn Hooker, who was moving ahead with her studies of male homosexuals. Hooker's earliest papers, published in the 1950s, suggested that the psychological profile of gay men not in therapy was indistinguishable from that of a comparable group of heterosexual males, that a deviant sexual orientation did not necessarily imply pathology, and that homosexuals adjusted to their situation in a multiplicity of ways. Hooker's prolific output and the originality of her work—she was virtually the only mental health professional studying nonpatient, noninstitutionalized homosexuals—guaranteed serious consideration, and her articles were widely reprinted.[33]

By the early 1960s Hooker's findings were propelling her to investigate the social life of gay men. Starting with the assumption that homosexuality did not constitute evidence of maladjustment, she explored the urban subculture in which some male homosexuals lived, fashioned their social identity, and created structures to enhance their self-acceptance. Hooker's description of the homosexual's world lacked the normative content that so often typified psychosexual literature. She wrote as an observer, more in the tradition of anthropology and sociology, and not as a clinician.[34]

In the mid-1960s, two collections of essays on homosexuality, the first ones intended for an educated lay audience, reflected these new theoretical directions. The articles in Hendrik Ruitenbeek's *Problem of Homosexuality in Modern Society* were weighted in favor of psychoanalysis, although not, as Ruitenbeek wrote, "because of the editor's preference, but rather because sociological studies are so rare." The psychoanalytic material in his volume emphasized social interpretations of sexual orientation, and Ruitenbeek pinpointed sociology as the key discipline for further exploration of homosexuality. Significantly, the opening and closing pieces disputed the classification of homosexuality as a disease.[35]

Although clinicians contributed the bulk of the material in Judd Marmor's *Sexual Inversion*, the work of social scientists was also included. Moreover, Marmor's introductory essay, coming as it did from a leading psychoanalyst, suggested the course of future opinion. Moderate and judicious in tone, it lent prestige to those findings that implicitly encouraged social tolerance of homosexuality. Marmor acknowledged that psychoanalytic theory rested on a skewed sampling of homosexuals. He accused clinicians who regarded homosexuality as undesirable of remaining imprisoned in the values of their culture, and he stamped Hooker's findings with his imprimatur. Marmor also

33. See above, chap. 7, n. 12, for references to Hooker's early work.
34. Evelyn Hooker, "Male Homosexuals and Their 'Worlds,' " in Judd Marmor, ed., *Sexual Inversion: The Multiple Roots of Homosexuality* (New York, 1965), pp. 83–107.
35. Ruitenbeek, ed., *The Problem of Homosexuality*, p. xi.

stressed that many of the "pathological" traits of homosexuals in treatment stemmed from "a total fabric that includes a specific kind of social mores . . . that deprecates and condemns homoerotic behavior and makes life much more difficult and hazardous for homosexuals." Marmor effectively sabotaged many of the essays in his volume by exposing the untested assumptions upon which they rested.[36]

Sociologists, particularly students of deviance, mounted the sharpest attack on traditional interpretations of homosexuality. The investigation of deviance had a long history, almost as old as the discipline itself, but until the 1950s American sociologists had tended to group the subject under the rubric of social pathology. The postwar era witnessed a significant shift, however, as a radical relativist perspective crept into the area. Social scientists came to view deviance not as evidence of social disorganization but, rather, as a sign of different norms of behavior. They examined deviant populations as members of a subculture, or they made use of labeling theory which emphasized the functions that the attribution of deviant status to a group served for the majority. During the 1960s deviance theory broke out of the confines of the university, as writers in the field consciously strove to reach a wider audience in order to exert an impact on public policy.[37]

Howard Becker's primer, *Outsiders* (1963), quickly became the standard text. In it Becker adopted a relativistic perspective from which he described deviance simply as "the failure to obey group rules." Social groups, Becker asserted, *"create deviance by making the rules whose infraction constitutes deviance. . . . Deviance is not a quality of the act the person commits, but* rather a consequence of the application by others of rules and sanctions to an 'offender.' " The ability to make rules and apply sanctions, according to Becker, reflected "power differentials" in society. Those groups "whose social position gives them weapons and power are best able to enforce their rules." He warned sociologists, in studying deviant populations, to avoid adopting the majority viewpoint. Investigators, he argued, should "see it simply as a kind of behavior some disapprove of and others value."[38]

Several social scientists applied this nonmajoritarian stance to the study of male homosexuality. Becker in *Outsiders* and Erving Goffman in *Stigma* (1963) frequently drew on the gay experience to illustrate their theoretical perspective.[39] Others gave the topic more extended treatment. In *Crimes Without Victims* (1965), Edwin Schur examined in detail the situation of drug users, women who sought abortions, and male homosexuals. He evaluated the

36. Judd Marmor, introduction to *Sexual Inversion*, pp. 1–24.

37. For an overview of deviance theory, see Stuart H. Traub and Craig B. Little, eds., *Theories of Deviance* (Itasca, Ill., 1975), especially the essays by Mills and Alexander.

38. Howard S. Becker, *Outsiders: Studies in the Sociology of Deviance* (New York, 1963), pp. 8–9, 17, 176.

39. Erving Goffman, *Stigma: Notes on the Management of Spoiled Identity* (Englewood Cliffs, N.J., 1963).

impact exerted on all three groups by legal penalties and argued that the criminal law, clearly ineffective as a means of preventing victimless crimes, instead served "positive functions for the conformists."[40] Doctor Martin Hoffman provided in *The Gay World* (1968) the first book-length portrayal of an urban homosexual community. Based on three years of observation of gay male life in San Francisco, Hoffman's book described the network of institutions that bound the community together, the patterns of interaction, the self-perceptions of his subjects, and the impact of legal penalties on gay men's lives. Hoffman's subtitle gave a clue to his point of view: *Male Homosexuality and the Social Creation of Evil.*[41]

Many of these writers conspicuously dropped the mantle of scientific neutrality and became partisans of reform. Schur derided the rationale on which antihomosexual laws rested, charged that the laws themselves created the social "problem," and urged the decriminalization of homosexual acts between adults in private. Hoffman, in his conclusion, went much further:

> The best solution to the problem of homosexuality is one which is modeled on the solution to the problem of religious difference, namely, *a radical tolerance for homosexual object-choice*, whether as a segment of an individual's sexual existence or as a full commitment to homosexuality as a way of life. . . . Society as a whole must significantly shift its attitudes towards homosexuals and homosexuality in American life.[42]

He proposed an end to all legal penalties and police activity against gay men and women as well as the abolition of discriminatory employment policies by private industry and the government, including the exclusion of homosexuals and lesbians from the armed forces. Becker, in the centenary issue of the *Nation*, penned a virtual manifesto for sexual liberation. He described his initially amused reaction to the appearance of DOB members whom he had addressed—"the group looked like a middle-class women's club having a meeting to decide how to run the next charity bazaar"—and the response that followed on his further reflection. "I stopped smiling when I realized the aggressiveness and courage it took to identify oneself publicly as the officer of a Lesbian organization and the risk these women were taking in doing so." Sex, he suggested, should be "the politics of the sixties," and he anticipated a time when sexual expression would be enshrined as an "inalienable" right.[43]

Important as these new perspectives on homosexuality and society were, one must beware of exaggerating their influence. In no sense did they displace the

40. Edwin M. Schur, *Crimes Without Victims: Deviant Behavior and Public Policy* (Englewood Cliffs, N.J., 1965), p. 4.

41. Martin Hoffman, *The Gay World: Male Homosexuality and the Social Creation of Evil* (New York, 1968).

42. Ibid., pp. 197–98.

43. Howard S. Becker, "Deviance and Deviates," *Nation*, September 20, 1965, pp. 115–19.

intellectually hegemonic view of the medical profession that a homosexual orientation was a sign of psychopathology. The most widely discussed books about the subject emanating from the scientific community in the 1960s were Irving Bieber's psychoanalytic study, *Homosexuality* (1962), and a report issued in 1964 by the New York Academy of Medicine. Both works held fast to the classification of same-gender sexuality as a disease, while the latter went even further by arguing that the phenomenon was becoming increasingly prevalent and endangering the welfare of society. The minority of dissenters, however, did offer an alternative way of looking at homosexuality, one that tended to affirm the proclivities of gay men and women, focused on their group social life, and typically identified the "problem" as one caused by society, not by the homosexual or lesbian. In doing so, they weakened the consensus surrounding homosexuality that had so hampered the efforts of homophile activists in the 1950s and that had helped to keep gay women and men away from the movement.[44]

IV

Although few critics of the status quo went as far as Hoffman and Becker in arguing for the social acceptance of homoerotic behavior, the two represented one end of a spectrum of dissent from the criminalization of homosexual acts. As portrayals of gay life multiplied, attention inevitably focused on the havoc that legal penalties wreaked upon homosexuals, especially males, who came more frequently into conflict with the law. Particularly within the legal profession, questions surfaced during the 1960s about the role of the state in regulating morality, the right to privacy, violations of due process, and arbitrary, capricious enforcement practices.

The decriminalization of private, consensual adult homosexual relations, the most basic of reforms, won prestigious supporters among jurists and attorneys. The American Law Institute, which drew its 1,500 members from the elite of the legal profession, completed work in 1962 on a model penal code that eliminated the sodomy statutes.[45] Two years later, the International Congress on Penal Law endorsed the ALI position.[46] Another voice in favor of reform came from England in 1957, with the Wolfenden report. The 1963

44. Irving Bieber et al., *Homosexuality: A Psychoanalytic Study of Male Homosexuals* (New York, 1962); and New York Academy of Medicine, Committee on Public Health, *Homosexuality* (New York, 1964). For discussions of the medical model in the press and in magazines, see *New York Times*, December 17, 1963, p. 1; May 19, 1964, p. 1; August 23, 1964, Section VI, p. 75; and January 31, 1965, p. 61. See also *Newsweek*, December 30, 1963, p. 42; and *Time*, February 12, 1965, p. 44.

45. See American Law Institute, *Model Penal Code* (Philadelphia, 1962); the "Commentary" on sodomy law repeal in *Model Penal Code Tentative Draft #4* (Philadelphia, 1955), pp. 276–91; and Louis B. Schwartz, "Morals, Offenses, and the Model Penal Code," *Columbia Law Review* 63 (1963): 669–86. For an overview of arguments for reform, see *The Challenge and Progress of Homosexual Law Reform* (San Francisco, 1968).

46. *New York Times*, August 30, 1964, p. 36.

publication of an American edition of the report and extended Parliamentary debates over its recommendations during the mid-1960s won coverage for the issue on this side of the Atlantic. Newspapers and magazines generally either endorsed Britain's progress toward decriminalization or adopted a neutral stance when reporting on the issue.[47] In legal journals, too, articles in favor of reform appeared steadily throughout the decade.

Writers within the legal profession advanced a number of arguments in support of sodomy law repeal. The most common approach simply questioned why the state should regulate private consensual behavior between adults. The purpose of the criminal law, this line of reasoning went, was to protect the person and property of citizens; sexual conduct in private endangered neither. Many of these writers took care to deny that they favored sexual license or advocated the abolition of laws punishing public solicitation or lewdness. Theirs was a defense based on notions of personal liberty bounded by the public welfare. Another rationale for change relied on expediency: the laws were impossible to enforce and hence ought to go. Some lawyers pointed out that poorly enforced laws gave rise to harmful side effects by encouraging disrespect and cynicism toward the law in general. Finally, a few attorneys who wrote about the sodomy statutes rested their case for repeal on the fickleness of sexual morality. As one of them commented, "yesterday's perversion is today's experiment and tomorrow's matter of taste."[48]

By the latter half of the 1960s, some lawyers moved beyond a narrow focus on the sodomy laws and began to address a wider range of issues concerning homosexuality and the law. A California study looked at the issue of public solicitation. It determined that most solicitation by gay men was practiced

47. On England see *The Wolfenden Report: Report of the Committee on Homosexual Offenses and Prostitution* (New York, 1963); *Newsweek*, June 7, 1965, p. 38, and February 21, 1966, p. 54; *Christian Century*, May 26, 1965, pp. 669–70; *Time*, December 30, 1966, p. 17, and July 14, 1967, p. 30; and *New York Times*, May 16, 1965, Section IV, p. 13; May 25, 1965, p. 1; May 27, 1965, p. 3; May 30, 1965, Section IV, p. 5; June 27, 1965, Section VI, p. 6; February 12, 1966, p. 1; May 11, 1966, p. 14; June 17, 1966, p. 34; July 6, 1966, p. 7; and December 20, 1966, p. 1. See also Jeffrey Weeks, *Coming Out: Homosexual Politics in Britain from the Nineteenth Century to the Present* (New York, 1977), pp. 156–82.

48. For articles in legal journals in favor of reform, see Douglas L. Custis, "Sex Laws in Ohio: A Need for Revision," *University of Cincinnati Law Review* 35 (1966): 211–41; Stephen D. Ford, "Homosexuals and the Law: Why the Status Quo?" *California Western Law Review* 5 (1969): 232–51; Jon J. Gallo et al., "The Consenting Adult Homosexual and the Law: An Empirical Study of Enforcement and Administration in Los Angeles County," *UCLA Law Review* 13 (1966): 644–832; Irving S. Goldman, "Bedroom Should Not Be Within the Province of the Law," *California Western Law Review* 4 (1968): 115–31; Robert N. Harris, Jr., "Private Consensual Adult Behavior: The Requirement of Harm to Others in the Enforcement of Morality," *UCLA Law Review* 14 (1967): 581–603; Graham Hughes, "Morals and the Criminal Law," *Yale Law Review* 71 (1962): 662–83; Ronald Johnson, "Sodomy Statutes: A Need for Change," *South Dakota Law Review* 13 (1968): 384–97; Paul S. Lamb, "Criminal Law—Consensual Homosexual Behavior—the Need for Legislative Reform," *Kentucky Law Journal* 57 (1968–69): 591–98; *Law and Contemporary Problems*, vol. 25, Spring 1960 issue; and J. Terry Moran, "Sex Offenses and Penal Code Revision in Michigan," *Wayne Law Review* 14 (1968): 934–69.

discreetly and in no way offended public decency. Yet it also found that a significant portion of the arrests of homosexuals in Los Angeles County came through decoy enforcement of solicitation statutes, on the basis of a few words exchanged between a gay man and a plainclothes officer. The authors of the study concluded that the use of decoys was not justified and that the police should leave homosexuals alone, except when they engaged in public sex or when they harassed heterosexual citizens. Such an approach would slash the number of arrests of gay men without compromising public safety. Another attorney compared the legal liabilities that homosexuals and lesbians suffered to the problems faced by racial minorities, enumerating as examples police brutality, unequal enforcement of laws, and the denial of employment opportunities. After examining the goals of homophile activists, the writer concluded that their activities assumed "many of the aspects of other struggles currently being waged to eradicate discrimination against minorities." His perspective was a long way from the limited call for consenting adult laws.[49]

Although the overwhelming weight of opinion articulated by attorneys and jurists in the 1960s favored the repeal of the sodomy statutes, little immediate progress was made in implementing their views. Only Illinois in 1961 and Connecticut in 1969 adopted the model penal code of the American Law Institute. In contrast, the attempt by the New York State legislature in the mid-1960s to eliminate the sodomy law met with disastrous defeat when an aroused Roman Catholic hierarchy mounted an effective lobbying campaign against the proposal. Moreover, the experience of Illinois revealed that the absence of criminal sanctions against private consensual relations was of little use to homosexuals by itself. Few men faced prosecution for acts committed in the privacy of their own homes. Far more common were arrests for vagrancy, disorderly conduct, public lewdness, and solicitation, and police enforcement of these laws against gays continued unabated.[50]

Still, the shift in professional opinion that took place during the decade was an important one. It represented a break from a centuries-long tradition in Anglo-American law. As such, one can hardly be surprised that penal code reform did not immediately occur, especially in the absence of large, well-organized campaigns in favor of it.

V

Not unexpectedly, the changes that took place during the 1960s passed largely unnoticed. In a decade that began with heroic sit-ins and freedom rides by civil

49. Gallo et al., "The Consenting Adult Homosexual and the Law"; and Ford, "Homosexuals and the Law," p. 250.

50. On the unsuccessful attempt at penal code reform in New York, see *Newsweek*, December 7, 1964, p. 90; *Life*, June 11, 1965, p. 4; and *New York Times*, March 17, 1964, p. 1; November 25, 1964, p. 43; November 26, 1964, p. 34; March 17, 1965, p. 1; June 4, 1965, p. 1; and July 23, 1965, p. 1. On Illinois, see *The Challenge and Progress of Homosexual Law Reform* (San Francisco, 1968); on Connecticut, see *New York Times*, March 3, 1969, p. 40, and June 3, 1969, p. 43.

rights activists in the South, that witnessed the assassinations of three charismatic leaders and the humbling of America's military power in the jungles of Southeast Asia, and that ended with violent convulsions on college campuses and in urban ghettos, articles in the press and magazines about an urban gay subculture created hardly a stir in the nation's consciousness. Besides, most of the discussion, novel and even daring as it was, came from the outside, from a heterosexual majority peering into a milieu that was strange, exotic, and different from its own. Throughout the 1960s, these observers mapped the terrain. They imposed their interpretations upon the lives they portrayed and the subculture they described. Even the few proponents of equality for lesbians and homosexuals spoke as allies, as defenders of a group of Americans whose perspective for the most part remained unexpressed. The challenges to the status quo lacked the passion of the aggrieved. The silence surrounding homosexuality was certainly ending, but the loudest voices were not yet those of gay men and women.

And yet, the developments of the 1960s held enormous significance. Barriers to discussion fell. The volume of material written about homosexuality grew large enough that the quantitative increase in itself represented a qualitative change. No longer the taboo topic of twenty years earlier, "sexual deviance" was losing its ability to shock and frighten. In addition, the familiarity that came from more open discussion bred not contempt but a variety of viewpoints. The formula that mixed sin, sickness, and crime into a jumbled consensus justifying opprobrium and punishment retained its dominance, but not without challenges. Conflicting models of homosexual behavior emerged among mental health professionals, while some social scientists, appropriating the phenomenon to their own discipline, constructed vastly different interpretations. Among leading lawyers and jurists, the criminalization of homosexual acts lost most of its support. The intellectual structure upon which the oppression of lesbians and homosexuals rested remained strong, but it also faced its first serious assault.

Ironically, the most important changes of the decade, the shifting self-perception and life-styles of gay men and women, defy easy measurement. Each novel, each physique magazine, each news report communicated to gay readers that their situation was widely shared. Homophile publications such as *The Ladder* and *ONE* offered the same message, but they reached too few people to carry much social significance. Popular novels and mass circulation weeklies, on the other hand, had audiences numbering in the millions. Regardless of their point of view, fictional renditions and journalistic accounts of lesbians and gay men filled in the outlines of a common predicament, a way of life experienced by millions. Self-hate drove Martha to suicide in *The Children's Hour*, but not before movie audiences heard Karen console her with the observation that there were other women who lived this way. Pulp novels informed readers of the existence of lesbian bars. Jess Stearn ridiculed and heaped contempt upon the male homosexuals whom he interviewed, but he also described the gyms where they met, the neighborhoods they inhabited, and the cities to which they flocked. At the very least, the growing discourse about lesbians and homosexuals strengthened a sense of belonging to a group, even when fear and guilt blocked any steps to act upon that awareness. For others, the new availability of information made the gay subculture of the nation's larger cities more accessible. News coverage and social scientific studies reflected an awareness that an urban gay world already existed. They also speeded its expansion.

Homophile activists in the 1960s thus worked in an altered social context. In some cases movement groups instigated change by offering their services to journalists or researchers, while in others they filled the role of interested onlookers who stood to benefit from the novel concern with homosexuality. Basic tasks of the 1950s—to break the "conspiracy of silence," to inform the public about the existence of a gay minority, to educate the lesbian and the homosexual—were proceeding apace, though often without the participation of activists and mostly from a perspective barely affected by the views of gay men and women. The movement needed to take advantage of the changing social climate, to transform an inchoate group consciousness composed of contradictory elements into a collective political force. The second decade of gay activism posed fresh challenges and opportunities.

NINE

Civil Rights and
Direct Action:
The New
East Coast Militancy,
1961–1965

In January 1962 Curtis Dewees of the New York Mattachine traveled to Los
Angeles to attend ONE's midwinter institute. Still troubled by the dissolution
of Mattachine's national structure and the conflicts between ONE and DOB,
he had spent much time mulling over their implications for the homophile
cause. In a speech to institute participants, he assessed the movement's work
in gloomy terms. Dewees acknowledged the failure to recruit many gay men
and women into the movement, but he attempted an optimistic interpretation
of the situation. The masses of "John Doe" homosexuals, he said, "rarely
produce the leadership so sorely needed" by the movement. He even questioned the value of trying to attract large numbers to the movement's banner.
"I believe the time is not yet ripe for a mass organization," Dewees announced.
"If such a group of organized homosexuals is suddenly thrust on the guardians
of public morality, the initial reaction would be indignation, horror, and a
general demand to crush such a despicable monster."

Instead, he offered as a model for the American movement the Homosexual
Law Reform Society of Great Britain, which had campaigned since 1958 for
the decriminalization of consensual sex acts between adults. The English
group, he said, "consisted of some of that country's most respected citizens.
. . . It was definitely not a group of organized homosexuals who pressed for
legal reform." For Dewees, the lesson of the comparison was clear. "First and
foremost we must lose the label of homosexual organizations." Progress for the
homophile cause required a movement staffed and led by "pillars of the
community." A small band of "strategically placed individuals can do more to

change public opinion in the next decade than many times that number of persons picked at random from society."[1]

Though Dewees had good reason to cast a critical eye on the experience of the previous few years, his prognostication placed him sadly out of step with the times. By 1962 the relatively quiescent, privatized mood of the 1950s was already rapidly yielding to a spirit of active, militant engagement by masses of Americans. For many, the election of John F. Kennedy to the presidency in 1960 symbolized the contrast between the previous decade and the current one. Young, articulate, and exuding confidence, he inspired reformers with his rhetoric. By telling Americans in his inaugural address to "ask not what your country can do for you, but what you can do for your country," Kennedy helped to legitimate social activism. Moreover, even before his election, civil rights forces in the South had resumed the offensive against white segregationists. The lunch counter sit-ins by black college students in 1960 and the freedom rides of the following year set in motion millions of black Americans who rejected the oppressed role of victim and drew a new pride and strength from their racial identity. The civil rights struggle quickly roused a generation of white college students to commit themselves to an effort to end racial injustice, poverty, and a host of other social evils. The accent in the protest movements of the 1960s was on self-activity, on ordinary men and women taking the initiative to seize from huge, impersonal structures the power to shape their lives. "Let the people decide" became a rallying cry for the new militants of the 1960s, as they rejected dependence on the "pillars of the community" for changes handed down from above.

Not surprisingly, the spirit of the times infected the gay movement as well. On the East Coast in the early 1960s, a militant wing of the movement emerged. Inspired by the example of civil rights activists, it abandoned the accommodationist approach of the 1950s. Militants adopted an ideology based on equal rights for minorities, engaged in direct action techniques of protest, and affirmed the propriety of homosexuals and lesbians leading their own struggle for justice. Their confidence and determination won for the movement and for gay women and men generally a visibility that their predecessors had failed to achieve.

I

Franklin Kameny spearheaded the new militancy in the gay movement. Born in 1925 to a middle-class Jewish family in New York City, the precocious Kameny entered college at the age of fifteen. After serving in the army during World War II, he finished college and went on to a Ph.D. program in astronomy at Harvard. During a year of research at the University of Arizona, Kameny came out as a homosexual and, with the companionship of an undergraduate, explored Tucson's gay subculture. "I took to it like a duck to water,

1. Curtis Dewees, "Address Read Before ONE's 10th Anniversary Meeting," January 27, 1962, typescript, ONE, Inc., file, Institute for Sex Research, Bloomington, Ind. (hereafter referred to as ISR).

as if it were made for me or I for it," he later recalled.[2] Kameny received his degree from Harvard in 1956 and, after teaching at Georgetown University for a year, began working for the U.S. Army map service in July 1957. But in December his government employment was abruptly terminated, when investigators uncovered a 1956 arrest on charges of lewd conduct. The following month, the Civil Service Commission barred him from further federal employment. After exhausting the internal appeal procedures of the commission, Kameny took his case to the courts, but by early 1961 that effort too had failed.[3]

For Kameny dismissal from government employment initiated a nightmarish period of hardship. "At the very first," he wrote, "I did not look for another job because I rather naively felt that this affair would quickly be resolved in my favor." As his plight became more serious, he began hunting for work, only to find himself "in the peculiarly ironic position of being in excessively great demand (as an astronomer at the commencement of the Space Age) and yet totally unable to get a job because of security problems." By the spring of 1959 he was penniless and living on handouts of food from the Salvation Army. Bills piled up, and malnutrition caused his health to deteriorate. Still he remained determined, as a letter written in the summer of 1960 revealed:

> I am not a belligerent person, nor do I seek wars, but having been forced into a battle, I am determined that this thing will be fought thru to a successful conclusion, come what may. . . . I will not be deprived of my proper rights, freedoms, and liberties, as I see them, or of career, profession, and livelihood, or of my right to live my life as I choose. . . .
>
> The past 2¾ years have not been easy ones. . . . The mills of justice in this country grind slow and exceedingly expensive, and unless the Government decides to surrender, there will be much time and money needed before victory is ours.[4]

The federal government did not surrender, and Kameny, with no further legal options, shifted course. "I felt I'd gone as far as I could go acting as an individual and that the time had come to act through an organization," he later recalled. Vaguely aware, as he put it, of the homophile movement during the mid-1950s, and later in touch with both ONE and Mattachine while his case wended its way through the courts, he resolved to form a homosexual rights group in Washington, D.C., to carry on his fight by other means.[5]

2. "Frank Kameny," in Kay Tobin and Randy Wicker, *The Gay Crusaders* (New York, 1972), pp. 90–92; and interview with Frank Kameny, November 3, 1978, in Washington, D.C.

3. Kameny to *ONE*, August 27, 1960, Legal Cases file, ONE, Inc., library, Los Angeles (Hereafter referred to as ONE Archives); interview with Kameny; and Tobin and Wicker, *The Gay Crusaders*, pp. 92–95. For the court rulings in Kameny's case, see Kameny v. Brucker, 365 U.S. 843 (1961), and Kameny v. Brucker, 282 F. 2d 823 (1960).

4. Kameny to *ONE*, August 27, 1960, ONE Archives; and Tobin and Wicker, pp. 93–95.

5. Interview with Kameny; and Tobin and Wicker, p. 95.

Kameny found a partner in Jack Nichols, a native of the capital. The son of a career FBI agent, Nichols acknowledged his gayness, to himself and to his family, while still in high school. Reading Cory's *The Homosexual in America*, he recalled, "revolutionized" his thinking, and when the twenty-two-year-old Nichols met Kameny at a party late in 1960, the two men became friends. During the summer of 1961, with Washington area names provided by the New York Mattachine, they began seeking recruits for a local homophile group. Finally, in November, about a dozen men and women met to form the Mattachine Society of Washington, electing Kameny its president.[6]

Kameny brought to his leadership role qualities that propelled the Washington Mattachine to the forefront of homosexual rights activity. His university credentials dispelled for him the awe in which many homophile leaders held the professional community, while his long, lonely fight against the federal government nourished a ferocious drive to lock horns with officialdom. During those years Kameny also acquired substantial knowledge of the labyrinthine workings of the Washington bureaucracy and the web of regulations and procedures that impinged upon gays. Better educated than most of his associates in the movement, he applied his intellectual skills to a rigorous analysis of the movement's goals, strategy, and tactics. Finally, Kameny owed much of his influence in the movement to his willingness to argue and articulate his stands aggressively.

Kameny's approach diverged markedly from the neutrality espoused by the homophile movement of the 1950s. "It is absolutely necessary," he wrote, "to be prepared to take definite, unequivocal positions upon supposedly controversial matters. We should have a clear, explicit, consistent viewpoint and we should not be timid in presenting it." He scorned the homophile movement's "genteel, debating society approach" which "impelled [it] to present impartially both or all sides" of every question. "We cannot stand upon an ivory-tower concept of aloof, detached dignity," he informed the Washington Mattachine members. "This is a movement, in many respects, of down-to-earth, grass-roots, sometimes tooth-and-nail politics." And, as he told a New York audience, "our opponents will do a fully adequate job of presenting their views, and will not return us the favor of presenting ours; we gain nothing in virtue by presenting theirs, and only provide the enemy . . . with ammunition to be used against us."[7]

6. "Jack Nichols," in Tobin and Wicker, pp. 178–80; interview with Kameny; interview with Curtis Dewees, January 29, 1979, in New York City; and New York Mattachine Society *Newsletter*, November 1961, p. 3. Nichols used the pseudonym of Warren Adkins in his Mattachine activities.

7. Frank Kameny, "Speech to the New York Mattachine Society," July 1964, New York Mattachine Society Archives (hereafter referred to as NYMS), New York City; Kameny, "Message to the Members of the Mattachine Society of Washington from the President of the Society on the State of the Society," April 1964, MSW file, ISR.

Kameny argued relentlessly for gay activists to embrace an aggressive direct action strategy modeled on the civil rights movement. As he saw it, the movement had three options: social service, information and education, and civil rights–direct action. The first two, he stated, must take a back seat to the third. "No LASTING good can be accomplished by administration of social services ALONE," he wrote. "One can supply virtually unlimited amounts of money, food, clothing and shelter to the poor, but unless one gets to the roots of poverty—the economic system which produces unemployment . . . one will accomplish little of lasting value." He also faulted the tendency to rely "solely on an intellectually-directed program of information and education . . . to change well-entrenched, emotionally-based attitudes." The prejudiced mind, he asserted, "is NOT penetrated by information, and is not educable." Kameny turned to the burgeoning civil rights movement to bolster his case. The black American, he declared, "tried for 90 years to achieve his purposes by a program of information and education. His achievements in those 90 years, while by no means nil, were nothing compared to those of the past ten years, when he tried a vigorous civil liberties, social action approach."[8]

Kameny's civil rights orientation led him to break decisively with the homophile movement's respect for professionals. "We cannot ask for our rights," he told an audience of New York activists, "from a position of inferiority, or from a position, shall I say, as less than WHOLE human beings." Kameny condemned the movement's receptivity to medical theories about the causes of homosexuality and about whether gay men and women were susceptible to cures. "I do not see the NAACP and CORE worrying about which chromosome and gene produced a black skin, or about the possibility of bleaching the Negro," he said.

I do not see any great interest on the part of the B'nai B'rith Anti-Defamation League in the possibility of solving problems of anti-semitism by converting Jews to Christians. . . . We are interested in obtaining rights for our respective minorities AS Negroes, AS Jews, and AS HOMOSEXUALS. Why we are Negroes, Jews, or Homosexuals is totally irrelevant, and whether we can be changed to Whites, Christians, or heterosexuals is equally irrelevant.

In contrast to the equivocation of Mattachine and DOB leaders in the late 1950s, Kameny could publicly declare, "I take the stand that not only is homosexuality . . . not immoral, but that homosexual acts engaged in by consenting adults are moral, in a positive and real sense, and are right, good, and desirable, both for the individual participants and for the society in which they live."[9]

8. Ibid.
9. Kameny, "Speech," NYMS.

Kameny's experience with the Civil Service Commission molded both the priorities he set and the tactics he espoused. He targeted the discriminatory policies of the federal government as the key problem, arguing that "a change in official policy is fundamental to any change in the status of our minority group." Armed with first-hand knowledge of bureaucratic intransigence, Kameny exhorted activists to take a "firm, no-nonsense approach" with public officials. "As citizens," he said, "we ALWAYS deserve the courtesy of a meaningful and constructive response from our public servants. . . . In a democracy a private citizen is more exalted than any office holder. We have the right to have our grievances heard." To those who suggested a meek, hat-in-hand posture, Kameny replied, "We owe apologies to no one—society and its official representatives owe us apologies for what they have done and are doing to us."[10]

The Washington Mattachine Society mirrored Kameny's outlook. The organization aimed its fire at the government, specifically the discriminatory policies of the U.S. Civil Service Commission, the armed forces' exclusion of homosexuals, and the blanket denial of security clearances to all homosexuals by the Pentagon. In August 1962 members wrote to every representative, senator, and Supreme Court justice, to the president and his cabinet, and to a long list of high-level Executive Department officials, requesting appointments to discuss their grievances. Although two liberal representatives, William Fitts Ryan of Manhattan and Robert Nix of Philadelphia, quickly arranged meetings between their staff and MSW members, most other elected officials and bureaucrats did not initially heed the society's request. As Kameny wrote soon after the start of the letter-writing campaign, "those doors which have been opened to us have been opened reluctantly and only with luck and after hard work on our part."[11]

The Washington Mattachine relentlessly pursued, pestered, and hounded federal officials in order to obtain meetings. In October 1962 Kameny and Bruce Scott, the organization's secretary and himself a victim of the government's exclusion policy, won access to Pentagon officials in charge of security clearances, only to be told by one that "all homosexuals are unstable" and by another that "all homosexuals are hedonists." On policy they did not budge an inch and disingenuously suggested that the Mattachine representatives "go to the President." In a May 1963 meeting with Selective Service chief General Lewis Hershey, Mattachine emissaries objected strenuously to the release of information pertaining to sexual orientation to other federal and state agencies. When Hershey adamantly refused to consider changes in this policy, they descended on the office of the secretary of the army, but with no better results.

10. Kameny, "Speech," NYMS, and "Message," ISR.

11. Press release, August 28, 1962, MSW file, ISR; Frank Kameny to Charles Hayden, September 15 and November 18, 1962, Randy Wicker papers, in the possession of Jonathan Katz, New York City. Charles Hayden was the real name of Randy Wicker. In the late 1960s, Hayden legally changed his name to Randolfe Wicker.

Repeated requests for a meeting with John Macy, the Civil Service Commission chairman who was a special target of Kameny's ire, elicited a curt reply that "there would be no useful purpose served" by a conference, since "homosexuals are not suitable for appointment or retention" in federal employment. Shifting course somewhat, Kameny then prepared a paper, "Discrimination Against the Employment of Homosexuals," which included a copy of Macy's refusal to meet with Mattachine members, submitted it to the U.S. Civil Rights Commission, and later testified before that body.[12]

In its campaign against government employment policies, the society managed to capture the support of the local affiliate of the American Civil Liberties Union. Established in November 1961 with Kameny as one of its charter members, the National Capital Area Civil Liberties Union was still searching during 1962 for a focus to its activities. Thus Mattachine members had the opportunity to influence its direction, and they regularly attended meetings of several NCA-CLU committees. At a meeting of the committee on discrimination in December 1962, Kameny suggested that it take up the cause of homosexuals. "They were very, very queasy about the subject," he recalled. "A lot of work needed to be done." But after he presented the committee with his paper on discrimination against the homosexual, the ACLU affiliate finally took on the issue and decided to fight the Civil Service Commission's exclusion policy. Hal Witt, who chaired the committee on discrimination, wrote to Macy in March 1964 to protest the commission's regulations and urge that they be changed. In August the union adopted a strongly worded resolution that condemned the exclusion of homosexuals as "discriminatory" and called upon the federal government to "end its policy of rejection of all homosexuals." The civil liberties group backed up its resolution by taking the case of Bruce Scott, whose application for federal employment had been rejected on the grounds of "convincing evidence" of homosexual conduct.[13]

The Scott case brought the movement its first victory in the area of federal employment policies. On June 16, 1965, the U.S. Court of Appeals ruled that the charges were too vague to justify Scott's disqualification for federal employment. "The Commission," the court stated, "must at least specify the

12. Minutes of meeting with Robert Applegate, director of Security Programs Division, and Herbert Lewis, director of Industrial Personnel Access Authorization Board, Office of the Assistant Secretary of Defense, October 23, 1962, typescript (hereafter cited as Pentagon meeting minutes), personal papers of Frank Kameny, Washington, D.C.; Bruce Schuyler to Randy Wicker, May 12, 1963, Wicker papers; John Macy to Bruce Schuyler, September 28, 1962, and "Discrimination Against the Employment of Homosexuals," February 28, 1963, both in MSW file, ISR; Kameny to Hayden, November 18, 1962, Wicker papers; see also Kameny, "Message," ISR, and "Speech," NYMS, for a summary of the society's activities.

13. Interview with Kameny; Kameny to Hayden, November 18, 1962, Wicker papers; Kameny, "Speech," and Kameny to Julian Hodges, August 1, 1964, both in NYMS; Hal Witt to John Macy, March 25, 1964; Resolution of National Capital Area Civil Liberties Union on Federal Employment of Homosexuals, August 7, 1964; David Carliner to Spencer Cox, May 20, 1964, all in Kameny papers; Scott v. Macy, 349 F. 2d 182 (1965). Carliner headed the ACLU group in Washington; Cox headed the Pennsylvania ACLU.

conduct it finds 'immoral' and state why that conduct related to occupational competence or fitness." Though the court failed to meet head on the issue of whether homosexual behavior was a proper reason for denial of employment, its ruling was the first to whittle away at the CSC's prerogatives. As the Washington *Post* reported, "no federal court has gone as far as this opinion in strongly suggesting that homosexual conduct may not be an absolute disqualification for Government jobs."[14]

The District of Columbia branch of the ACLU also pressed the national organization to reverse its previous stands on homosexual-related issues and to begin to champion the rights of gay men and women. Throughout the 1950s the union's national office had received inquiries from gays who suffered discrimination and were seeking legal assistance. Politely but firmly, the ACLU had refused to handle their cases, on the grounds that "no constitutional right to practice homosexual acts" existed and that behavior "can be regulated or prohibited . . . as distinguished from belief and speech protected by the Constitution." Using psychiatric opinion to bolster its argument, the national office also acquiesced in the exclusion of lesbians and homosexuals from the armed forces, government jobs, and private employment since sexuality, it claimed, unlike race and religion, did have a "functional relevancy" to job performance. In January 1957 the ACLU board of directors adopted a national policy statement that sustained the constitutionality of the sodomy statutes and the federal security regulations denying employment to gay men and women.[15] With the support of other affiliates, notably those in New York and southern California, the Washington branch persuaded the parent body to repeal the 1957 statement. At its national convention in 1964, the ACLU took the stand that no sexual behavior between consenting adults in private ought to be subject to criminal penalties. The Washington group's resolution on federal employment also initiated further study by the national ACLU in the entire area of homosexuality and civil liberties, and it encouraged other affiliates to take on gay rights cases.[16]

The assertive, self-assured style of the Washington Mattachine precipitated an attempt in Congress to throttle the society. In May 1963 Representative John Dowdy, a conservative east Texas Democrat, introduced a bill to revoke Mattachine's permit to raise funds. At hearings during the summer, Kameny

14. Scott v. Macy, 349 F. 2d 182 (1965); and Washington *Post*, June 17, 1965, p. 3.

15. Herbert Levy to Mrs. Thomas Manly Dillingham, September 20, 1955, and Levy to Thurburn, November 23, 1955, in General Correspondence, vol. 27, 1955; and "ACLU Statement on Homosexuality," January 7, 1957, in General Correspondence, vol. 16, 1957 (all in ACLU Papers, Princeton University).

16. Resolution on Federal Employment of Homosexuals, August 7, 1964, Kameny papers; Kameny to Julian Hodges, August 1, 1964, NYMS; *Civil Liberties*, September 1965; and *Tension, Change and Liberty: American Civil Liberties Union 45th Annual Report, 1964–65* (New York, 1965), p. 55. For more on the ACLU and the civil liberties and civil rights of homosexuals, see below, Chap. 11.

came well prepared to do battle, having secured supporting testimony from the ACLU, the D.C. board of commissioners, and the Family and Child Services Agency of Washington, D.C. But committee members exhibited little interest in listening to talk about job discrimination. Instead, Dowdy used the forum to rail against homosexuality as "revolting to normal society . . . [and] banned under the laws of God." Other committee members pressed Kameny repeatedly with questions about bestiality, incest, and homosexual orgies. In August 1964 an amended version of the bill passed the House.[17]

However, the Mattachine Society ultimately emerged from the ruckus unscathed and with its prestige enhanced. The city's press gave the controversy extensive coverage that presented the homophile group in a positive light. Kameny persuaded the ACLU to monitor the bill's progress and to lobby on Capitol Hill against its passage. The affair seemed to substantiate the claims of homophile leaders that gays were the target of irrational prejudice. When the bill died in the Senate, the favorable outcome boosted the movement's self-confidence by proving that it could survive conservative attacks. Kameny even facetiously suggested an award proclaiming Dowdy "the man who contributed the most to the homophile movement in 1963."[18]

The Washington Mattachine also aggressively challenged police practices in the District of Columbia, responding to harassment with action rather than ineffective editorials in the homophile press. On May 25, 1963, the police raided the Gayety Buffet restaurant and randomly arrested several gay male patrons, without specifying the charges or informing the men of their legal rights. Taken to a local station, they were fingerprinted, charged with disorderly conduct, interrogated for details about their personal life, and subjected to verbal abuse. One man who asked what the charges were was told by an officer that he had been arrested for "winking at my friend." He was then vilified as a "queer" and a "cock-sucker" and beaten badly enough to require hospitalization. When Kameny heard of the affair, he hunted down the victims, collected affidavits, and lodged a complaint with the police department and the D.C. board of commissioners. The ACLU also registered a complaint and provided the arrested men with an attorney. Several meetings with high-level police officials ensued, until Kameny felt he had established a "modus operandi" with the department.[19]

17. U.S. Congress, House of Representatives, *Hearings Before Subcommittee No. 4 of the Committee on the District of Columbia, on H.R. 5990*, August 1963 and January 1964 (Washington, 1964), esp. pp. 2, 58–59, 70–73, 85, and 88.

18. For press coverage, see the editorial in the Washington *Post*, August 8, 1963, p. 14. See also Washington *Post*, August 9 and 10, October 4, and November 9, 1963; Washington *Star*, August 4, 8, 9, 10, September 18, and November 9, 1963, and August 12, 1964; Washington *Daily News*, August 9 and 10, 1963, and August 10, 1964 (all clippings in Kameny papers); and Kameny, "Message," ISR.

19. "Gayety Buffet Affair," file with affidavits, Kameny papers; and Kameny, "Message," NYMS, and "Speech," ISR.

II

While Kameny and the Washington Mattachine Society were breaking new ground in the nation's capital, Randy Wicker was shaking up the homophile establishment in New York. A native of Plainfield, New Jersey, Wicker had his first contact with the movement during his student days at the University of Texas in Austin when he found a copy of *ONE*. He spent a summer in Los Angeles, where he frequented ONE's offices; in 1958 he came to New York to participate in Mattachine activities. In his last two years in Austin, Wicker became active in the civil rights movement. During a campaign for the presidency of the student body, he found himself in trouble after word reached his college dean that Wicker and his roommate were gay. Several students, including his roommate, were quietly expelled, but Wicker's prominence on campus protected him from the wrath of an administration that wanted to hush up the affair. The experience bolstered his conviction that homosexuals needed a militant movement, comparable to the Southern civil rights struggle, to protect them from such actions.[20]

When Wicker settled in New York City in 1961, he initially brought his political enthusiasm into the city's gay male bars. The brash campus activist would impulsively carry Mattachine literature with him on his cruising forays. Soon he was the target of ridicule:

I couldn't understand why every homosexual did not actively support gay groups. . . . [Instead,] I was belittled. "There's Miss Mattachine," they would say. They didn't want to hear about it. They would give you arguments: "We don't want people to know we [look like] everybody else. As long as they think everyone's a screaming queen with eyelashes, we're safe. We're not suspected. We don't want publicity."

Although the reaction at first dampened his optimism, it eventually bred an even stronger desire to capture publicity for the movement and for the city's secretive gay subculture. The glare of the media spotlight, he reasoned, would shake the complacency of homosexuals and make it difficult for them to hide behind stereotypical images of "sexual deviants."[21]

Wicker resumed his involvement in the New York Mattachine but found his proposals to attract media attention frustrated by the caution of Curtis Dewees and his lover, Al de Dion, who was then president of the society. They were still seeking professionals who would represent the movement and were concerned that a visible homosexual organization might stimulate a hostile reaction by society. Differences in approach and temperament fanned a personal

---

20. Jonathan Katz, interview with Randy Wicker, February 21, 1974, in New York City; Dan Wakefield, "The Gay Crusader," *Nugget*, June 1963, pp. 51–52; and Wicker to Gaeton Fonzi, January 31, 1963, Wicker papers. I am indebted to Jonathan Katz for letting me use the tape of his interview with Wicker.

21. Interview with Wicker.

antipathy that made it impossible for Wicker to work with them. Early in 1962 he created the Homosexual League of New York, a one-man organization designed to give him a free hand to pursue his own plans.[22]

In April 1962, when WBAI radio broadcast a discussion by psychiatrists on homosexuality, Wicker seized it as the opportunity to launch his media campaign. He convinced the station's public affairs director to air a program in which male homosexuals spoke for themselves and then sent out a press release announcing the show. Jack O'Brian, a conservative columnist for the New York *Journal-American*, picked up the story. He lambasted WBAI for "scraping the sickly barrel-bottom" and denounced Wicker as an "arrogant card-carrying swish." Wicker could hardly have asked for more. The next day, the station was swamped with calls asking about the broadcast. With the O'Brian column in hand, Wicker visited the offices of the city's press in the hope of getting mileage out of the controversy. He succeeded; *Newsweek* gave Wicker and the program a sympathetic full-page spread, and the *New York Times* favorably reviewed it in two articles.[23]

Wicker used his sudden visibility to induce further media coverage. Paul Krassner's *Realist* published a complete transcript of the show, and *Escapade*, one of a spate of *Playboy* imitators, printed a condensed version. Wicker persuaded the *Village Voice* to run a series on the homosexual rights movement and the Greenwich Village gay scene; he shepherded the writer Dan Wakefield on a tour of gay male bars and cruising areas for an article on Wicker and the gay movement; he convinced the editors of *Harper's* to publish a piece on homosexual life in New York; and he supplied a New York *Post* reporter with material for a major series on sex and the law.[24]

Wicker's achievements had a snowballing effect. Each one of the articles expanded his ability to present himself as a spokesperson for the movement and provided him with added leverage in gaining a hearing for the homophile cause. After the *Voice* gave play to his claim that homosexuals were a powerful political constituency, he wrote to such liberal political groupings as the Americans for Democratic Action and the Village Independent Democrats and requested the chance to speak to them as a representative of the homosexual "voting bloc." He secured speaking engagements at the American Human-

22. Interview with Wicker; interview with Curtis Dewees, January 29, 1979, in New York City; Wicker to Barbara Gittings, "Wed. the 17th," Wicker papers; NYMS *Newsletter*, July 1963, p. 2.

23. Interview with Wicker; New York *Journal American*, July 9, 1962, p. 18; *Newsweek*, July 30, 1962, p. 48; *New York Times*, July 16, 1962, p. 47, 48; and "Conversation on a Taboo Subject," *Escapade*, February 1963, pp. 20–22.

24. *Realist*, August 1962, September 1962, October 1962; *Escapade*, February 1963; Stephanie Gervis, "Politics: A Third Party for the Third Sex?" and "The Homosexual's Labyrinth of Law and Social Custom," *Village Voice*, September 27, 1962 and October 11, 1962; Dan Wakefield, "The Gay Crusader," *Nugget*, June 1963, pp. 51–52; William Helmer, "New York's Middle-Class Homosexuals," *Harper's*, March 1963, pp. 85–92; and New York *Post*, June 17–21, June 23, 1963.

ist Association, the New York Ethical Culture Society, Rutgers University, the City College of New York, and the Judson Memorial Church in Greenwich Village. The new visibility soon had publishers and broadcasters coming to Wicker and the city's other homophile organizations for information, as they sought not to be outdone by their competitors. The number of articles on homosexuality increased markedly from 1962 to 1965. Even the staid *New York Times* contributed to the trend toward more open discussion with a front page article on the "homosexual problem" in New York.[25]

Wicker keenly appreciated the impact that even one visible homosexual could have on the lives of gay men and women. As he explained in a letter to his mother shortly before appearing on national television,

> I will be talking to millions of people about things they never heard before. My participation on the panel will help mothers like you to understand the problems of their children. I will be reaching dozens, perhaps hundreds, even thousands of young men and women who are lost and confused, who are thinking of suicide, who are laden with guilt, who cannot face the world, who think they are the only ones in the world who feel as they do. I will be a "symbol" of hope to these people—a living example that they can have a life unracked by depravity. . . . [This] is the greatest chance I have ever had in my life to do something *really important, really noble*, and *really satisfying*.

Evidence that his efforts were worthwhile accumulated in the steady stream of correspondence that articles about him and the movement provoked. Letters kept arriving—from Hillsboro, Oregon, and Clearwater, Florida; from De-Kalb, Illinois, and Everett, Massachusetts—written by gay women and men who blessed Wicker for his courage. One man promised to move to New York to work with Wicker. Another expressed gratitude over finally learning the location of a gay bar in Manhattan. Now, he wrote, "I hope to get up the guts to visit one." A lesbian from Brooklyn asked Wicker "where the gay bars are for girls." A two-line ad placed by Wicker in the *Voice*—"Sample Packet of Homosexual Publications Mailed in a Plain Wrapper"—elicited 600 orders. The media breakthrough achieved by Wicker in the early 1960s alleviated for many the emotional trauma of coming out and provided information that eased entry into the urban gay subculture.[26]

25. See Wicker to John McDermit, Americans for Democratic Action, September 27, 1962; Wicker to William Fox, Village Independent Democrats, May 10, 1963; Joseph Duffey to Wicker, May 31, 1963; Wicker to New York Society for Ethical Culture, July 12, 1963, all in Wicker papers; Dan Wakefield, "The Gay Crusader," p. 71; NYMS *Newsletter*, July 1962, p. 2; August 1962, p. 4; April 1964, p. 12; and May 1964, pp. 9–10; *New York Times*, December 17, 1963, p. 1; and October 18, 1963, p. 28; *Newsweek*, December 30, 1963, p. 42; and *Life*, June 26, 1964, pp. 66–74. The number of articles listed in the *Readers' Guide to Periodical Literature* under "homosexuality" and "lesbianism" is as follows: 1959, 3; 1960, 1; 1961, 3; 1962, 1; 1963, 6; 1964, 7; 1965, 17.

26. Wicker [Charles Hayden] to his mother, November 16, 1964; "File of Letters from Readers;" and file of letters in response to *Village Voice* ad, all in Wicker papers.

III

The new militancy of Kameny and Wicker stimulated a hostile reaction from the old guard in New York. Each of them posed a challenge to the perspectives of the Mattachine Society and the Daughters of Bilitis. Kameny's attitude toward professionals, for instance, diverged sharply from the New York Mattachine's propensity to listen to pronouncements from doctors and lawyers, while Wicker's willingness to display any and all aspects of the gay subculture to public scrutiny contrasted with DOB's preoccupation with a respectable image. In October 1962 DOB held a discussion on the "new publicity break" that highlighted the gulf between Wicker's views and those of homophile leaders like Meredith Grey, a founder and officer of DOB, and Curtis Dewees.[27]

Undaunted by this negative reaction, both Wicker and Kameny sought mechanisms to expand their influence. Taking advantage of Mattachine's disposition to air every conceivable position, Wicker secured a regular column in the organization's newsletter. "The Wicker Basket" provided the readership with a militant exposition of the gay crusader's views that excited many members. One man informed him that he "made more sense than a lot of the hodge podge that I've heard in many a Mattachine meeting." Kameny suggested meanwhile that homophile groups in the East confer regularly. At a meeting in January 1963 in Philadelphia, representatives of four organizations—DOB and the New York Mattachine, the Janus Society of Philadelphia, and the Washington Mattachine—agreed to form a loosely structured coalition, East Coast Homophile Organizations (ECHO), to "explore ways of closer intergroup cooperation."[28]

Over the succeeding two years, ECHO played a critical role in solidifying a militant wing of the movement. Through its monthly meetings, activists who were enthusiastic about the achievements of the Washington Mattachine and the media breakthroughs—notably Kameny, Jack Nichols, Lilli Vincenz, and John Marshall in Washington; Joan Fraser, Marge McCann, Clark Polak, and Barbara Gittings in Philadelphia; and Dick Leitsch, Craig Rodwell, Julian Hodges, Kay Tobin, and Randy Wicker in New York—developed an informal communications network. They exchanged information, debated tactics, and concocted schemes for pushing their groups toward greater militancy. Small steps were taken toward binding the organizations more closely together. Militants in one group maintained memberships in others. The New York and Washington Mattachines embarked upon a jointly published magazine. And the militants' stronger commitment to intergroup cooperation gave them a

27. New York Mattachine Society *Newsletter*, October 1962, p. 7, and November 1962, pp. 7–9; *Ladder*, December 1962, pp. 16–17, and June 1963, pp. 19–20.

28. Wicker's column first appeared in the April 1963 issue of the New York Mattachine Society *Newsletter*; on ECHO see NYMS *Newsletter*, February 1963, p. 8; and Bill Brown to Wicker, July 17, 1962, Wicker papers.

disproportionate voice in ECHO that allowed them to attract more adherents to their banner.[29]

As those advocating an aggressive public posture drew closer to one another, they developed the confidence to push the movement even farther along their chosen path and thus sharpened antagonisms within organizations. The old guard members in the New York Mattachine and the Daughters of Bilitis found themselves beleaguered by an activist wing whose zeal, daring, and assertiveness appalled them. By 1965 the conflict between the accommodationist stance of the early leadership and the civil rights–direct action approach of the new militants was barely containable. The militants' decision in 1965 to press for an unequivocal stand against the medical establishment's sickness theory and to initiate public picketing on behalf of gay rights brought antagonisms to the breaking point.

For Kameny and his allies, the medical model of homosexuality hung like a millstone around the movement's neck. Dealings with the Washington bureaucracy impressed upon Kameny the sickness theory's deleterious impact on efforts to combat institutionalized inequality. Federal officials, he found, rarely invoked the danger of blackmail to justify discriminatory policies. Instead, they relied on psychiatric advice that gay men and women were "unstable." Moreover, the notion of homosexuality as mental illness was receiving greater dissemination during the early 1960s. In this regard, the movement's relatively successful effort to foster discussion of homosexuality in print proved a mixed blessing. Weakening inhibitions against writing about homosexuality in the press and magazines led to wider circulation of current medical opinion. In particular, Irving Bieber's 1962 psychoanalytic study, *Homosexuality*, and the New York Academy of Medicine's 1964 report both argued that homosexuality was an acquired illness susceptible to cure, and both received extensive favorable commentary in newspapers and popular periodicals.[30]

29. See, e.g., the following correspondence between militants: Leitsch to Adkins, January 26 and March 16, 1965, NYMS, and February 2, 1965, Kameny papers; Adkins to Leitsch, January 24, February 9, April 1, and June 2, 1965, NYMS; Hodges to Kameny, December 14, 1964, NYMS; Kameny to Leitsch, June 29, July 12, and August 15, 1965, NYMS; Gittings to Kameny, June 12, June 20, June 23, and November 26, 1965, Kameny papers; Gittings to Wicker, October 12 and December 12, 1962, Wicker papers; Tobin to Kameny, August 5, 1965, Kameny papers; Kameny to Hodges, July 18, 1965, NYMS; Kameny to Wicker, March 30, 1963, NYMS; Leitsch to Vincenz, October 26, 1964, November 3, 1964, and January 19, 1965, NYMS, Leitsch to Kameny, October 20, 1964, NYMS; [Marge McCann] to Leitsch, January 19, 1965, NYMS; Leitsch to [McCann], January 21, 1965, NYMS; Kameny to McCann, January 30, 1965, NYMS.

30. Pentagon meeting minutes, October 23, 1962, Kameny papers; Irving Bieber et al., *Homosexuality: A Psychoanalytic Study of Male Homosexuals* (New York, 1962); and New York Academy of Medicine, Committee on Public Health, *Homosexuality* (New York, 1964). For discussions of the medical model in the press and in magazines, see *New York Times*, December 17, 1963, p. 1; May 19, 1964, p. 1; August 23, 1964, Section VI, p. 75; and January 31, 1965, p. 61; *Newsweek*, December 30, 1963, p. 42; *Christian Century*, September 11, 1963, pp. 1099–1101; *Time*, February 12, 1965, p. 44; and *Science News Letter*, February 13, 1965, p. 102.

By the early 1960s, rumblings of discontent were coming from rank-and-file activists who were growing intolerant of the willingness of old guard leaders to give doctors a forum. When Ernest Harms, editor of the prestigious *International Monographs of Child Psychiatry*, told a New York Mattachine audience late in 1961 that 80 percent of male homosexuals were curable and advised Mattachine to try an "Alcoholics Anonymous" approach, a disgruntled clamor arose from the assembled crowd. Later, a chagrined officer scolded the audience: "Surely a professional psychiatrist has every right to disapprove of homosexual practices." Two years later, after Albert Ellis announced at an ECHO convention that "the exclusive homosexual is a psychopath," an enraged listener retorted, "Any homosexual who would come to you for treatment, Dr. Ellis, would *have* to be a psychopath!" When Samuel Hadden remarked in a lecture at the University of Pennsylvania Medical School that "I can always recognize a homosexual," a gay activist in the audience exploded, "This is not science, Dr. Hadden; this is faith!"[31]

It took persistence on the part of the militants to persuade the majority in their organizations to reject the medical establishment's authority. Jack Nichols first broached the subject in October 1963, in a letter urging the organization's executive board to adopt the position that homosexuality was not a disease. "The mental attitude of our own people toward themselves," he observed,

> that they are not well—that they are not whole, that they are LESS THAN COMPLETELY HEALTHY— is *responsible* for UNTOLD NUMBERS OF PERSONAL TRAGEDIES AND WARPED LIVES. By failing to take a definite stand, a strong stand . . . I believe that you will not only weaken the movement ten-fold, but that you will fail in your duty to homosexuals who need more than anything else to see themselves in a better light.[32]

Nothing, however, came immediately of Nichols' plea. As Lilli Vincenz, a militant stalwart of the organization, recalled, "people just weren't ready for it." By the following summer, the situation was changing. The currency given to Bieber's views and the publication of the New York Academy of Medicine report alerted activists to the medical model's subversive impact on the movement's efforts to win social acceptance. When Kameny delivered the 100th monthly lecture of the New York Mattachine Society in July 1964, he devoted a substantial part of his speech to precisely this issue. "The entire homophile movement," he asserted, "is going to stand or fall upon the question of whether homosexuality is a sickness, and upon our taking a firm stand on it." He assailed the literature of the mental health profession, and the Bieber study

31. NYMS *Newsletter*, November 1961, pp. 4–5; *Ladder*, December 1963, pp. 8–10; *Ladder*, May 1965, pp. 20–21.
32. Warren Adkins [Jack Nichols] to Executive Board, October 14, 1963, Kameny papers.

in particular, for its "appalling incidence of loose reasoning, of poor research, of . . . conclusions being derived from an examination of non-representative samplings, of conclusions being incorporated into initial assumptions, and vice versa, with the consequent circular reasoning." He challenged his audience to take his stand that, "until and unless valid positive evidence shows otherwise, homosexuality *per se* is neither a sickness, a defect, a disturbance, a neurosis, a psychosis, nor a malfunction of any sort."[33]

Kameny's speech galvanized the membership in New York and those from Washington who had come to listen. Five months later Julian Hodges, the New York Mattachine president and a recent convert to the militant wing, wrote Kameny that his address "caused, and is still causing, more active participation in our projects, and a more positive, actionist attitude in those who direct our projects." In Washington Nichols, Vincenz, and Kameny initiated a carefully orchestrated campaign to have their organization adopt an antisickness resolution. With the help of the New Yorkers, they amassed quotes and letters from dozens of doctors in support of their position. In February 1965 the Washington Mattachine opened debate on the policy statement. Nichols reported that he was "very pleased with the reaction of the members—even the more timid ones." In the following month, more than two-thirds of the membership approved the militants' resolution:

> The Mattachine Society of Washington takes the position that in the absence of valid evidence to the contrary, homosexuality is not a sickness, disturbance, or other pathology in any sense, but is merely a preference, orientation, or propensity, on par with, and not different in kind from, heterosexuality.[34]

The militants barely had time to enjoy their victory when new frontiers beckoned. On April 16 the press reported that the Cuban government was confining homosexuals in labor camps. Craig Rodwell in New York and Jack Nichols in Washington seized upon the announcement to organize impromptu demonstrations in front of the United Nations headquarters and the White House. Lest anyone mistake the event as an anti-Castro action, the pickets displayed signs that made their target clear: "Fifteen Million U.S. Homosexuals Protest Federal Treatment," one placard read, while another charged that "Cuba's Government Persecutes Homosexuals. U.S. Government Beat Them to It." At the May 1965 ECHO meeting, the militants won agreement to mount a series of picket lines during the spring and summer, choosing as sites the Civil Service Commission building, the State Department, the Pentagon,

33. Interview with Lilli Vincenz, November 5, 1978, in South Arlington, Virginia; Kameny, "Speech," NYMS. Vincenz used the pseudonym of Lily Hansen in her Mattachine activities.

34. Hodges to Kameny, December 14, 1964; Adkins [Nichols] to Leitsch, January 24, 1964; Leitsch to Adkins and Kameny, February 2, 1965; Leitsch to Adkins, January 26, 1965; Adkins to Leitsch, February 9, 1965 (all in NYMS); "Policy of the Mattachine Society of Washington," adopted March 4, 1965, MSW file, ISR.

the White House, and, for the fourth of July, Independence Hall in Philadelphia.[35]

Though hardly earth shattering in their impact, the demonstrations marked another important step forward. In comparison with the civil rights marches of the early 1960s or the first wave of antiwar protests that spring, the public actions staged by homophile militants were tiny. On the same day that Students for a Democratic Society attracted 20,000 to an antiwar demonstration at the Washington Monument, seven men and three women paraded at the White House for gay rights; at a repeat performance in October, the numbers had only risen to forty-five. Picketing implicitly involved an open avowal of one's homosexuality, and though many might applaud it, few were prepared to risk the possible consequences of a public stand. That some did, however, signaled a change and provided a model for others to emulate. Despite their paltry size, moreover, the demonstrations produced some welcome results. The day before the picketing of the State Department, for instance, Secretary of State Dean Rusk had to field a question from a reporter on the department's policy toward employing homosexuals. And the Civil Service Commission finally agreed to a meeting with Mattachine representatives after a day of marching in front of its offices. The public actions also garnered some much coveted media attention. Television cameras from ABC filmed the White House demonstration of May 29, and local affiliates in at least nine states used the film on their newscasts. The wire services also sent out a story that was picked up by papers in several cities around the country. Thus even small public actions could make known to many homosexuals and lesbians the existence of a gay rights movement.[36]

IV

In New York, meanwhile, where tensions between the militants and the old guard had reached the breaking point, battle lines were being drawn in preparation for the Mattachine Society's May 1965 elections. The contest promised a clear test of the respective strength of the two factions as they struggled for control of the organization. Each side presented a slate of

35. *New York Times*, April 16, 1965, p. 2, and May 27, 1965, p. 9; "News Bulletin," April 17, 1965, MSW file, ISR; Tobin and Wicker, *The Gay Crusaders*, pp. 181–82; New York DOB, Minutes of Business Meeting, June 6, 1965, in NYDOB *Newsletter*, July 1965; and news release, June 24, 1965, MSW file, ISR. Demonstrations were held on May 29 at the White House, June 26 at the Civil Service Commission building, July 4 at Independence Hall in Philadelphia, July 31 at the Pentagon, August 28 at the State Department, and October 23 at the White House. Copies of news releases issued prior to each event and information bulletins issued immediately after can be found in the Kameny papers and the MSW file, ISR.

36. See *New York Times*, May 30, 1965, p. 42; and Washington *Post*, August 29, 1965, p. 27. The New York and Washington Mattachine Societies received clippings and letters from readers concerning coverage of the demonstrations outside of Washington and New York. See NYMS *Newsletter*, May 1965, p. 3, and August 1965, p. 4; and Kameny to DOB Governing Board, June 8, 1965, Kameny papers.

candidates, and the campaign revealed the sharp differences in perspective between the camps. The militants pledged themselves to "a program of action" and vowed to transform the society into the "champion of the homosexual community." The old guard faction, on the other hand, based its campaign on "helping the individual homosexual adjust to society."[37]

Julian Hodges headed the militant slate. A member of a prominent North Carolina family, Hodges had originally been a protegé of Curtis Dewees, but Kameny's hard-hitting address in the summer of 1964 influenced him profoundly and won him over to militancy. At the October 1964 ECHO convention, Hodges delivered a speech that urged gay activists to plunge into the political arena. His conversion to the civil rights–direct action perspective of Kameny earned him the enmity of his old guard sponsors.[38]

Running with Hodges were Dick Leitsch, Kameny, and Dr. Hendrik Ruitenbeek. Leitsch too had been swayed by Kameny's philosophy. By his own admission, he had read the Washington activist's speech "about fifteen times" until convinced that if Mattachine did not become a "social protest organization," it was "useless, silly, and [had] no reason to exist." As editor of the organization's newsletter, Leitsch played a critical role in transforming it into an organ for the militants' views. Kameny and Ruitenbeek were seeking positions on the board of directors. A psychoanalyst and a faculty member at New York University, Ruitenbeek had supported the movement's drive against the medical model and had lent his prestige to the Washington militants' efforts to adopt an antisickness policy statement.[39]

The oldtimers in Mattachine found the accelerating shift toward a civil rights orientation distressing. Older than most of the militants by a decade or more, they remembered the atmosphere of heightened anxiety engendered by the McCarthy era and found it difficult to cast off their fears of the repression they believed militancy would provoke. Leaders of the old guard faction had also experienced more years of living "discreetly," and the openness of younger activists threatened their ingrained habits. Finally, to accept the positions espoused by the militants required that they repudiate as ineffective their own ideas about strategy and acknowledge their ambivalence about homosexuality. Undoubtedly, wounded egos contributed to their intransigence.

The old guard seized upon the elections as a last-ditch attempt to stop the militants. Early in 1965 some of them constituted themselves as "the committee" and began holding strategy sessions. Four past presidents and two current members of the board of directors were represented. As its candidates the

37. Hodges, Leitsch, and Kameny to NYMS members, n.d., and David Goldberger to NYMS members, May 12, 1965 (both in NYMS file, ISR).

38. Interview with Dewees; Adkins [Nichols] to Leitsch, January 24, 1965, NYMS; *Ladder*, January 1965, p. 9.

39. Leitsch to Vincenz, January 12, 1965, NYMS; Leitsch to Kameny and Adkins, February 2, 1965, Kameny papers.

committee put forward David Goldberger, who ran the Mattachine's West Side discussion group, Donald Webster Cory, and Curtis Dewees and aggressively sought proxies from inactive members of the society.[40]

The presence of Cory on the old guard's slate put into bold relief the issues in the campaign. As the author of *The Homosexual in America* in 1951, Cory was almost worshiped by participants in the movement. In succeeding years, he published a number of other books, spoke frequently at conferences on sexuality, addressed homophile conventions, and became more and more active in the New York Mattachine Society. But the intervening years had also wrought a profound shift in Cory's perspective. In his writing and public speeches, he increasingly propounded the view that homosexuals were disturbed and that cure was desirable. Though he believed that persecution should end—"the alcoholic is disturbed, but is not expelled from the society of man," he argued by analogy in 1959—Cory took issue with the militants' drive against the medical model. At the 1964 DOB convention in New York, Cory accused the movement of "alienating itself from scientific thinking . . . by its constant, defensive, neurotic, disturbed denial" that homosexuals were sick. The following year, when told that the Washington Mattachine had just adopted an antisickness resolution, he promised Dick Leitsch that he would "quit the Society if we ever pass such a statement here."[41]

The militants pulled out the stops in their struggle for control, leaving no room for confusion about the issues in the campaign. In private dialogue and public statements they posed the conflict sharply. Kameny wrote to Cory that

you have left the mainstream for the backwaters . . . you have fallen by the wayside, lost most of your effectiveness . . . you have become no longer the vigorous Father of the Homophile Movement, to be revered, respected and listened to, but the senile Grandfather of the Homophile Movement, to be humored and tolerated at best; to be ignored and disregarded usually; and to be ridiculed, at worst.

Hodges sent the membership a letter urging a vote for the entire militant slate in order to avoid electing a board of directors "split down the middle on such vital issues as whether or not homosexuality is an illness, whether or not the Society should be primarily a 'civil rights' organization, and whether the Society should aim its program to the homosexual community in general or to the individual homosexual." Leitsch, meanwhile, distributed a campaign flyer liberally sprinkled with Cory's most damaging comments about homosexuals

40. Al de Dion to members of the Committee, February 24, 1965 and April 20, 1965; the Committee to members of NYMS, March 5, 1965; Goldberger, Cory, and Kilpatrick to NYMS members, n.d. (all ISR).

41. Donald Webster Cory [pseud.], "A Preface to the Second Edition: One Decade Later," in *The Homosexual in America*, 2d ed. (New York, 1959); *Ladder*, August 1964, p. 21, and NYMS *Newsletter*, August 1964, p. 4; and Leitsch to Adkins [Nichols], March 16, 1965, NYMS.

as "disturbed individuals" and "borderline psychotics." In the May balloting, the militants captured two-thirds of the votes and routed the old guard. A jubilant Nichols sent Leitsch his congratulations: "It is very much a victory for all of us who are working hard and who don't want to see the clock turned backwards by the stick-in-the-muds and the 'sickniks.' "[42]

The election decisively closed a chapter in the New York Mattachine's history. The old guard departed en masse. For some like Curtis Dewees, who had spent almost ten years working in the Society, it marked the end of their involvement in the movement. Others shifted their allegiance to the West Side Discussion Group, which dropped its Mattachine affiliation and became an independent organization for homosexuals and lesbians to enjoy "informal but dignified fellowship."[43]

The outcome of the election had its most dramatic effect upon Cory. After 1965 the pseudonymous Cory ceased to exist and was replaced by Edward Sagarin, a sociologist of deviance. In 1966 Sagarin submitted as a doctoral dissertation at New York University a study of the New York Mattachine Society. Under the guise of academic objectivity, he described at length the functioning of the society and its recent upheavals, though without revealing that he was anything but a detached social scientist recording his observations. Sagarin was scathing in his criticism of the organization. He attributed the 1965 election battle to the desire to end manipulative tyranny by a small clique and dismissed the possibility that serious philosophical differences over the direction of a social change movement were at stake. In succeeding years, Sagarin continued to write about the homophile and later the gay liberation movement. Rarely did he have kind words for the movement that he helped launch and that later launched him into a career as a sociologist of "deviance."[44]

V

In the Daughters of Bilitis, meanwhile, Barbara Gittings provoked the first waves of conflict between militants and old guard. Founder and first president of the New York chapter, Gittings was born in Vienna in 1932, where her father served as a member of the United States diplomatic corps. She enrolled

42. Kameny to Cory, April 7, 1965, Kameny papers; Julian C. Hodges, campaign statement, and Dick Leitsch, campaign statement, both in NYMS file, ISR; Adkins [Nichols] to Dick Leitsch, June 2, 1965, NYMS; and NYMS *Newsletter*, May 1965, p. 1.

43. Interview with Dewees; Goldberger to NYMS members, May 12, 1965, NYMS file, ISR.

44. Edward Sagarin, "Structure and Ideology in an Association of Deviants," Ph.D. diss., New York University, 1966, esp. chap. 14; "Homosexuals: the Many Masks of Mattachine," in *Odd Man In: Societies of Deviants in America* (Chicago, 1969); "Good Guys, Bad Guys, and Gay Guys: Survey Essay," *Contemporary Sociology* 2 (1973): 3–13; and "Is 'Gay' as Good as 'Straight'?" *Sexology*, February 1970, p. 22. Sagarin's dissertation has been published in a 1975 Arno Press reprint edition. For a discussion of Cory/Sagarin from a gay liberationist perspective, see John Kyper and Steven Abbott, "The Betrayal of Donald Webster Cory?" *Fag Rag/Gay Sunshine: Stonewall 5th Anniversary Issue*, Summer 1974, p. 23.

in Northwestern University to study theater and, because of her close friendship with another woman student, found herself the target of rumors that she was a lesbian. The incident prompted a time of self-examination in which vague and confusing feelings coalesced gradually into an awareness that her sexuality departed from the norm. Gittings spent the rest of her freshman year searching for information—in texts on abnormal psychology, encyclopedias, medical books, and whatever studies of human sexuality she could find. "Everything," she recalled, "was so alien, so remote. It didn't give me any sense of myself or what my life and experience could be. It was mostly clinical-sounding—disturbance, pathology, arrested development—*and* it was mostly about men." Eventually she stumbled upon novels about lesbians. "They had more realism than all the case histories I'd read put together!" she reminisced. "At last here were lesbians shown as real people! They didn't exactly have lives of bliss, but at least they were functioning people and had their happinesses. . . . Finding the fiction literature of my people was a godsend to me."[45]

Gittings dropped out of college and moved to Philadelphia, where she made her way into the bar subculture of the early 1950s. For a time she adopted what seemed the only available option, the butch-femme roles that dominated the lesbian bar scene. But from her point of view they were no better than the case histories in a medical textbook, and she continued to search for alternatives. After reading *The Homosexual in America*, she wrote to Cory, who told her about the Mattachine Society. In the summer of 1956, Gittings traveled to San Francisco, where Don Lucas and Hal Call put her in touch with the newly formed Daughters of Bilitis. The contact marked a turning point in her life. "Del Martin and Phyllis Lyon provided me with a much better sense of lesbianism and the lesbian community than I'd ever had before," she said. Two years later, in September 1958, Gittings initiated a New York chapter and served as its president for three years. In December 1962 she took on the editorship of the *Ladder*.[46]

The militancy of Kameny and Wicker made a strong impression on Gittings. After hearing Wicker speak in October 1962, she thanked him "for sparking—and sparkling in—the panel discussion" and complimented him on his "clear and intelligent message." Kameny exerted an even greater influence. Meeting him at an ECHO meeting early in 1963, she recalled that he was "the first gay person I met who took firm, uncompromising positions about homosexuality and homosexuals' right to be considered fully on a par with heterosexuals. He was more positive than any other gay activist on the scene." A close, harmonious work relationship developed between them, and

---

45. "Barbara Gittings," in Kay Tobin and Randy Wicker, *The Gay Crusaders* (New York, 1972), pp. 206–8; see also the interview with Gittings in Jonathan Katz, ed., *Gay American History* (New York, 1976), pp. 420–33.

46. Tobin and Wicker, pp. 208–12.

before long Gittings was arguing in DOB for Kameny-style tactics, strategies, and perspectives.[47]

Gittings used her position as *Ladder* editor to give DOB a more militant appearance. She instituted a "Living Propaganda" series that urged gay women to come out, she included the word "lesbian" on the magazine's cover, and she further adorned it with photos of women taken by her lover, Kay Tobin. She commissioned articles by militant converts that had no pretense to objective journalism and took on doctors such as Albert Ellis and Irving Bieber. The *Ladder*'s coverage of the 1964 ECHO conference, written by Jack Nichols, Lilli Vincenz, Gittings, and Kay Tobin, was an unabashedly partisan presentation of the militant viewpoint. "I'm an activist," the article began. "I've read nearly 75 books in the New York Mattachine library, and I'm fed up with reading on the subject of homosexuality."[48]

Gittings's position as editor of the *Ladder* became precarious after she initiated debate at DOB's 1964 convention about the organization's dependence on the medical profession. She tried to convince the membership that "the only authorities on homosexuality as a way of feeling and living . . . are homosexuals themselves." But she found to her dismay that most DOB members held firm to the belief "that only the recognized experts can effectively influence public opinion, that we won't be given a hearing if we pooh-pooh the acknowledged 'authorities.' " Her strong statements at the convention and her choice of material for the *Ladder* antagonized the more conservative leaders in the organization. Florence Conrad, research director of DOB, wrote a long defense of the need for scientific studies to counter Gittings's stance. Shirley Willer, who succeeded Gittings as president of the New York chapter, directed members to send letters to DOB's governing board about the "crisis" facing the *Ladder*.[49]

However, Gittings refused to back down. In May 1965 she printed a lengthy article by Kameny, who presented the arguments behind the antisickness stand and exhorted his readers to "move away from the comfortingly detached respectability of research into the often less pleasant rough-and-tumble of political and social activism." Florence Conrad responded with an attack on the Mattachine position—"very foolish," she called it—and revealingly defined the difference between Kameny and herself as one of "audience." She

47. Barbara Gittings to Randy Wicker, October 12, 1962, Wicker papers; Tobin and Wicker, p. 213; interview with Kameny.

48. See "Living Propaganda," *Ladder*, November 1963, pp. 4–6; December 1963, pp. 15–16; and January 1964, pp. 18–19. "Lesbian" appears for the first time on the cover of the January 1964 issue, and photos in September 1964. See also "Ellis and the Chestnuts," *Ladder*, November 1963, pp. 13–15; "Faith and Fury," May 1965, pp. 20–22; "Editorial," August 1964, pp. 4–5; "ECHO Report, 64," January 1965, pp. 4–11.

49. Gittings to Don Slater, September 21, 1964, DOB file, Homosexual Information Center Library, Los Angeles (hereafter referred to as HIC); Florence Conrad, "How Much Research—and Why?" *Ladder*, September 1964, pp. 20–24; and NYDOB Minutes of Business Meeting, February 21, 1965, and Gittings to ONE, March 9, 1965, DOB file, HIC.

preferred a "dialogue" with "those whose opinions count," while Kameny geared his strategy toward "the unthinking masses." Gittings let Kameny have the final word, however, and in his rejoinder he rose to the challenge. "If there are no other reasons for our taking the position on sickness . . . than bolstering the morale of our own people, we would have justification enough."[50]

Gittings's aggressive use of the *Ladder* to champion the militant position may have influenced some readers, but it did nothing to change the views of the San Francisco–dominated governing board. In August 1965 Kay Tobin despairingly complained to Kameny about the "non-think DOB members in San Francisco." The DOB leadership, she informed him, remained "so impressed by 'experts' with credentials that . . . [it] forgets completely that minority groups with legitimate grievances are also among the best and most legitimate social critics." After Kameny's rebuttal to Conrad appeared in the *Ladder*, Gittings wryly described to him the "letters-and-letters-about-letters which comprise the latest DOB mess that I've been swatted with" and conceded that her hold on the editorship was "very precarious." The following summer the inevitable happened. The board removed Gittings "in a nasty debacle" that, she speculated, might "have the good effect of damaging the DOB Establishment's power grip and false image."[51]

While controversy swirled around Gittings, another political storm gathered force within the New York DOB. The decision of a majority of ECHO delegates to support picketing precipitated a clash in the chapter between an old guard and a militant wing that was as sharply defined, and as bitter, as the one experienced by the New York Mattachine over the antisickness resolution. In the case of DOB, however, the conservative faction could enlist the founders in San Francisco, whose power to veto chapter decisions transformed the picketing issue from a question of tactics into a test of loyalty. Militant women felt pressured to choose between their attachment to an all-lesbian organization and their allegiance to a civil rights–direct action perspective.

Meredith Grey and Shirley Willer led the old guard forces in New York. A friend and hiking companion of Barbara Gittings in the mid-1950s, Grey also was a founding member of DOB in New York. Years later she recalled how her skepticism about the effort was overcome by Gittings. When Grey questioned her about the venture's feasibility, Gittings quipped, "Don't ask a bee how it flies," and Grey succumbed to the faith of her friend. Willer had uprooted herself to participate in the lesbian organization. A registered nurse in Chicago, where she had been born and raised, she had come out in the 1940s and moved to New York at the end of the 1950s to join DOB, after failing to form a

50. Frank Kameny, "Does Research into Homosexuality Matter?" *Ladder*, May 1965, pp. 14–20; Florence Conrad, "Research Is Here to Stay," *Ladder*, July–August 1965, pp. 15–21; and Kameny, "Emphasis on Research Has Had Its Day," *Ladder*, October 1965, pp. 10–14, 23–26.

51. Tobin to Kameny, August 5, 1965; Gittings to Kameny, November 26, 1965, and July 18, 1966 (all in Kameny papers).

branch in the Midwest. She soon became president of the chapter as well as Grey's lover.[52]

The vote in favor of picketing distressed the two women, and Willer contacted the San Francisco leadership for guidance. Informed that demonstrations were "against DOB policy on political intervention," she brought to the next ECHO meeting a resolution that the coalition "not engage in any activity contrary to the policy or welfare of any participating organization." When the motion was defeated, Willer and Grey angrily pulled DOB out of ECHO. The decision reflected not merely the execution of a directive from San Francisco but personal conviction as well. As Grey wrote later that summer, the Washington demonstrations were "the most discouraging action yet undertaken by the homophile community."[53]

For the next year militants and old guard fought over the decision. In July, the rank and file overruled the leadership and approved participation in the picketing. The following month, Grey challenged the vote and raised the specter of disaffiliation by the national governing board if the New York group contravened its policy. The membership retreated and instead asked San Francisco to "revise its present non-participatory policy and adopt a full-scale progressive program of direct action to push the drive for full equality for the homosexual citizen." When the national office refused to budge, DOB's withdrawal from ECHO became permanent.[54]

In the short run Willer and Grey's tactics backfired. That October the membership voted them out of office and installed in their place "Emma Van Cott" and "Ernestine Eckstein," who had played conciliatory roles during the summer. Temperament motivated Eckstein's peacemaking; her convictions were pure militant. A black woman, Eckstein had studied journalism at Indiana University in the late 1950s and had joined the campus NAACP, the only civil rights organization in Bloomington. When she settled in New York after graduation, she shifted her involvement to the more action-oriented CORE. By the time she joined the Daughters in 1965, Eckstein felt that picketing was "almost a conservative activity," the least one could do to attract public notice. Disturbed by the "premium placed on psychologists and therapists" by some sectors of the homophile movement, she also enthusiastically supported the antisickness stand.[55]

Sensitive to the conflicting pulls on DOB members, Eckstein set herself a modest goal, "to get these people to realize there is such a thing as the homophile *movement*." But even her small initiatives, such as inviting Kameny

52. Toby Marotta, interviews with Shirley Willer and Meredith Grey, 1975. "Meredith Grey" is a pseudonym. I am indebted to Toby Marotta for letting me have access to his tapes.

53. Minutes of NYDOB business meeting, June 6, 1965, in NYDOB *Newsletter*, July 1965; and Grey to Elver Barker, August 20, 1965, Kameny papers.

54. Minutes of NYDOB meeting, July 11, 1965, in NYDOB *Newsletter*, August 1965; and minutes of August 8, 1965, meeting in *Newsletter*, September 1965.

55. "Interview with Ernestine," *Ladder*, June 1966, pp. 4–11. "Ernestine Eckstein" and "Emma Van Cott" are pseudonyms.

to speak to a DOB meeting, faltered before the strenuous objections of the ousted officers. Kameny warned her of the pitfalls of compromise—"you are running into a *very* firmly entrenched 'old guard' opposition . . . [who] are fighting tooth and nail to remain in power"—and predicted that Willer and Grey would impede "every progressive move you try to make." He was right. By June 1966 Eckstein found her efforts so frustrated that she resigned from the organization. Unwilling to go its own way, the New York DOB remained loyal to the directives of the governing board in San Francisco and kept its distance from the militant wing on the East Coast.[56]

The triumph of the old guard cost DOB dearly. In addition to Eckstein, other militant women with energy and drive departed from the organization. After Gittings's ouster from the editorship of the *Ladder*, she and Kay Tobin left DOB and worked in close alliance with East Coast militants as "independent activists." Joan Fraser and Marge McCann dropped their DOB affiliation and transferred their allegiance to the Philadelphia Mattachine Society, which they helped found in 1965. Lilli Vincenz, who joined the Washington Mattachine when it was the only organization in the city, had her impressions of DOB confirmed. "It was," she said, "a lesbian YWCA, a social service group, protective of women." The alienation from DOB was painful, since the women's group offered safe, comfortable socializing with other lesbians. But if DOB initially provided fertile soil in which political consciousness could sprout, it failed to offer continuing nourishment.[57]

VI

By 1965 the shift toward militancy showed unmistakable signs of attracting new adherents to the movement. In the spring of 1963, more than seven years after its founding, the New York Mattachine Society still had fewer than 100 members. Over the succeeding twelve months the numbers doubled, reaching almost 200. By the summer of 1965, with the militants' triumph complete, and despite the defection of a sizable portion of the old guard, membership stood at 445. DOB, in contrast, where the militants remained on the defensive, had only twenty-two women voting on the key resolutions of the summer of 1965; it is unlikely that total membership was much more than twice that number.[58]

Figures for other organizations are difficult to unearth, but evidence of growth does exist. Lilli Vincenz recalled that when she joined the Washington Mattachine in 1963, it had perhaps twenty members. By April 1964 Kameny reported that the society desperately needed larger meeting quarters and that it was fast losing its cozy, "family-like" quality. The upsurge of militancy also sparked a revival of the moribund Chicago Mattachine group in the summer of

56. Ernestine [Eckstein] to Kameny, February 12 and February 19, 1966; and Kameny to [Eckstein], March 2, 1966 (all in Kameny papers), *Ladder*; June 1966, p. 4.

57. Interview with Vincenz.

58. New York Mattachine Society *Newsletter*, September–October 1965, p. 5; and minutes of NYDOB business meeting, August 8, 1965, in NYDOB *Newsletter*, September 1965.

1965. The group immediately endorsed ECHO's call for picketing, sent participants to the July 4 demonstration in Philadelphia, and won the dismissal of all charges against a group of male homosexuals rounded up on charges of disorderly conduct. During April and May 1965, the Janus Society of Philadelphia conducted sit-ins at a local restaurant after the manager refused to serve several men and women whom he suspected of being gay "on the basis of appearance." Four persons, including Janus president Clark Polak, were arrested at the first action, but the distribution of 1,500 flyers and television coverage by a local station made the action well worth the costs. By November the organization's lectures were drawing crowds of more than 400, almost triple the attendance of the previous spring. In 1964 a homophile group took root in Miami after a state legislative investigating committee issued a report that urged an intensive crackdown on homosexual activity. The group's president, Richard Inman, adopted a Kameny-like tone in his dealings with public officials, and in 1965 the Mattachine Society of Florida affiliated with ECHO.[59]

It would be difficult to overestimate the significance of the militants' position. Their decisive break with the accommodationist spirit of the 1950s opened important options for the homophile cause. The militants' rejection of the medical model, their assertion of equality, their uncompromising insistence that gays deserved recognition as a persecuted minority, and their defense of homosexuality as a viable way of living loosened the grip of prevailing norms on the self-conception of lesbians and homosexuals and suggested the contours of a new, positive gay identity. The militant viewpoint also made possible the adoption of tactics that widened the horizons of the movement and magnified the expectations of its participants. By solidly grounding themselves in righteous anger over perceived injustice, they could seek allies among church leaders, civil libertarians, and mental health professionals from a foundation of moral rectitude, instead of approaching potential sympathizers "hat-in-hand," as Kameny had caustically described the old guard's methods. If the militants sometimes antagonized prospective supporters, they at least guaranteed that those who aided the movement did so on their terms. In addition, affirmation of their own worth allowed gay activists to challenge head on the discriminatory policies of the federal government. When the bureaucracy remained intransigent, homophile leaders could model their response on the direct-action techniques of the headline-making black civil rights movement. Although the accommodationist leaders of the 1950s had also argued that gay men and women suffered from persecution, their receptivity to negative points of view often suggested uncertainty about the justice of their

59. Interview with Vincenz; Kameny, "Message," ISR; *Eastern Mattachine Magazine*, July 1965, p. 16, and September–October 1965, p. 10; Janus Society of America *Newsletter*, April 1965, May 1965, and November 1965; and the assorted flyers in the Mattachine Society of Florida file, ISR. For the legislative investigation, see Florida Legislative Investigation Committee, *Homosexuality and Citizenship in Florida* (Tallahassee, Fla., 1964).

cause and about the moral integrity and psychological health of a homosexual way of life. The militants betrayed no such doubts.

What remained to be seen was whether the new breed of gay activists could successfully mobilize their hidden constituency. Although the organizations were growing, by the mid-1960s the movement had won the allegiance of only the tiniest fraction of gay men and lesbians. Yet the militants looked to the future with confidence. The first picket lines had generated some much needed publicity for the cause. More importantly, by making the gay world more visible, the breakthrough in the press and media was increasing the accessibility of the subculture to isolated lesbians and homosexuals. If most gay men and women still kept their distance from the movement, at least the bonds of group life were becoming stronger.

TEN

The Movement and the Subculture Converge: San Francisco During the Early 1960s

Though the movement on the East Coast had undoubtedly gathered strength through the debates over tactics, strategy, and ideology, it still found itself largely isolated from the mass of gay women and men. Homophile organizations were attracting more adherents, but the new recruits arrived as individuals, one by one. The world of the bars, the one place where large numbers of urban homosexuals and lesbians congregated, remained unaffected by the perspectives of an activist minority. A seemingly unscalable barrier existed between the two. Indeed, despite the huge gulf that separated militants and accommodationists on most issues, in one important area the militants shared the views of their predecessors. They projected on to patrons of the bars the stereotypical image of homosexuals and lesbians as decadent, frivolous, or cynical, and they maintained a distance from the gay subculture. With the notable exception of Randy Wicker, who canvassed the New York bars with homophile literature, activists never looked upon the bars as recruiting stations where they might swell the movement's ranks. Instead of going themselves to where their potential constituency gathered, they expected that their public actions and media visibility would bring gay men and women to the movement.

In San Francisco, on the other hand, the gay subculture and the movement began to converge in the early 1960s. An unusual configuration of circumstances—a burgeoning beat subculture in the North Beach section of the city, two homosexual-related scandals involving the mayor and the police department, and an intensive three-year-long crackdown against gays by law enforcement agencies—propelled politics into the bars and the bars into the orbit of the movement. The result was a dynamism that benefited both. The movement grew, gained allies, and achieved visibility; while the world of the bars increasingly took on the contours of a self-conscious, cohesive community.

I

San Francisco in the 1940s and 1950s was the setting of a remarkable literary "renaissance" that deviated from the norms of the era. The poets and writers who gathered there—Kenneth Rexroth, Robert Duncan, Lawrence Ferlinghetti, and others—saw themselves in many cases as cultural dissenters from the prevailing ethos of Cold War society. Rexroth, described as the "high priest and spokesman" of the Golden Gate's literary bohemia, attributed the renaissance to the survival in northern California of a strong anarchist-pacifist radical tradition explicitly at odds with the times. In the cafés and bars of San Francisco's North Beach section, poets met, talked, and read their work, as they self-consciously fashioned a poetics that allowed them to express through verse their opposition to the bland conformity and consumerism of the postwar years. Along with artists and musicians, they took cultural work out of the universities, museums, and concert halls and brought it into the streets, taverns, and coffeehouses of North Beach.[1]

By the mid-1950s, San Francisco was sustaining an extraordinary output of poetry. In October 1955 Allen Ginsberg, an unknown, little published writer from New York who had settled in San Francisco two years earlier, scheduled a reading of several poets at the Six Gallery in North Beach. He capped the evening with a long, drunken recital of a just-completed Whitmanesque poem, *Howl*, that sent the packed crowd into a frenzy. As Ginsberg described it later,

> like this was the end of the McCarthy scene, and here I was talking about super-Communist pamphlets on Union Square and the national Golgotha and the Fascists. . . . The evening ended with everybody absolutely radiant and happy, with talk and kissing and later on big happy orgies of poets. It was an *ideal* evening, and I felt so proud and pleased and happy with the sense of—the sense of "at last a community."[2]

1. *Saturday Review*, August 3, 1957, p. 10. For contemporary descriptions of the San Francisco Renaissance, see Kenneth Rexroth, "San Francisco's Mature Bohemians," *Nation*, February 23, 1957, pp. 159–62; *Evergreen Review* no. 2 (1957), an entire issue devoted to San Francisco; *Saturday Review*, August 3, 1957, p. 10, and October 5, 1957, pp. 5–7; and "The New San Franciscans," *Harper's*, January 1958, pp. 21–22. For a sampling of the poetry and poetics of the San Francisco writers, see Donald M. Allen, ed., *The New American Poetry* (New York, 1960); and Donald Allen and Warren Tallman, eds., *The Poetics of the New American Poetry* (New York, 1973). An excellent retrospective evaluation of the West Coast literary movement is found in Robert E. Johnson, ed., *Rolling Renaissance: San Francisco's Underground Art in Celebration, 1945–1968*, 2d ed. (San Francisco, 1975). See also Bruce Cook, *The Beat Generation* (New York, 1971), esp. pp. 40–67 and 117–32; and Neeli Cherkovski, *Ferlinghetti: A Biography* (Garden City, N.Y., 1979), pp. 75ff. For historical background on bohemian subcultures in San Francisco, see Albert Parry, *Garrets and Pretenders: A History of Bohemianism in America*, rev. ed. (New York, 1960); Richard C. Miller, *Bohemia: The Protoculture, Then and Now* (Chicago, 1977); and Idval Jones, *Ark of Empire: San Francisco's Montgomery Block, San Francisco's Unique Bohemia, 1853–1953* (Garden City, N.Y., 1972).

2. Quoted in Jane Kramer, *Allen Ginsberg in America* (New York, 1969), p. 48.

The event at the Six Gallery galvanized this inchoate community of poets. Over the next year or so, as one participant recalled, "this Dionysian, public confessional, Howl-type reading caught on like the Plague." Young writers, attracted by word of what was happening, flocked to the area. Among the avant-garde, San Francisco acquired a reputation as "the Paris of this generation." The fledgling *Evergreen Review* devoted an entire issue to the San Francisco renaissance. Kenneth Rexroth extolled the achievements of the North Beach scene. "Our underground isn't underground here," he said. "It's dominant—in fact, almost all there is."[3]

This small literary movement soon found itself the object of national media attention. In June 1957 Captain William Hanrahan of the San Francisco police department confiscated copies of *Howl and Other Poems* from City Lights bookstore and arrested its owner, Lawrence Ferlinghetti, a well-respected poet in North Beach, on charges of selling obscene literature. The case became a local cause célèbre, winning the support of the ACLU and a host of writers and book dealers. Spectators jammed the courtroom, which, as the *Chronicle* reported to its curious readers, contained "more beards and baggy jackets . . . than the Hall of Justice has seen in its history," and they cheered when the judge ruled against the prosecution. The hapless Captain Hanrahan had made *Howl* a bestseller.[4] Simultaneously with the trial came the publication of Jack Kerouac's *On the Road.* Though critics were divided over the novel's merits, none took it lightly. The fact that Ginsberg was one of the book's characters and that it was set in part in San Francisco guaranteed that more eyes would turn toward the city by the bay. Wittingly or not, Kerouac also gave the media a label to attach to the North Beach scene. A "beat generation" was born, *On the Road* became its bible, Kerouac and Ginsberg its mythic heroes, and San Francisco its home.[5]

Over the next three years, the media's spotlight glared upon North Beach. A diffuse and diverse literary movement, bound together more by locale and by what it stood against than by anything else, suddenly became "beat," representative of a nationwide generational rebellion against the values of the middle class. Journalists collapsed the San Francisco renaissance and the beat

3. J. F. Goodwin, "Dress Rehearsal: Or, Life Among the Founding Fathers," in Johnson, *Rolling Renaissance*, pp. 45–47; John Clellon Holmes, "The Philosophy of the Beat Generation," *Esquire*, February 1958, pp. 35–38; and Kenneth Rexroth, "San Francisco's Mature Bohemians," *Nation*, February 23, 1957, pp. 159–62.

4. San Francisco *Chronicle*, September 6, 1957, p. 3. On the arrest and trial, see the *Chronicle*, June 4, 6, and 7, August 16, 17, and 23, September 6 and 20, and October 4, 1957; "New Test for Obscenity," *Nation*, November 9, 1957, p. 314; and David Perlman, "How Captain Hanrahan Made 'Howl' a Best-Seller," *Reporter*, December 12, 1957, pp. 37–39. The controversial poem appears in Allen Ginsberg, *Howl and Other Poems* (San Francisco, 1956).

5. The literature on the beat generation is large and growing. The best general account remains that of Cook, *The Beat Generation.* See also John Tytell, *Naked Angels* (New York, 1976); Barry Gifford and Lawrence Lee, *Jack's Book: An Oral Biography of Jack Kerouac* (New York, 1978); Dennis McNally, *Desolate Angel: Jack Kerouac, the Beat Generation and America* (New York, 1979); and Jane Kramer, *Allen Ginsberg in America.*

generation into one and then outdid each other in casting furious, scornful invective at it. The beats, Bruce Bliven wrote in a special *Harper's* issue on San Francisco, were "young hedonists who don't really care whether something is good or evil, as long as it is enjoyable." One reviewer in the *Nation* saw in the San Francisco scene nothing but "a pack of unleashed zazous who like to describe themselves as Zen Hipsters—poets, pushers, and panhandlers, musicians, male hustlers, and a few marginal esthetes seeking new marginal directions." Another tried to discredit the whole phenomenon by characterizing it as "overrun with homosexuals."[6] Before long, the mass circulation weeklies entered the fray. *Time* called the beats "a pack of oddballs who celebrate booze, dope, sex, and despair." Labeling North Beach the "international headquarters of the so-called 'Beat Generation,'" *Look* jolted its audience with the observation that beat philosophy "consists merely of the average American's value scale—turned inside out." Local papers titillated and shocked their readers with lurid exposés of wild orgies, rampant sexual perversion, and outrageous experimentation of the most sordid kind. San Francisco, an *Examiner* headline announced, was "Mecca" for a generation in revolt.[7]

The heavy concentration of media attention transformed the North Beach milieu beyond recognition. A quiet bohemian community became a magnet for would-be writers, artists, and disenchanted youth from around the country. Weekends saw a massive influx of tourists eager to catch a glimpse of a bearded beatnik. City officials, alarmed at the notoriety the city was receiving, directed law enforcement agencies to clean up the area. The police tripled their surveillance of North Beach, invaded beat "pads" in search of drugs and illicit sexual activity, and harassed beat gathering places. California's Alcoholic Beverage Control Department declared North Beach a "problem area," ceased granting new liquor licenses, and dispatched agents to swoop down upon suspected violators of state liquor regulations. Meanwhile, many of the writers who had given North Beach its special bohemian quality departed from the area, resettling in the Haight, on Potrero Hill, or across the bay.[8]

The unique visibility of the burgeoning beat subculture in North Beach had a more than incidental impact upon gay male consciousness in San Francisco. Homosexuality weaved its way through descriptions of the North Beach scene as a persistent, albeit minor, motif. Literary critics used homosexuality as a labeling device that allowed them to dismiss out of hand the work of San

6. Bruce Bliven, "San Francisco: New Serpents in Eden," *Harper's*, January 1958, pp. 38–44; Herbert Gold, "Hip, Cool, Beat—and Frantic," *Nation*, November 16, 1957, pp. 349–55; and Bernard Wolfe, "Angry at What?" *Nation*, November 1, 1958, pp. 316–22.

7. *Time*, quoted in Morris Dickstein, *Gates of Eden: American Culture in the Sixties* (New York, 1977), p. 12; "The Bored, the Bearded, and the Beat," *Look*, August 19, 1958, pp. 64ff; and San Francisco *Examiner*, May 4–6, 1958, and *Chronicle*, June 15 and 22, 1958.

8. The changes in North Beach are documented in Francis J. Rigney and L. Douglas Smith, *The Real Bohemia: A Sociological and Psychological Study of the "Beats"* (New York, 1961), esp. chap. 10. See also the *Chronicle*, June 20, 1958, p. 1, and September 17, 1958, p. 2; and Johnson, *Rolling Renaissance*, pp. 12–14, 19.

Francisco writers and others who were lumped into that category. Journalistic exposés employed sexual perversion as a sure-fire method of shocking their readers, as in the *Chronicle*'s discovery that the city's beats were "divided into only two big groups, the heterosexual and the homosexual." The association of homosexuality and the beat scene in North Beach was so commonplace that defenders of the new bohemians felt compelled to disprove the charges. But, in a decade when homosexuality generally made its way into print through concern over national security or in stories about vice squad arrests, its discussion within the context of a major social phenomenon guaranteed a receptive, and attentive, ear among gays.[9]

The bohemian and, later, the beat culture of North Beach did in fact hold special relevance for San Francisco's gay male population. In addition to Allen Ginsberg, several of the San Francisco writers—Robert Duncan, Jack Spicer, Robin Blaser, and perhaps others—were homosexual. Duncan, already a well-respected poet in the mid-1950s, had written a pioneering essay in the 1940s on the destructive effect of antihomosexual prejudice upon gay artists. Spicer, considered by many a poet's poet, was a pivotal figure around whom others in the San Francisco renaissance gathered. When he held forth at The Place, a popular North Beach rendezvous for writers, "the cast at the Spicer table," one participant recalled, "really was something to rival 'Grand Hotel.' "[10] Duncan, Spicer, and Blaser formed a tight circle of mutual support and met almost daily for years. According to one younger poet under their tutelage, they

> not only kept alive a public homosexual presence in their own work, but kept alive a tradition, teaching us about Rimbaud, Crane, and Lorca. . . . They *carried* into the contemporary culture the tradition of homosexual art and were sensitive to the work of European homosexual contemporaries. There was a conscious searching out, in fraternity, of homosexual writers. Thus, in my "training" as a poet, homoerotic novels would be recommended to me. . . . This was at a time when the English departments of the country told us that Walt Whitman *wasn't* gay.

Because of their local stature, the three men helped to create "a social milieu in which it was possible to be gay."[11]

9. *San Francisco Chronicle This World Sunday Magazine*, June 15, 1958, pp. 4–6. For some other examples of the association of homosexuality with the beat scene, see Gold in the *Nation*, November 16, 1957, pp. 349–55; Wolfe in the *Nation*, November 1, 1958, pp. 316–22; and the *Chronicle*, June 22, 1958. For the denial of homosexuality, see Rigney and Smith, *The Real Bohemia*, p. 48. Even where homosexuality was not specifically mentioned, writers almost invariably referred to sexual experimentation, promiscuity, orgies, and hedonism when describing the beats.

10. J. F. Goodwin, "Dress Rehearsal," in Johnson, *Rolling Renaissance*, p. 46.

11. Stan Persky to author, March 26 and May 31, 1979. On Duncan, Spicer, and Blaser, see Cook, *The Beat Generation*, pp. 126–30; Allen, *The New American Poetry*, pp. xii, 432–35; Allen and Tallman, *The Poetics of the New American Poetry*, pp. 242–43; "The Jack Spicer Issue,"

While some poets carved out a small enclave of tolerance in a bohemian setting, Allen Ginsberg was influencing a far larger audience. The much publicized obscenity trial made *Howl* a bestseller throughout San Francisco; by the time the verdict on the poem came in, three more printings had rolled off the press. Ginsberg later called *Howl* a "crucial moment of breakthrough, . . . a breakthrough in the sense of a public statement of feelings and emotions and attitudes." Its description of gay male sexuality as joyous, delightful, and indeed even holy turned contemporary stereotypes of homosexuality upside down. *Howl*, along with other poems in Ginsberg's first collection, offered gay male readers a self-affirming image of their sexual preference. And, as the San Francisco writer most clearly identifiable as "beat," Ginsberg served as a bridge between a literary avant-garde tolerant of homosexuality and an emerging form of social protest indelibly stamped by the media as sexually deviant.[12]

To the extent that the beats expounded a coherent philosophy, their outlook resonated with the gay male experience in ways that tended to legitimate the life choice of homosexuals. Among the white middle class, the beats presented a significant challenge to the conformist pressures of the decade. Paul Goodman, one of the few social critics who took beat protest seriously, considered the beat generation "socially important out of proportion to its numbers . . . [since] they act out a critique of the organized system that everybody in some sense agrees with." When Goodman described the structural characteristics of this new youth subculture, he could just as easily have been referring to gay life: outcasts; objects of prejudice; protective exclusiveness; in-group loyalty; fear of the police; exotic, or at least nonstandard, art and folk ways. In their rejection of the nuclear family, their willingness to experiment sexually, and, most importantly, their definition of these choices as social protest, the beats offered a model that allowed homosexuals to view their own lives from a different angle. Through the beats' example, gays could perceive themselves as nonconformists rather than deviates, as rebels against stultifying norms rather than immature, unstable personalities.[13]

Manroot, no. 10 (Fall 1974–Winter 1975); "Interview: Robert Duncan," *Gay Sunshine*, no. 40/41 (Summer/Fall 1979), pp. 1–8; and Robert Duncan, "The Homosexual in Society," *Politics*, August 1944, pp. 209–11. For an excellent discussion of how homosexual writers can use "gay language" that speaks to a gay audience and helps build a culture of resistance without, however, revealing the sexual identity of the authors to the majority culture, see Bruce Boone, "Gay Language as Political Praxis: The Poetry of Frank O'Hara," *Social Text*, no. 1 (Winter 1979), pp. 59–92.

12. *Allen Ginsberg: Gay Sunshine Interview with Allen Young* (Bolinas, Calif., 1974), pp. 11–12, originally published in *Gay Sunshine*, no. 16 (January 1973). For the impact of the obscenity trial on sales, see Kramer, *Allen Ginsberg in America*, p. 159; and *Reporter*, December 12, 1957, pp. 37–39. For more on Ginsberg's influence on American society and culture, see Dickstein, *Gates of Eden*, pp. 3–24; Kramer, *Allen Ginsberg in America*; Theodore Roszak, *The Making of a Counterculture* (Garden City, N.Y., 1969), pp. 124–54; Tytell, *Naked Angels*, pp. 79–107; and Cook, *The Beat Generation*, pp. 40–67.

13. Paul Goodman, *Growing Up Absurd* (New York, 1960), pp. 170, 64.

The last thread connecting beats and homosexuals in San Francisco was one of space—the geography of the two subcultures overlapped considerably. North Beach contained gay male and lesbian bars as well as beat cafés, with homosexual taverns and cruising areas spreading outward from North Beach to the Polk Street area and down into the Tenderloin. Some of the most popular gay bars of the 1950s had earlier histories as bohemian meeting places and retained something of their original atmosphere. With beats and homosexuals coexisting easily on the streets and in the bars, the world view of one could easily sway the other.[14]

II

While the beats exerted their influence upon the consciousness of the local gay population and the city's elite worried about the ruinous image that beats were giving San Francisco, two homosexual-related scandals rocked the city. In the midst of the 1959 mayoral campaign, respectable residents received a jolt when Russell Wolden accused Mayor George Christopher and his police chief, Thomas Cahill, of allowing San Francisco to become "the national headquarters of the organized homosexuals in the United States." Despite the angry chorus of denials in the city's newspapers and Wolden's failure to capture votes with his charges, civic leaders and local officials worried about this new blow to San Francisco's reputation. The affair was especially embarrassing to Christopher, who prided himself on his efforts to root out vice and corruption. Not surprisingly, the votes had been barely counted and Mayor Christopher safely reelected when announcement was made of "a vigorous new campaign" against gay bars in San Francisco.[15]

Before the dust could settle on the election controversy, the mayor and his chief of police suffered another embarrassment: a "gayola" scandal hit the police department. In December, the California Supreme Court affirmed the right of homosexuals to congregate in taverns and stipulated that the Alcoholic Beverage Control Department (ABC) needed proof of illegal sexual activity on the premises of a bar in order to revoke a liquor license. Shortly after the ruling, the department restored the license of the Handlebar, a gay tavern on California Street. Emboldened by the protection that the law seemed to provide, the owner reported to the district attorney in February that for almost two years the police had extorted payoffs from him in order to stay in business.

14. See Henry Evans, *Bohemian San Francisco* (San Francisco, 1955); Johnson, *Rolling Renaissance*, pp. 15–16; Thomas Albright, "A Nostalgic Plea for the Artists' Bar," *Chronicle*, July 26, 1979, p. 47; *Allen Ginsberg: Gay Sunshine Interview*, pp. 20, 33; and Allen Brown, "Life and Love Among the Beatniks," *Chronicle*, June 15 and 22, 1958; see also the discussion of the Black Cat bar below. My determination of where gay bars were located comes from a perusal of the San Francisco *Chronicle* and *Examiner* for 1955–1961 for notices of actions taken against gay bars, and from a partial list of bars compiled by Bois Burk of Berkeley, Calif.

15. See San Francisco *Progress*, October 7, 1959, and Chap. 7 above for a discussion of the 1959 election controversy. On Christopher, see George Dorsey, *Christopher of San Francisco* (New York, 1962), pp. 92, 103, 106ff.

During the grand jury investigation that followed, several other bar owners testified about shakedowns by the police and the ABC. Throughout the spring and summer, accusations of police corruption filled the newspapers.[16]

The "gayola" scandal, as the press dubbed it, led to indictments against seven police officers and a liquor department investigator. Although two of the indicted men who were caught with marked money pleaded guilty, the other officers opted for a protracted trial, in which the defense capitalized on antihomosexual prejudice. A parade of prominent character witnesses testified for the accused, who portrayed themselves as "honest men devoted to defending public morals," painted repellent scenes of gay bar life, and charged the tavern owners with fabricating their tales of shakedowns. The defense lawyer cast aspersions on the credibility of the prosecution witnesses, claimed that the whole case represented a conspiracy of bar operators, and deplored a legal system in which "the most notorious homosexual may testify against a policeman." Persuaded by this line of argument, the jury acquitted all of the defendants.[17]

The combination of headline-making events spelled trouble for San Francisco's gay population. Acting on orders from the mayor and police chief, law enforcement officers turned their attention away from beatniks on Columbus Avenue and embarked upon an extended and intensive crackdown against any public display of homosexuality, focusing especially on the bars. On the day of the bribery indictment, Christopher complained at a press conference that the taverns "are protected by law" and that "there is very little [we] can do." He had the police "consult with the District Attorney and the ABC . . . to devise more strict measures" to control the establishments. In October 1960, shortly after the resolution of the last gayola indictment, Cahill announced that he had reorganized the police force's sex detail "for an attack on San Francisco's homosexual problem." Although the ABC and the police already had a long history of harassing gay bars, the rules laid down by the court made this round especially pernicious. To meet the requirement that illegal acts be proved, the ABC "stepped up [its] liaison" with the police and trained young officers "how to act and dress" for their new line of work. As Bill Plath, a bar owner, described it, "police would send in plainclothesmen in tight pants, very handsome guys, and they'd go to work on some older number who was available for almost anything."[18]

Statistics tell the story of the campaign's effectiveness. The *Ladder* reported that felony convictions of male homosexuals, which stood at zero in the first half of 1960, rose to twenty-nine in the next six months and to seventy-six in

16. Vallerga and Azar v. Department of Alcoholic Beverage Control, 347 P. 2d 909; and *Chronicle*, February 12, May 3, May 18 (p. 1), May 24 (p. 3), and June 23, 1960 (p. 1).

17. *Chronicle*, August 11, 1960, and July 23, 1960, p. 14; for more on the indictments and the trials see the *Chronicle*, July 12, 26–28; August 5, 6, 9, 11, and 20 (p. 1); and September 8 and 24, 1960.

18. *Chronicle*, June 23, 1960, p. 1; *Examiner*, October 17, 1960, p. 1, and October 12, 1961; interview with Bill Plath in San Francisco, December 7, 1976.

the period from January to June 1961. Misdemeanor charges against men and women stemming from sweeps of the bars ran at an estimated forty to sixty per week. In August 1961 the police conducted the biggest gay bar raid in San Francisco's history and arrested eighty-nine male and fourteen female patrons of the Tay-Bush Inn. The *Chronicle* described the scene as "vaguely reminiscent of leading sheep from a packed corral." Although a municipal judge dismissed the charges and harshly criticized the police action, the mayor applauded the raid as "justified" and praised the police for being "on the right track." In October 1961 the ABC, acting on evidence gathered by plainclothes police, announced that it had revoked the liquor licenses of twelve of the city's estimated thirty gay bars, with proceedings underway against another fifteen. Every establishment that had made charges against the police during the gayola scandal lost its license.[19]

The San Francisco police cast a wide net in their antihomosexual campaign. After the *Examiner* demanded that they flush out the "sex deviates who haunt [Buena Vista Park] at all hours of the day and night," the police dispatched decoys to patrol the city's parks, public squares, and transportation depots where gay men normally cruised. With the assistance of federal agents, San Francisco detectives revealed that they had uncovered the "World Center of [the] Filthy Book Trade" and stemmed a "tidal wave" of "cheaply printed paperbacks specializing in homosexuality, Lesbianism, masochism and the wildest eroticism." When a theater advertised *Fireworks*, an underground movie about a young homosexual by Kenneth Anger, vice officers raided the establishment, arrested the manager, and confiscated the film and projector, even though a Los Angeles court had previously cleared *Fireworks* of obscenity charges. No manifestation of homosexuality appeared safe from attack.[20]

The unrelenting assault upon "sex deviates" offered San Francisco's homophile organizations an unparalleled chance to recruit adherents. Far from experiencing the conspiracy of silence that had so hampered their work during the preceding decade, the Mattachine Society and the Daughters of Bilitis in the early 1960s confronted a barrage of headlines. The 1959 election controversy, as one veteran reporter commented, placed San Franciscans "uncomfortably alone among the fathers and mothers of America . . . in having to field such questions from eleven-and-twelve-year-olds as 'Daddy, what is a homosexual?' "[21] The gayola scandal and the ensuing police crackdown made the topic of homosexuality an almost daily staple in the city's diet of news, while simultaneously intensifying a sense of grievance within the gay subculture. Just as importantly, the stepped-up harassment followed on the

19. *Ladder*, October 1961, p. 19; on the Tay-Bush raid, see the *Chronicle*, August 14–16 and September 8, 1961, and the *Examiner*, August 15–16, 1961; on ABC actions against bars, see the *Examiner*, October 12, 1961, and *Mattachine Review*, February 1963, p. 32.

20. *Examiner*, June 17 and October 17, 1960, p. 1; *News-Call-Bulletin*, September 12, 13, 14, 16, 17, 1960; and *Chronicle*, May 19 and 24 and June 2, 1961.

21. Dorsey, *Christopher*, p. 187.

heels of a growing awareness of the beat rebellion, the legitimacy that the beats gave to nonconformity, and the subtle impact their presence exerted on gay consciousness in San Francisco. Conditions were right to encourage a political response to the antigay campaign.

Neither Mattachine nor DOB, however, seized the opportunity. Still ensconced in their accommodationist position of the 1950s and, like their counterparts in the East, detached from the world of the bars, they failed to appreciate the glimmerings of a new outlook that the cultural dissent of the beats was fostering. Instead, they remained wedded to a gradualist approach that emphasized patiently educating the public, projecting a respectable middle-class image, seeking professional endorsement, and regenerating the individual lesbian and homosexual. Moreover, the movement's internal upheavals during 1961 pushed both San Francisco groups into a period of retrenchment. With discontent simmering among the gay population, the Mattachine Society and the Daughters of Bilitis persevered in their old ways.

Ironically, the dissolution of the Mattachine Society's national structure in March 1961 had a disastrous impact on the San Francisco chapter that was responsible for it. The former national office suffered a precipitous decline. A fund-raising letter sent by Hal Call and Don Lucas in the spring netted a meager $270, as opposed to the more than $2,500 raised by a similar appeal the preceding year. The *Review* relied increasingly on reprints to fill its pages and contained less and less material that could be considered movement news. Early in 1964 it abandoned its monthly publication schedule. Behind Call's grandiose statement about the society "making a mark upon the modern social scene" lay the more sober reality of a few individuals preoccupied with a poorly selling journal.[22]

As the city's male homosexual population suffered under police attacks, the society continued to dissociate itself from the bar scene and to cultivate a responsible public image. The *News-Call-Bulletin*, for instance, which fanned the drive against "sex deviates," could nonetheless find sympathetic words for Mattachine. In an interview with Call at the height of the antigay campaign, the paper favorably described the society as an organization that helped "distraught homosexuals . . . understand themselves." Some homosexuals, the article continued, "have rejoined the ranks of the heterosexuals." Such a picture could hardly inspire allegiance among gay men more distraught over police harassment than over sexual orientation.[23]

The Daughters of Bilitis also failed to chart a course suited to the rapidly changing social climate of San Francisco. Instead, the estrangement from *ONE* after the homosexual bill of rights debacle in January 1961 and the shake-up within Mattachine made DOB more self-absorbed than before. Over the next two years, the *Ladder* several times reiterated DOB's stance as a

22. *Mattachine Review*, June 1961, p. 26; January 1963, pp. 34–35; April 1963, p. 20; and October 1963, pp. 4–5.
23. *News-Call-Bulletin*, July 25, 1961, p. 25.

"self-help" organization to "enable [the lesbian] to understand herself and make an adjustment to society." Acknowledging that "DOB has been more conservative than any other organization," it exhorted lesbians "to stop the breeding of defiance toward society" and strongly advocated "outward conformity." The emphasis on personal regeneration carried a corollary. If individual adjustment were possible, then perhaps the problem lay within each lesbian. Thus the *Ladder*, in defining the philosophy of DOB, declared, "While it is true that if there were less public pressure there would be less crippling effects, it is also true that the homosexual's 'affliction' stems more from Self—self-pity, self-consciousness, self-abasement."[24]

DOB also continued to keep its distance from the lesbian bar subculture, just at the time when bar patrons were suffering intensified attacks from the police. "Bars," DOB's president Jaye Bell wrote in October 1961,

> have their place, yes, but only the people with real strength can fight their way out of the example they see there that reeks of defiance, disillusionment, and despair. The defiance, disillusionment, and despair, we all know, lie there under the mask of "gaiety" which [patrons] of the bars put on![25]

In criticizing the bars and the women who congregated there, DOB glossed over the importance of bars in fashioning a lesbian identity. The environment may or may not have been oppressive, but the bars offered a place for lesbians to meet, to form networks of friendship and support, and to gain a sense of themselves as members of a *group*. Women who patronized the bars made an implicit affirmation of their sexual identity. By creating a dichotomy between "good lesbians" and "bar dykes," DOB like Mattachine cut itself off from the most organized, most group-conscious segment of the lesbian population.

III

A political response to the antigay campaign did finally emerge, and when it occurred it came out of the place where gay men, bohemian nonconformity, and police harassment most clearly converged—the Black Cat bar. Located on Montgomery Street just a few blocks from the center of North Beach, the Black Cat had a venerable history stretching back to the early twentieth century. During the 1940s it commanded the allegiance of the city's bohemian underground and provided the setting for part of Kerouac's *On the Road*. After World War II the Black Cat began drawing more of a gay male clientele, but in the 1950s it still remained a place where several worlds intersected. Allen Ginsberg, who patronized the bar in the mid-1950s, described it as "the

24. Jaye Bell, "DOB Anniversary Message from the President," *Ladder*, October 1961, pp. 4–9; "The Dare of the Future: An Appraisal of the Homophile Movement," *Ladder*, May 1962, pp. 4–10; "The Philosophy of DOB: The Evolution of an Idea," *Ladder*, June 1962, pp. 4–8.
25. *Ladder*, October 1961, p. 5.

greatest gay bar in America. It was really totally open, bohemian, San Francisco . . . and everybody went there, heterosexual and homosexual. It was lit up, there was a honky-tonk piano; it was enormous. All the gay screaming queens would come, the heterosexual gray flannel suit types, longshoremen. All the poets went there."[26]

Unwilling to make the standard payoffs expected of bar proprietors whose clientele included homosexuals, the Black Cat's owner, Sol Stoumen, found himself in trouble with the law. Faced with the loss of his liquor license, he filed suit and in 1951 won a favorable ruling from the state supreme court. In response to the court's finding that no state law prohibited homosexuals from gathering in taverns, the legislature eventually enacted in 1955 a statute that allowed the ABC to revoke the liquor license of a premise that served as a "resort for sexual perverts." For the next several years the police and the liquor control board watched the Black Cat with a vengeance and more license revocations and court proceedings ensued. The cost to Stoumen in legal fees eventually surpassed $38,000.[27]

The special zeal expended on the Black Cat by law enforcement officials may have stemmed in part from the unique atmosphere created by José Sarria, an employee. Sarria first visited the Black Cat in the 1940s with his family, became the lover of one of the waiters, and soon began waiting tables himself. A master of male homosexual camp humor, Sarria often dressed in drag and enlivened evenings at the Black Cat with parodies of popular torch songs. By the early 1950s his impromptu performances had evolved into a regular Sunday afternoon satirical opera. But Sarria's act departed dramatically from the female impersonation found in some gay male circles. Donning an outlandish hat to sing *Carmen*, for example, he reworked the script for his audience and its milieu. The heroine would be in Union Square, a gay cruising area in downtown San Francisco, scurrying through the bushes in an attempt to avoid capture by the vice squad. An overflow crowd of 200 or more cheered Carmen's escape.[28]

Sarria took the primitive protest implicit in his theatrics a step further. At the end of each opera, he made his listeners stand and, with their arms around one another, sing "God Save Us Nelly Queens." George Mendenhall, one

26. *Allen Ginsberg: Gay Sunshine Interview*, p. 33. On the Black Cat, see Evans, *Bohemian San Francisco*, p. 16; Johnson, *Rolling Renaissance*, pp. 15–16; *Chronicle*, July 26, 1979, p. 47; and "Gay Life in the 1950s: Interview with Jose Sarria," KPFA-FM, Berkeley, Calif., March 14, 1979.

27. Stoumen v. Reilly, 234 P. 2d 969; Del Martin, "The Gay Bar: Whose Problem Is It?" *Ladder*, December 1959, pp. 4–13ff.; and "Tenth Life for the Black Cat?" *Mattachine Review*, November 1963, pp. 5–7. For incidents of police and ABC actions against the Black Cat, see the *Chronicle*, August 28 and November 28–30, 1956; January 29, March 2, and September 19, 1957; and March 31, 1961.

28. Nancy and Casey Adair, *Word Is Out* (New York, 1978), pp. 73–74; and "Gay Life in the 1950s," KPFA-FM, March 14, 1979.

frequent patron of the Black Cat who later became active in the homophile movement, reminisced about the meaning of this Sunday ritual:

> You must realize that the vice squad was there. . . . They used to park their police cars outside of gay bars and they used to take down the names of people. . . . They used to come in and stand around and just generally intimidate people and make them feel that they were less than human. It was a frightening period. . . .
>
> But José would make these political comments about our rights as homosexuals. . . . If you lived at that time and had the oppression coming down from the police department and from society . . . , to be able to stand up and sing, "God Save Us Nelly Queens"—we were really not saying "God Save Us Nelly Queens." We were saying "We have our rights too."

For Mendenhall, as for others who attended the Black Cat, Sarria's comments marked the "beginning of my awareness of my rights as a gay person."[29]

In 1961, at the height of the police crackdown and with Stoumen appealing another ABC action against the Black Cat, Sarria took his political message out of the bars. He decided to run for city supervisor in the fall elections. As an open homosexual and a drag queen, Sarria initially had trouble collecting sufficient signatures to qualify for the ballot, but he eventually found enough "very bold queens," as he put it, who were willing to overcome their fear of exposure and sign his candidate's petition. Sarria had no chance of winning, but victory was not his goal. "I was trying to prove to my gay audience," he recalled, "that I had the right, being as notorious and gay as I was, to run for public office, because people in those days didn't believe you had rights." He was in a good position to make his point. Sarria's operas made him the best known and loved gay man in San Francisco; his reputation extended far beyond the regulars at the Black Cat, to the entire bar-going population. His candidacy, although it garnered only 6,000 votes, was the hot topic in the bars that fall, forcing patrons to think about their identity, their sexual orientation, in political terms.[30]

Unlike the later Stonewall Riot in New York City in 1969, Sarria's symbolic candidacy did not spark nationwide organizing among gays; but it did help set in motion developments that fed a steadily growing stream of gay political activity in San Francisco throughout the 1960s. In April 1961, shortly after Mattachine's restructuring, a new homophile group, the League for Civil Education, appeared in San Francisco. Originally conceived as a "democratic" alternative to the tightly controlled operation run by Hal Call, LCE boldly canvassed in the bars for members. However, its initiator, Guy Strait, proved as incapable (or undesirous) of presiding over a participatory organization as

29. Nancy and Casey Adair, *Word Is Out*, pp. 73–74.
30. "Gay Life in the 1950s," KPFA-FM, March 14, 1979; and *Chronicle*, November 8, 1961, p. 1.

the Mattachine leadership, and LCE's membership had only a paper status. But in October 1961, spurred by Sarria's campaign, Strait began printing the *LCE News* and circulating it in the city's gay bars to publicize the effort.[31]

LCE News constituted the first sustained attempt to bring the movement into the world of the gay bar. Financing the endeavor through advertising from tavern owners, Strait distributed the free paper in the city's bars. By the spring of 1962 its circulation in San Francisco alone exceeded the nationwide figures of *ONE*, the *Ladder*, and the *Mattachine Review*—7,000 copies came off the presses. Even the *Mattachine Review*, which disapproved of the paper's inflammatory copy, conceded that "*LCE News* captured the fancy of the gay bar crowd." Lengthy articles about police abuses filled its pages, and Strait emblazoned the cover with headlines like "WE MUST FIGHT NOW." The paper encouraged its readers to exercise their potential political muscle by registering to vote and casting their ballots as a bloc. In 1963, three mayoral candidates purchased ads in the paper. When police targeted Strait's advertisers and coerced one into cancelling, the irrepressible publisher exposed that, too, and threatened to file suit in court.[32]

Under these circumstances, it was natural that bar owners would begin to organize. In 1962 the proprietors and employees of several of the city's gay bars formed the Tavern Guild. Bill Plath, who ran the D'Oak Room bar, became president on the condition that members stop "fighting among themselves and [start] fighting the system." Through fund-raising social events and regular dues, the guild retained a lawyer and bail bondsman for anyone arrested in or near a gay bar and coordinated the efforts of owners to fight the capricious procedures of the ABC. At election time the bars became the scene of voter registration drives. The Tavern Guild financed the printing and distributed copies of the "Pocket Lawyer," a wallet-sized legal guide on what to do in case of harassment or arrest. The very existence of the guild was a statement that gay bars were a legitimate form of business enterprise that deserved freedom from arbitrary harassment. Its activities added a political dimension to the bar milieu and kept alive among patrons a sense of grievance and a spirit of questioning about their status initially aroused by Sarria's campaign and the *LCE News*.[33]

31. *LCE News*, December 25, 1961, p. 1; *Mattachine Review*, October 1962, p. 17, and April–September 1964, p. 18; New York Mattachine Society *Newsletter*, December 1961, p. 3; and Guy Strait to Randy Wicker, May 16, 1962, Wicker papers, in the possession of Jonathan Katz, New York City.

32. New York Mattachine Society *Newsletter*, May 1964, pp. 13–14; *Mattachine Review*, April–September 1964, p. 18; *LCE News*, October 15, 1962, p. 1; October 29, 1962, p. 1; December 10, 1962, p. 1; and January 7, 1963, p. 1. Toward the end of 1963, Strait changed the paper's name to the *Citizens' News*.

33. Bill Plath, quoted in Roxanne B. T. Sweet, "Political and Social Action in Homophile Organizations," Ph.D. diss., University of California, Berkeley, 1968, p. 123. On the Tavern Guild, see Sweet, pp. 122–24; *Mattachine Review*, April–September 1964, p. 20; and the author's interview with Plath, December 7, 1976, San Francisco.

The activity surrounding the bars in San Francisco highlighted the need for a politically effective gay male membership organization. Early in 1964, Bill Plath, William Beardemphl, a chef at one of the city's more elegant restaurants, Jim Foster, and Mark Forrester began discussions among themselves about the kind of organization that was needed. After several months of meetings, during which they drew in other friends, they formed the Society for Individual Rights in September 1964.[34]

From its inception, SIR distinguished itself from earlier homophile organizations in San Francisco. Its leaders possessed a degree of self-assertion and confidence comparable to that exhibited by the new breed of activists in the East. "We find ourselves scorned," SIR's statement of policy declared, "our rights as persons and citizens before the law imperiled, our individuality suppressed by a hostile social order, and our spirit forced to accept a guilt unwarranted by the circumstances of our existence." SIR took for granted the "worth of the homosexual . . . and [his] right to his own sexual orientation." Learning from the experience of Mattachine and the League for Civil Education, where near-dictatorial control over decisionmaking, activities, and policies kept membership small and apathetic, SIR pledged itself to a "democratic process" that would include "*all* expressions of the homosexual community." The very use of the word "community" suggested the close connection between SIR's origins and the world of the bars, the one manifestation of gay life that could be considered a community institution. SIR's founders, themselves regular patrons of the bars, understood that if the movement were to grow, it needed to affirm the impulses that brought many gay men into the bars. "There is not now, and never has been, a 'Homophile Movement,' " wrote Beardemphl, SIR's first president. "Our work is to create a Community feeling that will bring a 'Homophile Movement' into being."[35]

SIR's perception of the importance of generating a "community feeling" translated into a recognition of the social needs of gay men. In the 1950s, Mattachine had vigorously denied that it was a social organization, a place where male homosexuals could meet, out of fear that its purposes would be construed as encouraging illegal sexual behavior. On the other hand, newer, more militant groups like the Washington Mattachine eschewed social functions and social service work as traps that would drain energy from the pressing demands of civil rights activity. SIR, in contrast, opened its doors to anything that members had the energy to organize. It held dances, parties, brunches, and drag entertainments. It sponsored bridge clubs, bowling leagues, outings in the country, meditation groups, and art classes. With goods collected from

34. *Vector*, February 1965, p. 6; interviews with William Beardemphl, November 26, 1976, and Mark Forrester, December 9, 1976, both in San Francisco; interview with Plath.

35. *Vector*, December 1964, p. 1; "SIR Statement of Policy," SIR file, Institute for Sex Research (hereafter referred to as ISR), Bloomington, Ind.; and *Vector*, December 1965, p. 2, and August 1966, p. 2.

the gay male community, it operated a thrift shop, staffed by volunteers, that provided a regular source of income for the organization. In April 1966, it opened a gay community center in San Francisco, the first of its kind in the country.[36]

Social functions were the drawing card that provided SIR with the manpower to carry out service activities and engage in political work as well. With the cooperation of the city's public health department, it ran a major education campaign on venereal disease aimed at the gay male population. SIR's monthly magazine, *Vector*, was sold on newsstands throughout the city. Its attractive, glossy format included news about the progress of gay rights as well as entertainment and gossip to widen its appeal. A political action committee surveyed California politicians on sex law reform and police practices, conducted voter registration drives, and, beginning in 1965, held candidates' nights every fall, when aspirants to elective office addressed a gay audience. SIR took stands on local contests and published its endorsements of politicians who promised action on gay issues.[37]

SIR's willingness to cater to the need for fellowship among gay men seemed to provide a winning formula. Within months after its founding, upward of 250 people were attending its organizational meetings. Membership climbed rapidly, to 581 by the end of 1966 and to almost 1,000 a year later, making it the largest homophile organization in the country.[38] As membership grew, the claims of San Francisco's inchoate gay community for recognition by the local political establishment likewise gained credence.

More than a wide range of activities, however, accounted for SIR's ability to tap a constituency that had ignored the call of other homophile groups. Its initial success rested in no small part on its willingness to acknowledge that the bars played a central role in the lives of many urban homosexuals and constituted the one site where large numbers of otherwise scattered, invisible gay men gathered. SIR maintained an easy, cooperative relationship with the Tavern Guild, while the bars, fighting for survival under state harassment, were receptive to the needs of the city's newest homophile group. SIR held fund-raising auctions in taverns, and bars often donated food and drink for SIR's parties. The Tavern Guild financed the printing of SIR's "Pocket Lawyer," and the VD testing campaign drew its effectiveness from the willingness of the bars to display educational posters and literature. By not forcing patrons to make a choice between the movement or the bars, SIR was manag-

36. For a sampling of SIR's activities, see "Calendar: October 1965," SIR file, ISR; *Vector*, December 1964, p. 1; May 1965, p. 1; June 1965, p. 2; August 1965, p. 1; October 1965, p. 4; March 1966, p. 10; and April 1966, p. 1.

37. *Vector*, December 1964, p. 3; January 1965, p. 12; March 1965, p. 1; August 1965, p. 1; September 1965, pp. 1 and 3. "Vote Today: November 2, 1965" and "In Case of Arrest: The SIR Pocket Lawyer," SIR file, ISR.

38. *Vector*, June 1965, p. 2, and December 1967, p. 34.

ing both to increase the strength of the movement in San Francisco and to stimulate a deepening of political consciousness in the bar milieu.[39]

IV

While political awareness infiltrated the subculture of gay bars, the homophile movement was finding allies in an unexpected quarter—among San Francisco's Protestant clergy. By the early 1960s a wave of activism was sweeping the nation's churches, set in motion by the civil rights struggle, the "rediscovery" of widespread poverty in the midst of abundance, and the idealistic rhetoric of the Kennedy presidency. Social concerns dominated the country's ministry in a way that they had not since the 1930s. Among black and younger clergy in particular, service to God and to the church increasingly meant active engagement in the world. In San Francisco, where homosexuality had achieved a greater visibility than elsewhere, it was perhaps natural that a portion of this social concern would be spent on behalf of the gay rights cause.

Glide Memorial Methodist Church had a pastor and a location that made activism inevitable. Its black minister, the Reverend A. Cecil Williams, had a long history of involvement in the struggle for racial justice. Situated in the heart of the Tenderloin district of San Francisco, Glide found itself surrounded by the castoffs of American society—the poor and the aged, alcoholics and addicts, prostitutes, petty criminals and male hustlers. Besides traditional pastoral activities, Glide operated a number of special programs, including a Young Adult project to cater to the needs of a growing population of teenaged runaways living on the streets in the Tenderloin. In 1962 Williams brought Ted McIlvenna, a young minister-social worker from Kansas City, to Glide to head the project.[40]

McIlvenna's work in the Tenderloin quickly brought him face to face with the issue of homosexuality. Many of the male runaways, he discovered, were homosexuals driven to street hustling by the hostility and ostracism of their parents and their peers. Knowing little about questions of sexual identity, McIlvenna turned to the Mattachine Society for help, only to discover that the organization, fearful of charges of corrupting youth, firmly closed its doors to anyone under the age of twenty-one. But the contact with Mattachine, and later with DOB, SIR, and the Tavern Guild, alerted McIlvenna to the existence of an entire population with real grievances against the church. As DOB's president Billie Tallmij curtly put it, "to retain sanity, [we] *must* forego the organized approach to God." As an offshoot of his work with gay street youth, McIlvenna took a crash course on society's treatment of gay men and

---

39. For examples of cooperation among SIR, the Tavern Guild, and the city's gay bars, see *Vector*, December 1964, pp. 1 and 3; March 1965, p. 1; August 1965, p. 1; September 1965, p. 1; and October 1965, p. 4.

40. Sweet, "Political and Social Action in Homophile Organizations," p. 118.

women. Before long, San Francisco's homophile leaders had a minister ready to do more than deliver a homily at a monthly meeting.[41]

Through McIlvenna's initiative, a group of ministers emerged in San Francisco prepared to work for social justice toward homosexuals and lesbians. Under the sponsorship of the Glide Urban Center, McIlvenna organized a four-day consultation at the end of May 1964 between gay activists in San Francisco and Protestant ministers from several denominations, including a few from other cities. After a "gay line" tour of the city that included visits to bars, drag shows, private parties, and homophile meetings, the sixteen ministers met for two days in a "face-to-face confrontation" with a group of gay women and men. For many, it was the first time they had ever knowingly talked with a homosexual or a lesbian. The weekend witnessed, according to Del Martin's glowing report, "the re-birth of Christian fellowship" and opened "unexpected avenues of communication and cooperation between the two groups." The ministers acknowledged the role that religion had played in the persecution of homosexuals and promised to initiate dialogue in their denominations on the church's stand toward same-gender sexuality. Those from other parts of the country left with a commitment to work with local homophile groups. The San Francisco contingent, meanwhile, continued to meet for several months until December 1964, when the ministers and homophile leaders formed the Council on Religion and the Homosexual.[42]

To kick off the new venture and to raise funds for the organization, the ministers planned a New Year's Eve dance for the gay community. Since the police used mere touching by members of the same sex as grounds for arrest or the revocation of a liquor license, the decision to hold a public gay dance held the makings of a confrontation. Against the advice of homophile activists, the ministers informed the police of their intentions. When the department tried to force the proprietors of California Hall to cancel the dance, several ministers, including Williams and McIlvenna, met with the police again. The police, according to one account, snidely "looked at the rings on our fingers and said, 'We see you're married—how do your wives accept this?' " and told the ministers to "leave morals and law enforcement to us." Undeterred, the CRH representatives stayed until they had extracted a promise from vice squad officers not to interfere with the dance.[43]

41. Ibid.; *Ladder*, September 1964, p. 11; and Del Martin and Phyllis Lyon, *Lesbian/Woman* (New York, 1972), p. 260.

42. Del Martin, "The Church and the Homosexual: A New Rapport," *Ladder*, September 1964, pp. 9–13; Sweet, pp. 118–19; *CRH: 1964/1968* (San Francisco, 1968), pp. 3–4; *Chronicle*, December 7, 1964, p. 1; Kay Tobin and Randy Wicker, *The Gay Crusaders* (New York, 1972), pp. 53–54; and Martin and Lyon, *Lesbian/Woman*, pp. 260–61.

43. *Ladder*, February–March 1965, pp. 4–5; *Mattachine Review*, January–February 1965, pp. 8–9; *Vector*, January 1965, p. 1; interview with Beardemphl; *Chronicle*, January 3, 1965; and Sweet, p. 154.

On the night of the dance the liberal ministers, as the *Mattachine Review* reported, were "treated to the most lavish display of police harassment known in recent times." Scores of uniformed officers stalked the area around California Hall, with police cars and paddy wagons in full view. When the police demanded entrance, lawyers for CRH tried to block their way and demanded a search warrant or evidence of criminal activity that would justify police action. Three lawyers and a woman ticket-taker were arrested on charges of obstructing an officer. Meanwhile, in a blatant attempt at intimidation, police photographers flashed pictures of each of the 600 guests as they entered and left the hall.[44]

Accustomed as they were to a free hand in dealing with homosexuals, the police could not have foreseen the consequences of their action. On January 2, the ministers held a press conference at Glide, in which they ripped into the police. Describing in detail the "strained" negotiations before the dance, they accused the department of "deliberate harassment and bad faith" and charged officers with "intimidation, broken promises and obvious hostility." By arresting lawyers, the police provoked the wrath of the ACLU, which saw the case as an effort to "intimidate attorneys who represent unpopular groups" and agreed to defend the victims. When the four came to trial in February, the city's gay population felt vindicated as the scales of justice for once tilted in their favor. As the *Chronicle* reported, "complaining officers sat with mouths agape" while the judge directed the jury to return a not-guilty verdict before the defense had even presented its case. "It's useless to waste everybody's time following this to its finale," he announced in court.[45]

Gay activists in San Francisco at the time and later perceived the New Year's Eve ball as a turning point for the movement there. "This is the type of police activity that homosexuals know well," Del Martin wrote,

> but heretofore the police had never played their hand before Mr. Average Citizen. It was always the testimony of the police officer versus the homosexual, and the homosexual, fearing publicity and knowing the odds were against him, succumbed. But in this instance the police overplayed their part.[46]

The ministers provided a legitimacy to the charges of police harassment that the word of a homosexual lacked. For once, the press had to take the side of homosexuals or else dispute the words of a group of clergy. As Martin's statement suggested, moreover, the incident graphically demonstrated in a

44. *Mattachine Review*, January–February 1965, pp. 8–9; *Ladder*, February–March 1965, pp. 4–5; *Vector*, January 1965, p. 1; and Martin and Lyon, *Lesbian/Woman*, pp. 261–62.

45. *Examiner*, January 3, 1965, p. 3; *Chronicle*, January 3, 1965; January 6, 1965, p. 7; and February 12, 1965, p. 3; *Vector*, February 1965, p. 1; and *CRH: 1964/1968*, pp. 4–5.

46. *Ladder*, February–March, 1965, p. 5; and Martin and Lyon, *Lesbian/Woman*, pp. 261–62. All of the activists whom I interviewed in connection with these events—Lyon, Martin, Plath, Beardemphl, Forrester, Kepner, and Legg—agreed on the importance of the CRH ball.

single night what activists had told the ministers for months—that homosexuals and lesbians faced arbitrary and pervasive harrassment from the police. The event strengthened the commitment of CRH members to take up the cause of justice for gay women and men and their involvement guaranteed that at last the issue would receive a hearing.

V

By the mid-1960s, the gay subculture in San Francisco, and the movement that made up one aspect of it, was assuming a significantly different shape from its counterparts in other urban areas. Nourished in the milieu created by bohemian writers and young beats, it came alive through the attacks mounted against it by a hostile city administration and police force. Scandals and police assaults kept homosexuality in the news in San Francisco to an extent that was unique for the times, while also intensifying a sense of grievance that fed a political consciousness. New organizations took root within the bar subculture, and the movement, breaking out of its isolation, at last found influential allies committed to work in its behalf.

Gay life in San Francisco had reached a qualitatively new stage in its evolution. Despite the survival of patterns of discrimination and police harassment, and despite the persistence within society at large of a view of homosexuals and lesbians as sinful, sick, or criminal, local events had conspired to initiate a profound change in the consciousness of gay San Franciscans. A "community" was in fact forming around a shared sexual orientation, and the shift would have important implications in the future for the shape of gay politics and gay identity throughout the nation. The media did not exaggerate when it began calling San Francisco the "gay capital" of the United States. The city that, by the 1970s, became a magnet for gay men and lesbians from around the country was already acquiring its distinctiveness a decade earlier.[47]

47. The reference to San Francisco as the country's gay capital comes from *Life*, June 26, 1964, pp. 66ff. For an analysis of the relationship between pre- and post-Stonewall San Francisco and of the contrast between San Francisco and other cities, see John D'Emilio, "Gay Politics, Gay Community: San Francisco's Experience," *Socialist Review*, no. 55 (January–February 1981), pp. 77–104.

ELEVEN

High Hopes
and Modest Gains

The changes that occurred in the early 1960s bred confidence among activists. The success of Eastern militants in winning control of homophile organizations, and their first round of public picketing in 1965, nurtured the conviction that they were now on the offensive. In San Francisco the scandals, the police crackdown, and most importantly the ferment these produced within the bar subculture not only brought homosexuality into the public spotlight but also seemed to be creating a politically self-conscious gay community. The new receptiveness of the media, literature, and film to the topic of homosexuality, and the proliferation of viewpoints about it, gave activists a leverage they had lacked in the 1950s, when the so-called conspiracy of silence sharply restricted the scope of discussion. By the end of 1965 the homophile movement was ready to escape the isolation and marginality of the past and to enter the mainstream of social and political reform.

For the moment, however, the optimism among activists remained a matter of faith, an untested belief that the signs of change they detected around them would in the coming years translate into substantial progress for homosexuals and lesbians. A lengthy agenda was still ahead. The movement needed to expand its organizational base enormously and improve coordination among its separate units. In order to maintain their momentum, militants had to produce victories, especially over police harassment, that improved the quality of gay life. Activists faced the challenge of influencing portrayals of homosexuality and lesbianism so that they not only informed gay men and women of the existence of a subculture but also bolstered self-esteem. Finally, the homophile cause needed to go beyond its oppositional stance toward the law, religion, and medicine and succeed in rupturing once and for all the negative consensus about homosexuality. Unless activists could parlay their first good cards into a winning hand, their expectations would yield only disappointment.

I

Except for the Daughters of Bilitis, whose local chapters remained part of a single organization, homophile groups in the East and West had had little contact with one another since the end of the 1950s. On each coast gay politics was taking a new turn, and the movement was growing; yet activists remained largely uninformed about what their colleagues were doing and were not taking advantage of the increased strength that cooperation would bring.

Early in 1966 homophile leaders took a first step toward reestablishing working interrelationships when representatives of fifteen organizations convened in Kansas City. San Francisco activists, unwilling as yet to resume formal ties with their eastern counterparts, were intent on moving very slowly toward cooperation. Militants from the Northeast, on the other hand, fresh from their triumphs over their accommodationist colleagues, approached the gathering as new territory to conquer. Kameny, Gittings, Clark Polak from Philadelphia, and others went to Kansas City with well-defined goals—to create a tightly structured national body, bound by a militant philosophy, that would let the movement speak with one voice and act on a unified agenda.[1]

Although the militants did not achieve their aim of a single national homophile organization, the Kansas City meeting—and annual conferences held every summer for the rest of the decade—allowed them to attain much of the substance, if not the form, of what they desired. In August 1966 movement groups formed the North American Conference of Homophile Organizations, a loose federation that encouraged common projects. Under NACHO's auspices they created a national legal fund that financed several court cases, including challenges of bar closings, the exclusion of homosexual immigrants, and the rights of gay military personnel. NACHO sponsored days of protest against federal employment policies and the exclusion of gay men and women from the military. Simultaneous demonstrations in several cities maximized the chances of getting press coverage. NACHO also produced studies of homosexuals and the law and of discrimination in employment. Finally, its regional gatherings became an effective means of initiating homophile organizations in places that still remained outside the orbit of the movement.[2]

1. On the planning of the Kansas City meeting and the expectation of activists, see Leitsch to Beardemphl, January 21, 1966, and Beardemphl to Leitsch, received February 9, 1966, New York Mattachine Society Archives (hereafter referred to as NYMS); Tobin to Kameny, December 14, 1965, and Gittings to Kameny, January 11, 1966, personal papers of Frank Kameny, Washington, D.C.; and Leitsch to Polak, undated reply to letter of December 27, 1965, NYMS.

2. On the formation and evolution of NACHO and its various activities, see minutes of the National Planning Conference of Homophile Organizations, Kansas City, February 19–20, 1966, and "Preliminary Summary of Substantive Actions Approved by the National Planning Conference of Homophile Organizations, Meeting in San Francisco, August 25–27, 1966," both in

More significantly, NACHO provided militants with a platform from which they hammered home their message that only protest techniques, insistence upon equality, and rejection of the medical model could bring the movement victories. At the Kansas City meeting in February 1966, Kameny argued that "all the problems of the homosexual are . . . questions of prejudice and discrimination." He urged his audience to stop "talking about homosexuality to other homosexuals" and to adopt the direct action strategy of the black civil rights movement. When activists from around the country convened again in San Francisco in August, militants resumed their rhetorical offensive. Dick Leitsch, president of the New York Mattachine Society, challenged his listeners to "stop whimpering and begin demanding. . . . Homophile organizations must be radical. . . . We must demand the right to cruise, the right to work, the right to public accommodations, and the other rights the homosexual lacks." Clark Polak went even further, subjecting all of the movement's leaders, except for a handful of militants, to stinging criticism. "The chief oppression faced by the homosexual," he argued, "is the cultural tone which says 'I despise you.' " Polak blamed activists for contributing to that oppression through their own internalized self-hatred:

> Few of the leaders in the movement have examined their innards sufficiently to be able to accept homosexuality in themselves and rid themselves of their own anti-homosexual sentiments. Anti-homosexuality is rampant within the organizations. . . . Your publications reek with anti-homosexuality, [are] groveling, obsequious . . . and seem almost designed to maintain the homosexual's position of inferiority.

Until the movement buried the vestiges of the accommodationist, self-deprecating approach of the 1950s, Polak asserted, its efforts were doomed to failure.[3]

Despite the personal enmity that such speeches provoked, militants succeeded in pushing the rest of the movement along the path they had cut. As the 1960s wore on, most movement groups recognized the need for direct action.

NACHO file, ONE, Inc., Archives, Los Angeles (hereafter referred to as ONE Archives); minutes of the North American Homophile Conference, Washington, D.C., August 16–18, 1967, and Minutes of the North American Conference of Homophile Organizations, August 12–17, 1968, both in Homosexual Organization Files—N.A.H. Clearinghouse, Institute for Sex Research, Bloomington, Indiana (hereafter referred to as ISR). For the NACHO studies, see *The Challenge and Progress of Homosexual Law Reform* (San Francisco, 1968) and *Homosexuals and Employment* (San Francisco, 1970). For coverage of NACHO activities, see the Kansas City *Times*, February 21, 1966, p. 10; *New York Times*, April 17, 1966, p. 12, and August 19, 1968, p. 29; *New Republic*, May 21, 1966, pp. 8–9; and San Francisco *Chronicle*, April 18, 1966, May 21, 1966, and May 22, 1966.

    3. Minutes, Kansas City, February 19–20, 1966, NACHO file, ONE Archives; Dick Leitsch, "Concrete Steps That Must Be Taken if the Homophile Movement Is to Be Successful," NYMS; portions of Polak's speech are reprinted in the September 1966 newsletter of the Janus Society.

Equality rather than "understanding" became the goal of homophile activists. Picketing and public rallies spread from the Northeast to Midwestern cities and the West Coast. Homophile groups disputed the authority of the medical profession to diagnose gay men and lesbians as diseased. Newer organizations as well as older ones displayed a willingness to challenge harassment by local police forces. At the 1968 NACHO conference in Chicago, delegates endorsed "Gay Is Good" as a slogan for the movement, a symbolic affirmation of their sexual identity that would have been unthinkable a decade earlier. Though Kameny and his allies failed to persuade their colleagues to create a national homophile organization, the militants had managed to set the standards that others in the movement felt compelled to meet.[4]

II

The organizational impulse spread noticeably during the late 1960s. When activists met in Kansas City in February 1966—a decade and a half after the founding of the Mattachine Society—only fifteen groups existed, and most of these were confined to San Francisco and the Northeast. By the spring of 1969 the number had grown to fifty. Although California and the Washington–New York corridor remained the dual centers of the movement, the intervening three years witnessed the emergence of gay political activity in the South and the Northwest and its spread beyond Chicago to several Midwestern cities.[5]

The Phoenix Society offers a good example of how these newer organizations operated. When Drew Schafer, who subscribed to ONE magazine, heard about the national meeting in Kansas City, he asked ONE's editors to help him start a homophile group there. He and his friends eventually decided against becoming a chapter of ONE, Inc., and instead formed the Phoenix Society for Individual Freedom in March 1966. Within just a few months, the all-male organization had an office with a lending library and was publishing a newsletter, sponsoring dances and selling tickets to them in gay bars in Kansas City, and compiling a pamphlet on venereal disease.[6]

Religion figured prominently in the calculations of Kansas City activists. With the San Francisco Council on Religion and the Homosexual as a model, they searched out local clergy and spoke frequently to groups of ministers and seminarians. Less interested in finding church leaders who would speak to homosexuals than in prodding them to agitate for change within their denominations, the Phoenix Society delivered a strong message to its clerical audiences:

4. For the "Gay Is Good" resolution, see minutes of NACHO, Chicago, August 12–17, 1968, Homosexual Organization Files—N.A.H. Clearinghouse, ISR.

5. Cities with homophile groups for the first time in the late 1960s included Kansas City; Rock Island, Illinois; Syracuse and Ithaca, New York; Cincinnati, Dayton, and Columbus; Richmond and Norfolk, Virginia; Dallas and Houston; and Seattle.

6. *Phoenix*, May 1966, p. 1; July 1966, p. 2; September–October 1966, pp. 2–3; and December 1966, p. 2.

It is high time that the church accept its responsibility for the deplorable, misinformed attitude of society toward the homosexual in America today. The laws which apply to sexual matters between consenting adults in private are based upon religious attitudes. . . . It is time the Church taught compassion and understanding, rather than condemnation.

In January 1968 the homophile group persuaded Kansas City's Metropolitan Inter-Church Agency to establish a task force on homosexuality.[7]

Law enforcement practices also captured the attention of the Phoenix Society. The police department in Kansas City had a hands-off policy toward gay bars, and one long-time resident of the area could recall only a single raid since the late 1940s. As a result, bar life flourished. But the police showed little tolerance of street cruising by gay men and often resorted to entrapment to secure arrests. When one victim contacted the Phoenix Society, Marc Jeffers, an officer, proceeded to gather evidence of other incidents and soon had several signed affidavits attesting to the prevalence of plainclothes entrapment of homosexuals. After a meeting with police officials elicited a brusque denial, Jeffers turned to the ACLU, which promised him assistance.[8]

Other cities exhibited patterns of organization and activity similar to Kansas City's. A western regional meeting of NACHO in Seattle in December 1967 gave a boost to the newly-formed Dorian Society. Its members met frequently with Protestant ministers to explore the possibility of a Seattle CRH and addressed the annual meeting of the Washington ACLU, which soon took the case of a gay Boeing employee who had lost his security clearance. Veteran activists of the Chicago Mattachine pulled together a homophile group in Rock Island, Illinois, while Frank Kameny flew to Cincinnati in July 1967 to advise local gays eager to start an organization. Their statement of purpose, with its militant tone and antisickness stand, attested to Kameny's influence. Gay men and women in Syracuse received help in 1968 from homophile leaders in New York. The president of the Syracuse Mattachine, a black university student, quickly won the ear of the city's ACLU, which offered aid in combating police harassment.[9]

Law enforcement practices preoccupied these newcomers to the homophile movement, and their organizations refused to acquiesce in the abuses suffered by lesbians and gay men. In March 1968, when Philadelphia police raided

7. *Phoenix*, June 1966, p. 4; September–October 1966, p. 11; November 1966, p. 13; February 1967, p. 3; May 1967, p. 8; and January 1968, p. 5.

8. *Phoenix*, August 1966, pp. 5–6; July 1967, p. 2; and August 1967, pp. 9–10.

9. Minutes of Western Regional Conference of Homophile Organizations, Seattle, December 1–3, 1967, in Homosexual Organization Files—W.R.C.H.O., ISR; *Columns* (newsletter of the Dorian Society of Seattle), December 1968, p. 4; March 1969, p. 3; and May 1969, pp. 2–3; "Society Advocating Mutual Equality [of Rock Island, Ill.]: Introduction," n.d., NYMS; news release of the Cincinnati Mattachine Society, n.d., Kameny papers; *The Insider* (newsletter of the Washington Mattachine Society), October 1967; NYMS *Newsletter*, August 1968, p. 2; memo to Board of Directors of New York Mattachine Society, n.d., NYMS.

Rusty's, the city's most popular lesbian bar, arrested twelve patrons, abused them verbally, and coerced them into providing information about their employment, DOB members trooped down to police headquarters with an ACLU lawyer. Though Frank Rizzo, the police chief, showed little sympathy, activists persuaded the district attorney to drop the charges. When Houston police arrested several lesbians in August 1968 on charges of cross-dressing (they were wearing fly-front pants), the president of the Promethean Society, Ray Hill, extracted from the mayor a promise to end such harassment. The Chicago Mattachine obtained ACLU legal aid for men who were arrested in a bath house raid in October 1968, and gays in Miami convinced the civil liberties union there to mount a court challenge of a city ordinance that prohibited homosexuals and lesbians from assembling, being served, or being employed in places providing liquor. Early in 1969, members of the Central Ohio Mattachine Society in Columbus sent a petition to the state's attorney general protesting the acquittal of the self-confessed killer of a forty-eight-year-old gay man, after a trial that featured much antihomosexual rhetoric. The same year, a homophile league formed in Richmond, Virginia, after the Alcoholic Beverage Commission took action against a number of gay bars. Members announced that they would patronize, as a group, every bar in the city until ABC regulations changed or Richmond went dry.[10]

Although most of these new groups won only isolated victories in particular incidents, they did begin to change the complexion of homosexual life in their respective cities. The defense of patrons arrested in lesbian and gay male taverns carried into the bars the message that it was possible to resist oppression. The activism of a few counteracted the resignation that pervaded the gay subculture and modeled for bar goers a different way of looking at their situation. Homophile initiatives also brought gay life further into the open, making it visible both to the heterosexual majority and to relatively isolated gay men and women. City officials were alerted to a new interest group, and though they were slow to respond, they could not avoid the fact that a portion of the homosexual population was agitating for justice.

III

San Francisco and New York, meanwhile, solidified their reputation as the centers of the most active, visible, and largest homophile groups. While other urban areas experienced their first taste of gay politics, homophile organizations in these two cities acquired a measure of influence and won tangible

10. On Philadelphia, see *Ladder*, May–June 1968, pp. 22–23; NYMS *Newsletter*, August 1968, p. 9; and Kameny to Philadelphia DOB, June 5, 1968, Kameny Papers. On Houston, see *Ladder*, October–November 1968, pp. 40–41; on Chicago see news release, October 9, 1968, in Homosexual Organization Files—Mattachine Midwest, ISR; on Miami, see *Ladder*, June 1966, p. 14; and *Phoenix*, June 1967, p. 13; on Richmond, see Kameny to Leitsch, April 22, 1969, Kameny papers. On Columbus see Columbus *Dispatch*, May 31, 1969, p. 3; and Central Ohio Mattachine Society to State Attorney General Paul Brown, June 3, 1969, Kameny papers.

victories for the movement at a local level. In both places activists especially targeted police harassment. Their success in limiting police abuses allowed social institutions such as bars to thrive and led to a more stable gay subculture, especially among men.

In San Francisco, tensions between gays and the police continued to escalate for several months after the police action at the dance sponsored by the Council on Religion and the Homosexual. Galvanized by the events of New Year's Eve, CRH initiated a major study of local law enforcement practices, while the police continued their provocations. In May 1965 officers tried to raid a fundraising party held by SIR. In June the police took into custody four young gay men who were leaving a bowling alley where the SIR league played, brutally beat them at a local station, and then, without filing any charges, dumped them on the street. Soon after, CRH released its report, *A Brief of Injustices*, with much fanfare. "We are helping," it began, "to expose a pattern of social, legal and economic oppression of a minority group." Its authors charged that "through deceit and inducement, lure and suggestion, both police and ABC undercover agents encourage solicitations for sexual acts." Their manner of enforcement, the writers continued, "fosters oppression, blackmail, and discrimination." After cataloging the range of police abuses toward the gay community, the report confirmed what activists had been claiming for years: "There is very little justice for the homosexual."[11] That fall CRH lent its backing to the gay organizations candidates' nights, where audiences repeatedly demanded that San Francisco politicians endorse a civilian review board. In October 1965, with the support of CRH, activists formed Citizens Alert, a twenty-four-hour hot line that provided lawyers, photographers, and other assistance to victims of police brutality. The effort won the endorsement of black groups in San Francisco, and much of the gay-staffed organization's work revolved around incidents affecting blacks, Chicanos, and hippies.[12]

Something had to give, and in this case the beleaguered police retreated. The department initiated meetings with homophile activists and arranged liaisons with the gay community. A minor concession, it nonetheless helped diffuse tensions, since homophile groups now had a way of airing their grievances. More importantly, San Francisco's police force abruptly halted its harassment of gay bars. Some officers occasionally violated department procedures, and the police still arrested men who cruised in public places, but the change did make it relatively safe for lesbians and homosexuals to patronize bars. The result was astonishing. The number of gay bars in the city, reduced to fewer than twenty in 1963, rose to fifty-seven by the beginning of 1968,

11. *Vector*, June 1965, pp. 3, 7; Roxanne B. T. Sweet, "Political and Social Action in Homophile Organizations," Ph.D. diss., University of California, Berkeley, 1968, pp. 157–58; CRH, *A Brief of Injustices* (San Francisco, 1965), pp. 10, 9, 8, 3; *News-Call-Bulletin*, August 17, 1965, p. 10; *Chronicle*, September 25, 1965, p. 1; and *Ladder*, November 1965, pp. 4–7.

12. *Vector*, September 1965, p. 3; October 1965, p. 7; November 1965, p. 3; *Ladder*, November 1965, pp. 13–14; February 1966, p. 17; and April 1967, pp. 20–21; and Sweet, pp. 171–72.

placing San Francisco far ahead of much larger cities such as New York, Los Angeles, and Chicago.[13]

San Francisco's homophile groups worked hard to acquire political influence. In August 1966 the Daughters of Bilitis, in conjunction with its national convention and the NACHO conference, scheduled a round of public forums where officials from several municipal departments addressed themselves to gay concerns. The "Ten Days in August," as DOB billed it, marked the first time that representatives of the city bureaucracy spoke *to* the gay community instead of expostulating *against* it. With the backing of Glide Methodist Church, activists persuaded Mayor John Shelley to designate the Tenderloin an antipoverty area qualifying for funds from the federal Office of Economic Opportunity. Two openly gay men, Don Lucas of Mattachine and Mark Forrester of SIR, were hired to staff an office that worked primarily with young male hustlers. Candidates' nights, jointly sponsored by all of San Francisco's gay organizations, became annual events, drawing as many as 500 homosexuals and lesbians. Local politicians took ads in movement publications and actively courted the gay vote. Some, like Representative Philip Burton, state legislators Willie Brown and John Burton, and city supervisors Jack Morrison and Robert Gonzalez, became committed supporters of the movement. The shift fostered a growing confidence among activists. "If politicians do not openly address themselves to homosexuals," William Beardemphl of SIR announced, "they do not need our 90,000 votes. We shall put into office public servants who talk to homosexuals."[14]

An array of movement initiatives kept homosexuality in the news in San Francisco. Homophile groups demonstrated against the exclusion of homosexuals and lesbians from the armed services and federal employment. When they were denied an information booth at the state fair in Sacramento in August 1966, they filed suit in court; when that failed, activists distributed 10,000 leaflets outside the entrance. The refusal of Pacific Telephone to provide a listing in the yellow pages under "homophile organizations" led to another court battle and a series of hearings in 1968 and 1969 before the Public Utilities Commission. In March 1969, activists persuaded Assemblyman Willie Brown to introduce a consenting adults bill in the state legislature. The city's press,

13. *Vector*, September 1965, p. 5; March 1967, pp. 5, 7; and February 1968, p. 6; interviews with Bill Plath, December 7, 1976, and Mark Forrester, December 9, 1976, both in San Francisco; and *Sunday Examiner and Chronicle*, April 28, 1968, p. 3.

14. On the "Ten Days," see *Ladder*, August 1966, pp. 4–7; September 1966, pp. 4–9; October 1966, pp. 7–13; November 1966, pp. 4–14; December 1966, pp. 18ff.; and January 1967, pp. 6–13, 21–28; and *Chronicle*, August 17, 1966, p. 4; August 20, 1966; and August 24, 1966. On OEO funding, see *Chronicle*, February 24, 1966, p. 1, and February 25, 1966, p. 1; on candidates' nights and local politicians, see *Vector*, November 1967, p. 5; *Ladder*, February 1967, p. 15; "Vote Today," SIR's endorsement of candidates, Homosexual Organization Files—SIR, ISR; minutes of Western Regional Conference of Homophile Organizations, December 1–3, 1967, Seattle, Homosexual Organization Files—WRCHO, ISR; and *Chronicle*, August 24, 1966. Beardemphl is quoted in the *Examiner*, August 21, 1966.

meanwhile, provided substantial coverage of gay-related developments occurring in the courts, churches, and the arts outside San Francisco.[15]

Despite its visibility, however, the movement's power never quite matched the expectations of 1965. The candidates' nights, for instance, tended to attract aspirants to elective office in need of votes rather than incumbents, while DOB's "Ten Days" drew lower-echelon bureaucrats. Moreover, activists could not yet deliver on their tantalizing claims of a homosexual voting bloc, as the 1967 mayoral election made clear. The campaign pitted Jack Morrison, a progay supervisor and Democratic party outsider, against Joseph Alioto who, having the support of both the business community and organized labor, spurned contact with homophile groups. After Alioto's landslide victory, a chagrined Bill Beardemphl gave the city's homosexuals a severe tongue lashing. Calling them "political masochists," he charged that every homosexual who cast a vote for Alioto "cast a vote against S.I.R.," and he predicted a deterioration in relations with the police.[16]

The movement's limits stemmed in large part from the inability of DOB and SIR to transform the sense of grievance that police harassment had provoked among the city's gay male and lesbian population into large-scale grassroots activism. The hard-core activists who ran the organizations remained leaders without many followers. At a critically important business meeting in August 1965, DOB had only eighteen voting members. Two years later, the chapter's president complained that there were not enough members to pay dues to cover the rent on DOB's office. "Self-help" and socializing occupied the women, while experienced leaders such as Phyllis Lyon and Del Martin shifted their energy to CRH, Citizens Alert, and the National Organization for Women rather than try to inject some militancy into DOB.[17]

Although SIR did succeed in attracting much larger numbers of gay men—it had 1,000 members by the end of 1967—its experience tended to confirm Kameny's critique that social events did not necessarily cut a path to political activism. Most of the members participated only in the fun and largely avoided direct political involvement. George Mendenhall, who joined SIR in 1965 and edited *Vector*, recalled the frustration induced by this state of affairs:

> As its peak, when SIR had 1,000 members, maybe 400 people would come twice a year, for a drag show or if there was something really controversial at election time. Another 600 only subscribed to *Vector*. But

15. On the demonstrations, see *Chronicle*, April 18, 1966, p. 16, and May 21–22, 1966; and *Vector*, August 1968, p. 5. On the state fair incident, see *Chronicle*, August 22, 1966, p. 1, and August 25, 1966; *Ladder*, October 1966, pp. 21–22; and *Vector*, August 1966, p. 9, and September 1966, p. 1. On the PT&T hearings, see *Chronicle*, July 12 and August 9 and 11, 1968; *Ladder*, December 1968–January 1969, pp. 30–32, and August–September 1969, p. 45; and *Vector*, October 1968, p. 5. On the consenting adults bill, see *Chronicle*, March 4 and April 17 and 22, 1969. The *Chronicle* editorialized in favor of the legislation on March 6, 1969.

16. *Vector*, November 1967, pp. 5 and 23, and December 1967, p. 4.

17. San Francisco DOB *Newsletter*, August 1965, p. 1, and August 1967, p. 2.

otherwise they stayed away in droves, and you had a very small group of people, maybe twenty to forty, who were doing things. You can imagine how I felt about tap dancing and rehearsing for a drag show. That's all very interesting, but to have it around you every day when you're trying to be an activist—it was depressing.

Mendenhall attributed the paucity of activists to the fear of exposure that still existed in the late 1960s and that SIR failed to overcome. "Why should you come up front and risk anything when you can play this game of a dual identity? In spite of all our [social] activities, we were still closeted. It was a collective closet, but it was still a closet."[18]

SIR's problems, however, went deeper than the closet. A specific set of circumstances had propelled SIR into existence. The excitement generated by the beats, political scandals, a police crackdown, and the example of a charismatic drag queen had temporarily shaken many male homosexuals out of their acquiescence to oppression. Ironically, the success of the movement in bringing an end to the harassment of bars took the edge off the anger that led to SIR's founding. The close working relationship between SIR and the Tavern Guild, moreover, further weakened the impulse toward militancy, since the bar owners, upon whom SIR relied for funds and publicity, had achieved their goal of ending police harassment of their businesses. As one of its presidents, Larry Littlejohn, acknowledged, the dependence on gay entrepreneurs encouraged SIR's leaders to cultivate a "respectable and established" image that ultimately crippled SIR's potential effectiveness. Homosexuals who saw themselves as mainstream, middle-class Americans intuited that the public avowal of their sexual preference could only threaten their status and security, while SIR's social events and the flourishing bar culture made militancy less urgent, since the quality of their personal life had improved. Those gay men in whom the beats' cultural protest and glorification of nonconformity had originally struck a responsive chord found little in SIR to claim their allegiance. Instead, the heirs of the beats—the burgeoning hippie movement and counterculture in the San Francisco area—offered them a more hospitable home. Large and successful as the homophile movement in San Francisco was, at least comparatively, by the late 1960s it seemed to be losing its dynamism.[19]

IV

Although New York had a history of homophile organizing almost as long as San Francisco's, by the mid-1960s the movement had barely touched the consciousness of the city's population, gay or nongay. Without the significant cultural influence of the beats or the intrusion of major homosexual-related

18. Author's interview with George Mendenhall, December 2, 1976, in San Francisco. For membership figures, see *Vector*, December 1967, p. 34.
19. Author's interview with Larry Littlejohn, December 7, 1976, in San Francisco; interview with Mendenhall.

scandals into local politics to shake up New York's homosexuals and lesbians, the Mattachine Society and the Daughters of Bilitis remained largely invisible and insignificant, divorced from both the gay subculture and the political process.

Some homophile activists, however, had reason to anticipate change. Randy Wicker's brashness had cracked the silence of the city's press, while debates in Albany in 1964 over a new penal code had at least brought the issue of law reform before the public. Mattachine was growing rapidly, and with the triumph of the militants' civil rights/antisickness position, it stood poised to move beyond internal squabbles and into action. Moreover, the mayoral election of November 1965 drew the curtain on twelve years of Democratic machine rule. John Lindsay, a liberal Republican with a reputation as a reformer, took office. His strong campaign stand in favor of a police civilian review board raised hope of some relief from persistent harassment of lesbian and gay male bars and the widespread practice of entrapment.[20]

Dick Leitsch became Mattachine president in the same month as Lindsay's election. A cleancut, handsome former school teacher from Kentucky, he won office on the strength of his allegiance to the militant reform perspective and his pledge to get Mattachine moving. In public, Leitsch encased an almost ruthless fighting sense within a deceptively sweet style of verbal dueling that often left his opponents speechless. As head of the New York Mattachine for the rest of the 1960s, he charted the organization's course.

Events quickly shattered any illusions that the liberalism of the city's newly elected mayor automatically extended to homosexuals. Motivated perhaps by a desire to mollify a police force hostile to his civilian review proposals, and also anxious to solidify his support within the business community, in late February 1966 Lindsay gave the green light to a massive crackdown in Times Square that aimed to rid the area of "honky tonks, promenading perverts, . . . homosexuals and prostitutes." The next month, the police extended the cleanup campaign to "undesirables" in Greenwich Village. There they concentrated on Washington Square Park, whose western edge was a gay male cruising area dubbed the "meat rack" by those who frequented the park. Street arrests rose sharply, and chief inspector Sanford Garelik announced that these were merely a "first step in a broader city program."[21]

Although city officials confidently predicted "no organized opposition" to the effort, the mayor and police soon found themselves on the carpet. The New York Civil Liberties Union, which had exhibited little concern in 1960 over a similar antihomosexual drive, responded favorably to a Mattachine request for

20. On the debates in Albany, see *New York Times*, March 17, 1964, p. 1; November 25, 1964, p. 43; November 26, 1964, p. 34; March 17, 1965, p. 1; May 28, 1965, p. 36; June 4, 1965, p. 1; June 10, 1965, p. 43; and July 23, 1965, p. 1; *Newsweek*, December 7, 1964, p. 90; and *Life*, June 11, 1965, p. 4.

21. *New York Times*, February 23, 1966, p. 41; March 3, 1966, p. 23; March 16, 1966, p. 1; and March 17, 1966, p. 41.

help. The union's director, Aryeh Neier, accused the police of infringing upon the rights of homosexuals and "confusing deviant social behavior with criminal activity." Judson Memorial Church, located on the edge of Washington Square Park, sponsored a community meeting addressed by Garelik and packed with Mattachine members and gay Village residents. The chief inspector came under fire for allowing his officers to entrap homosexuals. His expression of surprise at the charges and his appeal to homosexuals to report instances of entrapment provoked a sharp retort from the NYCLU. Garelik, a spokesperson responded, "shows a certain naiveté. . . . It's alarming to think that the chief inspector doesn't know that a large number of police spend their duty hours dressed in tight pants, sneakers and polo sweaters to bring about solicitations." Lindsay, meanwhile, reportedly upset over "complaints that his administration was acting illiberally," agreed to meet with Neier, Leitsch, and representatives of a committee of artists, writers, and coffeehouse owners whom Allen Ginsberg organized to protest police harassment.[22]

The quick vocal reaction of the Mattachine Society and civil libertarians paid off. Early in May, police commissioner Howard Leary instructed officers not to lure homosexuals into breaking the law and, more importantly, required that plainclothesmen have a civilian witness when they made a gay arrest. The directive was fairly well observed, and entrapment, for years a scourge of gay men in New York, came to an end. The NYCLU termed the change an "extremely important victory," and Leitsch described it as "the best thing that ever happened."[23]

Other forms of harassment proved more difficult to curb. Though entrapment ended, officers continued to hassle gay men on Village streets, and on summer evenings the police presence was ubiquitous. Commissioner Leary's directive, moreover, did not apply to transit patrolmen, and Mattachine continued to report incidents of blackmail, shakedowns, and beatings. In one extreme instance, an off-duty transit police officer shot and killed two unarmed gay men who were cruising the waterfront area at night. A grand jury failed to issue an indictment in the case.[24] As in San Francisco, bar raids by the police and license revocations by the state liquor authority occurred regularly; during local elections, closings took place almost daily until virtually every bar shut its doors at least temporarily. In April 1966, with reporters and photographers trailing them, Leitsch and two other Mattachine members, Craig Rodwell and John Timmons, conducted a "sip-in" of Village drinking spots to test

22. *New York Times*, March 16, 1966, p. 1; March 18, 1966, p. 42; April 2, 1966, p. 1; and May 3, 1966, p. 49. See also memo and letter drafted by Leanne Golden, n.d., vol. 34, General Correspondence, 1961, ACLU papers, Princeton University; Leitsch to Polak, November 29, 1965, and Leitsch to Clarence Colwell, April 29, 1966, both in NYMS.

23. *New York Times*, May 11, 1966, p. 36; and NYMS *Newsletter*, June 1966, p. 3; September 1966, p. 1; and June 1967, p. 4.

24. NYMS *Newsletter*, February 1969, p. 14; September 1968, p. 14; October 1968, pp. 1–3; November 1968, pp. 14–15; March 1969, pp. 1–4; and April 1969, p. 1.

the SLA policy of closing taverns that served homosexuals. When the bartender turned them away at Julius, a gay bar of many years' standing, they had their case. The head of the city's human rights commission promised to investigate, and the incident prompted the chairman of the SLA to deny that his department prohibited the sale of liquor to homosexuals. The next year, in two separate cases involving gay bars, the state's appellate court ruled that "substantial evidence" of indecent behavior was necessary to revoke a license and that kissing between two men did not constitute indecency. Raids and closings became considerably less frequent, although they by no means ceased. As a result, the number of taverns in New York City rose, and a trend developed toward investment in gay bars by legitimate businessmen.[25]

Employment practices in New York also changed during the Lindsay administration, partly through the initiative of the city government and partly through court challenges. In 1966, the Civil Service Commission began quietly approving the hiring of homosexual men and women, whereas previously interviewers could reject an applicant who "by appearance, actions or attitudes" struck them as gay. Certain "sensitive" jobs remained closed to homosexuals and lesbians, however, and when the commission refused to hire two men as welfare case workers on grounds of homosexuality, the Mattachine Society asked for legal aid from the NYCLU. The men eventually won their suit against the city and were hired by the Department of Social Services. The *New York Times* called the outcome a significant advance for homosexual rights.[26]

The shift in hiring policies, however, was not quite complete. Although the civil service commission no longer regarded homosexuality as an "absolute disqualification" for employment, it retained wide discretionary power to exclude gay men and women from city jobs. It continued to utilize "provisions which authorize disqualification for either mental or physical disability, or for guilt of a crime, or infamous and notoriously disgraceful conduct." The commission refused to hire "an admitted homosexual, when the acts are frequent and recent," for positions such as corrections officer, children's counselor, or playground attendant. Finally, major city departments, including the police, the fire department, and the school system, remained entirely unaffected by the actions of the CSC.[27]

25. On raids at election time, see NYMS *Newsletter*, January 1966, p. 2, and September 1966, p. 2; on the sip-in see *New York Times*, April 26, 1966, p. 55, and *Village Voice*, May 5, 1966, p. 66; See also press release, April 22, 1966, in Homosexual Organization Files—New York Mattachine Society, ISR. On court cases, see *New York Times*, March 9, 1967, p. 33, and December 30, 1967, p. 6. On changes in police policy as well as continuing harassment, see *New York Times*, March 18, 1967, p. 15; November 26, 1967, p. 69; and November 30, 1967, p. 1; NYMS *Newsletter*, June 1969, p. 10; and Leitsch to Kameny, March 11, 1969, and NYMS press release, January 6, 1967, both in Kameny papers.

26. *New York Times*, January 7, 1967, p. 1; NYMS *Newsletter*, January–February 1967, p. 1, and October 1968, p. 4; and *New York Times*, May 7, 1967, Section IV, p. 5.

27. *New York Times*, May 9, 1969, p. 1.

The experience of Doctor Howard Brown reveals the limits of tolerance under Mayor Lindsay. Appointed health services administrator in June 1966, he felt compelled to have his lover of five years move out of their home in order to minimize suspicions of homosexuality. Brown knew several other gay men who held high positions in city government, but they never dared to meet socially as a group. Fear of exposure, the doctor recalled in his memoirs, ruled their lives, and they took extraordinary precautions:

> We could not be too careful. We could not talk in our official cars because of the chauffeurs. We came to be wary of telephones—a secretary might pick up while we were talking, or our phones might even be tapped. One gay commissioner regularly sent a technician around to check out my office telephone. . . . At home I had two telephones, one of which was connected to an answering service. My commissioner friend warned me never to use the service phone to call a homosexual and never to speak of homosexuality. . . . My other phone was, like my office phones, regularly checked out by the commissioner's assistant.

Brown survived one rumor that he was gay because Lindsay dismissed it as untrue, but he was led to resign in December 1967 on a tip from John Sibley, his brother-in-law and a reporter for the *New York Times*, about a forthcoming exposé of homosexuals in the administration. Despite some favorable changes under Lindsay, according to Brown the mayor "was not particularly sympathetic to homosexuals, although many New Yorkers assumed the contrary."[28]

The homophile movement in New York made its presence known in a variety of other ways during the late 1960s. In warm weather, the Mattachine Society set up information tables and gave out literature in the Village and on the upper west side of Manhattan. Reports of arrests on Fire Island, a summer resort that drew an increasingly gay male crowd, provoked the society to distribute on the beaches copies of a pamphlet on legal rights in case of arrest. When a Brooklyn Heights newspaper attempted to fan sentiment against male homosexuals in the neighborhood, members picketed its offices and organized an advertising boycott. From June 1966 to June 1967, Mattachine representatives appeared on 100 local television and radio shows and sent speakers to approximately 425 nongay groups in the metropolitan area.[29]

Other groups contributed to awareness of the gay movement's presence in New York. In the spring of 1967, Columbia University chartered a student homophile league (SHL), the first of its kind in the country. SHL created quite a stir on campus, received a great deal of media coverage, and aided the

28. Howard Brown, *Familiar Faces, Hidden Lives: The Story of Homosexual Men in America Today* (New York, 1976), pp. 9, 12, and passim in chap. 1.

29. NYMS *Newsletter*, June 1966, p. 4; September 1966, p. 1; May 1967, p. 5; June 1967, p. 4; September 1968, p. 8; and October 1968, p. 19; and *New York Times*, July 24, 1967, p. 19.

formation of similar groups at Cornell, NYU, and Stanford. In November 1967 Craig Rodwell, a Mattachine militant, opened the Oscar Wilde Memorial Bookshop in Greenwich Village. Stocking only gay and lesbian material, the store became a popular meeting place where news was exchanged and gay politics discussed. Its viability as a business testified both to the new availability of homosexual-related books and to the hunger of gay men and lesbians to read them. The Daughters of Bilitis also engaged in educational activities. For a time it appeared that DOB might take a more activist stance. Martha Shelley, a young woman who became president of the chapter in the fall of 1968, had a militant temperament as well as experience in campus politics and the antiwar movement. Articles by Shelley in the *Ladder* drew analogies between the condition of gay women and men and other oppressed minorities, and she continually urged a more forthright, less apologetic posture. But Shelley relinquished her leadership role early the next year, and DOB in New York remained primarily a support group for lesbians.[30]

Mattachine's visibility and its important, if limited, achievements ought to have attracted a substantial number of new members; but Leitsch hewed to a strategic line that bypassed recruitment and active membership involvement, thus keeping the organization's growth small. "We have to accumulate power and use it sensibly," he wrote.

> Power lies not in the number of members or the total of names on a list. . . . It lies in how effective your organization is in achieving the goals of the homophile movement. This is not a plea for "gay power" or "lavendar power." It is a plea for those charged with leadership positions in homophile organizations to accumulate enough power to implement social change, to make the voice of the homosexual heard in the community.

To Leitsch, the willingness of city officials to open their doors to him was evidence of his influence. Once inside, he explained, "I keep my demands reasonable, and learn how much they can give, given their power limitations, before asking." Leitsch apparently never considered that the limitations were his own, that by choosing to represent the homosexual community rather than mobilize it, he circumscribed the victories he did achieve. Leitsch negotiated concessions from those who wielded power, but he did not try to accumulate power within the gay community.[31]

---

30. On SHL, see *New York Times*, May 3, 1967, p. 1; May 11, 1967, p. 58; and June 3, 1967, p. 30; and material in Homosexual Organization Files—SHL, ISR. On Rodwell and the Oscar Wilde Memorial Bookstore, see Kay Tobin and Randy Wicker, *The Gay Crusaders* (New York, 1972), pp. 65–76. On Shelley and DOB see *Ladder*, August 1968, pp. 6–7, and April–May 1969, pp. 42–43; and New York DOB *Newsletter*, November 1968, p. 2, and March 1969, p. 2.

31. Dick Leitsch, "Concrete Steps That Must Be Taken if the Homophile Movement Is to Be Successful," August 1966, and Leitsch to Kameny, June 27, 1968, both in NYMS.

V

The growth in the number of homophile organizations, the trend toward cooperative efforts, and the acceptance by most groups of the strategy and perspectives of Eastern militants allowed the movement to push forward in its assault on the ideological structure that supported the oppression of lesbians and homosexuals. In the latter half of the 1960s, evidence of change in the law, the clergy, and the mental health profession appeared with accelerating frequency. Activists gained the backing of civil libertarians. They succeeded in opening debate within the churches, continued their attack upon the mental health profession, and saw the authority of the medical establishment rejected by a national task force on homosexuality. Each of these developments made the movement newsworthy, and by the end of the decade, press coverage of gay political initiatives was reshaping public discourse on homosexuality.

The strongest attack on the status quo emerged in the realm of law, where antihomosexual prejudice received institutionalized expression. Change came less in elimination of criminal statutes or discriminatory practices than in a broadening of support for law reform and civil rights and in the proliferation of court challenges of legalized inequality. For example, in the 1960s only Connecticut followed the lead of Illinois in repealing its sodomy statute, but the consenting adults principle received endorsement from the ACLU, Americans for Democratic Action, New York's Liberal party, Wisconsin's Young Democrats, and a number of church groups. By the end of the decade most legal writers on the topic expressed opinions in favor of decriminalization.[32] Although in 1967 the Supreme Court sustained the constitutionality of an immigration law that excluded aliens or denied them citizenship on the grounds of homosexuality, several appellate court decisions were won, particularly in the area of employment. More significantly, the number of gay-related cases reaching federal appeals courts grew from twelve in the first half of the 1960s to thirty between 1965 and 1969. The rise suggests a new conviction that appeal might bring victory.[33]

The legal status of gay bars offers one clear indicator of progress. By the end of the decade, courts in New York, New Jersey, and Pennsylvania had followed the lead of California in establishing the constitutional right of lesbians and homosexuals to assemble and be served in places providing liquor. A 1967 decision of the New Jersey Supreme Court, in a case financed by movement groups, was especially significant, since it laid out a historical argument, applicable to other states, that both explained previous liquor

---

32. *New York Times*, April 10, 1966, p. 80; June 3, 1969, p. 43; and March 3, 1969, p. 40; and *Ladder*, February–March 1969, p. 35.

33. Boutillier v. Immigration and Naturalization Service, 387 U.S. 118 (1967); Scott v. Macy, 402 F. 2d. 644 (1968); Norton v. Macy, 417 F. 2d. 1161 (1968); on the number of appellate court cases see Lawrence M. Goldwyn, "Legal Ideology and the Regulation of Homosexual Behavior," Ph.D. diss., Stanford University, 1979, p. 40.

authority action against gay bars and justified its discontinuation. The court acknowledged that in the 1930s, when national prohibition was repealed and the regulation of alcoholic beverages reverted to the states, it was understandable that the interests of patrons received "little consideration and were in any event overwhelmed by the highly felt transitional need for sweeping restraint." Three decades later, the court reasoned, state regulation had proved itself workable, and attention could focus on constitutional safeguards. As in other gay bar cases, the New Jersey decision only protected the right of homosexual men and women to patronize an establishment. Regulatory agencies could still suspend a license if they gathered evidence that solicitations for sexual acts had occurred on the premises. Yet the mere acknowledgment of a right to socialize in a public space was no small victory. Court decisions were giving gay bars greater freedom from harassment and thus making it safer for men and women to participate in an urban gay subculture.[34]

The movement received a considerable boost when the American Civil Liberties Union finally reversed its position on homosexuality and took on the issue of gay rights. Early in the 1960s the ACLU had begun to reevaluate its support of the sodomy statutes and its refusal to consider homosexual expression as a civil liberties issue. Letters inquiring about the union's stand elicited a different response from what was offered in the 1950s. "I expect that the Union in the coming years will be more actively involved in this area," wrote Alan Reitman, associate director of the national office in 1962. The ACLU had a case testing the constitutionality of Connecticut's anticontraception law and was waiting for a Supreme Court ruling. "Once we have the high court's opinion in this area, we will be in a position to determine our policy on the civil liberties aspect of a variety of sexual practices, including homosexuality," Reitman informed a correspondent. In June 1965, when the court struck down the law on the grounds that it infringed upon a right to privacy, the civil liberties group decided that it had a constitutional footing at least to oppose the laws penalizing homosexual behavior.[35]

Meanwhile, under mounting pressure from gay movement groups, a few local affiliates were racing ahead of the national office. Prodded by the Washington Mattachine Society, the ACLU branch in the nation's capital aggressively championed the rights of homosexuals. In consultation with homophile activists, ACLU chapters in southern California, Philadelphia, and New York also pushed forward on gay issues. When the District of Columbia

34. Kerma Restaurant Corporation v. State Liquor Authority, 278 N.Y.S. 2d. 951 (1966); Re Revocation of License of Clock Bar, Inc., 85 Dauphin County Reports, 125 (Pa., 1966); and One Eleven Wines and Liquors, Inc. v. Division of Alcoholic Beverage Control, 235 A. 2d. 12 (New Jersey, 1967).

35. Reitman to Kameny, May 28, 1962, and Reitman to E. A. Dioguardi, May 10, 1962, General Correspondence, vol. 59, 1962, ACLU Papers; and Griswold v. Connecticut, 381 U.S. 479 (1965). For an analysis of the Griswold decision and its implications for the constitutionality of laws regulating consensual sexual behavior, see Irv S. Goldman, "Bedroom Should Not Be Within the Province of the Law," *California Western Law Review* 4 (1968): 115–31.

group circulated among participants at the 1964 ACLU conference a position paper on the government employment issue, the delegates referred it to the national office for study and urged as well a "reconsideration of the Board's 1957 statement on laws punishing homosexual behavior."[36]

In 1967, after more than two years of careful deliberation, the union's due process committee recommended and the national board adopted a policy on gay rights that reversed its previous stand. The union disputed the propriety of any government regulation of private, consensual sexual behavior between adults, on the grounds that it infringed upon a constitutionally protected right to privacy. It also opposed police harassment of gay male and lesbian bars, challenged the ban on immigration of homosexuals, and argued that the government had the burden of proving the relevance of sexual orientation to job performance. With the expansion of the field of civil liberties to include homosexuality, the union could begin the long, slow process of finding test cases, amassing a corpus of favorable lower court rulings, and chipping away at the system of legal penalties and discriminatory practices.[37]

By the late 1960s the ACLU was leading the fight in the courts against discrimination in employment, violations of due process, and unequal enforcement of law. In California it commenced the first empirical study of arrests and prosecutions of gay men and challenged the use of peepholes for surveillance of public toilets. In Washington state and the District of Columbia, ACLU affiliates took on the Civil Service ban against the employment of homosexuals and lesbians and the denial of security clearances in defense production. In several states the civil liberties group supported the right of gay women and men to assemble in bars and provided legal aid for victims of bar and bath house raids. Union lawyers often accompanied homophile activists when they conferred with police and city officials.[38]

The ACLU played a critical role in halting a vast post office operation aimed at male homosexuals. In 1965, with the aid of homophile groups, the union began gathering evidence of snooping, entrapment, and deliberate exposure of

36. On the Washington Mattachine and the ACLU, see above, Chap. 9. On southern California, see minutes of meetings and reports of the ACLU Committee on Civil Liberties and Unusual Sex or Gender Behavior, Box 124, ACLU of Southern California Papers, UCLA. On Philadelphia, see Spencer Coxe to Alan Reitman, August 5, 1965, General Correspondence, vol. 1, 1965, ACLU Papers; and Coxe to Clayton Montgomery, March 22, 1966, Coxe to Reitman, March 29, 1966, and Coxe to Speiser, May 10, 1966, all in General Correspondence, vol. 1, 1966, ACLU Papers. On the 1964 ACLU conference, see "Summary Report of 1964 ACLU Biennial Conference," July 9, 1964, p. 12, in General Correspondence, vol. 71, 1964, ACLU Papers.

37. "ACLU Statement on Homosexuality," in General Correspondence, vol. 7, 1965, ACLU Papers; other materials on the new policy statement and its formulation can be found in General Correspondence, vols. 7 and 30, 1965; vols. 11 and 27, 1966; and vol. 5, 1967, all in ACLU Papers.

38. *Vector*, April 1965, p. 1; *Columns* (newsletter of the Dorian Society of Seattle), May 1969, p. 2; Chicago DOB *Newsletter*, April 1966, p. 2; Florida Civil Liberties Union press release, June 20, 1966, in General Correspondence, vol. 12, 1966, ACLU Papers, and press release, February 17, 1967, in General Correspondence, vol. 5, 1967, ACLU papers; and *Civil Liberties*, no. 245, April 1967, p. 6.

individuals' sexual orientation to employers. Mail inspectors, the ACLU charged, "have been visiting recipients of allegedly obscene mail for the 'friendly' purpose of warning them that they may get themselves into trouble. The Post Office apparently obtains names by subscribing to pen clubs, by reading personal columns in various magazines, and by mail watches." Postal employees initiated correspondence with unsuspecting gay men, and according to the Michigan civil liberties union, "once they had a basis for an arrest of a particular person they would then go through his mail and begin correspondence with persons who had been in communication with the arrested person to set . . . further arrests." The union accumulated cases of gay men who had lost their jobs because of information supplied to employers by the post office. A postal worker who refused to inform on an employee of Michigan State University, the union discovered, was threatened with dismissal by his supervisor. The ACLU extracted a promise from a Senate committee studying government invasions of privacy to investigate the operation. In 1966 the combined pressure by the union and its allies on Capitol Hill brought the surveillance to an end.[39]

Within the churches, the formation in 1964 of the San Francisco Council on Religion and the Homosexual provided the spark that ignited debate on homosexuality. CRH members were able to take advantage of the theological ferment and social activism that infected American religion in the 1960s in order to press for a reconsideration of Christian attitudes toward same-sex eroticism. CRH brought ministers together from around the country for symposia on homosexuality. It spawned councils in cities like Dallas, Los Angeles, Washington, and Seattle, and put clerics in touch with local gay activists in several other places. CRH members met with national decision-making bodies and influential personnel of the United Church of Christ, the Protestant Episcopal Church, the Lutheran Church in America, and the Methodist Church. Both UCC and the California Episcopal Diocese gave financial support to CRH.[40]

The reassessment of religious teachings that had been fixed for several hundred years naturally proceeded slowly and, in the 1960s, remained confined to discussion rather than extend to formal changes in creed. The National Council of Churches first considered the issue at an all-day meeting of clergy, laity, and gay activists in January 1966 and followed it with a larger three-day gathering in the fall. Similar interdenominational conferences occurred at a local level, including places such as Philadelphia and Kansas City. Among

39. Alan Reitman to Affiliates, memo, September 1, 1965; Ernest Mazey to Reitman, September 10, 1965; and Spencer Coxe to Reitman, August 5, 1965, all in General Correspondence, vol. 1, 1965, ACLU papers; Coxe to Clayton Montgomery, March 22, 1966, General Correspondence, vol. 1, 1966, ACLU papers; *New Republic*, August 21, 1965, pp. 6–7; and *Newsweek*, June 13, 1966, p. 24.

40. *CRH: 1964/1968* (San Francisco, 1968), pp. 7–9; *Ladder*, September 1966, p. 9; and Don Lucas to Don Slater, May 19, 1965, CRH file, HIC.

individual faiths, UCC and Presbyterians devoted issues of their journals to homosexuality, with gays speaking for themselves. At a symposium in New York in November 1967, Episcopal priests in the Northeast urged that homosexuality be classified as morally neutral and that gay relationships be judged by the same criteria applied to heterosexual marriages.[41]

Although no religious bodies repudiated the moral opprobrium attached to homosexual behavior, some sectors of the religious community were willing to question its criminalization. Following the example of England, where both the Anglican and Roman Catholic churches had endorsed law reform, a few American church leaders called for a separation of morality from law and the elimination of legal prohibitions against private sexual relations. In a lecture at Duke University, outspoken Episcopal Bishop James Pike ridiculed "the general assumption that if something is naughty there should be a law against it." He urged the repeal of laws against the sexual behavior of consenting adults and of statutes restricting access to abortions. The Diocesan Council of the Episcopal church in California extended Pike's appeal to include an end to entrapment, fair treatment for gay bars, and special training programs for police who dealt with homosexuals. Sometimes a call for reform coexisted with a defense of traditional moral teachings. The influential *Christian Century* magazine, for instance, found merit in proposals for law reform, equal employment opportunity, and an end to police abuses, even as it described as "highly dubious" the notion that homosexuality might be morally desirable.[42]

Although gay activists were inclined to pursue dialogue with the churches, they were more disposed to confrontation with the medical establishment. Despite the appearance of dissenting viewpoints that questioned the classification of homosexuality as mental illness, paradoxically the proponents of the sickness model reached the high point of their influence during the late 1960s. Besides the publication of new studies alleging the pathological character of homosexual behavior, mass circulation magazines carried articles popularizing the medical approach by psychiatrists like Irving Bieber, Samuel Hadden, and Lawrence Hatterer. Millions of American parents learned of the supposed perils confronting their children's sexual development by distant fathers and domineering mothers.[43] To homophile leaders the psychiatrists seemed an

41. *Ladder*, April 1966, p. 13; Greater Philadelphia Council of Churches, *Consultation on the Church and Homosexuality* (Philadelphia, 1965); *Social Action*, December 1967, and *Social Progress*, November–December 1967; *New York Times*, November 29, 1967, p. 1; and *Chronicle*, May 2, 1968, p. 1E, and March 16, 1968, p. 26.

42. *New York Times*, May 30, 1965, Section IV, p. 12; and October 11, 1966, p. 35; *Chronicle*, April 9, 1967; *Ladder*, January 1967, pp. 19–21; and *Christian Century*, June 5, 1968, pp. 744–45.

43. See, e.g., Charles Socarides, *The Overt Homosexual* (New York, 1968); Lionel Ovesey, *Homosexuality and Pseudo-Homosexuality* (New York, 1969); Lawrence Hatterer, *Changing Homosexuality in the Male: Treatment for Men Troubled by Homosexuality* (New York, 1970); *New York Times Magazine*, August 23, 1964, pp. 75ff; *Harper's*, March 1967, pp. 107–8; *Parents' Magazine*, March 1968, pp. 56–57; and Peter and Barbara Wyden, *Growing Up Straight: What Every Thoughtful Parent Should Know About Homosexuality* (New York, 1968).

omnipresent enemy thwarting their efforts at every turn. In February 1967, for instance, when Barbara Gittings and Frank Kameny acted as co-counsels at a Defense Department hearing concerning a gay employee, Doctor Charles Socarides testified for the government that the homosexual "is frightened of his own body. . . . He does not know the boundary of his own body. . . . He does not know where his body ends and space begins. . . . He will believe that parts of his body are missing." Anger and bitterness accumulated as testimony of this nature from mental health professionals became commonplace in court cases and other legal battles.[44]

Activists in the late 1960s challenged the medical profession in ways that the movement had been reluctant to undertake a decade earlier. In April 1968 a gay student group at Columbia University picketed a forum on homosexuality sponsored by the medical school after the planners refused to include a homosexual on the program. "It is time that homosexuality be pulled out of the morass of psychiatry, 'abnormality' and 'emotional disturbance' . . . and placed into its proper setting as a sociological problem of deeply entrenched prejudice and discrimination against a minority group," the Student Homophile League wrote. In the same year, the American Medical Association provided activists in San Francisco with a ready-made opportunity to speak out against the profession. As the AMA prepared for its annual convention there in June 1968, the editor of the San Francisco Medical Society *Bulletin* warned the arriving doctors to "be on guard against brigades of harlots and homosexuals." At the convention itself, Socarides spoke of homosexuality as "a dread dysfunction, malignant in character, which has risen to epidemic proportions." When he called upon the federal government to finance national centers for the cure and rehabilitation of the "sexually deviant," homophile leaders held a well-received press conference where they likened his proposal to a "final solution."[45]

In a few cases homophile activists were able to confront their medical opponents from the inside. The editors of *Psychiatric Opinion* gave space to Dick Leitsch to reply to a series of articles on homosexuality. His piece shifted the terms of discussion from the individual's psychosexual development to the sociology of prejudice and the politics of minority struggles for civil rights. In another situation Leitsch resorted to ridicule to counter one of the movement's most determined foes. Invited by NBC to appear with several doctors on a television special, Leitsch asked Socarides if his proposed treatment centers could be located in Florida and Hawaii. In response to the doctor's puzzlement, Leitsch explained that "they'd end up being government sponsored Fire Islands anyway and I'd like a warm climate. If that was arranged, I'd be

44. Kameny to Leitsch, March 9, 1969, and transcript of Defense Department Security Clearance Hearing, February 23, 1967, both in Kameny papers.
45. "We Protest the Kolb Panel," SHL flyer, Homosexual Organization Files—SHL, ISR; *Chronicle*, June 8, 1968, p. 4; June 19, 1968, p. 1; and June 21, 1968, p. 1; flyer distributed at AMA convention, Homosexual Organization Files—SIR, ISR; and *Ladder*, September 1968, pp. 29–30.

the first to sign up. . . . I figure it'd take about two days before we established a meat rack, a month to turn the center's commissary into a gay bar, and three months to 'bring out' all of the personnel." The activist's reply probably only confirmed for Socarides his view of homosexuals as pathological, but Leitsch was directing his remarks at gay viewers whose respect for the medical profession he wished to challenge.[46]

Despite the dissemination of the medical model to a lay audience and the outspoken adherence of prominent doctors, gay activists found signs even in the area of mental health that the negative consensus surrounding homosexuality was dissolving. In September 1967 the National Institute of Mental Health appointed Evelyn Hooker to chair a committee charged with investigating the subject. Most members of the panel, which included doctors and mental health professionals as well as lawyers, social scientists, and sexologists, had in one way or another broken with traditional views of homosexuality, and several had already aided the gay movement. The composition of the committee cheered most homophile leaders, who spoke of it as "stacked" in their favor. And in fact the final report of the task force, issued after two years of study, fashioned the liberal position on homosexuality into a cohesive whole. Human sexuality, it noted, extended across a continuum of behavior, homosexuality was not a unitary phenomenon, a homosexual personality did not exist, gay women and men came from all walks of life, and as many as 4 million Americans were primarily homosexual. The report also urged a reassessment of employment practices that discriminated against gay men and lesbians. Although the task force stopped short of positively endorsing homosexuality as a life choice—it urged, for instance, "an intensive effort . . . to understand better the factors involved in effective primary prevention"—its report did dissent from the medical approach that labeled homosexuals and lesbians as diseased and implied that tolerance of those persons who were already gay was the best social policy.[47]

As homophile activists left behind the isolation of the 1950s, they discovered that the press responded accordingly. Movement initiatives assumed a newsworthy quality. On a local level, San Francisco papers naturally far outdistanced those of other cities in their coverage of gay-related news, but homosexual reform efforts were also slowly attracting notice beyond the metropolitan page of urban dailies. The *New York Times*, for instance, carried a lengthy piece on the homosexual rights movement in its Sunday magazine in November 1967. The feature made only passing reference to traditional negative views of homosexuality and instead explored the oppressive conditions of gay

46. Dick Leitsch, "The Psychotherapy of Homosexuality: Let's Forget Jocasta and Her Little Boy," *Psychiatric Opinion*, June 1967, pp. 28–35; and Leitsch to Kameny, March 11, 1969, Kameny papers.

47. National Institute of Mental Health, *Final Report of the Task Force on Homosexuality* (Washington, D.C., 1969), and *New York Times*, October 21, 1969, p. 32. The quote can be found on page 5 of the *Final Report*.

life, the difficulties of organizing homosexuals, and the goals of movement
leaders. Mass circulation weeklies as well as the daily press reported at length
on the extended debates in the British parliament on law reform. The articles
lacked the sneering tone with the suggestion of depravity that had characterized coverage of the Wolfenden report ten years before.[48]

The significance of these changes lay more in the content of the communication than in the quantity of material. Articles about gay life and about
homophile politics still remained exceptional and could hardly be considered
part of the average American's weekly diet of news. But their relative infre-
quency almost guaranteed that the items would have a greater impact upon gay
readers who encountered a secret, perhaps shameful, part of their lives in
print. Even occasional coverage of the movement's efforts took homosexuality
out of the shadowy realm of deviance and criminality and placed it in the light
of social reform. Press attention represented more than simple reporting of the
day's events. It was reshaping in a qualitative way the public discourse on
homosexuality and in the process was transforming the self-perceptions of gay
men and lesbians.

VI

Movement participants who remembered the dreary times of the previous
decade—when activists wondered if it was legal to meet, when a single newspaper article represented a major achievement, and when homophile groups
went begging for a lawyer, minister, or doctor simply to speak to them—could
only marvel at the progress they had made during the 1960s. The survival of
the movement was no longer in doubt as homophile groups sank roots in a few
cities and spread to many more. In New York and San Francisco the movement had sharply restricted police abuses, while in other cities activists had
initiated challenges to long-standing practices of harassment. Magazines,
newspapers, television, radio, books, plays, and movies discussed male
homosexuality and to a lesser extent lesbianism and presented images of gay
life that reached a wide audience. Activists had to cope with the more welcome
problem of what *kind* of coverage gays and the homophile movement received
rather than with breaking through an informal system of censorship that kept
the subject unmentionable. In law, religion, and medicine the homophile
cause had allies whose support, though ranging from enthusiastic to only
lukewarm and still representing a minority viewpoint, nonetheless spelled an
end to the consensus on homosexuality that had existed when the Mattachine
Society was founded only twenty years earlier.

48. The *New York Times Magazine* article can be found in the edition of November 12, 1967,
p. 44. On law reform in England, see *Newsweek*, June 7, 1965, p. 38; February 21, 1966, p. 54; and
January 2, 1967, p. 28; *Time*, December 30, 1966, p. 17, and July 14, 1967, p. 30; *Christian
Century*, May 26, 1965, pp. 669–70; *New York Times Magazine*, June 27, 1965, pp. 6–7; and *New
York Times*, May 25, 1965, p. 1; May 27, 1965, p. 3; June 17, 1966, p. 34; July 6, 1966, p. 7;
December 20, 1966, p. 1; and July 5, 1967, p. 1.

The gains the movement had made by the end of the 1960s became all the more remarkable when placed alongside its undeniable failure in one critical area. The homophile cause still had not captured the support of the constituency that it claimed represented America's second largest minority. After two decades, membership in gay organizations barely surpassed 5,000 men and women, and of these only a few hundred could be said to have come out of the closet by publicly identifying themselves as homosexuals or lesbians. Although the work of activists in the latter years of the 1960s suggested that a hardy band of pioneers could initiate important changes, the goal of equality would remain elusive until the ranks of gay organizations swelled and the movement had a visible presence throughout America.

4 The Liberation Impulse

TWELVE

A New Beginning:
The Birth of
Gay Liberation

The homophile movement had escaped the doldrums of its first decade in large part through the influence of the emerging protest movements that appeared near the end of the 1950s and the early 1960s. To Kameny and other East Coast militants the civil rights struggle, from the Montgomery bus boycott to the sit-ins and freedom rides, offered compelling evidence of the success of direct action techniques in combating discrimination. Randy Wicker had participated in civil rights efforts in Texas before coming to New York, while other activists like Barbara Gittings, Kay Tobin, Dick Leitsch, and Jack Nichols peppered their speeches and articles with references to the movement for racial equality. In San Francisco, the cultural dissent of the beats, though less overtly political, helped shake a segment of the male homosexual subculture out of its acceptance of the status quo. Although the homophile movement never managed to fire the imagination of its constituency during the 1960s, it owed whatever dynamism it did possess to the example set by other discontented groups.

By the late 1960s, however, a distinctively new culture of protest had taken shape in the United States, with which the reform orientation of the gay movement contrasted oddly. At Columbia University, for instance, the student homophile league peacefully picketed a forum on homosexuality on the same day that black and white student radicals initiated a week-long occupation of campus buildings. Two weeks after delegates to the 1968 NACHO convention in Chicago conducted parliamentary debates according to Robert's Rules of Order, police battled antiwar activists in the city's streets. In San Francisco, members of SIR and DOB sat through candidates' nights and registered voters while the hippie counterculture—the heirs of the beats—

staged colorful, flamboyant be-ins in Golden Gate Park. The gay movement continued to pursue equality through the courts at a time when militant civil rights workers were shifting toward a strategy of community organizing and an ideology of black power. As homophile activists marched with neatly lettered placards in front of federal buildings, urban ghettos burst into flame, bombs exploded in banks and military-connected university facilities, and Black Panthers and Weathermen called for "armed struggle" against American imperialism. A generation of blacks and whites, men and women, was rising in revolt, but for the most part homophile activists remained curiously detached from the rebellions that were rocking the nation.

Despite the distance between gay activists and young radicals, the protests of the 1960s had more than superficial relevance to the situation of homosexuals and lesbians. Each of the separate strands of the "Movement"—black power, the student New Left, the counterculture, and women's liberation—spoke in a special way to gay women and men. Taken together and appropriated by those stigmatized for their sexuality, the ideology and tactics of the mass movements of the 1960s had the power to transform not only the organized struggle of homosexuals and lesbians for freedom but also the everyday quality and condition of gay life in the United States.

I

Young black militants in organizations like the Student Nonviolent Coordinating Committee and the Congress of Racial Equality led the move from the exuberant, optimistic reform spirit of the early 1960s to the angry, confrontational politics of the second half of the decade. By 1965 the successes of the civil rights movement had provoked a "crisis of victory," as racial inequality proved more intractable than the Southern legal codes that buttressed it. The combination of violent attacks by Southern whites, a sense of betrayal by Northern liberals and Democratic politicians, the explosive anger of ghetto residents, the growing appeal of the nationalist Black Muslims, and the war in Vietnam aroused impatience among many civil rights veterans and bred a cynicism toward the integrationist goals and nonviolent tactics that initially characterized the struggle for racial justice.[1]

When SNCC leader Stokely Carmichael raised the black power cry in June 1966, he voiced more than a slogan. Black power quickly came to embody a distinctive form of politics and culture. In many ways it represented a reversal of the dominant, long-term trend in American society, the assimilation of ethnic and cultural minorities in the American melting pot. Black power

---

1. On the civil rights movement, see August Meier and Elliott Rudwick, *CORE: A Study in the Civil Rights Movement* (New York, 1973); David L. Lewis, *King: A Critical Biography* (Chicago, 1978); Howard Zinn, *SNCC: The New Abolitionists* (Boston, 1964); and Benjamin Muse, *Ten Years of Prelude: The Story of Integration Since the Supreme Court's 1954 Decision* (New York, 1965). The phrase "crisis of victory" comes from a speech by A. Philip Randolph in January 1965, quoted in Meier and Rudwick, p. 329.

advocates began speaking about structural racism and systematic oppression rather than prejudice and discrimination. As their goals, liberation replaced equality, and self-determination superseded integration. They talked of organizing the black community, fashioning an independent power base, and preserving their autonomy and separateness from white society. Instead of minimizing the differences between the races, these new militants celebrated them. Black became beautiful, as young radicals took the stigma out of skin color and made it a source of pride.[2]

Comparable changes in the white student movement paralleled the shift among blacks. After first acting in support of the Southern civil rights movement, activists in Students for a Democratic Society switched toward organizing among the white poor in northern cities. But the Berkeley campus uprising in the autumn of 1964 revealed depths of discontent with the quality of their own lives, the kind of education they received, and the adult roles that awaited them in society. The war in Vietnam, with its sharp rise in draft calls, intensified the disaffection of college youth. Idealism and, for male students, self-preservation worked together to create in quick fashion a massive antiwar movement that targeted both the government and the institutions of higher learning that students accused of complicity in the war. As the decade wore on, New Left activism moved rapidly along a line from reform to resistance and, at least rhetorically, revolution.[3]

While many of the young channeled their energy into political protest and directed their fury toward institutions, others adopted a cultural radicalism. In some ways the hippie counterculture and the New Left worked at cross purposes, but in other ways they complemented and reinforced one another. In rebelling against the hypocrisy and alienation of modern American life, counterculture enthusiasts rejected the detached, objective mode of scientific inquiry that seemed to lead inexorably to the conflagration in Vietnam and pursued instead a politics of experience that celebrated the subjective. The counterculture sought a revolution in consciousness, a transformation of self that would create a personality, ethics, and style of living consistent with the political and social criticism of the New Left. Young hippies refused to conform to the expectations and values of white middle-class America. They constructed alternative living arrangements, adopted new styles of dress, ingested mind-expanding drugs, and embraced a sexual morality that often shocked ordinary Americans. Embedded in this experimentation was the

2. On the black power movement, see Stokely Carmichael and Charles V. Hamilton, *Black Power* (New York, 1967); Benjamin Muse, *The American Negro Revolution: From Non-Violence to Black Power, 1963–1967* (Bloomington, Ind., 1967); and Allen J. Matusow, "From Civil Rights to Black Power: The Case of SNCC, 1960–1966," in Barton J. Bernstein and Allen J. Matusow, eds., *Twentieth Century America: Recent Interpretations* (New York, 1969).

3. On the white student movement, the New Left, and the antiwar movement, see Kirkpatrick Sale, *SDS* (New York, 1973); Priscilla Long, ed., *The New Left: A Collection of Essays* (Boston, 1969); Michael Ferber and Staughton Lynd, *The Resistance* (Boston, 1971); and Paul Jacobs and Saul Landau, *The New Radicals* (New York, 1966).

conviction that one *could* remake one's self, that the quest for authenticity and fulfillment in a corrupt society *was* attainable—in short, that one could live the revolution now.[4]

Eventually, white women in the New Left took many of the key concepts that underlay the radicalism of the decade, applied them to their own situation, and, out of the tension between rhetoric and reality, created a women's liberation movement. The stress within the civil rights movement and among early SDS members on equality, self-determination, and participatory democracy almost demanded a resurgence of feminism, as young radical women found their contributions to the New Left devalued, their leadership capacity inhibited, and their identities submerged in those of the men with whom they were intimate. Moreover, the peculiar combination of politics and culture that characterized protest in the 1960s gave a boost to the women's movement. By rejecting traditional forms of family life, the counterculture delegitimized the normative female role of housewife and mother. Yet, paradoxically, its pursuit of a free-flowing, unrestricted sexuality also intensified for young women the experience of sexual objectification. Under the guise of liberation, politicized women endured new forms of alienating human relationships.[5]

Women's liberation added another dimension to political protest. Radical feminists questioned the very categories of male and female upon which most individuals' sense of self could rest securely. Women placed gender alongside race and class as a systematically enforced, socially constructed form of inequality. The injustices committed by fathers, husbands, and lovers were no more excusable than those of generals at the Pentagon. Intimate relationships became arenas of struggle, the bedroom and the kitchen battlegrounds, as women's liberationists fashioned a sexual politics that encompassed every aspect of personal life.[6]

Though much of the decade's rhetoric was overblown and never delivered what it promised, it nonetheless proved rousing enough to prod millions of the young and the not so young into action against social injustice or into revamping their own lives. In fact, the radicalism of the 1960s derived its force in no small part because it bound the personal and the political so tightly together that the two could no longer be distinguished. Even the vocabulary of the Movement had dual meanings. The right of self-determination could be applied to individuals as well as to a people; revolutions occurred in both consciousness and society; the future shape of the country could be found not

4. On the counterculture, see Theodore Roszak, *The Making of a Counter Culture* (Garden City, N.Y., 1969).

5. On the radical origins of the women's liberation movement, see Sara Evans, *Personal Politics* (New York, 1979); Judith Hole and Ellen Levine, *Rebirth of Feminism* (New York, 1971); and Jo Freeman, *The Politics of Women's Liberation* (New York, 1975).

6. For the writings of early women's liberationists, see Robin Morgan, ed., *Sisterhood Is Powerful* (New York, 1970); Ann Koedt, Ellen Levine, and Anita Rapone, eds., *Radical Feminism* (New York, 1973); Kate Millet, *Sexual Politics* (Garden City, N.Y., 1970); and Shulamith Firestone, *The Dialectic of Sex* (New York, 1970).

only in alternative institutions but in alternative styles of living. The affirmation of subjective personal experience as a primary source of knowledge and a reliable guide to action encouraged many Americans to make decisions they might otherwise not have risked and to see those choices as part of a vast movement for social change.

II

The homophile movement did not, of course, remain untouched by the radical politics of the 1960s. Here and there one could detect evidence of a new outlook, a desire to push beyond the civil rights integrationist orientation that made up the militant wing of the movement. Early in 1967, for instance, a stepped-up police campaign in Los Angeles against gay bars, including two New Year's Eve raids that left a bartender hospitalized with a ruptured spleen and a number of gay male patrons beaten by officers, provoked the largest gay demonstration of the decade. Several hundred homosexuals rallied on Sunset Boulevard, where they listened to angry speakers intoning the phrases of confrontational politics. The turmoil at Columbia University in the spring of 1968 radicalized the campus homophile group, which joined the student strike and, later, brought its New Left perspective to the NACHO convention in Chicago. Rebuffed by their more moderate colleagues, the student activists turned their attention to organizing gay groups on other campuses. Alternative institutions, premised on the special needs of a distinctive gay community, started to appear. In Los Angeles in 1968, Dick Michaels and Bill Rand began publishing the *Advocate*, a hard-hitting newspaper whose contents evinced an aggressive pride in being gay. That October, Troy Perry officiated at the first service of the Metropolitan Community Church before a gay congregation responding to an announcement in the *Advocate*. In New York, the success of Craig Rodwell's Oscar Wilde Memorial Bookstore proved that lesbians and gay men wanted a retail outlet that catered to their reading tastes. Now and then individual activists such as Martha Shelley in New York and Morgan Pinney in San Francisco contributed articles to organizational magazines that tried to make connections between the situation of gay men and lesbians and the burgeoning protest movements of blacks, students, and women. For the most part, however, these efforts were harbingers of the future, and the dissenters remained solitary voices that failed to alter the direction of the homophile movement.[7]

7. On the Los Angeles bar raids and rallies, see *Concern* (newsletter of the Southern California Council on Religion and the Homophile), January 1967, p. 3, and February 1967, pp. 1–2; and press release, Tavern Guild of Southern California, January 5, 1967, in New York Mattachine Society Archives (hereafter referred to as NYMS); *Los Angeles Free Press*, February 17, 1967, p. 6, and March 10, 1967, p. 5. On the Student Homophile League at Columbia, see "Student Homophile League Joins Strike," flyer, May 4, 1968, and SHL memo to NACHO convention, August 16, 1968, both in NYMS. On alternative institutions, see the chapters on Dick Michaels, Troy Perry, and Craig Rodwell in Kay Tobin and Randy Wicker, *The Gay Crusaders* (New York, 1972). See also Morgan Pinney, "Telling It Like It Is: State College from a Homosexual

The experience of both DOB and SIR illustrates the resistance of gay reformers to the radical spirit of the late 1960s. In the case of DOB the issue was feminism—what it meant for the organization and how best to adapt its insights to the situation of lesbians. By 1966 a new women's movement was taking shape in the United States, and its ideas allowed DOB members to reinterpret the conflicts that occasionally erupted between them and gay male activists. Instead of justifying their organizational autonomy by pointing to the lesbian's need for a space of her own, officers defended their independence on the grounds of political interest. "The lesbian is discriminated against not only because she is a lesbian, but because she is a woman," Shirley Willer told delegates to the 1966 NACHO convention. "Lesbian interest is more closely linked with the women's civil rights movement than with the homosexual civil liberties movement." Del Martin, who joined the San Francisco chapter of the National Organization for Women in 1967, quickly became one of its officers and shifted her energy from the homophile movement to women's issues. She too questioned the wisdom of DOB's continuing alliance with the gay rights cause. "The Lesbian," she wrote in the *Ladder*,

> is first of all a *woman*. . . . It is time that the Daughters of Bilitis and the Lesbian find and establish a much broader identification than that of the homosexual community or the homophile movement. The "battle of the sexes" which predominates in American Society prevails in the homosexual community as well and the Lesbian finds herself relegated to an even more inferior status.

After 1966 feminist concerns arose frequently in DOB. The *Ladder* devoted considerable space to articles about the status of women, sex discrimination, and the activities of women's rights groups such as NOW.[8]

However, oldtimers in DOB also displayed an ambivalence about an alliance with women's rights organizations, especially if it meant making a choice between heterosexual women and gay men. Shirley Willer, for instance, did not believe that heterosexual women would ever "give up their pedestals," and she preferred working with male homosexuals despite the many instances of "chauvinism." Meredith Grey also expressed serious reservations over the wisdom of lesbians working within feminist organizations. She doubted that "Miss Friedan's group . . . would accept my sisters as happily as [it] would accept my money" and rejected Del Martin's suggestion that DOB leave the homophile fold. Even Martin waffled on the question of where lesbians should

---

Perspective," *Vector*, January 1969, pp. 5–6; and Martha Shelley, "Homosexuality and Sexual Identity," *Ladder*, August 1968, pp. 6–7.

8. Shirley Willer, "The Lesbian, the Homosexual and the Homophile Movement," *Vector*, October 1966, pp. 8–9; and Del Martin, "The Lesbian's Majority Status,"*Ladder*, June 1967, pp. 24–26. For other examples of the *Ladder*'s interest in women's status, see issues of December 1966, pp. 15–16; February 1967, pp. 2–5; August 1967, pp. 2–4; October–November 1968, pp. 18–24; and December 1968, pp. 16–17.

place their primary allegiance. After a homophile conference in which lesbian grievances received an airing, she declared herself "happy to eat my words" about the need to disengage from the gay movement. Initially, the developing interest in feminism caused barely a ripple in the placid surface of either DOB or the larger homophile movement.[9]

The situation changed abruptly late in 1968, when new women came to the helm of DOB, and the terms of the debate shifted from women's rights to women's liberation. Rita Laporte, who by her own admission became president of DOB largely because "no one else wants the job," brought a radical feminist perspective to the office. "As I see it," she wrote to Barbara Gittings,

> when you've accomplished your aims in the homophile movement, you can proudly point to the fact that now lesbians have *full* second class citizenship, along with all women. That's nowhere near enough for me. I was not only born a lesbian, but a feminist as well! My first cry was one of fury at being considered second rate because of being female.[10]

Along with Barbara Grier, who became editor of the *Ladder*, she transformed the magazine into a publication that blazed a distinctly lesbian-feminist trail. More polemical and less compromising, the *Ladder* now presented lesbianism as the embodiment of feminist principles. "No heterosexual woman can match the passion some of us lesbians have for our rights," Laporte wrote. She also pressed for a withdrawal of DOB from NACHO. "It needs to be said over and over again that the real gap within humanity is that between men and women, not that between homosexual and heterosexual," she declared. Among women, lesbians alone could fight for the liberation of their sisters, unhampered by ties with men, Laporte argued, and she urged DOB members not "to dissipate this force by, in effect, a sort of group 'marriage' . . . to the male homophile community."[11]

Though sentiments such as these would soon mobilize tens of thousands of lesbians across the country, they ended up destroying DOB and the *Ladder*. Oldtimers were especially furious at what was happening to the magazine. In their view, the *Ladder* belonged to the women of DOB collectively, not to a few leaders, and should speak to all lesbians, particularly those who were taking their first tentative steps toward self-recognition. Sten Russell came to see the election of Laporte as "a damned debacle, a damned disaster. The thing that we believed in and loved was cracking up. . . . The women's lib movement was coming very much to the fore [with] a whole new bunch of people who

9. Interview with Shirley Willer, conducted by Toby Marotta, 1975; Meredith Grey, letter, *Ladder*, August 1967, pp. 20–21; and Del Martin, letter, *Ladder*, July 1967, p. 27.

10. Rita Laporte to Barbara Gittings, August 20, 1968, personal papers of Frank Kameny, Washington, D.C. Laporte's comment on why she was elected president can be found in a letter to Gittings dated August 4, 1968, also in the Kameny papers.

11. Rita Laporte, "An Open Letter to Mary Daly," *Ladder*, October–November 1968, p. 25; and Rita Laporte, "Of What Use NACHO?" *Ladder*, August–September 1969, pp. 18–19.

were talking a language that we didn't understand. . . . DOB was dying. It took from 1968 to 1970 to pound the nails into the coffin." When DOB members, including Martin and Lyon, laid plans to recover control of the *Ladder* at the 1970 convention, Laporte and Grier simply boycotted the gathering, made off with the organization's membership and subscription list, and began publishing the magazine independently. Without the *Ladder* to subsidize, DOB had little reason to maintain its national structure. The membership sadly agreed to dissolve the national organization, letting each chapter survive as best it could. The *Ladder*, meanwhile, without financial support, ceased publication a short while later. The lesbian wing of the homophile movement proved unable to cope with the intrusion of the new radicalism.[12]

SIR also came face to face with the political style of the late 1960s after its members, early in 1969, chose Leo Laurence to edit the organization's magazine. A staffer at KGO radio in San Francisco, the thirty-six-year-old Laurence had covered the 1968 Democratic convention in Chicago, where he witnessed the bloody confrontations between police and antiwar demonstrators. He returned to San Francisco "radicalized," impressed by the willingness of the young protesters to put themselves on the line for their beliefs. Laurence began writing for the Berkeley *Barb*, a New Left weekly, and for SIR's *Vector*. Extolling the importance of being honest about one's sexuality, he posed with his lover for a semi-naked photo that appeared in the *Barb*. Shortly after his election to the editorship of *Vector*, he wrote that "this is the beginning of a new revolution in San Francisco, the Homosexual Revolution of 1969. When the black man became proud, he became more militant. That same power is starting to hit the homosexual movement in the Bay Area." Laurence argued that gays should form coalitions with the Black Panthers, the antiwar movement, and other radical groups. He counseled homosexuals not to wait for "the right political climate" but to "demand our personal liberty and freedom right NOW!" In the language of the counterculture, he equated revolution with changes in consciousness. "We have to get over this bullshit of guilt, the feeling we are degenerates," he said in an interview. "After we can admit to ourselves 'gay is good,' the revolution will come." Laurence called on homosexuals to "come out from behind a double-life. . . . Say you're gay at work, at home, at church, wherever you go."[13]

Laurence might have survived in SIR if he had confined his rhetoric to a general call to arms, but when he turned his fire on the homophile movement, SIR's other officers acted decisively. In the April issue of *Vector* Laurence

---

12. Interview with Sten Russell, October 24, 1976, in Costa Mesa, Calif. Martin, Lyon, and Helen Sanders also commented at length on the conflict with Laporte and Grier in my interviews with them. See also Meredith Grey to Frank Kameny, September 8, 1968, Kameny papers. For a report on the 1970 DOB convention, see New York DOB *Newsletter*, August 1970, p. 1.

13. Leo Laurence to Dorr Legg, March 3, 1969, SIR file, ONE, Inc., Archives, Los Angeles; and *Berkeley Barb*, March 28, 1969, p. 5; February 7, 1969; and April 4, 1969, p. 11.

accused "timid leaders" of "enormous ego-trips, middle-class bigotry and racism," of "hurting almost every major homosexual organization." The same month, in the *Barb*, he dismissed homophile activists as "a bunch of middle-class, uptight, bitchy old queens." In May Laurence found himself out of the editorship and out of the organization. SIR persevered in its reform brand of civil rights politics, while Laurence went on to form the Committee for Homosexual Freedom, which tried to adapt New Left perspectives to the struggle for homosexual equality.[14]

Although homophile leaders could hold the line against the incursion of radical politics into the movement, they could not block its entry to the larger gay community. Especially among the young, the influence of the new culture of protest was too pervasive for the gay male and lesbian subculture to remain immune. Instead, the unresponsiveness of homophile activists guaranteed that when the decade's radicalism did reach homosexual men and women, it would spawn a movement that would rapidly overwhelm its predecessor.

III

On Friday, June 27, 1969, shortly before midnight, two detectives from Manhattan's Sixth Precinct set off with a few other officers to raid the Stonewall Inn, a gay bar on Christopher Street in the heart of Greenwich Village. They must have expected it to be a routine raid. New York was in the midst of a mayoral campaign—always a bad time for the city's homosexuals— and John Lindsay, the incumbent who had recently lost his party's primary, had reason to agree to a police cleanup. Moreover, a few weeks earlier the Sixth Precinct had received a new commanding officer who marked his entry into the position by initiating a series of raids on gay bars. The Stonewall Inn was an especially inviting target. Operating without a liquor license, reputed to have ties with organized crime, and offering scantily clad go-go boys as entertainment, it brought an "unruly" element to Sheridan Square, a busy Village intersection. Patrons of the Stonewall tended to be young and nonwhite. Many were drag queens, and many came from the burgeoning ghetto of runaways living across town in the East Village.[15]

However, the customers at the Stonewall that night responded in any but the usual fashion. As the police released them one by one from inside the bar, a crowd accumulated on the street. Jeers and catcalls arose from the onlookers when a paddy wagon departed with the bartender, the Stonewall's bouncer, and three drag queens. A few minutes later, an officer attempted to steer the

14. *Vector*, April 1969, p. 11; and *Berkeley Barb*, April 11, 1969, p. 11. On the action taken against Laurence and his ouster from SIR, see "Gold Sheet," newssheet for SIR members, May 1969, in SIR file, ONE, Inc., Archives.

15. The description of the Stonewall riot in this and succeeding paragraphs is drawn from the following sources: *Village Voice*, July 3, 1969, p. 1; *New York Times*, June 29, 1969, p. 33, and June 30, 1969, p. 22; and New York Mattachine *Newsletter*, July 1969, pp. 21–25, and August 1969, pp. 1–6.

last of the patrons, a lesbian, through the bystanders to a nearby patrol car. "She put up a struggle," the *Village Voice* reported, "from car to door to car again." At that moment,

> the scene became explosive. Limp wrists were forgotten. Beer cans and bottles were heaved at the windows and a rain of coins descended on the cops. . . . Almost by signal the crowd erupted into cobblestone and bottle heaving. . . . From nowhere came an uprooted parking meter—used as a battering ram on the Stonewall door. I heard several cries of "let's get some gas," but the blaze of flame which soon appeared in the window of the Stonewall was still a shock.[16]

Reinforcements rescued the shaken officers from the torched bar, but their work had barely started. Rioting continued far into the night, with Puerto Rican transvestites and young street people leading charges against rows of uniformed police officers and then withdrawing to regroup in Village alleys and side streets.

By the following night, graffiti calling for "Gay Power" had appeared along Christopher Street. Knots of young gays—effeminate, according to most reports—gathered on corners, angry and restless. Someone heaved a sack of wet garbage through the window of a patrol car. On nearby Waverly Place, a concrete block landed on the hood of another police car that was quickly surrounded by dozens of men, pounding on its doors and dancing on its hood. Helmeted officers from the tactical patrol force arrived on the scene and dispersed with swinging clubs an impromptu chorus line of gay men in the middle of a full kick. At the intersection of Greenwich Avenue and Christopher Street, several dozen queens screaming "Save Our Sister!" rushed a group of officers who were clubbing a young man and dragged him to safety. For the next few hours, trash fires blazed, bottles and stones flew through the air, and cries of "Gay Power!" rang in the streets as the police, numbering over 400, did battle with a crowd estimated at more than 2,000.

After the second night of disturbances, the anger that had erupted into street fighting was channeled into intense discussion of what many had begun to memorialize as the first gay riot in history. Allen Ginsberg's stature in the 1960s had risen almost to that of guru for many counterculture youth. When he arrived at the Stonewall on Sunday evening, he commented on the change that had already taken place. "You know, the guys there were so beautiful," he told a reporter. "They've lost that wounded look that fags all had ten years ago."[17] The New York Mattachine Society hastily assembled a special riot edition of its newsletter that characterized the events, with camp humor, as "The Hairpin Drop Heard Round the World." It scarcely exaggerated. Before the end of July, women and men in New York had formed the Gay Liberation

16. *Village Voice*, July 3, 1969, p. 18.
17. Ibid.

Front, a self-proclaimed revolutionary organization in the style of the New Left. Word of the Stonewall riot and GLF spread rapidly among the networks of young radicals scattered across the country, and within a year gay liberation groups had sprung into existence on college campuses and in cities around the nation.

IV

The Stonewall riot was able to spark a nationwide grassroots "liberation" effort among gay men and women in large part because of the radical movements that had so inflamed much of American youth during the 1960s. Gay liberation used the demonstrations of the New Left as recruiting grounds and appropriated the tactics of confrontational politics for its own ends. The ideas that suffused youth protest found their way into gay liberation, where they were modified and adapted to describe the oppression of homosexuals and lesbians. The apocalyptic rhetoric and the sense of impending revolution that surrounded the Movement by the end of the decade gave to its newest participants an audacious daring that made the dangers of a public avowal of their sexuality seem insignificant.

In order to make their existence known, gay liberationists took advantage of the almost daily political events that young radicals were staging across the country. New York's Gay Liberation Front had a contingent at the antiwar march held in the city on October 15, 1969, and was present in even larger numbers at the November moratorium weekend in Washington, where almost half a million activists rallied against American involvement in Southeast Asia. Gay radicals in Berkeley performed guerrilla theater on the campus during orientation that fall and carried banners at the November antiwar rally in San Francisco. In November 1969 and again the following May, lesbians from GLF converged on the Congress to Unite Women, which brought to New York women's liberationists from around the East. Gay activists ran workshops at the 1969 annual convention of the National Student Association. In May 1970 a GLF member addressed the rally in New Haven in support of Bobby Seale and Ericka Huggins, the imprisoned Black Panther leaders. A large contingent of lesbians and gay men attended the national gathering called by the Panthers in the fall of 1970, and the next year a gay "tribe" took part in the May Day protests in Washington against the war. In raising the banner of gay liberation at these and other local demonstrations, radical gays reached closeted homosexuals and lesbians in the Movement who already had a commitment to militant confrontational politics. Their message traveled quickly through the networks of activists created by the New Left, thus allowing gay liberation to spread with amazing rapidity.[18]

18. On the gay liberation presence at radical demonstrations, see Donn Teal, *The Gay Militants* (New York, 1971), pp. 52–53, 68–69, 98, 165–74, 179–83, 218–19; *Berkeley Tribe*, September 12, 1969, p. 5; *Berkeley Barb*, October 10, 1969, p. 12; and "March in San Francisco November 15th," Gay liberation flyer in the possession of Bois Burk, Berkeley, California.

The first gay liberationists attracted so many other young radicals not only because of a common sexual identity but because they shared a similar political perspective. Gay liberationists spoke in the hyperbolic phrases of the New Left. They talked of liberation from oppression, resisting genocide, and making a revolution against "imperialist Amerika." GLF's statement of purpose, printed in the New Left newspaper *RAT*, sounded like many of the documents produced by radicals in the late 1960s, except that it was written by and about homosexuals:

> We are a revolutionary group of men and women formed with the realization that complete sexual liberation for all people cannot come about unless existing social institutions are abolished. We reject society's attempt to impose sexual roles and definitions of our nature. We are stepping outside these roles and simplistic myths. We are going to be who we are. At the same time, we are creating new social forms and relations, that is, relations based upon brotherhood, cooperation, human love, and uninhibited sexuality. Babylon has forced us to commit ourselves to one thing—revolution![19]

Gay liberation groups saw themselves as one component of the decade's radicalism and regularly addressed the other issues that were mobilizing American youth. The Berkeley GLF, for instance, passed a resolution on the Vietnam War and the draft demanding that "all troops be brought home at once" and that homosexuals in the armed forces "be given Honorable discharges immediately." Its Los Angeles counterpart declared its "unity with and support for all oppressed minorities who fight for their freedom" and expressed its intention "to build a new, free and loving Gay counter-culture." Positions such as these made it relatively easy for previously closeted but already radicalized homosexuals and lesbians to join or form gay liberation organizations, and the new movement quickly won their allegiance.[20]

Gay liberationists targeted the same institutions as homophile militants, but their disaffection from American society impelled them to use tactics that their predecessors would never have adopted. Bar raids and street arrests of gay men in New York City during August 1970 provoked a march by several thousand men and women from Times Square to Greenwich Village, where rioting broke out. Articles hostile to gays in the *Village Voice* and in *Harper's* led to the

---

19. GLF Statement of Purpose, July 31, 1969, reprinted in *RAT*, August 12, 1969.

20. Berkeley GLF, "Resolution on the War and Draft," May 4, 1970; and Los Angeles GLF, "What Is Gay Liberation? A Statement of Purpose," n.d., both in Homosexual Organization Files, Institute for Sex Research, Bloomington, Indiana. For other early gay liberation writings, see Karla Jay and Allen Young, eds., *Out of the Closets* (New York, 1972). Of the influential early radical gay liberation newspapers, see esp. *Gay Liberator* (Detroit), *Gay Sunshine* (San Francisco), *Fag Rag* (Boston), *Body Politic* (Toronto), and *Come Out!* (New York). The best analysis of the political perspective of gay liberation remains that of Dennis Altman, *Homosexual: Oppression and Liberation* (New York, 1972). See also Toby Marotta, *The Politics of Homosexuality* (Boston, 1981).

occupation of publishers' offices. In San Francisco a demonstration against the *Examiner* erupted into a bloody confrontation with the police. Chicago Gay Liberation invaded the 1970 convention of the American Medical Association, while its counterpart in San Francisco disrupted the annual meeting of the American Psychiatric Association. At a session there on homosexuality a young bearded gay man danced around the auditorium in a red dress, while other homosexuals and lesbians scattered in the audience shouted "Genocide!" and "Torture!" during the reading of a paper on aversion therapy. Politicians campaigning for office found themselves hounded by scruffy gay militants who at any moment might race across the stage where they were speaking or jump in front of a television camera to demand that they speak out against the oppression of homosexuals. The confrontational tactics and flamboyant behavior thrust gay liberationists into the public spotlight. Although their actions may have alienated some homosexuals and lesbians, they inspired many others to join the movement's ranks.[21]

As a political force, the New Left went into eclipse soon after gay liberation appeared on the scene, but the movement of lesbians and gay men continued to thrive throughout the 1970s. Two features of gay liberation accounted for its ability to avoid the decline that most of the other mass movements of the 1960s experienced. One was the new definition that post-Stonewall activists gave to "coming out," which doubled both as ends and means for young gay radicals. The second was the emergence of a strong lesbian liberation movement.

From its beginning, gay liberation transformed the meaning of "coming out." Previously coming out had signified the private decision to accept one's homosexual desires and to acknowledge one's sexual identity to other gay men and women. Throughout the 1950s and 1960s, leaders of the homophile cause had in effect extended their coming out to the public sphere through their work in the movement. But only rarely did they counsel lesbians and homosexuals at large to follow their example, and when they did, homophile activists presented it as a selfless step taken for the benefit of others. Gay liberationists, on the other hand, recast coming out as a profoundly political act that could offer enormous personal benefits to an individual. The open avowal of one's sexual identity, whether at work, at school, at home, or before television cameras, symbolized the shedding of the self-hatred that gay men and women internalized, and consequently it promised an immediate improvement in one's life. To come out of the "closet" quintessentially expressed the fusion of the personal and the political that the radicalism of the late 1960s exalted.

Coming out also posed as the key strategy for building a movement. Its impact on an individual was often cathartic. The exhilaration and anger that surfaced when men and women stepped through the fear of discovery pro-

21. Donn Teal provides in *The Gay Militants* an extensive chronicle of gay liberation demonstrations from 1969 to 1971. On the "zaps" of the AMA and APA conventions, see Gary Alinder, "Gay Liberation Meets the Shrinks"; and Chicago Gay Liberation Front, "A Leaflet for the American Medical Association," in Jay and Young, *Out of the Closets*, pp. 141–46.

pelled them into political activity. Moreover, when lesbians and homosexuals came out, they crossed a critical dividing line. They relinquished their invisibility, made themselves vulnerable to attack, and acquired an investment in the success of the movement in a way that mere adherence to a political line could never accomplish. Visible lesbians and gay men also served as magnets that drew others to them. Furthermore, once out of the closet, they could not easily fade back in. Coming out provided gay liberation with an army of permanent enlistees.

A second critical feature of the post-Stonewall era was the appearance of a strong lesbian liberation movement. Lesbians had always been a tiny fraction of the homophile movement. But the almost simultaneous birth of women's liberation and gay liberation propelled large numbers of them into radical sexual politics. Lesbians were active in both early gay liberation groups and feminist organizations. Frustrated and angered by the chauvinism they experienced in gay groups and the hostility they found in the women's movement, many lesbians opted to create their own separatist organizations. Groups such as Radicalesbians in New York, the Furies Collective in Washington, D.C., and Gay Women's Liberation in San Francisco carved out a distinctive lesbian-feminist politics. They too spoke in the radical phrases of the New Left, but with an accent on the special revolutionary role that lesbians filled because of their dual oppression as women and as homosexuals. Moreover, as other lesbians made their way into gay and women's groups, their encounters with the chauvinism of gay men and the hostility of heterosexual feminists provided lesbian liberation with ever more recruits.[22]

Although gay liberation and women's liberation both contributed to the growth of a lesbian-feminist movement, the latter exerted a greater influence. The feminist movement offered the psychic space for many women to come to a self-definition as lesbian. Women's liberation was in its origins a separatist movement, with an ideology that defined men as the problem and with organizational forms from consciousness-raising groups to action-oriented collectives that placed a premium on female solidarity. As women explored their oppression together, it became easier to acknowledge their love for other women. The seeming contradiction between an ideology that focused criticism on men per se and the ties of heterosexual feminists to males often provoked a crisis of identity. Lesbian-feminists played upon this contradiction. "A lesbian is the rage of all women condensed to the point of explosion," wrote New York Radicalesbians in "The Woman-Identified Woman," one of the most influential essays of the sexual liberation movements:

22. On the emergence of a lesbian–feminist movement, see Teal, *The Gay Militants*, pp. 179–94; Sidney Abbott and Barbara Love, *Sappho Was a Right-on Woman* (New York, 1972); Jay and Young, *Out of the Closets*, pp. 172–203; and Nancy Myron and Charlotte Bunch, eds., *Lesbianism and the Women's Movement* (Baltimore, 1975). *The Furies* (Washington, D.C.) and *Lesbian Tide* (Los Angeles) are two of the influential lesbian–feminist periodicals from the early 1970s.

Lesbian is the word, the label, the condition that holds women in line. . . . Lesbian is a label invented by the man to throw at any woman who dares to be his equal, who dares to challenge his prerogatives, who dares to assert the primacy of her own needs. . . . As long as women's liberation tries to free women without facing the basic heterosexual structure that binds us in one-to-one relationships with our own oppressors, tremendous energies will continue to flow into trying to straighten up each particular relationship with a man. . . . It is the primacy of women relating to women, of women creating a new consciousness of and with each other which is at the heart of women's liberation, and the basis for the cultural revolution.[23]

Under these circumstances many heterosexual women reevaluated their sexuality and resolved the contradiction between politics and personal life by coming out as lesbians. Lesbian-feminist organizations were filled with women who came not from the urban subculture of lesbian bars but from the heterosexual world, with the women's liberation movement as a way station. As opponents of feminism were quick to charge, the women's movement was something of a "breeding ground" for lesbianism.[24]

Besides the encouragement it provided for women to come out, women's liberation served lesbians—and gay men—in another way. The feminist movement continued to thrive during the 1970s. Its ideas permeated the country, its agenda worked itself into the political process, and it effected deep-seated changes in the lives of tens of millions of women and men. Feminism's attack upon traditional sex roles and the affirmation of a nonreproductive sexuality that was implicit in such demands as unrestricted access to abortion paved a smoother road for lesbians and homosexuals who were also challenging rigid male and female stereotypes and championing an eroticism that by its nature did not lead to procreation. Moreover, lesbians served as a bridge between the women's movement and gay liberation, at the very least guaranteeing that sectors of each remained amenable to the goals and perspectives of the other. Feminism helped to remove gay life and gay politics from the margins of American society.

V

By any standard of measurement, post-Stonewall gay liberation dwarfed its homophile predecessor. In June 1970 between 5,000 and 10,000 men and women commemorated the first anniversary of the riot with a march from Greenwich Village to Central Park. By the second half of the decade, Gay

23. Radicalesbians, "The Woman-Identified Woman," reprinted in Jay and Young, Out of the Closets, pp. 172–77.

24. For the phenomenon of women who came out as lesbians via the women's liberation movement, see the autobiographical essays in Myron and Bunch, eds., Lesbianism and the Women's Movement; Julia Penelope Stanley and Susan J. Wolfe, eds., The Coming Out Stories (Watertown, Mass., 1980); and Nancy and Casey Adair, Word Is Out (San Francisco, 1978).

Freedom Day events were occurring in dozens of cities, and total participation exceeded half a million individuals. The fifty homophile organizations that had existed in 1969 mushroomed into more than 800 only four years later; as the 1970s ended, the number reached into the thousands. In a relatively short time, gay liberation achieved the goal that had eluded homophile leaders for two decades—the active involvement of large numbers of homosexuals and lesbians in their own emancipation effort.

Numerical strength allowed the new breed of liberationists to compile a list of achievements that could only have elicited awe from homophile activists. In 1973 the American Psychiatric Association altered a position it had held for almost a century by removing homosexuality from its list of mental disorders. During the 1970s more than half the states repealed their sodomy laws, the Civil Service Commission eliminated its ban on the employment of lesbians and homosexuals, and several dozen municipalities passed antidiscrimination statutes. Politicians of national stature came out in favor of gay rights. Activists were invited to the White House to discuss their grievances, and in 1980 the Democratic party platform included a gay rights plank.

The stress gay liberation placed upon coming out also gave the movement leverage of another kind. Not only did men and women join groups that campaigned for equality from outside American institutions; they also came out within their professions, their communities, and other institutions to which they belonged. Gay Catholics, for instance, formed Dignity, and gay Episcopalians, Integrity. In some denominations gay men and women sought not only acceptance but also ordination as ministers. Military personnel announced their homosexuality and fought for the right to remain in the service. Lesbian and gay male academicians, school teachers, social workers, doctors, nurses, psychologists, and others created caucuses in their professions to sensitize their peers to the needs of the gay community and to combat discrimination. Openly gay journalists and television reporters brought an insider's perspective to their coverage of gay-related news. The visibility of lesbians and gay men in so many varied settings helped make homosexuality seem less of a strange, threatening phenomenon and more like an integral part of the social fabric.

Finally, the post-Stonewall era witnessed a significant shift in the self-definition of gay men and women. As pressure from gay liberationists made police harassment the exception rather than the rule in many American cities, the gay subculture flourished as never before. The relative freedom from danger, along with the emphasis the movement placed on gay pride, led not only to an expansion of the bar world but also to the creation of a range of "community" institutions. Gay men and lesbians formed their own churches, health clinics, counseling services, social centers, professional associations, and amateur sports leagues. Male and female entrepreneurs built record companies, publishing houses, travel agencies, and vacation resorts. Newspapers, magazines, literary journals, theater companies, and film collectives gave expression to a distinctive cultural experience. The subculture of homosexual men and women became less exclusively erotic. Gayness and lesbianism began to encompass an identity that for many included a wide array of private and public activities.

Stonewall thus marked a critical divide in the politics and consciousness of homosexuals and lesbians. A small, thinly spread reform effort suddenly grew into a large, grassroots movement for liberation. The quality of gay life in America was permanently altered as a furtive subculture moved aggressively into the open.

THIRTEEN

Conclusion

Young gay radicals exhibited as little respect toward the homophile movement as they did toward the institutions of American society. They scorned its moderation and reformist politics. Gay liberationists disrupted the conferences of homophile organizations, shouted outside their meeting halls, and shed few tears when groups like SIR, the Mattachine Society and DOB—unable to adapt to the politics of the 1970s—faded from the scene. Except for a few men and women such as Kameny, Gittings, Martin, and Lyon, most of the stalwarts of the movement in the late 1950s and 1960s retired to private pursuits. As lesbian-feminism and gay liberation came to dominate the struggle for homosexual freedom, the accomplishments of the first two decades were either forgotten or ignored.

Although the discontinuities between the pre- and post-Stonewall eras are glaring and undeniable, the tendency of liberationists to dismiss their forebears has obscured how much they owed the homophile effort and how much it achieved. Mass movements for social change do not spring into existence fully grown, nor do institutional arrangements and cultural beliefs generally alter as suddenly as those that pertained to homoeroticism in the 1970s. Many of the shifts that occurred in the decade were due to the weakening of traditional centers of power caused by the protest movements of the 1960s, but the relative ease with which gay liberationists accumulated victories can only be explained by the persistent, plodding work of the activists who preceded them. The homophile movement deserves kinder treatment than it has received. The popular wisdom of gay liberation needs to be reevaluated.

I

In mid-twentieth-century America, there existed a consensus that devalued homosexual behavior and justified its punishment. A religious tradition stretching back at least to the Middle Ages excoriated it as a heinous sin and an unnatural act; legal codes dating from the earliest years of English settlement stipulated harsh penalties for it; and the medical profession diagnosed it as pathological. In the popular mind, the homosexual and the lesbian were at best a target of ridicule and at worst a social menace. Police harassment made life dangerous for gay men and women, and the ostracism and punishment that almost surely followed exposure of one's sexual identity imposed a heavy burden of secrecy upon them. Condemnation of homosexuality so permeated the culture that gay men and women could not easily escape it. They too internalized negative attitudes about their sexuality.

Although American society evinced an unbroken history of hostility toward homosexual behavior, the forms and meaning of homoerotic expression changed considerably in the few generations before World War II. As the United States became a nation of cities in the late nineteenth and early twentieth centuries, and as wage labor replaced the family farm and the plantation for millions of Americans, what had once been a discrete transgression, a criminal act, metamorphosed into a characteristic descriptive of its possessor. Ironically, aided by a medical profession that reconceptualized homosexual behavior as a condition inhering in a person, some men and women took on a sexual self-definition that distinguished them from the majority. Even as many homosexuals and lesbians led lives isolated from those who shared their sexuality, others gradually found ways of meeting and staked out a corner of urban society where a rudimentary gay subculture slowly took shape.

The founding of the Mattachine Society occurred at a critical moment in the collective existence of gay men and lesbians. On the one hand, World War II had sufficiently disrupted social life so that many men and women could come out, discover others who shared their erotic inclinations, and encounter expanded possibilities for being gay. Although traditional patterns of heterosexual family life reasserted themselves in the postwar years, the changes set in motion by military mobilization did not come to a halt when the conflict ended. Gay men and women who had located their peers during the war preserved those connections afterward. In the process, they helped expand an urban gay subculture that made it easier for those who followed them to come out.

On the other hand, homosexuals and lesbians in the Cold War era found themselves scapegoated by anticommunist politicians bent on attacking not only political dissenters but sexual nonconformists as well. The image of the "sexual pervert" as a social menace sharpened during the McCarthy years, and with it came greater penalties. The exclusion of gay women and men from government employment was written into law, the military intensified its purges, the FBI initiated widespread surveillance, and urban police forces harassed the sexually different in bars, on the street, and sometimes in their homes. Just as a group life was growing stronger for homosexuals and lesbians, they confronted a thickening web of oppression.

Any prospective effort to mobilize gay men and women faced enormous obstacles. Most homosexuals and lesbians possessed the ability to "pass" as heterosexual. Involvement in a gay emancipation group threatened to remove their cover and subject them to penalties in return for the uncertain promise of a better future, at best. Moreover, the dominant view of homosexuality presented it as an individual problem, not as an instance of systematic injustice. Most gay men and women discovered their sexuality in relative isolation, and the furtiveness that characterized the gay subculture tended to reinforce the belief that their sexual identity was a personal matter. In general, homosexuals and lesbians lacked the experience of belonging to a cohesive social group.

The founders of the Mattachine Society attempted to tackle both of these difficulties. They drew upon their experience with the Communist party to devise a complex secret structure that preserved the anonymity of participants. In the discussion groups that they sponsored, they encouraged gay men and women to reevaluate their condition and perceive themselves as members of an oppressed minority. The enthusiasm elicited by the discussion groups suggested that the question of consciousness—of how gay men and women interpreted their experience—was indeed critical to building a movement. The relatively rapid growth of the organization in southern California seemed to demonstrate that gays could be motivated to act on their own behalf.

The anticommunism of the Cold War era brought an end to Mattachine's radical orientation. Secrecy could serve the movement's purposes only for a time, and the leftist background of Hay and the other founders cast suspicion upon the motives behind the group's structure. Moreover, the leaders' emphasis on collective political action and mass militancy placed them out of step with the times. The early 1950s were not hospitable to such initiatives, especially if they came from sexual nonconformists. When the founders departed, their vision of a cohesive, proud gay community also faded, but at least they had bequeathed to their successors an organization that was strong enough to survive.

The men who came to the helm of the Mattachine Society and the women who later established the Daughters of Bilitis were ill equipped to build a movement. Although their involvement in gay organizations evinced courage in itself, they acquiesced too readily to the circumstances in which they found themselves. Convinced that America would not tolerate agitation for gay rights, they maintained the lowest of profiles and advised their constituency against mounting any challenges to the status quo. In their effort to accommodate themselves to a conservative political climate and a society antagonistic to homosexuality, they oftentimes abetted the attitudes and policies that stigmatized homosexuals and lesbians. Whatever their private convictions about gay life may have been, the leaders of the homophile movement during the 1950s betrayed an uncertainty about their own self-worth that made it difficult to attract supporters. Although they were almost certainly right in believing that they had little room in which to maneuver, the distinction between a reasonable caution with tactical merit and an acceptance of their inferior condition was too often lost in their words and actions.

However, even during its weakest phase, the movement achieved something of value for lesbians and homosexuals. In several cities, small chapters of Mattachine and DOB were established, to serve as the base from which the movement would grow. For each minister and doctor who sustained the negative view of homosexuality before a gay audience, there was another who dissented and whom the movement might enlist in its behalf. Homophile activists also initiated what became a tradition of openly gay publishing and, through ONE's challenge of postal censorship, saw their constitutional right to freedom of speech upheld by the Supreme Court. Although the circulation of the magazines remained small, most of the movement's recruits came from men and women who had happened upon a copy of one of the journals. Furthermore, at a time when few lesbians and homosexuals ever contemplated speaking openly about their sexual identity, stumbling upon even a single issue of a gay periodical could affect their perceptions of their situation. As dismal as the movement's prospects appeared during most of the 1950s, its mere existence was a force for change.

The scope and pace of activity increased considerably during the 1960s. The idealistic rhetoric of the Kennedy presidency implicitly legitimated attempts at social reform, while the civil rights movement vividly demonstrated not only that all was not right in America but also that change was possible. Southern blacks provided an inspiring example of courage in the face of an entrenched, even violent opposition. Under these circumstances, it was not surprising that a new breed of gay activists emerged, with a willingness to take greater risks than their predecessors.

The militancy of some activists in the 1960s also reflected changes in the structure of gay life. Except for Kameny, whose battle with the government had nourished a ferocious determination to see justice done, the homophile militants were considerably younger than the leaders of the previous decade. Born in the late 1930s as most of them had been, they came of age after the persecutions of the McCarthy era had become part and parcel of the gay experience. Not having lived through the years when the situation of lesbians and homosexuals was clearly deteriorating, they lacked the typical fear of their elders that their condition could get worse. They benefited, too, from the expansion of the urban gay subculture that had occurred in the 1940s and from the McCarthy era's preoccupation with the homosexual menace, which, however damaging to self-esteem it may have been, allowed younger gay men and women to recognize more easily their sexual impulses. Hence the movement's new recruits had been able to find their way into the gay subculture while still young. Fewer years of isolation, a more clearly articulated system of oppression, and involvement in the subculture at an impressionable age gave them a more pronounced awareness of their sexuality as a widely shared condition.

Homophile militants broke with the movement's past in two critical ways. First of all, they entertained no doubts about the integrity of their sexual preferences. In their view, homosexuality was a valid form of erotic and emotional expression, and anything less than the full rights of citizenship represented unjust discrimination against them. Second, with the model of the civil rights movement in front of them, they argued that political action, rather than self-help or education, was the path to equality. Together, these two differences expanded the movement's options. Militants approached professionals not to solicit their views about homosexuality or their sympathy but to win their aid in a struggle for social justice. Allies acted on behalf of an agenda set by the aggrieved, reversing the pattern of the 1950s, when movement participants followed the lead of professionals. Willingness to take action, whether in picket lines, repeated visits to public officials, press conferences to expose bigotry and harassment, or court cases to challenge discrimination, brought the movement into the open. It also meant that nongay supporters could help in specific, concrete ways.

The movement soon reaped the benefits of its militant civil rights perspective. It won the backing of civil libertarians, who took up the gay rights cause in the courts and supported homophile groups in their confrontations with urban police forces. Within American Protestantism, clerical allies opened a debate on church teaching about homosexuality. The movement's rejection of the sickness model gave it added leverage in its dealings with the medical profession. The number and influence of the dissenting voices within the mental health field grew to the point where they could shape the conclusions of a national task force on homosexuality. Homophile groups in New York and San Francisco amassed enough strength to curtail police harassment significantly. In a number of states court decisions protected gay bars from capricious law enforcement practices. Movement organizations spread to more than a score of cities where they imitated on a smaller scale the work of their counterparts in New York, San Francisco, and Washington. By the end of the decade, homosexuality had become an arena of contention in American society. Though the forces advocating change still had the longest part of their journey ahead, they had succeeded in breaking the consensus that guaranteed an inferior status to gay men and women. Sin, crime, and sickness no longer monopolized the discourse on homoeroticism.

The militancy of activists also allowed the movement to exploit the sexual permissiveness that characterized American culture in the 1960s. The nationwide debate about sexual matters sparked by the Kinsey reports, along with the series of Supreme Court decisions on obscenity, cleared away the residue of proscriptions on sexual discourse that was the legacy of Victorianism. Sex was marketed not only in pornography but also in Hollywood movies, mass circulation magazines, popular fiction, the theater, and the metropolitan press. The birth control pill was heralded—prematurely, as it later turned out—as the perfect contraceptive, freeing women from the fear of pregnancy and weakening constraints on the pursuit of erotic pleasure. Human growth therapies proliferated as Americans sought release from the inhibitions that blocked sexual enjoyment. Sex—if not engaging in it, then certainly talking about it—became a national pastime.

It would be a mistake to conclude that the sexual liberalism of the decade would automatically have included homoeroticism without the initiatives taken by gay activists. Heterosexual mores had been in flux at least since the first decades of the twentieth century, as birth control advocates, sex radicals of the post–World War I generation, adherents of Freudianism, modern writers, and others mounted challenges to Victorian orthodoxy. In the 1960s several decades of gradual change came together in a new synthesis that legitimated nonprocreative heterosexuality and affirmed erotic expression as a part of the good life. But the shifts in sexual mores that occurred throughout the twentieth century had not extended to homosexuality. Popular attitudes remained hostile, censors enforced the obscenity statutes with more vigor when it came to same-gender sexuality, and the professionals who elaborated upon sexual ideology stood firm in their conviction that homosexual behavior was neither desirable nor tolerable.

The homophile movement stretched the boundaries of sexual discourse until they encompassed homosexuality. Randy Wicker had cracked the silence of the printed media in New York, so that the gay subculture became a topic of discussion. Popular writers looking for a new angle on the sexual revolution turned to the Mattachine Society and the Daughters of Bilitis for easy entry to the gay world. Social scientists amenable to new interpretations of homosexual behavior found activists to be cooperative informants able to shepherd them through the twists and turns of an unfamiliar life-style. Even when the finished product evinced hostility, as the journalistic exposés of Jess Stearn certainly did, for instance, they brought to countless readers information about the homosexual rights movement and the gay subculture.

Inability to measure precisely the influence of these materials on gay women and men should not obscure their significance. Homosexuals still struggled alone when they first acknowledged their sexual impulses, but in the 1960s the catalyst might well have been a color spread in *Life* describing the meeting places of gay men in several cities. Lesbians too faced an initial time of sexual isolation, but a pulp novel in a rack at the corner drugstore could lighten the burden with its portrayal of a woman-centered world. For the first time, gay men and lesbians had substantial resources not only for naming their sexuality but for finding the gay subculture in which they could take a place. Their decisions to act upon this knowledge strengthened the collective life of the gay world and affected the consciousness of its individual members. However negative their self-image might be, association with others solidified their gay identity. It also let them know that they were not isolated freaks.

Information about the homosexual rights movement infiltrated this subculture. In New York and San Francisco the existence of homophile groups was common knowledge, but even in places without a gay organization, word of the movement had arrived. The picket lines, the court cases, the statements of religious leaders, and other homophile initiatives were picked up by *Time* and *Newsweek*, by the wire services, and by television network affiliates around the country. No gay man or woman who saw it could forget the image of homosexuals marching in front of the White House. If most homosexuals and lesbians were as yet unwilling to join the tiny band of activists, they could not escape the awareness that for some sexual identity had become a political cause.

II

The homophile movement remained small in numbers because, despite the changes in gay life and consciousness, the penalties attached to discovery continued intact. Homosexual behavior was still a criminal activity, exposure virtually guaranteed the termination of employment, and the revelation of one's sexual identity could easily rupture family ties and friendships. The short-term losses seemed to outweigh clearly the future gains that political action might bring. For the overwhelming majority of lesbians and homosexuals, a rational consideration of their own self-interest indicated that their precarious but familiar secret life was preferable to the calamities that openness would bring.

Gay liberation was able to break through the barrier that held the movement back by appealing to a very particular gay constituency of recent origin and beyond the reach of the civil rights politics of homophile activists. The men and women who responded to the image of drag queens rioting in Greenwich Village were for the most part young radicals. Whether as New Left activists or as counterculture enthusiasts, they had already decided that American society was corrupt and oppressive, and they had adopted an oppositional stance toward authority. The threat of exclusion from the military or the loss of a government job meant little to them. To have themselves labeled as criminal or deviant was a badge of honor that they sported with pride. When the banner of gay power was held aloft on Christopher Street, they were prepared to rally behind it. Young gay radicals could act on the slogan "Out of the Closets and into the Streets" because they did not fear the consequences.

The gay liberation movement permanently altered the shape of homosexual and lesbian life. The courage of young radicals proved infectious. Before long, their proliferating organizations were attracting not only the politically disaffected but also many of the gay men and women who had observed the homophile movement from a distance and refrained from taking part in it. Early gay liberationists not only provided a model to imitate but offered at last the safety of numbers. The benefits of coming out were no longer so tenuous, and its risks began to pale beside the sense of community and self-respect that a liberation movement offered. Gay liberation affected the self-image even of those men and women who never joined a gay organization or participated in a demonstration. Its ideas permeated the subculture of lesbians and homosexuals so that pride and openness became common characteristics. Gay liberation transformed homosexuality from a stigma that one kept carefully hidden into an identity that signified membership in a community organizing for freedom.

If the homophile movement broke the monopoly that traditional negative views held over the discourse on homoeroticism and the shaping of public policy, gay liberation amassed enough strength to make a serious bid for supremacy. During the 1970s, in virtually every area of American life, debates raged and battles were fought over homosexuality. In some places, gay liberation emerged with clear-cut victories, as in the case of the American Psychiatric Association's removal of homosexuality from its list of mental disorders and the steadily growing number of states that decriminalized private consensual sex between adults. In other situations, the record was mixed. The federal government eliminated the ban on the employment of homosexuals and lesbians, but the question of security clearances remained murky, and the military stood firm in its exclusion policy. Some movement goals proved amenable to a two-pronged strategy. Although the mass media exhibited a willingness to cover homosexual-related news and often presented the subject sympathetically, in many cities the lesbian and gay male community expended considerable resources to sustain its own newspapers and magazines. Gays organized within the various religious faiths with different degrees of success, but they also formed their own churches and synagogues, where they could worship as they pleased. Gay liberation made least progress in its quest for legal protection against discrimination. Only one state, Wisconsin, added sexual and affectional preference to its civil rights statutes, and after the mid-1970s the number of cities passing gay rights bills slowed considerably. Some of those that had done so repealed them through bitterly contested referendum campaigns. Yet even in the realm of mainstream politics, activists continued to make some headway. In many states they persisted in lobbying for bills prohibiting discrimination, and in 1980 the Democratic party included a gay rights plank in its national platform. The situation of lesbians and homosexuals had changed significantly from a generation earlier, when legal penalties could be enacted without debate.

Although the rise of an organized opposition to homosexual freedom has stimulated concern about the gay movement's prospects, and although the movement itself shows no unanimity as to the social rearrangements that equality would require, the record of the past suggests an even better future for lesbians and homosexuals. During the 1960s and 1970s, certain long-term demographic trends accelerated, and these, together with the self-conscious political activity of gay men and lesbians, tended to blur the distinction between homosexual and heterosexual.

A gay identity and subculture had evolved from the late nineteenth century onward because of structural changes in the economy and the society that made it possible to live beyond the boundaries of the family. Men and, to a lesser extent, women with a strong attraction to their own gender understandably were among the first to pursue that option. In the last twenty years, however, birth rates have plummeted, average household size has declined, divorce rates have risen, and the variety of living arrangements that Americans are choosing has multiplied. Though most heterosexuals still marry and have children, fewer and fewer of them can expect a lifetime of participation in a nuclear family. Small families and long life expectancies guarantee many years of adulthood without the task of rearing children. Contemporary heterosexuality is clearly no longer primarily procreative, and the desire for sexual pleasure figures in the life choices of many heterosexuals. Stable families survive not because their members have no alternative but because the relationships bring personal fulfillment. As the life cycle of heterosexuals exhibits greater variety and less predictability, they have come to face many of the choices and experiences that gay men and women confront.

If heterosexual life is coming to resemble in some ways its gay counterpart, the experience of homosexual men and women likewise shows signs of converging with the heterosexual norm. An urban gay subculture originally took shape to bring together men and women with a common sexual identity. The harsh reality of oppression formed both the identity and the subculture. Sexuality loomed large as the primary component of an individual's sense of self, and the institutions of the gay subculture served mainly to promote erotic liaisons. The gay liberation movement allowed many lesbians and homosexuals to break out of the ideological prison that confined them to a sexual self-definition. It also began the transformation of a sexual subculture into an urban community. The group life of gay men and women came to encompass not only erotic interaction but also political, religious, and cultural activity. Homosexuality and lesbianism have become less of a sexual category and more of a human identity.

III

When Harry Hay, Chuck Rowland, and a few other leftist homosexuals formed the Mattachine Society in 1950, they defined their primary task as the creation of an "ethical homosexual culture." The founders of the gay emancipation movement in the United States discarded the conventional view of homosexuals and lesbians as flawed individuals. In its place, they posited that gay men and women were an oppressed minority and that, like other minorities, they possessed a culture of their own. The dominant ideology made it difficult for gays to see this. Instead, it instilled a shame and self-hatred that often produced distorted, unhappy lives. Hay and his fellows sought to transform the consciousness of homosexuals and lesbians, to replace an isolated, secret existence with a cohesive community that would then be able to take its place proudly in American society. For almost twenty years that vision was lost, until a new generation of gay radicals built a liberation movement motivated by similar goals of pride, openness, and community.

Gay liberation was able to give substance to the dreams of the Mattachine founders because of the work of homophile activists in the intervening years. However little the homophile movement seemed to have achieved in the way of specific goals, the pioneering activists of the 1950s and 1960s had managed to disseminate throughout American culture information about homosexuality that reshaped the consciousness of gay men and women. The idea that homosexuals and lesbians were a minority no longer remained confined to the living rooms of a few gays meeting secretly but was there to be taken from the pages of newspapers, books, and magazines. Gay liberation propelled hundreds of thousands of men and women to act upon that belief, but two decades of work by homophile activists had made the individuals who were ready to respond. At the time of the Stonewall riot in 1969, homosexuality had already ceased being an invisible phenomenon, and gay men and lesbians more easily participated in the collective life of the gay subculture. In attempting to build a politics based on sexual preference, the homophile movement in effect helped create the community that, later, was able to sustain a liberation effort.

Index